Moreton Morrell Site

Simply **Marketing** Communications

Visit the *Simply Marketing Communications* Companion Website at **www.pearsoned.co.uk/fill** to find valuable **student** learning material including:

- Multiple choice questions with feedback to test your knowledge
- Links to relevant sites on the World Wide Web
- Link to a regularly-updated website containing interesting journal articles, news and events
- Extra mini case studies from recent Chartered Institute of Marketing Diploma examinations

Chris Fill

University of Portsmouth

Simply Marketing Communications

FT Prentice Hall
FINANCIAL TIMES

An imprint of Pearson Education
Harlow, England • London • New York • Boston • San Francisco • Toronto
Sydney • Tokyo • Singapore • Hong Kong • Seoul • Taipei • New Delhi
Cape Town • Madrid • Mexico City • Amsterdam • Munich • Paris • Milan

Pearson Education Limited
Edinburgh Gate
Harlow
Essex CM20 2JE
England

and Associated Companies throughout the world

Visit us on the World Wide Web at:
www.pearsoned.co.uk

First published 2006

ISBN-13: 978-0-273-70405-8
ISBN-10: 0-273-70405-2

British Library Cataloguing-in-Publication Data
A catalogue record for this book is available from the British Library

Library of Congress Cataloging-in-Publication Data
A catalogue record for this book is available from the Library of Congress

10 9 8 7 6 5 4 3 2 1
10 09 08 07 06

Typeset in 9.5/12.5pt Stone Serif by 35
Printed and bound by Mateu Cromo Artes Graficas, Spain

The publisher's policy is to use paper manufactured from sustainable forests.

This book is dedicated to:

all those people throughout the world who do simple and kind things to help other people,

political leaders who simply defend peace and avoid war,

my simply brilliant family who understand me.

Brief Contents

Part 4 Industry, relationships and operations

Contents

15 Agency operations: selection, personnel and practice   378

Supporting resources

Visit **www.pearsoned.co.uk/fill** to find valuable online resources

Companion Website for students
- Multiple choice questions with feedback to test your knowledge
- Links to relevant sites on the World Wide Web
- Link to a regularly-updated website containing interesting journal articles, news and events
- Extra mini case studies from recent Chartered Institute of Marketing Diploma examinations

For instructors
- Complete, downloadable Instructor's Manual
- PowerPoint slides that can be downloaded and used as OHTs
- Teaching schemes
- Additional mini case studies

Also: The Companion Website provides the following features:

- Search tool to help locate specific items of content
- E-mail results and profile tools to send results of quizzes to instructors
- Online help and support to assist with website usage and troubleshooting

For more information please contact your local Pearson Education sales representative or visit **www.pearsoned.co.uk/fill**

Preface

Thank you for reading *Simply Marketing Communications*. It has been drawn from the fourth edition of *Marketing Communications* and is intended to help you understand the increasingly complex world of marketing communications. This book has been written partly to meet the needs of students studying for professional qualifications such as the Professional Diploma offered by the Chartered Institute of Marketing. In addition, students studying marketing communications for the first time on university- and college-based courses should also find this book helpful. I have tried to present the material in a straightforward manner, with a minimal amount of supporting conceptual frameworks, theories and models. I hope that you will enjoy the material, be stimulated to want to know more and wish to engage further with the exciting world of marketing communications.

A world of marketing communications

All organisations, large and small, commercial, government, charities, educational and other not-for-profit organisations, need to communicate with a range of stakeholders. This may be in order to get materials and services to undertake their business activities or to collaborate and coordinate with others to secure suitable distribution of their goods and services. In addition, there are consumers, you and me, people who are free to choose among the many hundreds and thousands of product and service offerings. Marketing communications provide a core activity so that all interested parties can understand the intentions of others and appreciate the value of the goods and services offered.

Traditionally, there are five main marketing communication disciplines or tools: advertising, sales promotion, personal selling, public relations and direct marketing. In addition, there are media in which time and space can be bought or used to deliver messages to target audiences. The appropriate mix of these tools and the choice of media have for a long time been largely predictable. Distinct mixes could be identified for business-to-consumer (b2c) and business-to-business (b2b) audiences. There were variations reflecting particular brand circumstances, but essentially in the b2c market advertising was used to build brand values, sales promotions were used to instil customer action and public relations sought to generate goodwill and interest about the company. Personal selling was regarded as the primary tool in b2b markets but also had a role to play in retail environments: for example, selling consumer durables. In the 1990s direct marketing became a more prominent tool in the mix because technology had enabled a new form of communication by appealing personally and directly to the target customer. This change introduced new media formats, and the subsequent development of the Internet and related digital technologies has accelerated change in the marketing communications industry. There are now a myriad of opportunities to reach audiences, with the Internet representing a new, yet challenging, form of communication channel.

At the same time as the media world has splintered into many different parts, so have the audiences with whom organisations need to communicate. Consumers now have a variety of different ways to spend their leisure time. Some of those that chose to incorporate the media as part of their relaxation now have not just three commercial television channels but nearly two hundred channels, all have access to an increasing number of general- and specific-interest magazines, a multitude of new cinema complexes and, of course, the Internet with an explosion of websites offering a seemingly endless source of information, opportunities to buy online and a form of global entertainment. The world of marketing communications is bright, exciting, sometimes unpredictable, challenging and evolving

Managers are now not only required to find new ways to communicate but do so on reduced budgets for which they are fully accountable. The development of long-term relationships with customers, whether this be in b2b or b2c markets, is now an essential aspect of marketing policy. Customer retention is crucial today and various devices, such as loyalty schemes, are used to shape long-term customer behaviour. Organisations now accept that the tools of the promotional mix are not the only way brands communicate. All parts of the marketing mix communicate: the behaviour of employees, the performance of products and the actions of competitors all serve to influence the way in which each customer perceives a brand. Corporate branding is now recognised as an integral part of the overall communication effort. Corporate reputation and the actions undertaken by organisations are perceived not only in terms of brand values and profits but also in terms of their ethics and the impact organisations have on the environment.

Marketing communication agencies are trying to adjust the way they can best serve the interests of their clients. One of the results is structural realignment (mergers and takeovers), which can lead to consolidation. Clients themselves are fighting to generate superior value for their customers and to find new ways of establishing competitive advantage. Globalisation and the development of partnerships, alliances and networks are all testimony to changing markets and expectations.

Where does this all lead? It leads to a new form and role for marketing communications and a vision that an organisation's entire marketing communications should be planned, coherent and consistent. The word 'consistency' applies to internal policies and strategies, to messages to and from internal and external stakeholders, to the values of their customers and to the relationships they forge with key suppliers and distributors.

This book introduces you to this changing world of marketing communications and should help you to appreciate some of the issues associated with marketing communications and associated aspects of integration, coordination and planning. There are examples of the practical application of marketing communications, and examples that demonstrate the application of theory in practice.

Overview of this book

A key topic in this book is engagement. Effective marketing communications enables audiences to engage with products, services, brands and organisations. Through engagement, relationships can develop and this enables customers, stakeholders and organisations to achieve their various goals. The degree to which engagement occurs reflects audience perception, interpretation and meaning of the messages delivered. Through engagement, brand value and equity can be developed or reduced. Engagement, therefore, encompasses a range of marketing communication activities and is referred to throughout the text.

This book seeks to provide a suitably consistent appraisal of the ever-expanding world of marketing communications. It seeks to stimulate thought and consideration about a wide range of interrelated issues, and to help to achieve this aim a number of theories and models are advanced. Some of these theories reflect marketing practice, while others are offered as suggestions for moving the subject forward. Many of the theories are abstractions of actual practice, some are based on empirical research and others are pure conceptualisation. All seek to enrich the subject, but not all need carry the same weight of contribution. Readers should form their own opinions based upon their reading, experience and judgement.

There are a number of themes running through the text, but perhaps the two main ones concern relationship marketing and integrated communications. I am of the view that organisations will in the future perceive communications as a core strategic activity, central to strategic management and thought. Corporate and marketing communications will inevitably merge and integrate, the need to build and sustain relationships with a variety of stakeholders inside and outside the organisation will become paramount and communications will be a vital source in making it all work – witness the branding developments at the grocery giants Procter & Gamble and Unilever to understand this point.

In this light, this text assumes relationship marketing to be essential and sees communication in the context of both transactional and relational exchanges. Corporate and marketing communications are considered as important components of the total process, which should always be Simply Marketing Communications.

Structure of the text

There are four main parts to this book:

Part 1 introduces fundamental ideas and concepts associated with marketing communications. Readers are introduced to the subject from a general perspective before the material seeks to establish some core information about communication theory and the importance of people and technology on the way in which communication is considered to work. The part closes with important underpinning material about audience and buyer behaviour.

Part 2 is concerned with the management of marketing communication activities. This section of the book considers some of the key issues management must address in order that the organisation's marketing communications are effective. The content starts with a view of marketing communications strategy and determines three strategic approaches based on the nature of the particular audiences. This is followed by an exploration of some of the ideas about integrated marketing communications, or IMC. The chapter concludes with a consideration of the marketing communications planning framework, used to develop campaigns and other relevant activities.

Chapter 5 is concerned with another important management process, segmentation. Marketing communications should be an audience-centred activity, and in that sense management needs to undertake segmentation, targeting and positioning activities.

The final chapter in this part considers the nature and impact of technology on marketing communications. Attention is given to a range of developments that include the role and nature of websites in contemporary marketing communications.

Part 3 focuses on the tools and media of the marketing communications mix. The characteristics and strengths and weaknesses of each tool are considered in turn, and each chapter contains a section dealing with the ways in which the particular discipline can be evaluated. The goal is to help readers to understand the ways in which the tools can be applied in order to communicate effectively with target audiences.

Part 4 considers the nature and significance of relationship marketing and the impact that marketing communications can have on the development and maintenance of certain relationships. Attention is given to relationships in the context of end-user customers, marketing channels, the marketing communications industry, employees and agency/client operations.

Chapter 12 explores ideas concerning value and the nature of relationship marketing. The concept of value as a basis for exchange provides the foundation for the spectrum of relationships. This is used to consider issues concerning trust, commitment, loyalty and retention. The final part of the chapter explores ideas concerning the involvement of employees as part of the marketing communications process.

Some of these ideas are taken further in the next chapter. Here, relationships and marketing communications are considered in the context of a range of stakeholders (channel intermediaries, business-to-business organisations and international clients and agencies).

The penultimate chapter focuses on the structure and dynamics of the marketing communications industry and the means by which the industry serves their audiences and their constituent players. Issues concerning industry structure provide an important underpinning to understand many of the current issues facing the industry. Other topics concern the way clients determine how much they should invest in marketing communications, how much agencies should be rewarded for their activities and finally how both agencies and clients should be controlled and regulated with regard to the messages delivered and media used to carry them. Legislation and voluntary controls provide the context within which organisations behave with varying degrees of responsibility.

The final chapter considers some of the principal processes and operations used by communication agencies to develop campaigns. This is important, because many readers may be (or become) involved in the development of marketing communications materials and campaigns as part of their work. Familiarity with the vocabulary and processes can facilitate both career and examination success.

Design features and presentation

In addition to the four-part structure of the book, there are a number of features that are intended to help readers navigate the material.

Chapter objectives

Each chapter opens with both the aims of what is to be covered and a list of (learning) objectives. This helps to signal the primary topics that are covered in the chapter and so guide the learning experience.

Navigation

Important key text is extracted and presented in the margin. This helps readers to locate relevant material quickly and highlight key issues. In addition, to assist readers through the various chapters, the left-hand page is used to identify the page number and in which part of the text it is located. To complement this, the right-hand page is used to flag the page number and the chapter title.

Visual supports

This book is produced in colour and throughout the text there are numerous colour and black-and-white exhibits, figures (diagrams) and tables of information that serve to highlight, illustrate and bring life to the written word. The pictures either serve to illustrate particular points by demonstrating theory in practice or complement individual examples. The examples are normally highlighted in the text as ViewPoints. These examples are easily distinguishable through the colour contrasts and serve to demonstrate how a particular aspect of marketing communications has been used by an organisation in a particular context. I hope you enjoy these ViewPoints of organisational practice.

Summaries and mini case studies

At the end of each chapter is a summary and a series of review and discussion questions. Readers are advised to test their own understanding of the content of each chapter by considering some or all of the discussion questions. In this sense the questions support self-study but tutors might wish to use some of these as part of a seminar or workshop programme.

In addition, each Part of the book contains an additional summary, which brings together many of the key points and themes that have run throughout the Part. This is followed by a further set of questions intended to help readers to understand how the different materials, ideas and concepts tie together. To assist this process, two mini case studies are included in the summaries. Many of these cases are very similar to those used in previous CIM Marketing Communication exams, and I have tried to maintain the same style and approach. Other cases have been written by marketing academics from a variety of universities and colleges, and some have been written by leading marketing practitioners. These short cases can be used in class for discussion purposes and to explore some of the salient issues that have been raised in the Part. Students working alone can use the mini case studies to test their own understanding and to consolidate their understanding. Readers intending to sit the CIM paper should practise using past papers.

Support materials

Students and lecturers who adopt this text have a range of support materials and facilities to help them.

Readers are invited to visit the companion website for the book at www.pearsoned.co.uk/fill. Here students have access to a range of mini case studies, including a selection of recent Chartered Institute of Marketing examination cases for both the Integrated Marketing Communications and the new Marketing Communications modules.

For lecturers and tutors, not only is there an Instructor's Manual containing a range of teaching schemes, slides and exercises in downloadable format but there is also a password-protected section of the companion website for their use. From this site a much larger range of PowerPoint slides, teaching schemes and additional mini cases can be downloaded.

A test bank of multiple-choice questions has also been developed for use by students and lecturers. In addition, there are hyperlinks to a range of related sites.

Acknowledgements

This book could not have been written without the support of a wide range of people. Contributions range from providing information and permissions, to writing mini-case studies, to answering my questions and tolerating my persistent nagging, sending through photographs, answering phone calls and emails and simply liaising with others. Finally there are those who have read, reviewed drafts, made constructive comments and provided moral support and encouragement.

The list of individuals and organisations involved with this book is extensive. My thanks is offered to all of you. I have tried to list everyone but if anyone has been omitted then I offer my apologies.

Marion Baker – Procter and Gamble
Anthony Byrne - Liverpool John Moores University
Eileen Buckwald – Wall's Ice Cream
Richard Christy – University of Portsmouth
Paul Collier – Hewlett Packard
Darren Feist – Photographer
Graham Hughes – Leeds Metropolitan University

Nigel Markwick – Wolff Olins
Mike Molesworth – Bournemouth University
Gordon Oliver – Horndean
Ben Pearman – Birds Eye Walls
Steve Pike – Photographer
Victoria Savill – Dyson
Lynn Sudbury – Liverpool John Moores University
Debra Weatherley - Findphoto

Above all perhaps are the various individuals at Pearson Education and their associates who have taken my manuscript, managed it and published it in this form. In particular I should like to thank Thomas Sigel for his constant support, professionalism and faith in my writing and to wish him well in the next stage of his career. I should also like to thank Andrew Harrison, for his never say no attitude and for always finding answers to questions. In addition I should like to thank Tim Parker and his inside and outside teams of editors, proof readers and production staff and printers, for transforming the manuscript into the final product. Thank you all.

The biggest thank you is, as ever for my wife Karen. Yet again she has been an absolute star, understanding, supportive and a thoughtful contributor to this book. I am a lucky man.

We would also like to thank the following for permission to reproduce copyright material:

Table 6.3 adapted from *Journal of Personal Selling & Sales Management*, vol. 22, no. 3 (Summer 2002): 189–198. Copyright © 2002 by PSE National Educational Foundation. Reprinted with permission of M.E. Sharpe, Inc. All Rights Reserved. Not for Reproduction; Table 6.7 from Web site characteristics and business performance: some evidence from international business-to-business organisations in *Marketing Intelligence and Planning*, 21, 2, Emerald Group Publishing Limited (Karayanni, D.A. and Baltas, G.A. 2003); Table 6.8 from *Internet Marketing Strategy, Implementation and Practice* by Chaffey, D., Mayer, R., Johnston, K. and Ellis-Chadwick, Pearson Education, 2003; Table 8.2 from Advertising Association's Advertising Statistics Yearbook published by the World Advertising Research Center; Table 11.2 adapted from *Rethinking the Sales Force: Redefining Selling to Create and Capture Customer Value, 1E*, N. Rackham & J. DeVincentis, © 1999 The McGraw-Hill Companies Inc.; Table 11.3 adapted from *Strategic Marketing, 5E*, D. Cravens, © 1997 The McGraw-Hill Companies Inc.; Table 12.1 Reprinted from *Business Horizons* (November–December), 46, 6, Wagner, S. and Boutellier, R., Capabilities for managing a portfolio of supplier relationships, pp. 78–79, Copyright (2002), with permission from Elsevier; Figure 12.4 Reprinted from Relationship Marketing: Creating Stakeholder Value, by Christopher, M., Payne, A. and Ballantyne, D., 48, Copyright (2002), with permission from Elsevier; Table 14.1 from Advertising Association's Advertising Statistics Yearbook published by the World Advertising Research Center.

Exhibit 1.1 reproduced with the kind permission of Dyson; Exhibits 1.2 and 1.3 reproduced with the kind permission of Little Chef; Exhibit 2.1 reproduced with the kind permission of Ronseal Ltd.; Exhibit 2.2 reproduced with the kind permission of Max Factor/ Leo Burnett; Exhibit 3.1 reproduced with the kind permission of the Coca-Cola Company; Exhibit 3.2 reproduced with the kind permission of Kimberley-Clark Ltd; Exhibit 3.3 reproduced with the kind permission of Adidas; Exhibit 4.1 reproduced with the kind permission of Makita UK Ltd.; Exhibit 4.2 reproduced with the kind permission of Bird's Eye Walls; Exhibit 13.1 reproduced with the kind permission of Solvite on behalf of Henkel Consumer Adhesives and BDHTBWA; Exhibit 13.5 reproduced with the kind permission of Green & Blacks; Exhibit 7.1 reproduced with the kind permission of No More Nails on behalf of Henkel Consumer Adhesives and BDHTBWA; Exhibit 7.2 reproduced with the kind permission of Duracell; Exhibit 10.1 reproduced with the kind permission of Hewlett Packard Ltd.; Exhibit 10.2 reproduced with the kind permission of Neil Tingle/Action Plus; Exhibit 11.1 reproduced with the kind permission of Dell.

Introduction

Part
1

Marketing communications: an introduction

1

Aims and objectives

The aims of this introductory chapter are to introduce some of the key concepts associated with marketing communications, to consider the scope and purpose of marketing communications and to develop an appreciation of the key characteristics of the main tools of the communications mix. There are four primary topics in this chapter:

Exchange, Engagement, Branding, Communication tools

The learning objectives are to enable readers to:

1. understand the tasks of contemporary marketing communications;
2. describe the process of exchange and relate marketing communications to both market and relational exchanges;
3. define and explain the scope of marketing communications;
4. explain how marketing communications works through engagement;
5. explain the range of issues that influence marketing communications;
6. write brief notes about the key characteristics of each major tool in the communications mix;
7. describe how marketing communications can be used to build brands;
8. identify the different influences placed on marketing communications when used in consumer and business markets.

Introduction

Everything that people and organisations do in the name of marketing communications should be, first and foremost, audience-centred.

What is marketing communications all about? Well, this book will try to explain, but one element is quite clear and it runs throughout the rest of this text: marketing communications is an audience-centred activity. Everything that people and organisations do in the name of marketing communications should be, first and foremost, audience-centred.

Now, just because that is what marketing communications should be about does not mean that what we all see, hear and read about is good, effective or appropriate marketing communications. So, just as we can identify some football teams that are truly great, some that are good, some that are average, some that are good within their league, and some that should not be invited to play again, so it is with marketing communications. Some of the works that are said to be examples of marketing communications are indeed great, some are average and some are pretty poor. And the reason why some of the less than satisfactory work fails is because what is presented in the name of advertising, public relations or direct marketing is anything but audience-centred. Quite often it is company- or product-oriented, discipline-driven or media-directed.

This book does not pretend to have all the answers. However, over the course of the four parts and fifteen chapters, marketing communications is presented and considered, wherever possible, from an audience perspective.

Organisations engage with a variety of audiences in order to pursue their marketing and business objectives.

Organisations engage with a variety of audiences in order to pursue their marketing and business objectives. Perkins Engines, Reebok, IBM, Save the Children, Dell, LG, Quantas, Ryanair, Honda, First-Direct, World Vision and IKEA all operate across a number of sectors, markets and countries and use a variety of marketing communications tools to engage with their various audiences. These audiences consist not only of people who buy their products and services but also of people and organisations who might be able to influence them, who might help and support them by providing, for example, labour, finance, manufacturing facilities, distribution outlets and legal advice or who are interested because of their impact on parts of society or the business sector in particular.

The organisations mentioned earlier are all well-known brand names, but there are hundreds of thousands of smaller organisations that also need and use marketing communications to convey the essence of their products and services and to engage their various audiences. Each of these organisations, large and small, is part of a network of companies, suppliers, retailers, wholesalers, value-added resellers, distributors and other retailers that join together, often freely, so that each can achieve its own goals.

Effective communication is critically important to organisations, which is why they use a variety of marketing communication tools. Advertising, sales promotion, public relations, direct marketing, personal selling and added-value approaches such as sponsorship are the most-used tools (or disciplines). To deliver their messages they use traditional media such as print and broadcast, cinema and radio; but increasingly digital media, and the Internet in particular, are used to 'talk' to and with their customers, potential customers, suppliers, financiers, distributors, communities and employees, among others. Tools and media are two separate elements of marketing communications although they often work together to deliver messages to target audiences.

Tools and media are two separate elements of marketing communications.

ViewPoint 1.1   FMCG marketing communications

Procter & Gamble (P&G) and Unilever are two of the largest fast-moving consumer goods manufacturers (FMCG). Both organisations own many of the most popular brands in their various categories: for example, P&G owns Pantene, Olay, Pringles, Lenor, Pampers and Gillette, and Unilever owns Sunsilk, Dove, Hellmans, Persil, Birds Eye and ice cream brands Magnum, Carte D'or and Solero, among many others. In order to communicate and develop their brands with retailers, customers and other stakeholders they use a variety of communication tools. Some of the main ones are set out below.

Advertising	Websites	Point of purchase	Packaging
Corporate identity	Direct marketing	Public relations	
Personal selling	Exhibitions	Trade promotions	Sponsorship
Product placement	Sales promotion	Field marketing	
Merchandising	Vending machines	Customer contact centres	
Videoconferencing	Discussion boards		

Marketing communications provides the means by which brands and organisations are first presented to their audiences and then to engage them over the longer term. The goal is to stimulate a succession of purchases, and the task of marketing communications is to engage audiences to enable transactions.

The term 'engagement' has been used, and this refers to the form of communication and whether the nature of the messages and media are essentially intellectual and/or emotional in character. Invariably, organisations use a mixture of these two elements in order that they be heard, understood and engage their audiences in interaction, dialogue and mutually beneficial relationships.

The concept of marketing as an exchange

The concept of exchange, according to most marketing academics and practitioners, is central to our understanding of marketing. For an exchange to take place there must be two or more parties, each of whom can offer something of value to the other and who are prepared to enter freely into the exchange process, a transaction. It is possible to identify two main forms of exchange: market (or transactional or discrete) exchanges and relational (or collaborative) exchanges.

Market exchanges (Bagozzi, 1978; Houston and Gassenheimer, 1987) are transactions that occur independently of any previous or subsequent exchanges. They have a short-term orientation and are primarily motivated by self-interest. When a consumer buys a bag of nails or a packet of branded crisps, one which they buy infrequently, then a market exchange can be identified.

In contrast to this, *relational exchanges* (Dwyer et al., 1987) have a longer-term orientation and develop between parties who wish to build long-term supportive relationships. So, whenever a consumer buys crisps, however infrequently, and buys the same brand and even flavour, relational exchanges are considered to be taking place.

These two types of exchange represent the extremes in a spectrum of exchange transactions.

These two types of exchange represent the extremes in a spectrum of exchange transactions. In industrial societies market exchanges have tended to dominate commercial transactions, although recently there has been a substantial interest in and movement towards relational exchanges. In other words, there are a mixture of exchanges that occur and each organisation has a portfolio of differing types of exchange that it maintains with different customers, suppliers and other stakeholders. Communication is an essential element, similar to an oil, that lubricates these exchanges and enables them to function. However, for these different exchanges to function properly, different types of communication are necessary.

Relational exchanges form the basis of the ideas represented in relationship marketing. Many organisations use relationship marketing principles, manifested in the form of customer relationship marketing, or loyalty marketing programmes. This book is developed on relationship marketing principles, and marketing communications is considered to be a means by which long-term relationships between organisations and between organisations and consumers can be developed.

The tasks of marketing communications

Marketing communications lies at the heart of this process of exchange. For market exchanges marketing communications should deliver messages through tools and media that are appropriate to the needs of the target audience. At the other end of the spectrum, where audiences are actively involved, marketing communications can be used to convey different types of messages. However, all marketing communications needs to deliver against one or more of the following four main tasks:

1. It can *inform* and make potential customers aware of an organisation's offering.

2. Communication may attempt to *persuade* current and potential customers of the desirability of entering into an exchange relationship.

3. Communications can also be used to *reinforce* experiences. This may take the form of *reminding* people of a need they might have or reminding them of the benefits of past transactions with a view to convincing them that they should enter into a similar exchange. In addition, it is possible to provide *reassurance* or comfort either immediately prior to an exchange or, more commonly, post-purchase. This is important as it helps to retain current customers and improve profitability. This approach to business is much more cost-effective than constantly striving to lure new customers.

4. Finally, marketing communications can act as a *differentiator*, particularly in markets where there is little to separate competing products and brands. Mineral-water products, such as Perrier and Highland Spring, are largely similar: it is the communications surrounding the products that have created various brand images, enabling consumers to make purchasing decisions. In these cases it is the images created by marketing communications that dissociates one brand from another and positions them so that consumers' purchasing confidence and positive attitudes are developed. Therefore, in order of the overall process, communication can inform, differentiate, persuade and then reinforce brand associations through reminder-based messages (see Table 1.1).

TABLE 1.1 DRIP elements of marketing communications

DRIP element	Examples
Differentiate – position/create standout	Burger King differentiates itself from market leader McDonald's by stating that its burgers are flame-grilled for a better taste.
Reinforce – remind/reassure	Specsavers Opticians work to bring people back into the eyecare market.
Inform – educate/make aware	The Environment Agency and Flood Action Week – to inform various organisations, such as the Met Office, local media and the general public of the new flood-warning codes.
Persuade	Drink organic milk because it is better for us than ordinary milk.

ViewPoint 1.2   Dyson DRIP

Dyson manufactures a revolutionary type of carpet cleaner and has 52 per cent of the UK market. It is based on a new cyclone technology that has effectively replaced the older vacuum-cleaner-based equipment. Its communications have needed to:

● *differentiate* it from conventional products – use of innovative technology;

● *remind/reassure* customers that the cyclone system works better than any other and to resist the competition's attempts to gain top-of-mind awareness;

● *inform* and educate the market about what is wrong with conventional appliances;

● *persuade* potential customers to consider Dyson as the only option when next purchasing floor-cleaning appliances.

EXHIBIT 1.1 Dyson: a floor cleaner with revolutionary cyclone technology
The manufacturer of this revolutionary new domestic appliance uses marketing communications to differentiate, remind, inform and persuade audiences. Picture reproduced with the kind permission of Dyson

Defining marketing communications

There is no universal definition of marketing communications and there are many interpretations of the subject. Some definitions draw out the added value that marketing communications can provide through enhanced product and organisational symbolism. Some interpretations understand that marketing communications occurs within a particular context that impacts upon the meaning and interpretation given to such messages. Others stress the need to change attitudes or behaviour, or indeed both.

Previous 'promotional' interpretations tended to focus on customers and products.

Previous 'promotional' interpretations tended to focus on customers and products. Now, in an age where the word 'integration' is used to express a variety of marketing and communication-related activities, where corporate marketing is emerging as the next important development within the subject (Balmer and Gray, 2003) and where relationship marketing is the preferred paradigm (Gronroos, 2004), marketing communications needs to embrace a wider remit, to become an integral part of an organisation's overall communications and relationship management strategy. This perspective embraces communications as a one-way, two-way, interactive and dialogic approach necessary to meet the varying needs of different audiences.

Two definitions of marketing communications follow. The first, the long version, seeks to reflect the breadth and scope of this exciting and dynamic aspect of an organisation's marketing activities. The second is a shorter version, designed to be recalled and acted upon as an aide-memoire.

Long version

Marketing communications is a management process through which an organisation seeks to engage with its various audiences. To accomplish this, the organisation develops, presents and evaluates a series of messages, which it sends to and receives from its different audiences. The objective of this process is to (re)position the organisation and its offerings in the minds of particular audiences and in doing so encourage the development of relationships that are of mutual value.

This definition has three main themes. The first concerns the word *engages*. Through recognition of the different transactional and relationship needs of the target audience, marketing communications can be used to engage with a variety of audiences in such a way that one-way, two-way and dialogic communications are used (Chapters 2 and 9) that meet the needs of the audience. It is incorrect to think that all audiences always want a relationship with your organisation, and for some, one-way communication is just fine.

It is incorrect to think that all audiences always want a relationship with your organisation, and for some, one-way communication is just fine.

However, messages should encourage individual members of target audiences to respond to the focus organisation (or product/brand). This response can be immediate through, for example, purchase behaviour or use of customer care lines, or it can be deferred as information is assimilated and considered for future use. Even if the information is discarded at a later date, the communication will have prompted attention and consideration of the message.

ViewPoint 1.3   Water communications

The growth in consumption of bottled water is well known: it now accounts for 10 per cent of the soft drinks market and is only surpassed by cola and fruit juice (ACNielsen). However, the market is evolving such that consumers do not want straight water just for hydration purposes; now they want bottled 'water-plus' products, for example with added minerals and vitamins, low carbonated for exercise (Lucozade Hydro Active) and functional, fortified and 'wellness' waters to support healthy lifestyles and to reduce or guard against obesity.

Marketing communications plays an active role in shaping our perception of these various bottled waters and helps construct brands. Vittel used 'reVittelise' to change perceptions of its brand beyond hydration. Malvern mineral water uses advertising to position itself as 'Not quite Middle England' and reinforces this with celebrities such as Ali G.

However, advertising spend on these bottled brands has fallen as more attention is given to other communication activities. For example, attention has been given to packaging in an attempt not only to achieve shelf stand-out but also to reflect changing social trends. Evian has introduced an 'easy-to-carry' Nomad bottle with a belt clip for 'active consumers'.

Source: Adapted from Sweney (2004)

The second theme concerns the *audiences* for marketing communications. Traditionally, marketing communications has been used to convey product-related information to customer-based audiences. Today, a range of stakeholders have connections and relationships of varying dimensions and marketing communications needs to incorporate this breadth and variety. Stakeholder audiences, including customers, are all interested in a range of corporate issues, sometimes product-related and sometimes related to the policies, procedures and values of the organisation itself. Marketing communications should be an audience-centred activity and in that sense it is important that messages be based on a firm understanding of both the needs and the environment of the audience. To be successful, marketing communications should be grounded in the behaviour and information-processing needs and style of the target audience. This is referred to as understanding the context in which the communications event is to occur (Chapters 5, 6 and 12). From this base it is easier to present and position brands in order that they are perceived to be different and of value to the target audience.

Marketing communications should be an audience-centred activity.

The third theme from the definition concerns the *relationship* between the parties. Different people (audiences) require different outcomes from the various brands they become involved with. Not everyone desires a long-term relationship with a company or brand, we do not always want more loyalty cards or streams of additional direct mail, email and other promotional messages. Therefore, marketing communications should be used with respect for the level of relationship the audience requires, the level of current trust and commitment, all of which is reflected in the term 'mutual value'.

Short version

Marketing communications is an audience-centred activity designed to encourage engagement between participants.

This shorter version focuses on the audience as the centre of interest and the role of communications as the means through which appropriate (to the audience) relationships are developed through engagement. Marketing communications, therefore, can be considered from a number of perspectives. It is a complex activity and is used by organisations with varying degrees of sophistication and success.

The role of marketing communications

From the above it is possible to deduce that marketing communications is partly about the communication and promotion of a brand (or products and services) with customer audiences, and partly about the organisation and the development of relationships with various stakeholder audiences. Marketing communications recognises the increasing role the organisation plays in the marketing process and the impact that organisational factors can have on the minds of members of target audiences. As the structure, composition and sheer number of offerings in some markets proliferate, so differences between products diminish, to the extent that differentiation between products has become much more difficult. This results in a decrease in the number of available and viable positioning opportunities. One way to resolve this problem is to use the parent organisation as an umbrella, to provide greater support and leadership in the promotion of any offerings. Hence the earlier reference to the emerging strength of corporate marketing.

Many organisations recognise the usefulness and importance of good public relations. This is because of the high credibility attached to the messages received and the relatively low operational costs. As a result, the use of corporate advertising has grown.

Marketing communications recognises the development of channel or trade marketing. Many organisations have moved away from the traditional control of a brand manager to a system that focuses upon the needs of distributors and intermediaries in the channel. The organisations in the channel work together to satisfy their individual and collective objectives. The degree of conflict and cooperation in the channel network depends upon a number of factors, among the most important of which are the form and quality of the communications between member organisations. This means that marketing communications must address the specific communication needs of members of the distribution network and those other stakeholders who impact on or who influence the performance of the network. Indeed, marketing communications recognises the need to contribute to the communications in the channel network, to support and sustain the web of relationships.

For example, many organisations in the airline industry have shifted their attention to the needs of the travel trade, customers and competitors. United Airlines, British Airways, KLM, Qantas and other airlines have changed their approach, attitude and investment priorities so that channel partnerships and alliances are of particular priority. Now there is a clear emphasis on working with their partners and their competitors (e.g. British Airways and KLM), and this entails agreement, collaboration and joint communication activity in order for all participants to achieve their objectives.

The primary role of marketing communications is to engage audiences. In doing so, market and relational exchanges can be developed. Engagement acts as a bridge, the mechanism through which brands and organisations link with target audiences and both parties' goals are achieved. Engagement enables understanding and meaning to be conveyed effectively. At one level, engagement through one-way communication enables target audiences to understand product and

The primary role of marketing communications is to engage audiences.

service offers to the extent that the audience is sufficiently engaged to want to enter into a market exchange. At another level, engagement through two-way communication enables information that is relationship-specific (Ballantyne, 2004) to be exchanged and in doing so build collaborative relationships. So, the role of marketing communications might be to engage audiences but this can be achieved in many different ways.

Marketing communications and the environment

The management of marketing communications is a complex and highly uncertain activity. This is due in part to the nature of the marketing communication variables, the fallibilities of information processing by different audiences and the influence of the environment. The first and second are considered later in this chapter and in Chapter 4 but it is the impact of the environment that is considered here before progressing.

The environment can be considered in many different ways. For the sake of simplicity, however, the external, intermediate and internal environments are considered here. See Table 1.2.

These influences are determined by the degree to which an organisation can control them. External influences are generally assumed to be uncontrollable and organisations need to anticipate, flex and adapt to prevailing conditions. Intermediate influences are characterised by an organisation's partial control over them, whereas internal influences are, theoretically, totally controllable.

Internal influences

The internal environment refers primarily to the organisation. Here various forces seek to influence an organisation's marketing communications. The overall *strategy* that an organisation adopts should have a huge impact: for example, how the organisation wishes to differentiate itself within its target markets will influence the messages and media used and, of course, the overarching positioning and reputation of the company. Brand strategies will influence such things as the way in which brands are named, the extent to which sales promotions are an integral part of the communication mix and how they are positioned. The prevailing *organisational culture* can also be extremely influential. For a long time the hierarchical management structure and power culture at Procter & Gamble led to the establishment of a pattern of behaviour whereby the marketing communication messages were largely product benefit-oriented rather than emotionally driven, as at their arch rival Unilever. The amount of money available to

TABLE 1.2 Influences that shape marketing communications

External	Intermediate	Internal
Political	Competitors	Strategy
Economic	Suppliers	Culture
Social	Agencies	Resources: financial and skills
Technological	Intermediaries	Socio-political
Legalistic	Customers	
	Stakeholders	

the marketing communications budget will influence the media mix or the size of the sales force used to deliver messages. Apart from the quality and motivation of the people employed, the level, preferences and *marketing skills* deployed can impact on the messages to media, agencies and support services that a brand communicates. Finally, the *socio-political* climate of the firm shapes not only who climbs the career ladder fastest but how and to which brands scarce (marketing) resources are distributed.

Marketing communications is regarded as one of the elements of the marketing mix and is primarily responsible for the communication of the marketing offer to the target market. Although recognising that there is implicit and important communication through the other elements of the marketing mix (through a high price, for example, symbolic of high quality), it is the task of a planned and integrated set of communication activities to communicate effectively with each of an organisation's stakeholder groups. Marketing communications is sometimes perceived as only dealing with communications that are external to the organisation, but it should be recognised that good communications with internal stakeholders, such as employees, are also vital if, in the long term, successful favourable perceptions and attitudes are to be established. Influences through the workforce and the marketing plan can be both positive and effective: for example, staff used in B&Q and Halifax advertising project strong internal values that in turn reflect positively upon the respective brands.

Intermediate influences

Intermediate influences are characterised by partial levels of control and are typified by the impact of competitors. Competitors occupy particular positions in the market and this shapes what others claim about their own products, the media they use, the geographic coverage of the sales force and their own positioning. Intermediaries influence the nature of business-to-business (b2b) marketing communications. The frequency, intensity, quality and overall willingness to share information with one another are significant forces. Of course, the various agencies an organisation uses can also be very influential. Marketing research agencies (inform about market perceptions, attitudes and behaviour), communication agencies (determine what is said and then design how it is said, what is communicated) and media houses (recommend media mixes and when it is said) all have considerable potential to influence marketing communications. However, perhaps the biggest single intermediate group consists of the organisation's customers and network of stakeholders. Their attitudes, perceptions and buying behaviours, although not directly controllable, (should) have a far-reaching influence on the marketing communications used by an organisation.

> The frequency, intensity, quality and overall willingness to share information with one another are significant forces.

External influences

As mentioned earlier, the external group of influencers are characterised by the organisation's near total lack of control. The well known PEST framework is a useful way of considering these forces. *Political* forces, which can encompass both legal and ethical issues, shape the use of marketing communications through legislation, voluntary controls and individual company attitudes towards issues of right and wrong, consequences and duties and the formal and informal communications an organisation uses. Indeed, increasing attention has been placed upon ethics and corporate social responsibility to the extent that in some cases a name and shame culture might be identified.

Economic forces, which include demographics, geographics and of course geodemographics, can determine the positioning of brands in terms of perceived value. For example, if the government raises interest rates then consumers are more inclined not to spend money, especially on non-staple products and services. This may mean that marketing communications needs to convey stronger messages about value and to send out strident calls-to-action.

Social forces are concerned with the values, beliefs and norms that a society enshrines. Issues to do with core values within a society are often difficult to change. For example, the American gun culture or the once prevalent me-orientation with respect to self-fulfilment set up a string of values that marketing communications can use to harness, magnify and align brands. The current social pressures with regard to obesity and healthier eating habits have forced fast-food companies such as McDonald's to introduce new menus and healthier food options (see ViewPoint 1.4). As a result, marketing communications not only has to inform and make audiences aware of the new menus but also convey messages about differentiation and positioning plus provide a reason to visit (the restaurant).

> *Social* forces are concerned with the values, beliefs and norms that a society enshrines.

ViewPoint 1.4   Social forces of obesity

The influence of social forces on marketing, and marketing communications in particular, can be immense. For example, in the past few years increasing media and public attention has been given to issues concerning healthy eating, obesity and the role food manufacturers and retailers play in helping us (or not) to be slimmer.

Little Chef, which owns several hundred roadside restaurants, has used the brand icon of a chef called Charlie, who has carried a discernible paunch (Exhibit 1.2) since he first appeared in the 1970s. As part of an overall marketing strategy to provide guests with a healthy range of menu items, using less salt and more fruit, it was decided to slim Charlie down (Exhibit 1.3). Part of Little Chef's research

EXHIBIT 1.2 Original Charlie with slight paunch

EXHIBIT 1.3 Proposed but rejected slimmed-down Charlie

programme included the use of focus groups and an online voting system for the public to decide which icon they preferred. The public decided, quite emphatically, that Charlie should not be slimmed down.

Source: Adapted from Gray (2004)

Technological forces have had an immense impact on marketing communications. New technology has revolutionised traditional forms of marketing communications and led to more personalised, targeted, customised and responsive forms of communications. What was once predominantly one-way communications based upon a model of information provision and persuasion, has now given way to a two-way model in which interaction with audiences and where sharing and reasoning behaviours are enabled by digital technology is now used frequently with appropriate target audiences. Chapter 6 considers the impact of technology on marketing communications in greater detail.

New forms of marketing communication have been developed in response to changing market and environmental conditions. For example, public relations are now seen by some to have both a marketing and a corporate dimension. Direct marketing is now recognised as an important way of developing closer relationships with buyers, both consumer and organisational, while new and innovative forms of communication through sponsorship, floor advertising, video screens on supermarket trolleys and checkout coupon dispensers plus the Internet and associated technologies mean that effective communication requires the selection and integration of an increasing variety of communication tools.

> **Direct marketing is now recognised as an important way of developing closer relationships with buyers.**

The marketing communications mix

The marketing communications mix consists of a set of tools (disciplines) that can be used in various combinations and different degrees of intensity in order to communicate with a target audience. In addition to these tools of communication, there is the media, or the means by which marketing communications messages are conveyed. Tools and media are different and, although related, should not be confused as they have different characteristics and seek to achieve different goals.

There are five principal marketing communications tools: these are advertising, sales promotion, public relations, direct marketing and personal selling. See Figure 1.1.

> **There are five principal marketing communications tools: these are advertising, sales promotion, public relations, direct marketing and personal selling.**

However, there have been some major changes in the environment and in the way organisations communicate with their target audiences. New technology has given rise to a raft of different media, and people have developed a variety of ways to spend their leisure time. This is referred to as media and audience fragmentation and organisations have developed fresh combinations of the communications mix in order to reach their audiences effectively. For example, there has been a dramatic rise in the use of direct-response media as direct marketing becomes adopted as part of the marketing plan for many products. The Internet and digital technologies have enabled new interactive

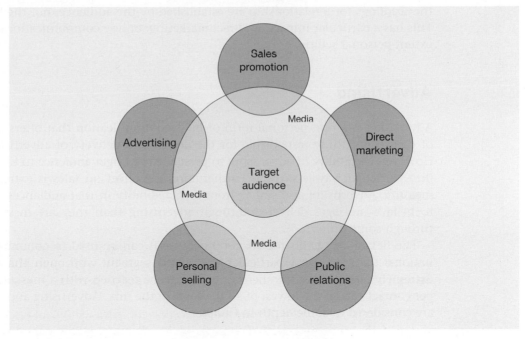

FIGURE 1.1 The tools of the marketing communications mix

forms of communication, where the receiver has greater responsibility for their part in the communication process. An increasing number of organisations are using public relations to communicate messages about the organisation (corporate public relations) and also messages about their brands (marketing public relations).

What has happened therefore is that the marketing communications mix has developed such that the original emphasis on heavyweight mass communication (above-the-line) campaigns has given way to more direct and highly targeted communication activities using direct marketing and the other tools of the mix. Using the jargon, through-the-line and below-the-line communications are used much more today than they have been in the past. Figure 1.2 brings these elements together.

The shift is from an *intervention*-based approach to marketing communications (one based on seeking the attention of a customer who might not necessarily be interested), towards *permission*-based communications (where the focus is upon communications with members of an audience who have already expressed an interest in a particular offering). In other words with permission-based communications

> With permission-based communications the seedlings for a relationship are established by the audience, not the brand owner.

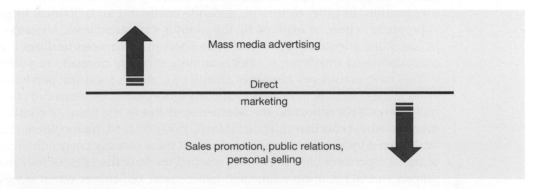

FIGURE 1.2 Above- and below-the-line communications

the seedlings for a relationship are established by the audience, not the brand owner. This has a particular impact on direct marketing, online communications and to some extent personal selling.

Advertising

Advertising is a non-personal form of mass communication that offers a high degree of control for those responsible for the design and delivery of advertising messages. However, the ability of advertising to persuade the target audience to think or behave in a particular way is suspect. Furthermore, the effect on sales is extremely hard to measure. Advertising also suffers from low credibility in that audiences are less likely to believe messages delivered through advertising than they are messages received through some other tools.

The flexibility of this tool is good because it can be used to communicate with a national audience or a particular specialised segment. Although the costs can be extremely large, a vast number of people can be reached with a message, so the cost per contact can be the lowest of all the tools in the mix. Advertising and related media are considered in some depth in Chapter 7.

Sales promotion

Sales promotion comprises various marketing techniques, which are often used tactically to provide added value to an offering, with the aim of accelerating sales and gathering marketing information. Like advertising, sales promotion is a non-personal form of communication but has a greater capability to be targeted at smaller audiences. It is controllable and, although it has to be paid for, the associated costs can be much lower than those of advertising. As a generalisation, credibility is not very high, as the sponsor is, or should be, easily identifiable. However, the ability to add value and to bring forward future sales is strong and complements a macroeconomic need, which focuses upon short-term financial performance. Sales promotion techniques are the subject of Chapter 9.

> The ability to add value and to bring forward future sales is strong.

Personal selling

Personal selling is traditionally perceived as an interpersonal communication tool that involves face-to-face activities undertaken by individuals, often representing an organisation, in order to inform, persuade or remind an individual or group to take appropriate action, as required by the sponsor's representative. A salesperson engages in communication on a one-to-one basis where instantaneous feedback is possible. The costs associated with interpersonal communication are normally very large.

This tool, considered further in Chapter 11, differs from the previous two in that, although still lacking in relative credibility and control, the degree of control is potentially lower. This is because the salesperson is free at the point of contact to deliver a message other than that intended (Lloyd, 1997). Indeed, many different messages can be delivered by a single salesperson. Some of these messages may enhance the prospect of the salesperson's objectives being reached (making the sale), or they may retard the process and so incur more time and hence costs. Whichever way it is viewed, control is lower than with advertising.

Public relations

Public relations is 'the art and social science of analysing trends, predicting their consequences, counselling organisations' leadership, and implementing planned programmes of action which will serve both the organisation's and the public interest' (Mexican Statement, 1978). This definition suggests that public relations should be a part of the wider perspective of corporate strategy, and this is discussed at length in Chapter 10. The increasing use of public relations, and in particular publicity, is a reflection of the high credibility attached to this form of communication. Publicity involves the dissemination of messages through third-party media, such as magazines, newspapers or news programmes. There is no charge for the media space or time but there are costs incurred in the production of the material (there is no such thing as a free lunch or free promotion). There is a wide range of other tools used by public relations, such as event management, sponsorship and lobbying. It is difficult to control a message once it is placed in the channels, but the endorsement offered by a third party can be very influential and have a far greater impact on the target audience than any of the other tools in the communications mix.

> The increasing use of public relations, and in particular publicity, is a reflection of the high credibility attached to this form of communication.

ViewPoint 1.5 Audi football placement

German car manufacturer Audi, a part of the Volkswagen group, has agreements with both Manchester United and Real Madrid to be their 'car partner' for several seasons, usually three. Not only does this provide Audi opportunities for its cars to be seen associated with some of the leading footballers (celebrities) but it gives Audi opportunities to be seen worldwide as well as inside Old Trafford and the Bernabéu stadiums.

When David Beckham was negotiating his contract to move to Real Madrid the media coverage was intense. He was provided with three Audis during his 36-hour stay, during which he undertook medicals, a contract signing event and an official reception. The cars were constantly on prime time news programmes and in newspaper photographs around the globe, to the extent that the equivalent advertising media costs would have been impossible to pay and would not have had the credibility that the product-placement event provided.

This non-personal form of communication offers organisations a different way to communicate, not only with consumers but also with many other stakeholders.

The four elements of the communications mix discussed so far have a number of strengths and weaknesses. As a response to some of the weaknesses that revolve around costs and effectiveness, direct marketing emerged in the 1990s as a new and effective way of building relationships with customers over the long term.

Direct marketing

The growing utilisation of direct marketing by organisations over recent years has been significant. It signals a shift in focus from mass to personalised communications.

> It signals a shift in focus from mass to personalised communications.

In particular, the use of direct mail, telemarketing and the fast-developing area of interactive communications represents through-the-line communications. By removing the face-to-face aspect of personal selling and replacing it with an email communication, a telephone conversation or a direct-mail letter, many facets of the traditional salespersons' tasks can be removed, freeing them to concentrate on their key skill areas.

Direct marketing seeks to target individual customers with the intention of delivering personalised messages and building a relationship with them based upon their responses to the direct communications. In contrast to conventional approaches, direct marketing attempts to build a one-to-one relationship, a partnership with each customer, by communicating with the customers on a direct and personal basis. If an organisation chooses to use direct marketing then it has to incorporate the approach within a marketing plan. This is because distribution is different and changes in the competitive environment may mean that prices need to change, such as charges for packing and delivery that may have to be incorporated. The product may also need to be altered or adapted to the market: for example, some electrical products are marketed through different countries on home shopping channels and websites, so the electrical requirements of each country or region need to be incorporated within the product specification of each country's offering. In addition to these changes, the promotion component is also different, simply because communication is required directly with each targeted individual. To do this, direct-response media must be used.

In many cases direct-response media are a derivative of advertising, such as direct mail, magazine inserts, and television and print advertisements that use telephone numbers to encourage a direct response. However, direct response can also be incorporated within personal selling through telemarketing and sales promotions with competitions to build market knowledge and develop the database, which is the key to the direct-marketing approach.

This text regards direct marketing as the management process associated with building mutually satisfying customer relationships through a personal and intermediary-free dialogue. Direct-response media are the primary communication tools when direct marketing is an integral part of the marketing plan. Further discussion of direct marketing and direct-response communications can be found in Chapter 11.

The Internet is a distribution channel and communication medium that enables consumers and organisations to communicate in radically different ways. It is not a communication tool, as it is so often presented. It allows for interactivity and is possibly the best medium to enable engagement and then dialogue. Communication is two-way and interactive, and is very fast, allowing businesses and individuals to find information and enter exchange transactions in such a way that some traditional communication practices and shopping patterns are being reconfigured.

The communications mix is changing.   The communications mix is changing: no longer can the traditional grouping of communication tools be assumed to be the most effective forms of communication. This brief outline of the elements of the promotions mix signals some key characteristics. These are the extent to which each element is controllable, whether it is paid for by the sponsor and whether communication is by mass medium or undertaken personally. One additional characteristic concerns the receiver's perception of the credibility of the source of the message. If the credibility factor is high then there is a greater likelihood that messages will be perceived to be believable and hence accepted by the receivers.

The 4Cs framework (Table 1.3) represents the key characteristics and shows the relative effectiveness of the tools of promotion across a number of different characteristics. The three primary groupings are the ability of each to communicate, the costs involved and the control that each tool can maintain.

TABLE 1.3 The 4Cs framework – a summary of the key characteristics of the tools of marketing communications

	Advertising	Sales promotion	Public relations	Personal selling	Direct marketing
Communications					
Ability to deliver a personal message	Low	Low	Low	High	High
Ability to reach a large audience	High	Medium	Medium	Low	Medium
Level of interaction	Low	Low	Low	High	High
Credibility given by target audience	Low	Medium	High	Medium	Medium
Credibility					
Given by the target audience	Low	Medium	High	Medium	Medium
Costs					
Absolute costs	High	Medium	Low	High	Medium
Cost per contact	Low	Medium	Low	High	High
Wastage	High	Medium	High	Low	Low
Size of investment	High	Medium	Low	High	Medium
Control					
Ability to target particular audiences	Medium	High	Low	Medium	High
Management's ability to adjust the deployment of the tool as circumstances change	Medium	High	Low	Medium	High

Effectiveness of the communication tools

Each element of the marketing communications mix has different capacities to communicate and to achieve different objectives. The effectiveness of each tool can be tracked against the purchase-decision process. Here consumers can be assumed to move from a state of unawareness through product comprehension to purchase. Advertising is better for creating awareness, and personal selling is more effective at promoting action and purchase behaviour.

Readers are encouraged to see the elements of the mix as a set of complementary ingredients, each drawing on the potential of the others. The tools are, to a limited extent, partially interchangeable and in different circumstances different tools are used to meet different objectives. For example, network marketing organisations, such as Avon Cosmetics, use personal selling to complete the majority of activities in the purchase-decision sequence. The high cost of this approach is counterbalanced by the effectiveness of the communications. However, this aspect of interchangeability only serves to complicate matters. If management's task were simply to identify problems and then select the correct precision tool to solve the problem, then the issue of the selection of the 'best' promotions mix would evaporate.

These five elements of the communications mix are supplemented by one of the most effective forms of marketing communication, *word-of-mouth* recommendation. As

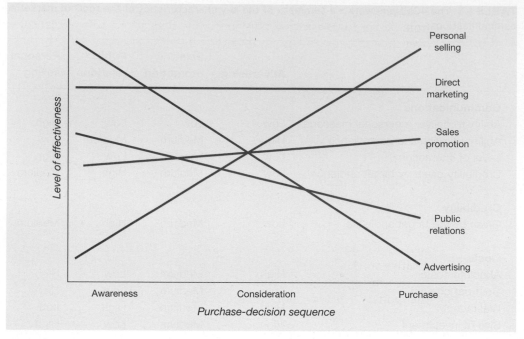

FIGURE 1.3 The effectiveness of the tools of the marketing communications mix

we shall see later, word-of-mouth recommendation is one of the most powerful marketing communications tools and, if an organisation can develop a programme to harness and accelerate the use of personal recommendation effectively, the more likely it will be that the marketing programme will be successful.

Selection criteria

The key criteria governing an organisation's selection and use of each tool are as follows:

1. the degree of control required over the delivery of the message;
2. the financial resources available to pay a third party to transmit messages;
3. the level of credibility that each tool bestows on the organisation;
4. the size and geographic dispersion of the target audiences.

Control

Control over the message is necessary to ensure that the intended message is transmitted to and received by the target audience.

Control over the message is necessary to ensure that the intended message is transmitted to and received by the target audience. Furthermore, this message must be capable of being understood in order that the receiver can act appropriately. Message control is complicated by interference or negative 'noise' that can corrupt and distort messages: an airline's advertising, for example, may be discredited by a major news story about safety checks or even an accident.

Advertising and sales promotion allow for a high level of control over the message, from design to transmission. Interestingly, they afford only partial control or influence over the feedback associated with the original message.

Financial resources

Control is also a function of financial power. In other words, if an organisation is prepared to pay a third party to transmit the message, then long-term control will rest with the sponsor for as long as the financial leverage continues. However, short-term message corruption can exist if management control over the process is less than vigilant. For example, if the design of the message differs from that originally agreed, then partial control has already been lost. This can happen when the working relationship between an advertising agency and the client is less than efficient and the process for signing off work in progress fails to prevent the design and release of inappropriate creative work.

Advertising and sales promotion are tools that allow for a high level of control by the sponsor, whereas public relations, and publicity in particular, is weak in this respect because the voluntary services of a third party are normally required for the message to be transmitted.

There is a great variety of media available to advertisers. Each media type (such as television, radio, newspapers, magazines, posters and the Internet) carries a particular cost, and the financial resources of the organisation may not be available to use particular types of media, even if such use would be appropriate on other grounds.

Credibility

Public relations scores heavily on credibility factors. This is because receivers perceive the third party as unbiased and to be endorsing the offering. They view the third party's comments as objective and trustworthy in the context of the media in which the comments appear.

At a broad level, advertising, sales promotion and, to a slightly lesser extent, personal selling are tools that can lack credibility, as perceived by the target audience. Because of this, organisations often use celebrities and 'experts' to endorse their offerings. The credibility of the spokesperson is intended to distract the receiver from the sponsor's prime objective, which is to sell the offering. Credibility, as we shall see later, is an important aspect of the communication process and of marketing communications.

Size and geographic dispersion

The final characteristic concerns the size and geographic dispersion of the target audience. A consumer audience, often national, can only be reached effectively if tools of mass communication are used, such as advertising and sales promotion. Similarly, various specialist businesses require personal attention to explain, design, demonstrate, install and service complex equipment. In these circumstances personal selling, one-to-one contact, is of greater significance. The tools of marketing communications can enable an organisation to speak to vast national and international audiences through advertising and satellite technology, or to single

Marketing communications can enable an organisation to speak to vast national and international audiences.

persons or small groups through personal selling and the assistance of word-of-mouth recommendation.

The tools of the communications mix have individual characteristics that enable each of them to achieve specific communication goals. However, they also overlap each other.

Branding and the role of marketing communications

Marketing communications plays a vital role in the development of brands and is the means by which products become brands, that is, how customers can see how a product is different and understand what a brand stands for and what its values are.

Brassington and Pettitt (2004) refer to a brand's function as the creation and communication of a multidimensional character for a product, one that 'is not easily copied or damaged by competitors' efforts'. In order to develop this character it is important to understand how brands are constructed. Brands consist of two main types of attributes: intrinsic and extrinsic (Riezebos, 2003). Intrinsic attributes refer to the functional characteristics of the product such as its shape, performance and physical capacity. If any of these intrinsic attributes were changed, it would directly alter the product. Extrinsic attributes refer to those elements that are not intrinsic and if changed do not alter the material functioning and performance of the product itself: devices such as the brand name, marketing communications, packaging, price and mechanisms that enable consumers to form associations that give meaning to the brand. Buyers often use the extrinsic attributes to help them distinguish one brand from another because in certain categories it is difficult for them to make decisions based on the intrinsic (product performance) attributes alone.

> Brands consist of two main types of attributes: intrinsic and extrinsic.

Using marketing communications to build brands

> Marketing communications can be used to enable customers and other stakeholders to make brand-related associations.

Marketing communications can be used to enable customers and other stakeholders to make brand-related associations. Two main approaches can be used to develop these associations, rational and emotional. One of advertising's main roles is to create and maintain brand values.

When a rational approach is used the functional aspects of a brand are emphasised and the benefit to the consumer is stressed. Very often product performance is the focus of the message and a key attribute is identified and used to position the brand. Typically, unique selling propositions are often used to draw attention to a single superior functional advantage that customers find attractive.

When an emotional approach is used, advertising should provide emotional selling points (ESPs). These can enable consumers to make positive brand associations based on both psychological and socially acceptable meanings, a psychosocial interpretation. Product performance characteristics remain relatively dormant while customers are encouraged to develop positive feelings and emotions with the brand. A further goal can be to create positive attitudes towards the advertising itself, which in turn can be used to make associations with the brand. In essence, therefore, emotional advertising is about people enjoying the advertisement (and complements expressive positioning; see Chapter 5).

ViewPoint 1.6	Diamond Trading Company

Through previous communications De Beers, now known as the Diamond Trading Company, established the idea that diamonds are forever. Diamonds have become a symbol of love and eternity as expressed through engagement rings. The problem facing the company was that they wanted new occasions in which expressions of love were made and the gift of a diamond would be appropriate.

Research showed that women need reaffirmation of love, and they perceive two aspects of the emotion. They acknowledge that love changes, yet at the same time it remains absolute. Using diamonds as a language rather than a luxury item JWT helped develop a new brand, 'The three stone diamond ring – for your past, your present and your future', which has subsequently helped drive sales of diamonds.

Source: http://www.jwt.com/case studies/; used with permission

Brand building through other techniques

When the marketing communications budget is limited or where the target audience cannot be reached reasonably or effectively through advertising, then it is necessary to use various other (below-the-line) communication tools to develop brands. Although sales promotion is traditionally perceived as a tool that erodes rather than helps build a brand, as it has a price rather than a value orientation, it can be used strategically. In recent years new technology has enabled innovative sales promotion techniques to be used as a competitive weapon and to help build brand presence. See Chapter 9 for more details about sales promotion.

Direct marketing and public relations are important methods used to build brand values, especially when consumers experience high involvement. The Internet offers opportunities to build new dot-com brands and the financial services sector has tried to harness this method as part of a multichannel distribution policy. What appear to be overridingly important for the development of brands operating with limited resources are the brand name and the merchandising activities, of which packaging, labelling and POP (point of purchase) are crucial. In addition, as differentiation between brands becomes more difficult in terms of content and distinct symbolism, the nature of the service encounter is now recognised as having a considerable impact on brand association. The development of loyalty schemes and carelines for FMCG, durables and service-based brands is a testimony to the importance of developing and maintaining positive brand associations.

When advertising is the main source of brand development consumers develop associations about the content and positioning of the brand through advertising messages. As a substitute for advertising, it is the merchandising, packaging and the brand name itself that need to convey the required symbolism in such a way that the content and positioning are understood by the target audience. Indeed, the brand name needs to be closely aligned with the brand's primary function, more so than when advertising is able to convey the product's purpose and role.

Where the brand name and merchandising needs to be the predominant force in enabling buyers to develop managed and positive brand associations.

There are many occasions where advertising funds are not available to develop brand associations and where the brand name and merchandising needs to be the predominant force in enabling buyers to develop managed and positive brand associations. An increasing number of organisations in the b2b sector are using branding approaches and recognise the benefits of co-branding in particular. Charities and organisations in the not-for-profit sector are increasingly using commercial organisations to co-brand. For example, the relationship between the NSPCC and Microsoft reflects strong co-branding. The former receive commercial expertise and funding while the latter gain in terms of association with good deeds, giving (rather than taking) and being seen to care.

Buyers can build trust and reduce perceived risk for buyers during the purchase-decision-making process. Marketing communications enable audiences to make associations immediately they become aware of a brand name and are the means by which products become brands. It is the brand manager's task to ensure that the associations made are appropriate and provide a means of differentiation. By communicating the key strengths and differences of a brand, by explaining how a brand brings value to a customer and by reinforcing and providing consistency in the messages transmitted, a level of integration can be brought to a brand, or rather the way it is perceived by the target market.

Communication differences in consumer and business markets

Having identified the need to communicate with a number of different audiences, it seems appropriate to conclude this opening chapter by examining the differences between communications used by and targeted at two very different and specific audiences. These are organisations (commonly referred to as business-to-business) and those aimed at consumer markets. Some writers (Brougaletta, 1985; Gilliland and Johnston, 1997) have documented a variety of differences between consumer and business-to-business markets. The following is intended to set out some of the more salient differences (see also Table 1.4):

1. *Message reception*
   The contextual conditions in which messages are received and ascribed meanings are very different. In the organisational setting the context is much more formal, and as the funding for the purchase is to be derived from company sources (as opposed to personal sources for consumer market purchases) there may be a lower orientation to the price as a significant variable in the purchase decision. The purchase is intended to be used by others for company usage, whereas products bought in a consumer context are normally intended for personal consumption.

> The purchase is intended to be used by others for company usage, whereas products bought in a consumer context are normally intended for personal consumption.

2. *Number of decision-makers*
   In consumer markets a single person very often makes the decision. In organisational markets decisions are made by many people within the buying centre. This means that the interactions of the individuals need to be considered. In addition, a variety of different individuals need to be reached and influenced and this may involve the use of different media and message strategies.

3. *The balance of the communications mix*
   The role of advertising and sales promotions in business-to-business communications is primarily to support the personal selling effort. This contrasts with the mix

that predominates in consumer markets. Personal selling has a relatively minor role and is only significant at the point of purchase in some product categories where involvement is high (cars, white goods and financial services), reflecting high levels of perceived risk. However, the increasing use of direct marketing in consumer markets suggests that personal communications are becoming more prevalent and in some ways increasingly similar to the overall direction of business-to-business communications.

4. *The constituents of the marketing communications mix*

Business-to-business markets have traditionally been quite specific in terms of the communication tools and media used to target audiences. Although the use of advertising literature is very important, there has been a tendency to use a greater proportion of below-the-line activities. This compares with consumer markets, where a greater proportion of funds have been allocated to above-the-line activities. It is interesting that the communications in consumer markets are moving towards a more integrated format, more similar in form to the business-to-business model than was previously considered appropriate.

TABLE 1.4 Differences between consumer and business-to-business marketing communications

	Consumer-oriented markets	**Business-to-business markets**
Message reception	Informal	Formal
Number of decision-makers	Single or few	Many
Balance of the promotional mix	Advertising and sales promotions dominate	Personal selling dominates
Specificity and integration	Broad use of promotional mix with a move towards integrated mixes	Specific use of below-the-line tools but with a high level of integration
Message content	Greater use of emotions and imagery	Greater use of rational, logic- and information-based messages, although there is evidence of a move towards the use of imagery
Length of decision time	Normally short	Longer and more involved
Negative communications	Limited to people close to the purchaser/user	Potentially an array of people in the organisation and beyond
Target marketing and research	Great use of sophisticated targeting and communications approaches	Limited but increasing use of targeting and segmentation approaches
Budget allocation	Majority of budget allocated to brand management	Majority of budget allocated to sales management
Evaluation and measurement	Great variety of techniques and approaches used	Limited number of techniques and approaches

5. *Message content*

Generally, there is high involvement in many business-to-business purchase decisions, so communications tend to be much more rational and information-based than in consumer markets. However, there are signs that businesses are making increased use of imagery and emotions in the messages (see Chapter 7).

6. *Length of purchase-decision time*

The length of time taken to reach a decision is much greater in the organisation market. This means that the intensity of any media plan can be dissipated more easily in this market.

7. *Negative communications*

The number of people affected by a dissatisfied consumer, and hence negative marketing communications messages, is limited. The implications of a poor purchase decision in an organisational environment may be far-reaching, including those associated with the use of the product, the career of participants close to the locus of the decision and, depending upon the size and spread, perhaps the whole organisation.

8. *Target marketing and research*

The use of target marketing processes in the consumer market has been more advanced and sophisticated than in the organisation market. This impacts on the quality of the marketing communications used to reach the target audience. However, there is much evidence that the business-to-business markets organisations are becoming more aware and sophisticated in their approach to segmentation techniques and processes.

9. *Budget allocation*

The sales department receives the bulk of the marketing budget in the organisation market and little is spent on research in comparison with the consumer market.

10. *Measurement and evaluation*

The consumer market employs a variety of techniques to evaluate the effectiveness of communications. In the organisation market, sales volume, value, number of enquiries and market share are the predominant measures of effectiveness.

There can be no doubt that there are a number of major differences between consumer and organisation communications. These reflect the nature of the environments, the tasks involved and the overall need of the recipients for particular types of information. Information need, therefore, can be seen as a primary reason for the differences in the way communications mixes are configured. Advertising in organisation markets has to provide a greater level of information and is geared to generating leads that can be followed up with personal selling, which is traditionally the primary tool in the communications mix. In consumer markets, advertising plays the primary role with support from the other tools of the communications mix. Interestingly, new media appear to be reconfiguring the marketing communications mix and perhaps reducing the gulf and distinction between the mix used in business-to-business and consumer markets. Throughout this book, reference will be made to the characteristics, concepts and processes associated with marketing communications and each of these two main sectors.

Summary of key points

1. Market and relational exchanges are the two key types of exchange. These can help to explain the communications used to oil the flow of exchanges between people and organisations.

2. Marketing communications has several roles and many tasks to achieve. The primary role is to engage audiences to encourage understanding and meaning through the communication of relationship-specific knowledge.

3. At one level engagement can occur through one-way communication that is focused on product, price and service offers. At another level, engagement can be through two-way communication where the communication is focused on the relationship. If successful, both forms of engagement enable the delivery of mutual value.

4. The main tasks of marketing communications concern the delivery of differentiated, persuasive, informative and reinforcing messages (DRIP). Each campaign requires the delivery and accomplishment of some of these tasks, not all of them at the same time.

5. To achieve these tasks marketing communications uses five traditional tools, collectively referred to as the communications mix: advertising, sales promotion, public relations, direct marketing and personal selling. In addition, some messages have to be conveyed through various media, whether they be print, broadcast, outdoor, cinema, in-store or through new media such as the Internet.

6. Each tool and each medium has strengths and weaknesses, each is used in different ways and they can all be combined or integrated in different ways to achieve different goals.

7. Marketing communications plays an important role in helping audiences to develop suitable brand-related associations. Whether this be accomplished through advertising or the use of below-the-line communication tools, it is important to base the associations people make on either rational or emotional messages.

8. Marketing communications has an important role to play in communicating and promoting the products and services not only to consumers but also to business-to-business audiences and other organisations that represent other stakeholders.

9. Marketing communications is, above all else, an audience-centred activity.

Review questions

1. Briefly compare and contrast market and relational exchanges.
2. How does marketing communications assist the exchange process?
3. Name the five main tools of the marketing communications mix and write a brief description of each tool.
4. What does engagement mean when applied to marketing communications?
5. How do each of the tools compare across the following criteria: control, communication effectiveness and cost?
6. Explain the role of marketing communications in building successful brands.

References

Bagozzi, R. (1978), 'Marketing as exchange: a theory of transactions in the market place', *American Behavioral Science*, **21**(4), pp. 257–61.

Ballantyne, D. (2004), 'Dialogue and its role in the development of relationship-specific knowledge', *Journal of Business and Industrial Marketing*, **19**(2), pp. 114–23.

Balmer, J.M.T. and Gray, E.R. (2003), 'Corporate brands: what are they? What of them?', *European Journal of Marketing*, **37**(7/8), pp. 972–97.

Brassington, F. and Pettitt, S. (2004), *Principles of Marketing*, 3rd edn, Harlow: Pearson.

Brougaletta, Y. (1985), 'What business-to-business advertisers can learn from consumer advertisers', *Journal of Advertising Research*, **25**(3), pp. 8–9.

Dwyer, R., Schurr, P. and Oh, S. (1987), 'Developing buyer–seller relationships', *Journal of Marketing*, **51** (April), pp. 11–27.

Gilliland, D.I. and Johnston, W.J. (1997), 'Toward a model of business-to-business marketing communications effects', *Industrial Marketing Management*, **26**, pp. 15–29.

Gray, R. (2004), 'Why the fatboys slimmed', *Marketing*, 25 August, p. 14.

Gronroos, C. (2004), 'The relationship marketing process: communication, interaction, dialogue, value', *Journal of Business and Industrial Marketing*, **19**(2), pp. 99–113.

Houston, F. and Gassenheimer, J. (1987), 'Marketing and exchange', *Journal of Marketing*, **51** (October), pp. 3–18.

Lloyd, J. (1997), 'Cut your rep free', *Pharmaceutical Marketing*, September, pp. 30–2.

Mexican Statement (1978), *The Place of Public Relations in Management Education*, Public Relations Education Trust, June.

Riezebos, R. (2003), *Brand Management: A Theoretical and Practical Approach*, Harlow: Pearson.

Sweney, M. (2004), 'Sector insight: bottled water – beyond the functional', *Marketing*. Retrieved 18 August 2004 from www.brandrepublic.co.uk/news/newsArticle.

Communication: theory, interactivity and people

2

Aims and objectives

The aims of this chapter are to introduce the fundamental elements of communication theory and then to examine how the context and personal influences on the communication process can bring complexity to the process of establishing meaning between the parties involved in the communication. There are four primary topics in this chapter:

Communication models, Source credibility, Word of mouth, Interactivity

The learning objectives are to enable readers to:

1. understand the basic model of the communication process;
2. appreciate how the components of the model contribute to successful communications;
3. explain the linkages between the various components in the process;
4. evaluate the impact of personal influences on the communication process;
5. describe how source credibility works and to explain how it can be developed;
6. examine the importance and characteristics of using source credibility;
7. consider the essential issues involved with interactive forms of communication;
8. explain how communication theory underpins our understanding of marketing communications.

An introduction to the communications process

Communication is the process by which individuals share meaning, so participants need to be able to interpret the meaning embedded in the messages they receive and be able to respond coherently, as far as the sender is concerned. The act of responding is important to complete an episode in the communication process. Sender–receiver communication is essentially a one-way process, whereas sender–receiver–sender becomes a two-way communication episode. For this overall process to work, information needs to be transmitted by all participants. It is important, therefore, that those involved with marketing communications understand the complexity of the transmission process. Through knowledge and understanding of the communications process they are more likely to achieve their objective of sharing meaning with each member of their target audiences and so have an opportunity to enter into a dialogue.

Sender–receiver–sender becomes a two-way communication episode.

Linear model of communications

Wilbur Schramm (1955) developed what is now accepted as the basic model of mass communications (Figure 2.1). The components of the linear model of communications are:

1. Source: the individual or organisation sending the message.
2. Encoding: transferring the intended message into a symbolic style that can be transmitted.

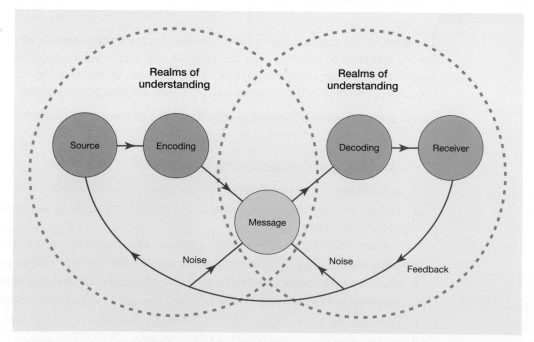

FIGURE 2.1 A linear model of communications. Based on Schramm (1955) and Shannon and Weaver (1962)

3. Signal: the transmission of the message using particular media.
4. Decoding: understanding the symbolic style of the message in order to understand the message.
5. Receiver: the individual or organisation receiving the message.
6. Feedback: the receiver's communication back to the source on receipt of the message.
7. Noise: distortion of the communication process, making it difficult for the receiver to interpret the message as intended by the source.

The linear model emphasises the 'transmission of information, ideas, attitudes, or emotion from one person or group to another (or others), primarily through symbols' (Theodorson and Theodorson, 1969). The model and its components are straightforward, but it is the quality of the linkages between the various elements in the process that determine whether the communication will be successful.

Source/encoding

The source, an individual or organisation, identifies a need to transmit a message and then selects a combination of appropriate words, pictures, symbols and music to represent the message to be transmitted. This is called encoding. The purpose is to create a message that is capable of being understood by the receiver.

There are a number of reasons why the source/encoding link might break down; for example, the source may fail to diagnose a particular situation accurately. By not fully understanding a stakeholder's problem or level of knowledge, inappropriate information may be included in the message that, when transmitted, may lead to misunderstanding and misinterpretation by the receiver. By failing to appreciate the level of education of the target receiver, a message might be encoded in words and symbols that are beyond the comprehension of the receiver. This is why some organisations spend a great deal of time and expense on marketing research, trying to develop their understanding of their target audience.

The source of a message is an important factor in the communications process. A receiver who perceives a source lacking conviction, authority, trust or expertise is likely to discount any message received from that source until such time that credibility is established.

> The source of a message is an important factor in the communications process.

Most organisations spend a great deal of time and expense recruiting sales representatives. The risk involved in selecting the wrong people can be extremely large. Many high-tech organisations require their new sales staff to spend over a year receiving both product and sales training before allowing them to meet customers. From a customer's perspective, salespersons who display strong product knowledge skills and who are also able to empathise with the individual members of the decision-making unit are more likely to be perceived as credible. Therefore, the organisation that prepares its sales staff and presents them as knowledgeable and trustworthy is more likely to be successful in the communications process than those that do not take the same level of care.

The source is a part of the communication process, not just the generator of detached messages. Patzer (1983) determined that the physical attractiveness of the communicator, particularly if it is the source, contributes significantly to the effectiveness of persuasive communications.

This observation can be related to the use by organisations of spokespersons and celebrities to endorse products. Spokespersons can be better facilitators of the communications process if they are able to convey genuine conviction,

> Spokespersons can be better facilitators of the communications process if they are able to convey genuine conviction.

if they are easily associated with the object of the message, if they have credible expertise and if they are attractive to the receiver, in the wider sense of the word.

This legitimate authority is developed in many television advertisements by the use of the 'white coat', or product-specific clothing, as a symbol of expertise. By dressing the spokesperson in a white coat, he or she is perceived immediately as a credible source of information ('they know what they are talking about'), and so is much more likely to be believed.

Signal

Once encoded, the message must be put into a form that is capable of transmission. It may be oral or written, verbal or non-verbal, in a symbolic form or in a sign. Whatever the format chosen, the source must be sure that what is being put into the message is what is wanted to be decoded by the receiver. The importance of this aspect of the communication process will be developed later when different message strategies are examined in Chapter 7.

The channel is the means by which the message is transmitted from the source to the receiver. These channels may be personal or non-personal. The former involves face-to-face contact and word-of-mouth communications, which can be extremely influential. Non-personal channels are characterised by mass-media advertising, which can reach large audiences.

Information received directly from personal influence channels is generally more persuasive than information received through mass media. This may be a statement of the obvious, but the reasons for this need to be understood. First, the individual approach permits greater flexibility in the delivery of the message. The timing and power with which a message is delivered can be adjusted to suit the immediate 'selling' environment. Secondly, a message can be adapted to meet the needs of the customer as the sales call progresses. This flexibility is not possible with mass-media messages, as these have to be designed and produced well in advance of transmission and often without direct customer input.

ViewPoint 2.1   Encoding/decoding problems

When developing names or taglines for global brands it is important to choose a name that translates appropriately into all the languages. The encoding process, the name of the car, cleaner, biscuit or fashion accessory should be well researched and capable of being decoded by the target audience in such a way that there is meaning, sense and value. The following are examples where the encoding process had not been properly considered:

- When the European hardware store chain 'Götzen' opened in Istanbul it had to change the name as 'Göt' means 'ass' in Turkish.
- Traficante is an Italian brand of mineral water. In Spanish, it means drug dealer.
- Clairol's 'Mist Stick' curling iron had problems when launched in Germany because 'mist' is slang for manure.

A mainstream UK bank informed audiences in a recent advertising campaign that to show the soles of your feet in Thailand is a very rude gesture, and to give the thumbs-up sign in Turkey has quite the opposite meaning to its symbolism of cool acceptance here in the UK.

Finally, workers in an African port saw a consignment with the international symbol for 'fragile' (a wine glass with snapped stem) on the side. They assumed it meant that they had been sent a cargo of broken glass and immediately pitched all the cases overboard into the harbour.

Source: Adapted from www.i18nguy.com/translations and http://www.sourceuk.net/indexf.html?03590; used with permission

Decoding/receiver

Decoding is the process of transforming and interpreting a message into thought. This process is influenced by the receiver's realm of understanding, which encompasses the experiences, perceptions, attitudes and values of both the source and the receiver. The more the receiver understands about the source and the greater his or her experience in decoding the source's messages, the more able the receiver will be to decode the message successfully.

Feedback/response

The set of reactions a receiver has after seeing, hearing or reading the message is known as the response. These reactions may vary from the extreme of dialling an enquiry telephone number, returning a coupon or even buying the product, to storing information in long-term memory for future use. Feedback is that part of the response that is sent back to the sender, and it is essential for successful communication. The need to understand not just whether the message has been received but also which message has been received is vital. For example, the receiver may have decoded the message incorrectly and a completely different set of responses may have been elicited. If a suitable feedback system is not in place then the source will be unaware that the communication has been unsuccessful and is liable to continue wasting resources. This represents inefficient and ineffective marketing communications.

Feedback is that part of the response that is sent back to the sender, and it is essential for successful communication.

The evaluation of feedback is, of course, vital if sound communications are to be developed. Only through evaluation can the success of any communication be judged. Feedback through personal selling can be instantaneous, through overt means such as questioning, raising objections or signing an order form. Other means, such as the use of gestures and body language, are less overt, and the decoding of the feedback needs to be accurate if an appropriate response is to be given. For the advertiser, the process is much more vague and prone to misinterpretation and error.

Feedback through mass-media channels is generally much more difficult to obtain, mainly because of the inherent time delay involved in the feedback process. There are some exceptions, namely the overnight ratings provided by the Broadcasters' Audience Research Board to television contractors, but as a rule feedback is normally delayed and not as fast. Some commentators argue that the only meaningful indicator of communication success is sales. However, there are many other influences that affect the level of sales, such as price, the effect of previous communications, the recommendations of opinion leaders or friends, poor competitor actions or any number of government or regulatory developments. Except in circumstances such as direct marketing, where immediate and direct feedback can be determined, organisations should use other methods to gauge the success of their communications activities, such as the level and quality of customer enquiries, the number and frequency of store visits, the degree of attitude change and the ability to recognise or recall an advertisement. All of these represent feedback but, as a rough distinction, the evaluation of feedback for mass communications is much more difficult to judge than is the case for interpersonal communications.

Noise

A complicating factor that may influence the quality of the reception and the feedback is noise. Noise, according to Mallen (1977), is 'the omission and distortion of information', and there will always be some noise present in all communications. Management's role is to ensure that levels of noise are kept to a minimum, wherever it is able to exert influence.

Noise occurs when a receiver is prevented from receiving the entire message.

Noise occurs when a receiver is prevented from receiving the entire message. This may be because of either cognitive or physical factors. For example, a cognitive factor may be that the encoding of the message was inappropriate, so making it difficult for the receiver to decode the message. In this circumstance it is said that the realms of understanding of the source and the receiver were not matched. Another reason why noise may enter the system is that the receiver may have been physically prevented from decoding the message accurately because the receiver was distracted. Examples of distraction are that the telephone rang, or someone in the room asked a question or coughed. A further reason could be that competing messages screened out the targeted message.

Some sales-promotion practitioners use the word 'noise' to refer to the ambience and publicity surrounding a particular sales promotion event. In other words, the word is being used as a positive, advantageous element in the communication process. This approach is not adopted in this text.

Realms of understanding

The concept of the 'realm of understanding' was introduced earlier. It is an important element in the communication process because it recognises that successful communications are more likely to be achieved if the source and the receiver understand each other. This understanding concerns attitudes, perceptions, behaviour and experience: the values of both parties to the communication process. Therefore, effective communication is more likely when there is some common ground, a realm of understanding between the source and receiver.

Some organisations, especially those in the private sector, spend a huge amount of money researching their target markets and testing their ads to ensure that their messages can be decoded and understood by the target audience. The more organisations understand their receivers, the more confident they become in constructing and transmitting messages to them. Repetition and learning are important elements in marketing communications. Learning is a function of knowledge, and the more we know, the more likely we are to understand.

Factors influencing the communications process

The linear, sequential interpretation of the communications process fails to represent accurately all forms of communication. Indeed, it is probable that there is not a single model or framework that is entirely satisfactory and capable of covering all forms of communication. However, there are three particular influences on the communications process that need to be considered. First, the media used to convey information, second, the influence of people on the communications process, and finally, the credibility of the source of the message as perceived by the receiver. These are considered in turn.

The influence of the media within the communications process

The interaction that marketing communications seeks to generate with audiences is partially constrained by an inherent time delay based upon the speed at which responses are generated by the participants in the communications process. Technological advances now allow participants to conduct marketing communication-based 'conversations' at electronic speeds. The essence of this speed attribute is that it allows for interactively based communications, where enquiries are responded to more or less instantly. This is explored later in this chapter.

New technology, and the Internet in particular, provide an opportunity for interaction and, for some, real dialogue with customers. With traditional media the tendency is for a monologue or at best delayed and inferred two-way communication. One of the first points to be made about these new media-based communications is that the context within which marketing communications occurs is redefined. Traditionally, interaction occurs in a context that is familiar (relatively) and which is driven by providers who deliberately present their messages via a variety of communication devices into the environments that they expect their audiences may well pass through or recognise. Providers implant their messages into the various environments of their targets. Yuan et al. (1998) refer to advertising messages being 'unbundled', such as direct marketing, which has no other content, or 'bundled' and embedded with other news content such as television, radio and Web pages with banner ads. Perhaps more pertinently, they refer to direct and indirect online advertising. Direct advertising is concerned with advertising messages delivered to the customers (email) while indirect advertising is concerned with messages that are made available for customers to access at their leisure (websites).

New media-based communications tend to make providers become relatively passive. Their messages are presented in an environment that requires targets to use specific equipment to actively search them out. The roles are reversed, so that the drivers in the new context are active information seekers, represented by the target audience (members of the public and other information providers such as organisations), not just the information-providing organisations.

The influence of people on the communications process

The traditional view of communication holds that the process consists essentially of one step. Information is directed and shot at prospective audiences, rather like a bullet is propelled from a gun. The decision of each member of the audience to act on the message or not is the result of a passive role or participation in the process (Figure 2.2).

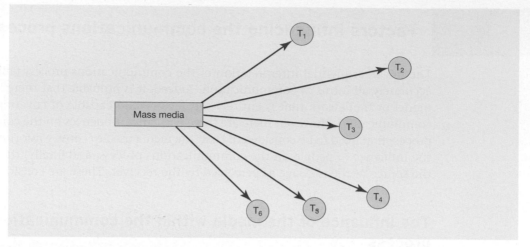

FIGURE 2.2 The one-step model of communications. T = member of the target audience

One-step flow of communications

Organisations can communicate with different target audiences simply by varying the message and the type and frequency of channels used. The one-step model has been criticised for its oversimplification, and it certainly ignores the effect of personal influences on the communication process and potential for information deviance.

The one-step model has been criticised for its oversimplification.

Two-step flow of communications

This model depicts information flowing via media channels to particular types of people (opinion leaders and opinion formers; see later) to whom other members of the audience refer for information and guidance. Through interpersonal networks, opinion leaders not only reach members of the target audience who may not have been exposed to the message, but may reinforce the impact of the message for those members that did receive it (Figure 2.3). For example, editors of travel sections in the Sunday press and television presenters of travel programmes fulfil the role of opinion former and can influence the decision of prospective travellers. It can be seen that targets 5

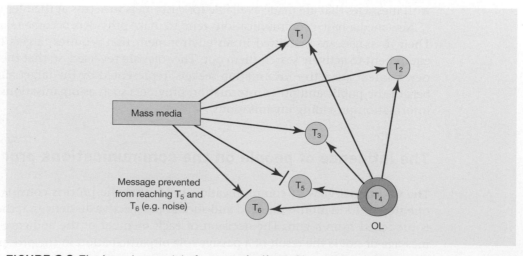

FIGURE 2.3 The two-step model of communications. OL = opinion leader

EXHIBIT 2.1 Brushing Wax print ad. This uses the principles of opinion leadership (a representative of the target audience) to convey product benefits

and 6 were not exposed to the original message, so the opinion leader (OL; T_4) acts as an original information source for them and as a reinforcer for targets 1, 2 and 3.

The implication of the two-step model is that the mass media do not have a direct and all-powerful effect on their audiences. If the primary function of the mass media is to provide information, then personal influences are necessary to be persuasive and to exert direct influence on members of the target audience.

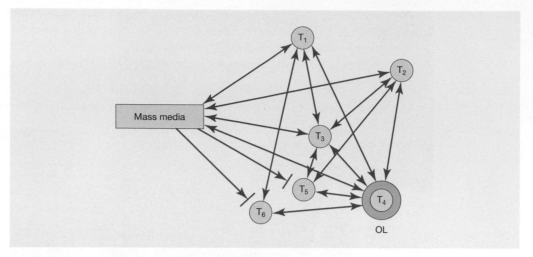

FIGURE 2.4 The multi-step model of communications

Multi-step flow of communications

This model proposes that the process involves interaction among all parties to the communication process; see Figure 2.4. This interpretation closely resembles the network of participants that are often involved in the communication process.

Message source

The third influence on the success of a marketing communication message concerns the credibility that is attributed to the source of the message itself. Kelman (1961) believed that the source of a message has three particular characteristics. These are: the level of perceived credibility as seen in terms of perceived objectivity and expertise; the degree to which the source is regarded as attractive and message recipients are motivated to develop a similar association or position; and the degree of power that the source is believed to possess. This is manifest in the ability of the source to reward or punish message receivers.

Kelman (1961) believed that the source of a message has three particular characteristics.

ViewPoint 2.2   Fear of Gas

Very often source power is reflected in fear appeals. British Gas, for example, was found by the Advertising Standards Authority to be running a campaign that induced fear in its customers. British Gas was trying to improve its retention rates and used a strap-line that said that 'Walk away from British Gas and wave goodbye to our engineers'. In other words, it was warning customers that if they left for another energy supplier they would no longer be entitled to use other British Gas services, most notably its service backup scheme.

British Gas holds a strong position in the market even though it has been deregulated and opened up. It might be argued that the power it has in terms of its stature and range of services was being used as leverage to frighten customers into staying. Unsurprisingly, competitors such as Npower, E.On and Scottish Power objected to this approach.

Source: Adapted from Carter (2005) and www.asa.org.uk

The two former characteristics are evident in various forms of marketing communications but the latter is directly observable in personal selling situations, and perhaps in the use of sales promotions.

Following this work on source characteristics, three key components of source credibility can be distinguished:

1. What is the level of perceived expertise (how much knowledge the source is thought to hold)?
2. What are the personal motives the source is believed to possess?
3. What degree of trust can be placed in the source concerning the motives for communicating the message in the first place?

No matter what the level of expertise, if the level of trust is questionable, credibility will be adversely affected.

Establishing credibility

Credibility can be established in a number of ways. One simple approach is to list or display the key attributes of the organisation or the product and then signal trustworthiness through the use of third-party endorsements and the comments of satisfied users.

A more complex approach is to use referrals, suggestions and association. The two principal elements of credibility are trustworthiness and expertise. These can be developed by using a spokesperson or organisation to provide testimonials on behalf of the sponsor of the advertisement. Credibility, therefore, can be established by the initiator of the advertisement or by a messenger or spokesperson used by the initiator to convey the message.

Effectively, viewers trade off the validity of claims made by brands against the perceived trustworthiness (and expertise) of the individuals or organisations who deliver the message. The result is that a claim may have reduced impact if either of these two components is doubtful or not capable of verification but, if repeated enough times, will enable audiences to accept that the products are very effective and of sufficiently high performance for them to try.

Credibility established by the initiator

The credibility of the organisation initiating the communication process is important. An organisation should seek to enhance its reputation with its various stakeholders at every opportunity. However, organisational credibility is derived from the image, which in turn is a composite of many perceptions. Past decisions, current strategy and performance indicators, level of service and the type of performance network members (e.g. high-quality retail outlets) all influence the perception of an organisation and the level of credibility that follows.

One very important factor that influences credibility is branding. Private and family brands in particular allow initiators to develop and launch new products more easily than those who do not have such brand strength. Brand extensions (such as Mars ice cream) have been launched with the credibility of the product firmly grounded in the strength of the parent brand name (Mars). Consumers recognise the name and make associations that enable them to lower the perceived risk and in doing so provide the platform to try the new product.

The need to establish high levels of credibility also allows organisations to divert advertising spend away from a focus upon brands to one that focuses upon the organisation. Corporate advertising seeks to adjust organisation image and to build reputation.

Credibility established by a spokesperson

People who deliver the message are often regarded as the source, when in reality they are only the messenger. These people carry the message and represent the true source or initiator of the message (e.g. manufacturer or retailer). Consequently, the testimonial they transmit must be credible. There are four main types of spokesperson: the expert, the celebrity, the chief executive officer and the consumer.

The expert has been used many times and was particularly popular when television advertising first established itself in the 1950s and 1960s. Experts are quickly recognisable because they either wear white coats and round glasses or dress and act like 'mad professors'. Through the use of symbolism, stereotypes and identification, these characters (and indeed others) can be established very quickly in the minds of receivers and a frame of reference generated that does not question the authenticity of the message being transmitted by such a person. Experts can also be users of products, for example professional photographers endorsing cameras, secretaries endorsing word processors and professional golfers endorsing golf equipment.

Entertainment and sporting celebrities were used increasingly in the 1990s, not only to provide credibility for a range of high-involvement (e.g. David Beckham for Vodafone and Linda Barker for DFS) and low-involvement decisions (e.g. Jamie Oliver for Sainsbury's) but also to grab the attention of people in markets where motivation to decide between competitive products may be low. The use of celebrities enables messages to stand out among the clutter and noise that typify many markets. It is also hoped that the celebrity and/or the voice-over will become a peripheral cue in the decision-making process: Joanna Lumley for Privilege car insurance, Gary Lineker for Walkers Crisps and Nicole Kidman for Chanel No. 5.

> The use of celebrities enables messages to stand out among the clutter and noise that typify many markets.

There are some potential problems that advertisers need to be aware of when considering the use of celebrities. First, does the celebrity fit the image of the brand and will the celebrity be acceptable to the target audience? Consideration also needs to be given to the longer-term relationship between the celebrity and the brand. Should the lifestyle of the celebrity change, what impact will the change have on the target audience and their attitude towards the brand?

ViewPoint 2.3   Max Factor's source credibility

Max Factor claims that its products are so good that they are used by the experts in their industry: 'The Make-up of Make-up Artists'. Many of its recent campaigns feature expert make-up artists who work on blockbuster Hollywood movies, although most of these experts themselves are not known to the general public. The development of 'trustworthiness' therefore relies on the film credential.

As with all use of spokespersons, Max Factor needs to ensure that its use of experts is perceived by the target audiences as genuinely believable. In this case Max Factor uses these experts because they are perceived to be objective and independent simply because their job gives them freedom of choice with regard to the products they use.

Potential new customers seeing these advertisements are challenged on the grounds that if the brand is good enough for these experts then it should be good enough for them. If a viewer is already a Max Factor customer, then product experience will contribute to a support argument and these advertising messages are used to reinforce previous brand choice decisions. Either way, these Max Factor advertisements are extremely powerful.

EXHIBIT 2.2 Max Factor. Used with the kind permission of Leo Burnett, London, Eugenia Silva and the photographer Darren Feist

ViewPoint 2.4   Running endorsement

According to the *Sunday Times* the athlete Paula Radcliffe who failed to complete the Marathon and 10,000 metres at the Athens Olympic Games in 2004, was dropped by Quaker Oats as the endorser of their Oatso Simple brand. The line 'Quaker Oats – helps you go the distance' might not have been in the best taste but the decision to cancel the ads was made because the Broadcast Advertising Clearance Centre would not pass the scripts.

The second problem concerns the impact that the celebrity makes relative to the brand. There is a danger that the receiver remembers the celebrity but not the message or the brand that is the focus of the advertising spend. The *celebrity* becomes the hero, rather than the product being advertised. Summers (1993) suggests that the Cinzano advertisements featuring Joan Collins and Leonard Rossiter are a classic example of the problem: 'The characters so dwarfed the product that consumers may have had trouble recalling the brand'.

Sir Richard Branson is used to promote Virgin Financial products and Victor Kiam 'so liked the razor that he bought the company' (Remington). Here, the CEO openly promotes his company. This form of testimonial is popular when the image of the CEO is positive and the photogenic and on-screen characteristics provide for enhanced credibility. Bernard Matthews has established authenticity and trustworthiness with his personal promotion of Norfolk Roasts.

The final form of spokesperson is the consumer. By using consumers to endorse products, the audience is being asked to identify with a 'typical consumer'. The identification of similar lifestyles, interests and opinions allows for better reception and understanding of the message. Consumers are often depicted testing similar products, such as margarine and butter. The Pepsi Challenge required consumers to select Pepsi from Coca-Cola through blind taste tests. By showing someone using the product, someone who is similar to the receiver, the source is perceived as credible and the potential for successful persuasion is considerably enhanced.

Word-of-mouth communications

The multi-step model suggests that opinion leaders/formers and members of the target audience all influence each other. Indeed, successful communication is characterised by interaction, and word-of-mouth (WoM) communications can assist and enrich this communication process.

Therefore, personal influence upon the communication process is important if communication is to be successful. Customers use word-of-mouth recommendations to provide information and to support and reinforce their purchasing decisions. At the heart of this approach is the source credibility that is assigned to people whose opinions are sought after and used in the purchase-decision process. In comparison to advertising messages, word-of-mouth communications are more robust (Berkman and Gilson, 1986).

Stokes and Lomax (2002) define word-of-mouth communication as 'interpersonal communication regarding products or services where the receiver regards the communicator as impartial'. This definition was developed from some of the more established interpretations that did not accommodate such communication through new media and restrictions concerning perceived independence of the communicator. Organisations now use WoM techniques commercially in order to generate a point of differentiation.

People like to talk about their product (service) experiences.

People like to talk about their product (service) experiences, for a variety of reasons that are explored in the next section. However, by talking with a neighbour or colleague about the good experiences associated with a new car, for example, the first-hand 'this has actually happened to someone I know' effect will be instrumental in the same views being passed on to other colleagues, irrespective of their validity or overall representation of similar cars. eViral marketing (see Chapter 6) is an electronic version of the spoken endorsement of a product or service where messages, screensavers and other information are targeted at key individuals who then voluntarily pass the message to friends and colleagues and in doing so bestow, endorse and provide the message with much-valued credibility.

Dichter (1966) determined that there were four main categories of output WoM:

1. *Product involvement*

   People, he found, have a high propensity to discuss matters that are either distinctly pleasurable or unpleasurable. Such discussion serves to provide an opportunity for the experience to be relived, whether it be the 'looking for' or the 'use' experience, or both.

2. *Self-involvement*

   Discussion offers a means for ownership to be established and signals aspects of prestige and levels of status to the receiver. More importantly, perhaps, dissonance can be reduced as the purchaser seeks reassurance about the decision.

3. *Other involvement*

   Products can assist motivations to help others and to express feelings of love, friendship and caring. These feelings can be released through a sense of sharing the variety of benefits that products can bestow.

4. *Message involvement*

   The final motivation to discuss products is derived, according to Dichter, from the messages that surround the product itself, in particular the advertising messages and, in the business-to-business market, seminars, exhibitions and the trade press, which provide the means to provoke conversation and so stimulate word-of-mouth recommendation.

It is interesting to note that Dichter's various forms of involvement, in particular the 'self' and 'other' categories, bear a strong similarity to the market exchanges and reciprocal exchanges explored in Chapter 1. However, word-of-mouth communications are often undertaken by those who identify very closely with a brand, to the extent that they might be termed brand advocates. Advocacy can be demonstrated not only through word-of-mouth communications but also through behaviour, such as by wearing branded clothing or using tools and equipment. Watts (2000) reports the claim made by the group marketing director of Dyson that 70 per cent of sales are generated through recommendation by family and friends, to the extent that some people would ring up others and offer to lend out their machine. The issue of advocacy is explored further in Chapter 15 in the section on loyalty and retention schemes.

ViewPoint 2.5   WoM to attract hotel guests

A hotel manager noticed that input WoM for his hotel given by travel agents was much stronger than the output WoM, even though the overseas guests reported very favourable satisfaction levels. In order 'to align the input WoM needs of potential customers with activities designed to encourage appropriate output WoM', a range of activities was introduced to prompt WoM opportunities.

One of these required guests to tell the agents of their experience, and the manager also communicated with the agents by sending them copies of the guest comment cards. He also provided complimentary rooms for the agents so that they could experience the hotel at first hand and then sent them teddy bears (a reminder of England) when they made a certain number of bookings. Later he sent them jars of honey. Guests were also given teddy bears on departure.

One other notable activity included restoring one of the hotel rooms to how it would have been when the hotel opened in 1860. People perceived this as novel, interesting, and it gave rise to extensive positive output WoM. This activity also gave rise to a number of public relations activities.

Source: Stokes and Lomax (2002); used with kind permission

For organisations it is important to target messages at those individuals who are predisposed to such discussion, as this may well propel word-of-mouth recommendations and the success of the communications campaign. The target, therefore, is not necessarily the target market, but those in the target market who are most likely to volunteer their positive opinions about the offering or those who, potentially, have some influence over members. There are three types of such volunteers: opinion leaders, formers and followers.

Opinion leaders

Katz and Lazerfeld (1955) first identified individuals who were predisposed to receiving information and then reprocessing it to influence others. Their studies of American voting and purchase behaviour led to their conclusion that those individuals who could exert such influence were more persuasive than information received directly from the mass media. These opinion leaders, according to Rogers (1962), tend 'to be of the same social class as non-leaders, but may enjoy a higher social status within the group'. Williams (1990) uses the work of Reynolds and Darden (1971) to suggest that they are more gregarious and more self-confident than non-leaders. In addition, they have a greater exposure to relevant mass media (print) and as a result have more knowledge/familiarity and involvement with the product class, are more innovative and more confident of their role as influencer (leader) and appear to be less dogmatic than non-leaders (Chan and Misra, 1990).

They are more gregarious and more self-confident than non-leaders.

Opinion leadership can be simulated in advertising by the use of product testimonials. Using ordinary people to express positive comments about a product to each other is a very well-used advertising technique.

ViewPoint 2.6	French fashion clothing

Vernette (2004) reports that a typical profile of an opinion leader in the French women's fashion market is aged 15 to 35 years, is female and is either employed or is a student. Their dominant values are that they are open-minded, full of wanderlust and they attach a high level of importance to their friends. They favour advertising more than non-leaders (or followers) and they prefer to talk about advertising more than non-leaders do. Vernette confirmed that (these) leaders read more women's magazines than non-leaders but also found that it is possible to rank these magazines according to the penetration among leaders. This suggests that media planning can be developed around those media vehicles that reach a disproportionately high number of opinion leaders.

Source: Adapted from Vernette (2004)

Opinion formers

Opinion formers are individuals who are able to exert personal influence because of their authority, education or status associated with the object of the communication process. Like opinion leaders, they are looked to by others to provide information and advice, but this is the formal expertise that opinion formers are perceived to hold. For example, community pharmacists are often consulted about symptoms and medicines, and film and theatre critics carry such conviction in their reviews that they can make or break a new production.

The formal expertise that opinion formers are perceived to hold.

ViewPoint 2.7	Delia followers

Many celebrities develop a band of followers, who are keen to support the opinion former or spokesperson. Sainsbury's was said to be able to predict the volume of ingredients and food it would sell the day following the broadcast of a Jamie Oliver advertisement. Delia Smith has a similar fan base to the extent that the day after she used fresh cranberries in a TV recipe, sales of cranberries rose 200 per cent. When she fried and boiled eggs on *How to Cook* average egg sales rose by 54 million.

Source: Adapted from Keating (2004)

The BBC radio programme *The Archers*, an everyday story of country folk, has been used to deliver messages about farming issues. The actors in the programme are opinion formers and they direct messages to farmers about farming techniques and methods. This educational use was very important after the Second World War.

Popular television programmes, such as *EastEnders*, *Emmerdale* and *Coronation Street*, all of which attract huge audiences, have been used as vehicles to bring to attention and open up debates about many controversial social issues, such as contraception, abortion, drug use and abuse, and serious illness and mental health concerns.

The influence of opinion formers can be great. For example, the editor of a journal or newspaper may be a recognised source of expertise, and any offering referred to by the editor in the media vehicle is endowed with great credibility. In this sense the editor acts as a gatekeeper, and it is the task of the marketing communicator to ensure that all relevant opinion formers are identified and sent appropriate messages.

However, the credibility of opinion formers is vital for communication effectiveness. If there is a suspicion or doubt about the impartiality of the opinion former, then the objectivity of their views and comments is likely to be perceived as tainted and not believed so that damage may be caused to the reputation of the brand and those involved.

Many organisations constantly lobby key members of parliament in an effort to persuade them to pursue 'favourable' policies. Opinion formers are relatively easy to identify, as they need to be seen shaping the opinion of others, usually opinion followers.

Opinion followers

The vast majority of consumers can be said to be opinion followers. The messages they receive via the mass media are tempered by the opinions of the two groups of personal influencers just discussed. Some people actively seek information from those they believe are well informed, while others prefer to use the mass media for information and guidance (Robinson, 1976). However, this should not detract from the point that, although followers, they still process information independently and use a variety of inputs when sifting information and responding to marketing stimuli.

Ethical-drug manufacturers normally launch new drugs by enlisting the support of particular doctors who have specialised in the therapy area and who are recognised by other doctors as experts. These opinion formers are invited to lead symposia and associated events to build credibility and activity around the new product. At the same time, public relations agencies prepare press releases with the aim that the information will be used by the mass media (opinion formers) for editorial purposes and create exposure for the product across the target audience, which, depending upon the product and/or the media vehicle, may be GPs, hospital doctors, patients or the general public. All these people, whether they be opinion leaders or formers, are active influencers or talkers (Kingdom, 1970).

Process of adoption

An interesting extension to the concept of opinion followers and the discussion on word-of-mouth communications is the process by which individuals become committed to the use of a new product. Rogers (1983) has identified this as the process of adoption and the stages of his innovation decision process are represented in Figure 2.5. These stages in the adoption process are sequential and are characterised by the different factors that are involved at each stage (e.g. the media used by each individual).

1. *Knowledge*
   The innovation becomes known to consumers, but they have little information and no well-founded attitudes. Information must be provided through mass media to institutions and people that active seekers of information are likely to contact. Information for passive seekers should be supplied through the media and channels

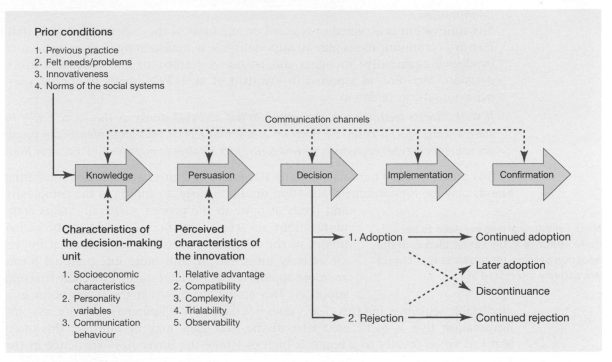

FIGURE 2.5 Stages in the innovation decision process of adoption. Reprinted from Rogers (1983) with the permission of the Free Press. Copyright 1962, 1971, 1983 by the Free Press

that this group habitually uses to look for other kinds of information (Windahl et al., 1992).

Jack cleans his teeth regularly, but he is beginning to notice a sensitivity to both hot and cold drinks. He becomes aware of an advertisement for Special Paste on television.

2. *Persuasion*

The consumer becomes aware that the innovation may be of use in solving known and potential problems. Information from those who have experience of the product becomes very important.

Jack notices that the makers of Special Paste claim that their brand reduces the amount of sensitive reaction to hot and cold drinks. Special Paste has also been recommended to him by someone he overheard in the pub last week. Modelling behaviour predominates.

3. *Decision*

An attitude may develop and may be either favourable or unfavourable, but as a result a decision is reached whether to trial the offering or not. Communications need to assist this part of the process by continual prompting.

Jack is prepared to believe (or not to believe) the messages and the claims made on behalf of Special Paste. He thinks that Special Paste is potentially a very good brand (or not). He intends trying Special Paste because he was given a free sample (or because it was on a special price deal).

4. *Implementation*

For the adoption to proceed in the absence of a sales promotion, buyers must know where to get it and how to use it. The product is then tested in a limited way. Communications must provide this information in order that the trial experience be developed.

Jack buys Special Paste and tests it.

5. *Confirmation*

The innovation is accepted or rejected on the basis of the experience during trial. Planned communications play an important role in maintaining the new behaviour by dispelling negative thoughts and positively reaffirming the original 'correct' decision. McGuire, as reported in Windahl et al. (1992), refers to this as post-behavioural consolidation.

It works; Jack's teeth are not as sensitive to hot and cold drinks as they were before he started using Special Paste. He reads an article that reports that large numbers of people are using these types of products satisfactorily. Jack resolves to buy Special Paste next time.

This process can be terminated at any stage and, of course, a number of competing brands may vie for consumers' attention simultaneously, so adding to the complexity and levels of noise in the process. Generally, mass communications are seen to be more effective in the earlier phases of the adoption process for products that buyers are actively interested in, and more interpersonal forms are more appropriate at the later stages, especially trial and adoption. This model assumes that the stages occur in a predictable sequence, but this clearly does not happen in all purchase activity, as some information that is to be used later in the trial stage may be omitted; this often happens when loyalty to a brand is high or where the buyer has experience in the marketplace.

> **Mass communications are seen to be more effective in the earlier phases of the adoption process for products that buyers are actively interested in.**

Process of diffusion

The process of adoption in aggregate form, over time, is diffusion. According to Rogers, diffusion is the process by which an innovation is communicated through certain channels over a period of time among the members of a social system. This is a group process, and Rogers again identified five categories of adopters. Figure 2.6 shows how diffusion may be fast or slow and that there is no set speed at which the process occurs. The five categories are as follows:

1. *Innovators:* these groups like new ideas and have a large disposable income. This means they are more likely to take risks associated with new products.

2. *Early adopters:* research has established that this group contains a large proportion of opinion leaders and they are therefore important in speeding the diffusion process. Early adopters tend to be younger than any other group and above average in education. Other than innovators, this group takes more publications and consults more salespeople than all others. This group is important to the marketing communications process because they can determine the speed at which diffusion occurs.

3. *Early majority:* usually, opinion followers are a little above average in age, education, social status and income. They rely on informal sources of information and take fewer publications than the previous two groups.

4. *Late majority:* this group of people is sceptical of new ideas and only adopts new products because of social or economic factors. They take few publications and are below average in education, social status and income.

5. *Laggards:* a group of people who are suspicious of all new ideas and set in their opinions. Lowest of all the groups in terms of income, social status and education, this group takes a long time to adopt an innovation.

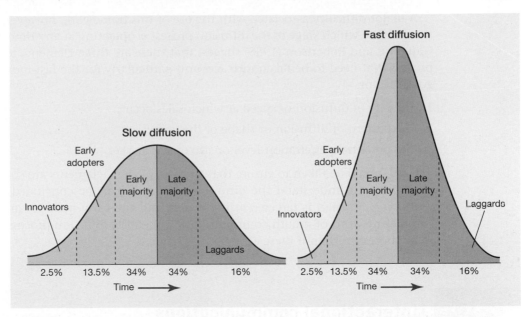

FIGURE 2.6 Fast and slow diffusion of an innovation. From Hawkins et al. (1989); used with kind permission

This framework suggests that, at the innovation stage, messages should be targeted at relatively young people in the target group, with a high level of income, education and social status. This will speed word-of-mouth recommendation and the diffusion process.

ViewPoint 2.8   Sugary WoM sweeteners

In an attempt to harness the power of word-of-mouth communications Sir Alan Sugar, chairman of Amstrad, used the WoM concept as the marketing communications platform to relaunch his 'Integra' face care system product. The principle is that customers are offered money as an incentive to recommend the product to others.

Interested customers can elect to join the Web-based scheme and observe which of their friends and contacts purchase the Integra. Sir Alan Sugar draws parallels with the eBay generation and suggests that the commission earned through this referral system might be perceived as a useful second income. Interestingly, Amstrad state that it is important that people must have direct product experience in order to join the referral programme. Presumably source credibility is stronger as product-related expertise rises steeply. Against this, the financial incentive reduces levels of objectivity, as it is clear why the contact is making the recommendation in the first place.

Source: Adapted from Murphy (2005) and material at http://www.amstrad.com/sases/

Mahajan et al. (1990) observe that the personal influence of word-of-mouth communications does not work in isolation from the other communication tools. Early adopters are more likely to adopt an innovation in response to 'external influences' and only through time will the effect of 'internal influences' become significant. In other words, mass-media communications need time to work before word-of-mouth communications can begin to build effectiveness.

A major difficulty associated with the use of this framework, however, is the inability to define which stage of the diffusion process is operating at any time. Furthermore, Gatignon and Robertson (1985) suggest that there are three elements to the diffusion process that need to be taken into account, particularly for the fast-moving consumer goods sector:

1. the rate of diffusion or speed at which sales occur;
2. the pattern of diffusion or shape of the curve;
3. the potential penetration level or size of the market.

Care should be taken to ensure that all three of these elements are considered when attempting to understand the diffusion process. It can be concluded that if a promotional campaign is targeted at innovators and the early majority and is geared to stimulating word-of-mouth communications, then the diffusion process is more likely to be successful than if these elements are ignored.

Interactional communications

The models and frameworks of the communication process discussed so far do not necessarily account for the whole process and spectrum of communications. The one-step model is linear, unidirectional and it suggests that the receiver plays a passive role in the process. The two-step and multi-step models attempt to account for the interactive nature of communication and they proffer a mutually participative role for all parties to the communication process.

Interaction is about actions that lead to a response, and new technology has further enabled the process of interaction. Goffman (1969) advocates an 'interactional' approach that focuses on the roles adopted by the players in the communication process. Through mutual understanding of each other's behaviour the rules of the communication process are established. McEwan (1992) suggests that this permits formal and informal communication procedures to be established. This interactivity enables the development of mutual understanding (Rogers and Kincaid, 1981), and increased levels of trust can be developed by the participants. Such interaction can be based around particular topics and interests, and the mutual understanding, which Ballantyne (2004) refers to as relationship-specific knowledge, develops. Once this is established it is argued that a dialogue occurs between communication partners.

Interactivity, therefore, is an important aspect of communication and is a prelude to dialogue, the highest or purest form of communication. This is an interesting perspective, as strands of the importance of source credibility can be identified in this approach. Evidence of Goffman's approach can be seen in personal selling. Sellers and buyers, meeting for the first time, often enter negotiations at a formal level, each adopting a justifiable, self-protective position. As negotiations proceed, so the two parties adjust their roles, and, as the likelihood of a mutual exchange increases, so the formal roles give way to more informal ones.

Interactivity has traditionally been regarded as the key characteristic and strength of personal selling. However, it can occur not only between people, as a result of a message conveyed through a particular medium, but also with machines or cyberspace. As Hoffman and Novak (1996) state, people interactivity is now supplemented by machine interactivity. This means that the interaction or indeed dialogue that previously occurred through machines

> The interaction or indeed dialogue that previously occurred through machines can now occur with the equipment facilitating the communication exchanges.

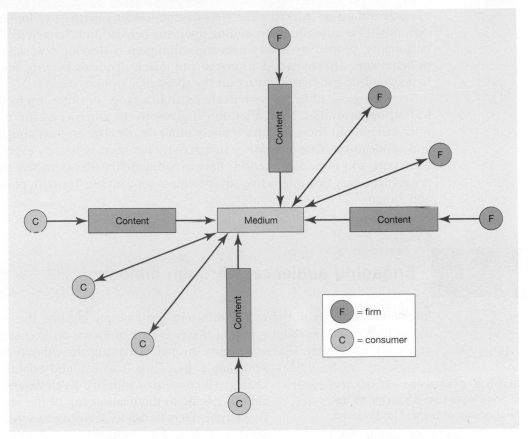

FIGURE 2.7 A model of marketing communications in a hypermedia, computer-mediated environment. From Hoffman and Novak (1996); reprinted with permission from the *Journal of Marketing*, published by the American Marketing Association

can now occur with the equipment facilitating the communication exchanges (see Figure 2.7).

These authors refer to the work of Steuer (1992), who suggests that the principal relationship is with what is referred to as a *mediated environment* and not between sender and receiver. This is important, as it is the potential of all participants in the communication activity to mediate or influence the environment (especially the message content) in which the dialogue occurs that makes interactive marketing communications so dynamic and such a radically revolutionary new promotional medium.

Digital technology allows for true interactively based communications, where messages can be responded to more or less instantly. Although there has been considerable media attention given to the development and potential of interactive services, the reality is that only a relatively small proportion of the public has become immersed in interactive environments, measured in terms of advertising space sold, usage and attitude research, and the number of transactions undertaken interactively. The development of interactive services may well be best served by the identification of those most likely to adopt such services and who will encourage others in their social orbits to follow their actions. This strategy would require communication with innovators and early adopters to speed the process of adoption (Rogers, 1983). This is quite crucial, as the infrastructure and associated heavy costs require an early stream of cash flows (Kangis and Rankin, 1996). The cost of equipment and time taken

Digital technology allows for true interactively based communications.

to learn and utilise interactive services does represent a barrier to adoption. These barriers might be substantial, depending upon the background characteristics, education, personality, propensity to take risks and willingness to develop new skills and patterns of behaviour. This reinvention process can take individuals varying amounts of time to accomplish and hence impact on the speed of adoption.

Technological advances have made possible a range of other interactive communication opportunities. Most attention is given to the Internet as the main source of interactivity, but there have been many other imaginative and exciting developments and applications. One area where interactivity has been subject to experimentation is television, and some organisations have experimented with interactive messages, most notably the very first interactive advertisement for Chicken Tonight, plus Dove, Mazda and Tango.

Engaging audiences through dialogue

Interaction alone is not always a sufficient goal, simply because the content of the interaction could be about a radical disagreement of views, an exchange of opinion or a social encounter. Dialogue occurs through reasoning and mutual understanding, one that is based on listening and adaptive behaviour. Dialogue is concerned with the development of knowledge that is specific to the relationship of the parties involved. Ballantyne refers to this as 'learning together' (Ballantyne, 2004, p. 119) and it is referred to by Gronroos (2004) as a critical aspect of marketing communication's role within relationship marketing (see Chapter 12).

> **Dialogue is concerned with the development of knowledge that is specific to the relationship of the parties involved.**

The adoption of dialogue as the basis for communication changes an organisation's perspective of its audiences. Being willing and able to enter into a dialogue indicates that there is a new emphasis on the relationships organisations hold with their stakeholders. For dialogue to occur, therefore, there must first be interaction, and it is the development and depth of the interaction that leads to meaningful dialogue. The rise and significance of direct marketing is a reflection of the way many organisations seek to encourage dialogue with particular audiences.

Ideas about how marketing communications works must be founded, in part, on the notion and significance of the level of interaction and dialogue that the organisation and its stakeholder audiences desire. One-way communication, as reflected in traditional planned mass-media-based communication, still has a significant role, especially for audiences who prefer transactional exchanges. Two-way communication based on interaction with audiences who desire continuing contact, or dialogue for those who desire a deeper, more meaningful relationship, will form an increasingly important aspect of marketing communications strategy in the future.

New technology and new communication infrastructures will give increasing numbers of people the opportunity to experience both interactive and dialogue-based marketing communications. The skill for marketing practitioners will be to know when to move from one-way, to two-way, to interactive and then dialogue-based marketing communications.

Summary of key points

1. The classic approach to communication views the process as linear, similar to the actions of a hypodermic syringe injecting its audience with information. Here the sender, message, channel, receiver approach is prevalent.

2. Subsequent models have attempted to reflect a two-way perspective and to account for the interpersonal components of communications, which stress mutuality and shared perceptions (Windahl et al., 1992).

3. The linear approach is not rejected, as there are circumstances where a one-way transmission of information is required, such as a flood warning by the National Rivers Authority or the announcement that a product specification has been altered to meet new legislative requirements. However, in the context of developing relational exchanges (Chapter 1), the interactional and dialogue approaches to communication are both justified and compatible.

4. Opinion formers are people whose expertise in a particular subject or topic is formalised through their position or career. Opinion leaders have informal expertise bestowed upon them because of their interest and in-depth knowledge of a topic or area of interest.

5. The manner in which receivers assign meaning to a message is, in part, a function of the degree to which they perceive the source as credible. The two principal elements of source credibility are trustworthiness and expertise.

6. Word-of-mouth communication is used by people to provide information and to support and reinforce their own purchasing decisions. This form of communication is regarded as highly credible and reliable, and organisations have developed ways of assigning part of their campaigns to the creation and stimulation of word-of-mouth communication, both on- and offline.

7. Communication can be one way or two way. The latter form can be considered in terms of both interactive and dialogue-based communications. Interaction implies response and increased response leads to information being shared that is specific to the parties involved in the communication. Dialogue emerges when relational conditions exist between those in the communication process.

Review questions

1. Name the elements of the linear model of communication and briefly describe the role of each element.

2. Make brief notes explaining why the linear interpretation of the communication process is not entirely valid.

3. Discuss the differences between one-step, two-step and interactional communications.

4. Explain the concept of source credibility.

5. How do opinion leaders differ from opinion formers and opinion followers?

6. Why is word-of-mouth communication so important to marketing communications?

References

Ballantyne, D. (2004), 'Dialogue and its role in the development of relationship-specific knowledge', *Journal of Business and Industrial Marketing*, **19**(2), pp. 114–23.

Berkman, H. and Gilson, C. (1986), *Consumer Behaviour: Concepts and Strategies*, Boston, Mass.: Vent.

Carter, B. (2005), 'British Gas slammed by ASA for playing on fears', *Marketing*, 19 October, p. 1.

Chan, K.K. and Misra, S. (1990), 'Characteristics of the opinion leader: a new dimension', *Journal of Advertising*, **19**(3), pp. 53–60.

Dichter, E. (1966), 'How word-of-mouth advertising works', *Harvard Business Review*, **44** (November/December), pp. 147–66.

Gatignon, H. and Robertson, T. (1985), 'A propositional inventory for new diffusion research', *Journal of Consumer Research*, **11**, pp. 849–67.

Goffman, E. (1969), *Strategic Interaction*, New York: Doubleday.

Gronroos, C. (2004), 'The relationship marketing process: communication, interaction, dialogue, value', *Journal of Business and Industrial Marketing*, **19**(2), pp. 99–113.

Hawkins, D.I., Best, R.J. and Coney, K.A. (1989), *Consumer Behaviour: Implications for Marketing Strategy*, Homewood, Ill.: Richard D. Irwin.

Hoffman, D.L. and Novak, P.T. (1996), 'Marketing in hyper computer-mediated environments: conceptual foundations', *Journal of Marketing*, **60** (July), pp. 50–68.

Kangis, P. and Rankin, K. (1996), 'Interactive services: how to identify and target the new markets', *Journal of Marketing Practice: Applied Marketing Science*, **2**(3), pp. 44–67.

Katz, E. and Lazerfeld, P.F. (1955), *Personal Influence*, Glencoe, Ill.: Free Press.

Keating, S. (2004), 'Food heroes: Delia Smith', *The Magazine*, 27 November, p. 122.

Kelman, H. (1961), 'Processes of opinion change', *Public Opinion Quarterly*, **25** (Spring), pp. 57–78.

Kingdom, J.W. (1970), 'Opinion leaders in the electorate', *Public Opinion Quarterly*, **34**, pp. 256–61.

McEwan, T. (1992), 'Communication in organisations', in *Hospitality Management* (ed. L. Mullins), London: Pitman.

Mahajan, V., Muller, E. and Bass, F.M. (1990), 'New product diffusion models in marketing', *Journal of Marketing*, **54** (January), pp. 1–26.

Mallen, B. (1977), *Principles of Marketing Channel Management*, Lexington, Mass.: Lexington Books.

Murphy, C. (2005), 'Money talks', *Marketing*, 28 September, p. 19.

Patzer, G.L. (1983), 'Source credibility as a function of communicator physical attractiveness', *Journal of Business Research*, **11**, pp. 229–41.

Reynolds, F.D. and Darden, W.R. (1971), 'Mutually adaptive effects of interpersonal communication', *Journal of Marketing Research*, **8** (November), pp. 449–54.

Robinson, J.P. (1976), 'Interpersonal influence in election campaigns: two-step flow hypothesis', *Public Opinion Quarterly*, **40**, pp. 304–19.

Rogers, E.M. (1962), *Diffusion of Innovations*, 1st edn, New York: Free Press.

Rogers, E.M. (1983), *Diffusion of Innovations*, 3rd edn, New York: Free Press.

Rogers, E.M. and Kincaid, D.L. (1981), *Communication Networks: Toward a Paradigm for Research*, New York: Free Press.

Schramm, W. (1955), 'How communication works', in *The Process and Effects of Mass Communications* (ed. W. Schramm), Urbana, Ill.: University of Illinois Press, pp. 3–26.

Steuer, J. (1992), 'Defining virtual reality: dimensions determining telepresence', *Journal of Communication*, **42**(4), pp. 73–93.

Stokes, D. and Lomax, W. (2002), 'Taking control of word of mouth marketing: the case of an entrepreneurial hotelier', *Journal of Small Business and Enterprise Development*, **9**(4), pp. 349–57.

Summers, D. (1993), 'Dangerous liaisons', *Financial Times*, 18 November, p. 12.

Theodorson, S.A. and Theodorson, G.R. (1969), *A Modern Dictionary of Sociology*, New York: Cromwell.

Vernette, F. (2004), 'Targeting women's clothing fashion opinion leaders in media planning: an application for magazines', *Journal of Advertising Research*, March, pp. 90–107.

Watts, J. (2000), 'Dyson abandons strategy of in-house advertising', *Campaign*, 11 August, p. 22.

Williams, K. (1990), *Behavioural Aspects of Marketing*, Oxford: Heinemann.

Windahl, S., Signitzer, B. and Olson, J.T. (1992), *Using Communication Theory*, London: Sage.

Yuan, Y., Caulkins, J.P. and Roehrig, S. (1998), 'The relationship between advertising and content provision on the Internet', *European Journal of Marketing*, **32**(7/8), pp. 667–87.

Audiences: behaviour, attitudes and decision-making

3

Aims and objectives

The aims of this chapter are, first, to consider some of the ways information is processed by people, and second, to examine the key issues associated with purchase-decision-making. There are four primary topics in this chapter:

Perception, Attitudes, Perceived risk, Involvement

The learning objectives are to enable readers to:

1. explain the nature of perception and how marketing communications can be used to influence the way people perceive and position brands;
2. describe the key components of attitudes and discuss ways in which marketing communications can be used to influence attitudes;
3. set out ideas concerning the nature of perceived risk and to relate ways in which marketing communications can be used to alleviate such uncertainty;
4. appreciate the nature of involvement and to explain how marketing communications can be used to reflect high- and low-involvement situations;
5. explain the various purchase-decision-making processes adopted by individuals and organisations.

Introduction

Marketing is about many things, but one of its central themes is the management of behaviour. It makes sense therefore to underpin marketing activities with an understanding of buyer behaviour, in order that marketing and communication activities in particular are more effective. The first part of the chapter deals with the way audiences process information and how this knowledge can influence marketing communications. The second part of the chapter deals with buyer decision-making. Understanding the ways in which buyers make decisions and the factors that impact upon the decision process can affect the effectiveness of marketing communications. In particular, it can influence message structure, content and scheduling. In this chapter, and indeed the book, reference is made to both buyers and audiences. This is because although all buyers constitute an audience, not all audiences are buyers.

Audience information processing

Marketing communications is an audience-centred activity so it is vitally important to understand the way in which audiences process information.

Marketing communications is an audience-centred activity so it is vitally important to understand the way in which audiences process information prior to, during and after making product/service purchase decisions. Here three main information processing issues are considered: awareness, perception and attitudes.

Awareness

Awareness of the existence and availability of a product/service or an organisation is necessary before information can be processed and purchase behaviour expected. Much of marketing communications activity is directed towards getting the attention of the target audience, simply because of the vast number of competing messages and 'noise' in the marketplace. Many different techniques and approaches have been developed, first through advertising and now in most aspects of marketing communications. The goal is to get the undivided attention of the audience, to create awareness of the key messages and induce engagement. Awareness, therefore, needs to be created, developed, refined or sustained, according to the characteristics of the market and the particular situation facing an organisation at any one point in time. See Figure 3.1.

In situations where the audience experiences high involvement and is fully aware of a product's existence, attention and awareness levels need only be sustained, and efforts need to be applied to other communication tasks that may be best left to the other elements of the communications mix: for example, sales promotion and personal selling are more effective at informing, persuading and provoking purchase of a new car once advertising has created the necessary levels of awareness.

Where low levels of awareness are found, getting attention needs to be a prime objective so that awareness can be developed in the target audience. Where low involvement exists, the decision-making process is relatively straightforward. With levels of risk minimised, buyers with sufficient levels of awareness may be prompted into purchase with little assistance from the other elements of the mix. Recognition and recall

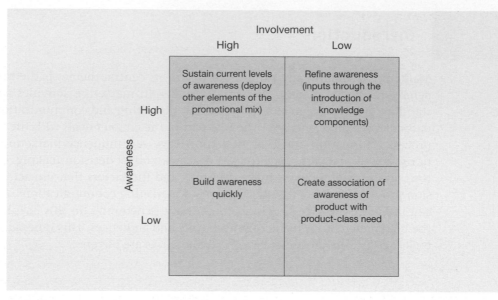

FIGURE 3.1 An awareness grid

of brand names and corporate images are felt by some (Rossiter and Percy, 1987) to be sufficient triggers to stimulate a behavioural response. The requirement in this situation would be to refine and strengthen the level of awareness in order that it provokes interest and stimulates a higher level of involvement during recall or recognition.

Where low levels of awareness are matched by low involvement, the prime objective has to be to create awareness of the focus product in association with the product class. It is not surprising that organisations use awareness campaigns and invest a large amount of their resources in establishing their brand or corporate name. Many brands seek to establish 'top-of-mind awareness' as one of the primary objectives for their advertising spend.

Many brands seek to establish 'top-of-mind awareness' as one of the primary objectives for their advertising spend.

ViewPoint 3.1   Changing names

One of the principal motivations for the online DVD retailer Blackstar to change its name was to secure a .com to replace its limiting .co.uk address. In order to compete more effectively with its main rivals, Amazon and Play, the new name, Sendit.com, would enable the company to reach a far greater audience.

However, one of the first tasks was to create name awareness and to then create the right brand associations and credibility to attract new customers.

Source: Adapted from Smith (2004)

Once awareness has been created in the target audience, it should not be neglected. If there is neglect, the audience may become distracted by competing messages and the level of awareness of the focus product or organisation may decline.

Perception

Perception is concerned with how individuals see and make sense of their environment. It is about the selection, organisation and interpretation of stimuli by individuals so that they can understand their world.

Selection

Individuals are exposed, each day, to a tremendous number of stimuli. De Chernatony (1993) suggested that each consumer is exposed to over 550 advertisements per day, while Lasn (1999) estimated that this should be 3,000 advertisements per day (cited by Dahl et al., 2003). In addition, there are thousands of other non-commercial stimuli that each individual encounters. To cope with this bombardment, our sensory organs select those stimuli to which attention is given. The nature of the stimuli, or external factors such as the intensity and size, position, contrast, novelty, repetition and movement, are factors that have been developed and refined by marketing communicators to attract attention. Animation is used to attract attention when the product class is perceived as bland and uninteresting, such as margarine or teabags. Unexpected camera angles and the use of music can be strong methods of gaining the attention of the target audience, as used successfully in the Bacardi Breezer and Renault commercials. Sexual attraction can be a powerful means of capturing the attention of audiences, and when associated with a brand's values can be a very effective method of getting attention (for example, the Diet Coke advertisement, Exhibit 3.1).

EXHIBIT 3.1 'Diet Coke'
Coca-Cola uses sexual overtones to gain the attention of the target market. Diet Coke is a registered trademark of the Coca-Cola Company. This image has been reproduced with kind permission of the Coca-Cola Company

Organisation

These selected stimuli are organised in order to make them comprehensible and are then given meaning. Stimuli therefore need to be presented in ways that we can understand or create meaning. The use of contour (Coke bottle), and grouping objects to convey meaning by association, enable easier organisation of stimuli.

Interpretation

Once stimuli are organised they need to be interpreted so that meaning can be attributed. As Cohen and Basu (1987) state, by using existing categories meanings can be given to stimuli. These categories are determined from the individual's past experiences and they shape what the individual expects to see. These expectations, when combined with the strength and clarity of the stimulus and the motives at the time perception occurs, mould the pattern of the perceived stimuli. Stimuli, therefore, are selected, organised and interpreted.

Stimuli are selected, organised and interpreted.

Marketing communication and perception

The ways in which individuals perceive, organise and interpret stimuli are a reflection of their past experiences, and the classifications used help to understand the different situations each individual frames every day. Individuals seek to frame or provide a context within which their role becomes clearer. Shoppers expect to find products in particular situations, such as rows, shelves or display bins of similar goods. They also develop meanings and associations with some grocery products because of the utility and trust/emotional satisfaction certain pack types evoke. The likelihood that a sale will be made is improved if the context in which a purchase transaction is undertaken does not contradict a shopper's expectations.

Marketing communications should attempt to present products (objects) in a frame or 'mental presence' (Moran, 1990) that is recognised by a buyer, such as a consumption or purchase situation. A product has a much greater chance of entering an evoked set if the situation in which it is presented is one that is expected and relevant. However, a new pack design can provide differentiation and provoke people into reassessing their expectations of what constitutes appropriate packaging in a product category.

ViewPoint 3.2   Changing times

The Times newspaper ran a campaign in 2004 to try to change the way the paper was perceived by people younger than the 42-year-old average reader. For infrequent readers The Times was a second-choice paper, and in order to make it their first choice the newspaper tried to change the way it was perceived.

To do this they developed a campaign using four celebrity spokespersons: Gordon Ramsay, Jonny Wilkinson, Gabby Logan and Jodie Kidd. With the strapline 'Join the Debate' the strategy was based on the personalities debating issues about health, sport and various forms of entertainment in order to broaden the perception of the topics covered by the newspaper.

Source: Sweney (2004)

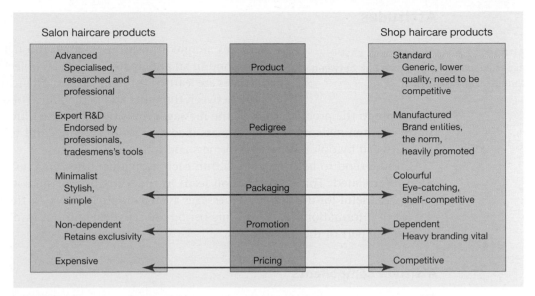

FIGURE 3.2 A comparison of salon and shop haircare products

Javalgi et al. (1992) point out that perception is important to product evaluation and product selection. Consumers try to evaluate a product's attributes by the physical cues of taste, smell, size and shape. Sometimes no difference can be distinguished, so the consumer has to make a judgement on factors other than the physical characteristics of the product. This is the basis of branding activity, where a personality is developed for the product that enables it to be perceived differently from its competitors. The individual may also set up a separate category or evoked set in order to make sense of new stimuli or satisfactory experiences. Consumer perception of salon- and shop-based haircare products shows important differences and indicates the different roles that marketing communication needs to play: see Figure 3.2. Within each of these sectors many brands are developed that are targeted at different segments based upon demographic, benefit and psychographic factors.

Individuals carry a set of enduring perceptions or images.

Finally, individuals carry a set of enduring perceptions or images. These relate to themselves, to products and to organisations. The concept of positioning the product in the mind of the consumer is fundamental to marketing strategy and is a topic that will be examined in greater depth in Chapter 5. The image an individual has of an organisation is becoming recognised as increasingly important, judging by the proportion of communication budgets being given over to public relations activities and corporate advertising in particular.

Organisations develop multiple images to meet the positioning requirements of their end-user markets and stakeholders. They need to monitor and adjust their identities constantly in respect of the perceptions and expectations held by the other organisations in their various networks. For example, the level of channel coordination and control can be a function of the different perceptions of channel members. These concern the perception of the channel depth, processes of control and the roles each member is expected to fulfil. Furthermore, the perception of an organisation's product quality and its associated image (reputation) is becoming increasingly important. Both end-user buyers and channel members are attempting to ensure that the intrinsic and extrinsic cues associated with their products are appropriate signals of product quality (Moran, 1990).

Attitudes

Attitudes are learned through past experiences and serve as a link between thoughts and behaviour.

Attitudes are predispositions, shaped through experience, to respond in an anticipated way to an object or situation. Attitudes are learned through past experiences and serve as a link between thoughts and behaviour. These experiences may relate to the product itself, to the messages transmitted by the different members of the channel network (normally mass-media communications) and to the information supplied by opinion leaders, formers and followers.

Attitudes tend to be consistent within each individual: they are clustered and very often interrelated. This categorisation leads to the formation of stereotypes, which is extremely useful for the design of messages as stereotyping allows for the transmission of a lot of information in a short time period (30 seconds) without impeding learning or the focal part of the message.

Attitude components

Attitudes are hypothetical constructs, and they are considered to consist of three components: a cognitive or learning component, an affective or feeling element and a conative or action component. See Figure 3.3.

1. *Cognitive component (learn)*
   This component refers to the level of knowledge and beliefs held by individuals about a product and/or the beliefs about specific attributes of the offering. This represents the learning aspect of attitude formation. Marketing communications are used to create attention and awareness, to provide information and to help audiences learn and understand the features and benefits a particular product/service offers.

2. *Affective component (feel)*
   By referring to the feelings held about a product – good, bad, pleasant or unpleasant – an evaluation is made of the object. This is the component that is concerned with feelings, sentiments, moods and emotions about an object. Marketing communications are used to induce feelings about the product/service such that it becomes a preferred brand. This preference may be based on emotional attachment to a brand, conferred status through ownership, past experiences and longevity of brand usage or any one of a number of ways in which people can become emotionally involved with a brand.

3. *Conative component (do)*
   This is the action component of the attitude construct and refers to the individual's disposition or intention to behave in a certain way. Some researchers go so far as to suggest that this component refers to observable behaviour. Marketing communications, therefore, should be used to encourage audiences to do something: for example, visit a website, phone a telephone number, take a coupon, book a visit, press red (on a remote control unit) for interactivity through digital television.

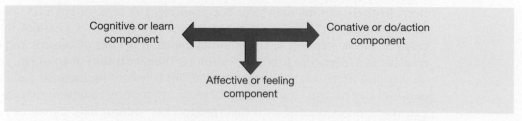

FIGURE 3.3 The three-component attitude framework

This three-component approach to attitudes is based upon attitudes towards an object, person or organisation. The sequence of attitude formation is learn, feel and do. This approach to attitude formation is limited in that the components are seen to be of equal strength. A single-component model has been developed where the attitude only consists of the individual's overall feeling towards an object. In other words, the affective component is the only significant component.

Multi-attribute attitude models

One of the difficulties with the three- and single-component attitude models is that they fail to explain why an individual has a particular attitude. A different approach views objects as possessing many different attributes, all of which are perceived and believed by individuals with differing strengths and intensity.

Attribute analysis is an important factor in the design and consistency of marketing communication messages. For example, the UK toilet tissue market has been dominated by two main players, Andrex with 24.2 per cent market share and SCA Hygiene's Double-Velvet with 10.4 per cent share (Brabbs, 2000). In 2000 Charmin entered the market. For many years Andrex has used a puppy (see Exhibit 3.2) to symbolise the softness, strength and length of its product. The strong attitudes held by Andrex's loyal customers have enabled market share to rise steadily and market leadership has been maintained. This has been achieved in the light of the increased number of high-quality products (often own label) that are now available, all of which communicate softness and strength as the key attributes.

In 2000 Procter & Gamble introduced Charmin to the UK from the USA where it has a 30 per cent market share. Apart from a huge £14 million ad spend and a strong outdoor, radio, press and direct marketing programme, the launch was notable for the

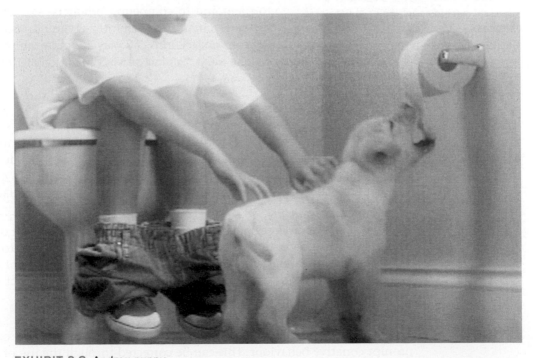

EXHIBIT 3.2 Andrex puppy
The use of product attributes in marketing communications is long established. Here the Andrex puppy is used to symbolise (through time) the length and strength of the brand. Picture reproduced with the kind permission of Kimberley-Clark Ltd

Charmin's approach has been to highlight a neglected attribute.

position it took in the market. Andrex positions itself by features, such as strength, length and softness as symbolised by the puppy. Double-Velvet adopts a similar position but appears to focus on features such as thickness as a surrogate for quality. Charmin's approach has been to highlight a neglected attribute, namely a comfortable cleaning proposition, smooth and strong, even when wet.

Changing attitudes with marketing communications

Marketing communications is important to either maintain or change attitudes held by stakeholders. It is not the only way as product and service elements, pricing and channel decisions all play an important part in shaping the attitudes held. However, marketing communications has a pivotal role in conveying each of these aspects to the target audience. Branding (Chapter 1) is a means by which attitudes can be established and maintained in a consistent way and it is through the use of the tools of the communication mix that brand positioning can be sustained. The final point that needs to be made is that there is a common thread between attributes, attitudes and positioning (Chapter 5). Attributes provide a means of differentiation and positions are shaped as a consequence of the attitudes that result from the way people interpret the associated marketing communications.

Environmental influences on the attitudes people hold towards particular products and services result from many elements. First, they are a reflection of the way different people interpret the marketing communications surrounding them; second, they are a result of their direct experience of using them; and third, a result of the informal messages received from family, friends and other highly credible sources of information.

Marketing communications can play an important part in changing or maintaining attitudes.

tion. These all contribute to the way people perceive (and position) products and services and the feelings they have to them and to competing products. Managing attitudes (towards a brand) is therefore very important and marketing communications can play an important part in changing or maintaining attitudes. There are a number of ways in which attitudinal change can be implemented:

1. *Change the physical product or service element*
   At a fundamental level, attitudes might be so ingrained that it is necessary to change the product or service. This may involve a radical redesign or the introduction of a significant new attribute. Only once these changes have been made should marketing communications be used to communicate the new or revised object. When VW bought Skoda it redesigned the total product offering before relaunch.

2. *Change misunderstanding*
   In some circumstances people might misunderstand the benefits of a particularly important attribute and marketing communications is required to correct the beliefs held. This can be achieved through product demonstration of functionally based communications. Packaging and even the name of the product may need to be revised.

3. *Build credibility*
   Attitudes towards a brand might be superficial and lack sufficient conviction to prompt conative behaviour. This can be corrected through the use of an informative strategy, designed to build credibility. Product demonstration and hands-on experience (e.g. through sampling) are effective strategies. Skoda supports a rally team to convey durability, speed and performance.

4. *Change performance beliefs*

    Beliefs held about the object and the performance qualities of the object can be adjusted through appropriate marketing communications. For example, by changing the perceptions held about the attributes, it is possible to change the attitudes about the object.

5. *Change attribute priorities*

    By changing the relative importance of the different attributes and ratings it is possible to change attitudes. Therefore, a strategy to emphasise a different attribute can change the attitude not only towards a brand but also to a product category. By stressing the importance of travel times, the importance of this attribute might be emphasised in the minds of potential holidaymakers. Dyson changed attitudes to floor-cleaning equipment by stressing the efficiency of its new cyclone technology rather than the ease of use, aesthetic design or generic name (Hoover) associations used previously.

6. *Introduce a new attribute*

    Opportunities might exist to introduce a radically different and new (or previously unused) attribute. This provides a means for clear differentiation until competitors imitate and catch up. For example, by making prominent new service levels that are coupled with guaranteed refunds in the event of performance failure, this new attribute may lead to greater success.

7. *Change perception of competitor products*

    By changing the way competitor products are perceived, it is possible to differentiate your own brand. This could be achieved by using messages that distance a competitor's brand from your own. For example, an airline could highlight a key competitor's punctuality record, and this might help change the way its own performance level is perceived. In much the same way, Thomson Holidays used this approach when it used copy that read, 'We go there, we don't stay there'.

8. *Change or introduce new brand associations*

    By using celebrities or spokespersons with whom the target audience can identify, it might be possible to change the way in which a brand is perceived. For example, a bread producer might use a well-known athlete to represent their brand as a healthy food.

    Alternatively, it may use children in its marketing communications to suggest that it is fun to eat and that all children love the brand.

9. *Use corporate branding*

    By altering the significance of the parent brand relative to the product brand, it is possible to alter beliefs about brands and their overall value. In some situations there is little to differentiate competitive brands and little credible scope to develop attribute-based attitudes. By using the stature of the parent company it is possible to develop a level of credibility and brand values that other brands cannot copy, although they can imitate by using their parent brand. Procter & Gamble has introduced its name to the packs of many of its brands.

10. *Change the number of attributes used*

    Many brands still rely on a single attribute as a means of providing a point of differentiation. This was popularly referred to as a unique selling proposition at a time when attribute- and information-based communications reflected a feature-dominated understanding of branding. Today, two or even three attributes are often combined with strong emotional associations in order to provide a point of differentiation and a set of benefit-oriented brand values.

ViewPoint 3.3   Land-Rover seeks to change attitudes

Following a brief to sell 300 Land-Rovers, research conducted by the direct marketing agency Craik Jones found that the attitudes held by prospective Land-Rover buyers were based on serious misconceptions about the brand. Not only did they feel that Land-Rovers were essentially a rural vehicle but also that they drove like a truck rather than a luxury car.

These attitudes had been developed as a result of information and perceptions of the brand, without the prospective buyers ever having driven the car. This is typical of the order in which attitudes are formed when there is high involvement (learn–feel–do). In order to overcome this, a direct marketing strategy was developed by the agency to encourage trial in order that attitudes could be based on direct experience (learn–do–feel). Direct mail was used to stimulate a test drive and this was followed up a week later to thank the drivers and to find out their reactions to the experience of actually driving a Land-Rover. Not only were over 700 orders placed as a direct result of this campaign but the reaction and knock-on effect on the dealer network was very positive. Direct marketing had been used as part of a pull strategy to change attitudes and increase sales.

Decision-making

Much of marketing communications activity has been orientated towards decision-making, and knowledge of a buyer's decision-making processes is vital if the correct type of information is to be transmitted at the right time and in the right or appropriate manner. There are two broad types of buyer: consumers and organisational buyers. Consideration will first be given to a general decision-making process, and then an insight into the characteristics of the decision-making processes for consumers and organisational buyers will be presented. Figure 3.4 shows that there are five stages in the general process whereby buyers make purchase decisions and implement them. Marketing communications can impact upon any or all of these stages with varying levels of potential effectiveness.

Problem recognition

Problem recognition occurs when there is a perceived difference between an individual's current position and their ideal state. Marketing communications can be used to encourage 'problem recognition' by suggesting that the current state is not desirable,

Marketing communications can be used to encourage 'problem recognition'.

by demonstrating how consumers can tell whether they have a similar problem (e.g. 'Is your hair dull and lifeless?') or by suggesting that their current brand is inferior.

Information search

Having identified a problem a prospective buyer will search for information in an attempt to resolve it. There are two main areas of search activity:

1. The internal search involves a memory scan to recall experiences and knowledge, utilising the perceptual processes to see whether there is an 'off-the-shelf' solution.

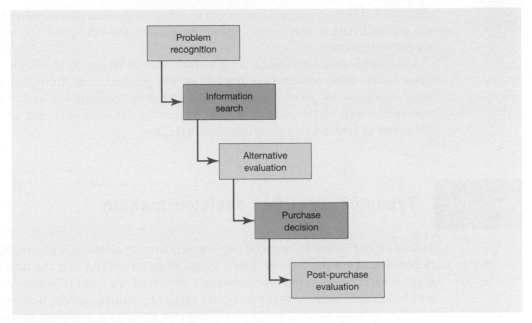

FIGURE 3.4 A general decision-making framework

2. If there is no 'off-the-shelf' solution, the prospective buyer will resort to an external search.

This will involve family and friends, reference sources and commercial guides and advertising.

Alternative evaluation

Potential solutions need to be evaluated in order that the optimum choice be made. Products considered feasible constitute the *preference set*, and it is from these seven or eight products that a smaller group of products is normally assembled. This is referred to as the *evoked set* (or repertoire) and it is from this that consumers make a choice. Attributes used to determine the sets are referred to as evaluative criteria. Very often these attributes are both objective and subjective in nature.

Attributes used to determine the sets are referred to as evaluative criteria.

Purchase decision

Having evaluated various solutions, the buyer may develop a predisposition to make a purchase. This will involve matching motives and evaluative criteria with product attributes. This necessitates the use of the processes of learning and attitude formation, discussed in the previous chapter.

Post-purchase evaluation

Direct experience of the product is an important part of the decision process. Feedback from use helps learning and attitude development and is the main contributor to long-run behaviour. Communication activity must continue to provide satisfaction and prevent the onset of cognitive dissonance. This is a state where, after the purchase decision has been made, a buyer might feel tension about a past decision either because the product fails to reach expectations or because the consumer becomes aware of a superior alternative.

Marketing communications, at this stage, should be aimed at reinforcing past decisions by stressing the positive features of the product, the emotional enhancement usage brings or by providing more information to assist its use and application. For example, much of the advertising undertaken by car manufacturers seeks to prevent the onset of tension and purchase dissatisfaction.

Types of consumer decision-making

Buyers do not follow the general decision sequence at all times. The procedure may vary depending upon the time available, levels of perceived risk and the degree of involvement a buyer has with the type of product. Perceived risk and involvement are issues that will be covered later. At this point three types of problem-solving behaviour (extended problem-solving, limited problem-solving and routinised response) will be considered.

Extended problem-solving (EPS)

Consumers considering the purchase of a car or house undertake a great deal of external search activity and spend a lot of time reaching a solution that satisfies, as closely as possible, the evaluative criteria previously set. This activity is usually associated with products that are unfamiliar, where direct experience and hence knowledge are weak, and where there is considerable financial risk.

Marketing communications should aim to provide a lot of information to assist the decision process. Marketing communications should aim to provide a lot of information to assist the decision process. The provision of information through sales literature, such as brochures and leaflets, websites for determining product and purchase criteria in product categories where there is little experience, access to salespersons and demonstrations and advertisements are just some of the ways in which information can be provided.

Limited problem-solving (LPS)

Having experience of a product means that greater use can be made of internal memory-based search routines, and the external search can be limited to obtaining up-to-date information or to ensuring that the finer points of the decision have been investigated.

Marketing communications should attempt to provide information about any product modification or new attributes and convey messages that highlight those key attributes known to be important to buyers. By differentiating the product, marketing communications provides the buyer with a reason to select that particular product.

Routinised response behaviour (RRB)

For a great number of products the decision process will consist only of an internal search. This is primarily because the buyer has made a number of purchases and has accumulated a great deal of experience. Therefore, only an internal search is necessary, so little time or effort will be spent on external search activities. Low-value items that are frequently purchased fall into this category, for example toothpaste, soap, tinned foods and confectionery.

Some outlets are perceived as suitable for what are regarded as distress purchases. Tesco Express and many petrol stations position themselves as convenience stores for distress purchases (for example, a pint of milk at 10 o'clock at night), whereas many garages have positioned themselves as convenience stores suitable for meeting the needs of RRB purchases. In doing so they are moving themselves away from the perception of being only a distress purchase outlet.

Communicators should focus upon keeping the product within the evoked set or getting it into the set. Learning can be enhanced through repetition of messages, but repetition can also be used to maintain attention and awareness.

Perceived risk

An important factor associated with the purchase-decision process is the level of risk perceived by buyers. This risk concerns the uncertainty of the consequences arising from a decision to purchase a particular brand.

Risk is perceived because the buyer has little or no experience of the performance of the product or the decision process associated with the purchase. Risk is related to not only brand-based decisions but also to product categories, an especially important aspect when launching new technology products, for example. The level of risk an individual experiences varies through time and across products, and is often a reflection of an individual's propensity to manage risk. Settle and Alreck (1989) suggest that there are five main forms of risk that can be identified; the purchase of a hi-fi unit demonstrates each element. These are set out in Table 3.1 with respect to the purchase of such a system.

> Risk is related to not only brand-based decisions but also to product categories.

A sixth element, time, is also considered to be a risk factor (Stone and Gronhaug, 1993):

Using the hi-fi example, will purchase of the unit lead to an inefficient use of my time? Or can I afford the time to search for a good hi-fi so that I will not waste my money?

What constitutes risk is a function of the contextual characteristics of each situation, the individuals involved and the product under consideration.

TABLE 3.1 Types of perceived risk

Type of perceived risk	Explanation
Performance	Will the unit reproduce my music clearly?
Financial	Can I afford that much or should I buy a less-expensive version?
Physical	Will the unit damage my other systems or endanger me in any way?
Social	Will my friends and colleagues be impressed?
Ego	Will I feel as good as I want to feel when listening to or talking about my unit?

A major task of marketing communications is to reduce levels of perceived risk. By providing extensive and relevant information a buyer's risks can be reduced substantially. Mass media, word of mouth, websites and sales representatives, for example, are popular ways to set out the likely outcomes from purchase and so reduce the levels of risk. Brand loyalty can also be instrumental in reducing risk when launching new products. The use of guarantees, third-party endorsements, money-back offers (some car manufacturers offer the opportunity to return a car within 30 days or exchange it for a different model) and trial samples (as used by many haircare products) are also well-used devices to reduce risk.

ViewPoint 3.4   Back-page risk reducers

Many print-based direct response advertisements use a variety of ways to reduce the risk inherent in buying 'off the back page'. Holiday companies, direct wine and book clubs use a variety of sales channels but website-based ecommerce and direct-response magazine advertisements provide a rich source of business.

Magazine advertisements, often to be found on or near the back of magazines and Sunday newspaper supplements, allow for a large amount of text as well as eye-catching visual work. The text is often used to reduce functional risk by explaining the features and extolling the benefits of the product or service. Social and ego risks are reduced by setting the right visual scene and depicting people using the product who may be seen as either aspirational or represent the target market. Financial risk is reduced through opportunities to buy now at a reduced or discounted price (credit card) and promises of warranties and money-back guarantees further reduce the uncertainty of this form of exchange. Finally, time risk is reduced through buy-now opportunities and delivery to the door, negating the need to travel, park, browse, compare, decide and carry home the purchase.

Many direct response magazine ads seek to reduce a number of different types of risk. Companies offering wine for direct home delivery, for example, try to reduce performance risk by providing information about each wine being offered. Financial risk is reduced by comparing their 'special' prices with those in the high street, social risk is approached by developing the brand name associations and trying to improve credibility, and time risk is reduced through the convenience of home delivery.

Involvement theory

Purchase decisions made by consumers vary considerably, and one of the factors thought to be key to brand choice decisions is the level of involvement (in terms of individual importance and relevance) a consumer has with either the product or the purchase process.

Involvement is about the degree of personal relevance and risk perceived by consumers in the target market when making a particular purchase decision (Rossiter et al., 1991). This implies that the level of involvement may vary through time as each member of the target market becomes more (or less) familiar with the purchase and associated communications. At the point of decision-making involvement is either high or low, not some point on a sliding scale or a point on a continuum between two extremes.

At the point of decision-making involvement is either high or low.

High involvement

High involvement occurs when a consumer perceives an expected purchase that is not only of high personal relevance but also represents a high level of perceived risk. Cars, washing machines, houses and insurance policies are seen as 'big ticket' items, infrequent purchases that promote a great deal of involvement. The risk described is financial but, as we saw earlier, risk can take other forms. Therefore the choice of perfume, suit, dress or jewellery may also represent high involvement, with social risk dominating the purchase decision. The consumer, therefore, devotes a great deal of time to researching the intended purchase and collecting as much information as possible in order to reduce, as far as possible, levels of perceived risk.

ViewPoint 3.5   Web-involved Mazdas

Loch (2003) refers to involvement branding, a concept that brings together direct response and value-added branding work. He cites work on the UK's Mazda 2 campaign where the company used a couple of Web-only video clips and distributed them through a network of targeted sites. By placing tracking codes in the clips Mazda could measure the number of occasions each clip was viewed, and on which sites.

At the end of the clips a 'hot spot' links to a landing page where visitors can request a brochure or even book a test drive. This in turn is linked to a tracking system, connected to Mazda HQ and its dealership network. Through this networked approach Mazda can not only identify how many brochures/test drives were requested directly as a result of the campaign, but also how many cars were sold on the back of it.

Source: Adapted from Loch (2003)

Low involvement

A *low-involvement* state of mind regarding a purchase suggests little threat or risk to the consumer. Low-priced items such as washing powder, baked beans and breakfast cereals are bought frequently, and past experience of the product class and the brand cues the consumer into a purchase that requires little information or support. Items such as alcoholic and soft drinks, cigarettes and chocolate are also normally seen as low involvement, but they induce a strong sense of ego risk associated with the self-gratification that is attached to the consumption of these products.

Two approaches to decision-making

From this understanding of general decision-making processes, perceived risk and involvement theory, it is possible to identify two main approaches to consumer decision-making.

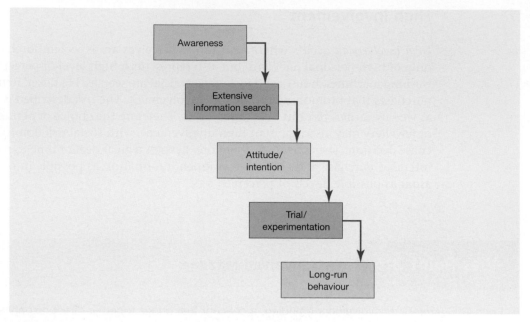

FIGURE 3.5 High-involvement decision-making

High-involvement decision-making

If an individual is highly involved with the initial purchase of a product, EPS is the appropriate decision sequence, as information is processed in a rational, logical order. Individuals who are highly involved in a purchase are thought to move through the process shown in Figure 3.5. When high-involvement decision-making is present individuals perceive a high level of risk and are concerned about the intended purchase. The essential element in this sequence is that a great deal of information is sought initially and an attitude is developed before a commitment or intention to trial is determined.

Information search is an important part of the high-involvement decision-making process. Because individuals are highly motivated, information is actively sought, processed and evaluated. Many media sources are explored, including the mass media, word-of-mouth communications and point-of-sale communications. As individuals require a lot of information, print media are more appropriate as a large volume of detailed information can be transmitted and this allows the receiver to digest the information at a speed they can control.

Low-involvement decision-making

If an individual has little involvement with an initial purchase of a product, LPS is the appropriate decision process. Information is processed cognitively but in a passive, involuntary way. Information is processed using right-brain thinking, so information is stored as it is received, in sections, and this means that information is stored as a brand association (Heath, 2000). An advertisement for Andrex toilet tissue featuring the puppy is stored as the 'Andrex puppy' without any overt thinking or reasoning. Because of the low personal relevance and perceived risk associated with this type of processing, message repetition is necessary to define brands and create meaningful brand associations. Individuals who have a low involvement with a purchase decision

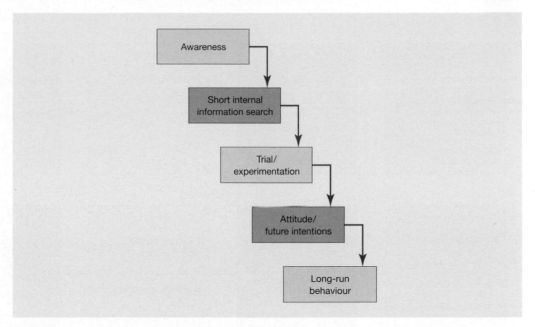

FIGURE 3.6 Low-involvement decision-making

choose not to search for information and are thought to move through the process shown in Figure 3.6.

Communications can assist the development of awareness in the low-involvement decision-making process. However, as individuals assume a passive problem-solving role, messages need to be shorter than in the high-involvement process and should contain less information. Broadcast media are preferred as they complement the passive learning posture adopted by the individual. Repetition is important because the receiver has little or no motivation to retain information, and his or her perceptual selection processes filter out unimportant information. Learning develops through exposure to repeated messages, but attitudes do not develop at this part of the process (Harris, 1987).

Where low involvement is present, each individual relies upon internal, rather than external, search mechanisms, often prompted by point-of-purchase displays.

Impact on communications

Involvement is a theory central to our understanding of the way in which information is processed and the way in which people make decisions about product purchases. We have established in the preceding section that there are two main types of involvement, high and low. These two types lead directly to two different uses of marketing communications. In decisions where there is high involvement, attitude precedes trial behaviour. In low-involvement cases this position is reversed.

> Where there is high involvement, consumers seek out information because they are concerned about the decision processes and outcomes.

Where there is high involvement, consumers seek out information because they are concerned about the decision processes and outcomes. This can be because of the levels of uncertainty associated with the high costs of purchase and usage, inexperience of the product (category) often brought about due to the infrequency of purchases, the complexity of product and doubts about its operational usefulness. Because they have these concerns, people develop an attitude prior to behaviour.

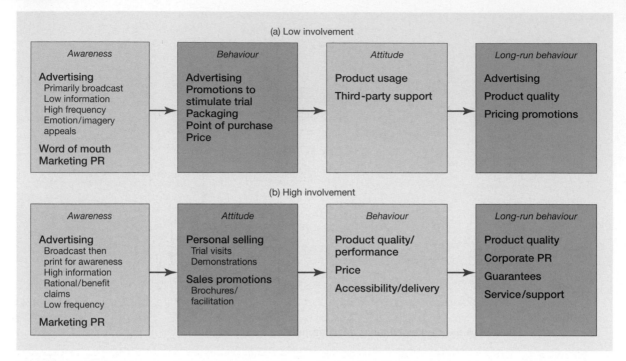

FIGURE 3.7 Marketing communications approaches for the two levels of involvement

Where there is low involvement, consumers are content to select any one of a number of acceptable products and often rely on those that are in the individual's evoked set. Low involvement is thought to be a comfortable state, because there are too many other decisions in life to have to make decisions about each one of them, so an opportunity not to have to seek information and make other decisions is welcome. See Figure 3.7, which indicates the marketing communication strategies best suited for each level within both involvement sequences.

Involvement, therefore, impacts on what is said, how it is said and when it is said.

Organisational buying-decision processes

Organisational buying, according to Webster and Wind (1972), is 'the decision-making process by which formal organisations establish the need for purchased products and services and identify, evaluate and choose among alternative brands and suppliers'. Of particular significance is the relationship that develops between organisations involved as buyers or sellers.

One way of examining the context is to compare organisational decisions with those made in consumer markets. There are far fewer buyers in the organisational context than in the consumer market, although there can be a number of people associated with a buying decision in an organisation. Orders are invariably larger and the frequency with which they are placed is much lower. It is quite common for agreements to be made between organisations for the supply of materials over a number of years. Similarly, depending upon the complexity of the product (photocopying paper or a one-off satellite), the negotiation process may also take a long time.

ViewPoint 3.6   Hospital buying decisions

The purchase of medical supplies and equipment by hospitals is an important decision, if only because of the implications of the decisions made with regard to patient welfare. However, the wide variety of people involved in the process can lead to buying decisions becoming overly complex, sometimes over budget and delayed. For example, purchasing decisions regarding infusion pumps are influenced by various stakeholder groups: medical experts (such as doctors and consultants), administrators (such as general managers and purchasing administrators), those with financial responsibilities, purchasing agents and of course certain direct government representatives, primary care trusts and other influential stakeholders.

Many of the characteristics associated with consumer decision-making processes can be observed in the organisational context. However, organisational buyers make decisions that ultimately contribute to the achievement of corporate objectives. To make the necessary decisions a high volume of pertinent information is often required. This information needs to be relatively detailed and is normally presented in a rational and logical style. The needs of the buyers are many and complex, and some may be personal. Goals, such as promotion and career advancement within the organisation, coupled with ego and employee satisfaction, combine to make organisational buying an important and complex task, one that requires professional training and the development of expertise if the role is to be performed optimally.

Buyclasses

Organisational buyers make decisions that vary with each buying situation and buyclass. Buyclasses, according to Robinson et al. (1967), comprise three types: new task, modified rebuy and straight rebuy (Table 3.2):

1. *New buy*
   As the name implies, the organisation is faced with a first-time buying situation. Risk is inevitably high at this point, and partly as a consequence there are a large number of decision participants. Each participant requires a lot of information and a relatively long period of time is required for the information to be assimilated and a decision to be made.

2. *Modified rebuy*
   Having purchased a product, the organisation may request through its buyer that certain modifications be made to future purchases, for example adjustments to the specification of the product, further negotiation on price levels or perhaps the arrangement for alternative delivery patterns. Fewer people are involved in the decision process than in the new task situation.

3. *Straight rebuy*
   In this situation, the purchasing department reorders on a routine basis, very often working from an approved list of suppliers. No other people are involved with the exercise until different suppliers attempt to change the environment in which the decision is made: they may, for example, interrupt the procedure with a potentially better offer.

TABLE 3.2 Main characteristics of the buyclasses

Buyclass	Degree of familiarity with the problem	Information requirements	Alternative solutions
New buy	The problem is fresh to the decision-makers	A great deal of information is required	Alternative solutions are unknown, all are considered new
Modified rebuy	The requirement is not new but is different from previous situations	More information is required but past experience is of use	Buying decision needs new solutions
Rebuy	The problem is identical to previous experiences	Little or no information is required	Alternative solutions not sought or required

Readers may have noticed the strong resemblance to the extended, limited and routinised response identified earlier with respect to the consumer market.

Reference has been made on a number of occasions to organisational buyers, as if these people are the only representatives of an organisation to be involved with the purchase-decision process. This is not usually the case, as very often a large number of people are involved in the purchase decision. This group is referred to as either the decision-making unit (DMU) or the buying centre.

Buying centres vary in size and composition in accordance with the nature of each individual task.

Buying centres vary in size and composition in accordance with the nature of each individual task. Webster and Wind (1972) identified a number of people who make up the buying centre.

Users are people who not only initiate the purchase process but will use the product, once it has been acquired, and evaluate its performance. *Influencers* very often help set the technical specifications for the proposed purchase and assist the evaluation of alternative offerings by potential suppliers. *Deciders* are those who make purchasing decisions. In repeat buying activities the buyer may well also be the decider. However, it is normal practice to require that expenditure decisions involving sums over a certain financial limit be authorised by other, often senior, managers. *Buyers* (purchasing managers) select suppliers and manage the process whereby the required products are procured. As identified previously, buyers may not decide which product is to be purchased but they influence the framework within which the decision is made. *Gatekeepers* have the potential to control the type and flow of information to the organisation and the members of the buying centre. These gatekeepers may be technical personnel, secretaries or telephone switchboard operators.

The size and form of the buying centre is not static. It can vary according to the complexity of the product being considered and the degree of risk each decision is perceived to carry for the organisation. Different roles are required and adopted as the nature of the buying task changes with each new purchase situation (Bonoma, 1982). It is vital for seller organisations to identify members of the buying centre and to target and refine their messages to meet the needs of each member of the centre.

The task of the marketing communications manager and the corresponding sales team is to decide which key participants have to be reached, with which type of message, with what frequency and to what depth contact should be made. Just as with individual consumers, each member of the buying centre is an active problem-solver and processes information so that personal and organisational goals are achieved.

Buyphases

The organisational buying-decision process consists of several stages or buyphases (Robinson et al., 1967). The following sequence of six phases or events is particular to the new-task buyclass. Many of these buyphases are ignored or compressed when either of the other two buyclasses are encountered.

Need/problem recognition

Products or services are purchased because of two main events (Cravens and Woodruff, 1983). Difficulties may be encountered first as a result of a need to solve problems, such as a stock-out or new government regulations, and second as a response to opportunities to improve performance or enter new markets. Essentially, the need/recognition phase is the identification of a gap. This is the gap between the benefits an organisation has now and the benefits it would like to have. For example, when a photocopier breaks down or fails to meet the needs of the organisation, the communication benefits the copier offers are missed by the users. This gap can be bridged by getting the machine mended, by using a different machine on a temporary basis or by buying a new machine that provides the range of benefits required.

Product specification

As a result of identifying a problem and the size of the gap, influencers and users can determine the desired characteristics of the product needed to resolve the problem. This may take the form of a general description or may require a much more detailed analysis and the creation of a specification for a particular product. What sort of photocopier is required? What is it expected to achieve? How many documents should it copy per minute? Is a collator or tray required? This is an important part of the process, because if it is executed properly it will narrow the supplier search and save on the costs associated with evaluation prior to a final decision.

Supplier and product search

At this stage the buyer actively seeks organisations who can supply the necessary product. There are two main issues at this point. Will the product reach the required performance standards and will it match the specification? Secondly, will the potential supplier meet the other organisational requirements? In most circumstances organisations review the market and their internal sources of information and arrive at a decision that is based on rational criteria.

Organisations work wherever possible to reduce uncertainty and complexity.

Organisations work wherever possible to reduce uncertainty and complexity. By working with others who are known, of whom the organisation has direct experience and who can be trusted, risk and uncertainty can be reduced substantially. This highlights another reason why many organisations seek relational exchanges and operate within established networks and seek to support each other.

The quest for suppliers and products may be a short task for the buyer; however, if the established network cannot provide a solution, the buying organisation has to seek new suppliers, and hence new networks, to be able to identify and shortlist appropriate supplier organisations.

Evaluation of proposals

Depending upon the complexity and value of the potential order(s), the proposal is a vital part of the communication plan and should be prepared professionally. The proposals of the shortlisted organisations are reviewed in the context of two main criteria: the product specification and the evaluation of the supplying organisation. If the organisation is already a part of the network, little search and review time need be allocated. If the proposed supplier is new to the organisation a review may be necessary to establish whether it will be appropriate (in terms of price, delivery and service) and whether there is the potential for a long-term relationship or whether this is a single purchase that is unlikely to be repeated.

Supplier selection

The buying centre will undertake a supplier analysis and use a variety of criteria depending upon the particular type of item sought. This selection process takes place in the light of the comments made in the previous section. A further useful perspective is to view supplier organisations as a continuum, from reliance on a single source to the use of a wide variety of suppliers of the same product.

Jackson (1985) proposed that organisations might buy a product from a range of different suppliers, in other words a range of multiple sources are maintained (a practice of many government departments). She labelled this approach 'always a share', as several suppliers are given the opportunity to share the business available to the buying centre. The major disadvantage is that this approach fails to drive cost as low as possible, as the discounts derived from volume sales are not achieved. The advantage to the buying centre is that a relatively small investment is required and little risk is entailed in following such a strategy.

At the other end of the continuum are organisations that only use a single-source supplier. All purchases are made from the single source until circumstances change to such a degree that the buyer's needs are no longer being satisfied. Jackson referred to these organisations as 'lost for good', because once a relationship with a new organisation has been developed, they are lost for good to the original supplier. An increasing number of organisations are choosing to enter alliances with a limited number or even single-source suppliers. The objective is to build a long-term relationship, work together to build quality and help each other achieve their goals. Outsourcing manufacturing activities for non-core activities has increased, and this has moved the focus of communications from an internal to an external perspective.

Evaluation

The order is written against the selected supplier and immediately the supplier is monitored and performance is evaluated against such diverse criteria as responsiveness to enquiries and modifications to the specification and timing of delivery. When the product is delivered it may reach the stated specification but fail to satisfy the original need. This is a case where the specification needs to be rewritten before any future orders are placed.

Organisational buying has shifted from a one-to-one dyadic encounter, salesperson to buyer, to a position where a buying team meets a selling team. The skills associated with this process are different and are becoming much more sophisticated, and the demands on both buyers and sellers are more pronounced. The processes of buying and selling are complex and interactive.

Readers are referred to the section at the end of Chapter 1 in which the differences between consumer and organisational marketing communications was highlighted. These differences reflect the various contextual issues that frame both the consumer and organisational environments. The nature of the environments, the tasks involved and the overall need of the recipients for particular types of information are some of the principal contextual issues.

Summary of key points

1. The way consumers process information prior to a purchase decision can involve a range of elements, issues and dimensions.

2. Perception is concerned with how individuals see and make sense of their environment. It is about the selection, organisation and interpretation of stimuli by individuals so that they can understand their world.

3. Marketing communications stimuli can be used to get people's attention and gain awareness, help consumers to understand the associations and meanings between a message and a brand and show them how the product (service) might solve a particular problem.

4. Attitudes are hypothetical constructs, and they are considered to consist of three components: a cognitive or learning component, an affective or feeling element and a conative or action component. Marketing communications has an important role to play in maintaining or changing attitudes towards products, organisations and brands.

5. Product purchase decisions can be simple or complex depending upon the context in which they are made. Purchase decisions are often the result of experience, knowledge and an interpretative view of the environment. Therefore, the decision processes used by buyers are not always sequential, nor do they reflect a rational approach to resolving problems and needs.

6. All purchase decisions involve a level of uncertainty about the consequences and outcomes of these decisions. Marketing communications can be used to reduce such risks.

7. The level of personal care people bring to purchase decisions is referred to as involvement. The level of involvement experienced by an individual can be regarded as either high or low.

8. Organisations purchase products and services through groups of people known as buying centres or a decision-making unit. The people who constitute these groups each have different roles to play in the purchase process.

9. Marketing communications needs to be based on an understanding of the decision processes used by buyers in the targeted market. This means that the content and style of messages and the form of delivery by the tools of the communication mix (Chapters 6–11) can be dovetailed closely to the needs of the receivers. This also demonstrates how the realm of understanding (Chapter 2) is an important issue in effective communications.

Review questions

1. Attitudes are believed to comprise three elements. Name them.
2. Make brief notes explaining how marketing communications are used to reduce perceived risk and change attitudes.
3. What are EPS, LPS and RRB?
4. Describe the high- and low-involvement decision-making processes.
5. What are buyclasses and buying centres?
6. How might a salesperson successfully utilise knowledge about the buying centre?

References

Bonoma, T.V. (1982), 'Major sales: who really does the buying?', *Harvard Business Review*, May/June, p. 113.

Brabbs, C. (2000), 'Charmin characters take on the Andrex puppy', *Marketing*, 3 February, p. 15.

Chernatony, L. de (1993), 'The seven building blocks of brands', *Management Today*, March, pp. 66–7.

Cohen, J. and Basu, K. (1987), 'Alternative models of categorisation', *Journal of Consumer Research*, March, pp. 455–72.

Cravens, D. and Woodruff, R. (1983), *Marketing*, Reading, Mass.: Addison-Wesley.

Dahl, D.W., Frankenberger, D. and Manchanda, R.V. (2003), 'Does it pay to shock?', *Journal of Advertising Research*, **43**(3) (September), pp. 268–80.

Harris, G. (1987), 'The implications of low-involvement theory for advertising effectiveness', *International Journal of Advertising*, 6, pp. 207–21.

Heath, R. (2000), 'Low-involvement processing', *Admap*, March, pp. 14–16.

Jackson, B. (1985), 'Build customer relationships that last', *Harvard Business Review*, **33**(3), pp. 120–8.

Javalgi, R., Thomas, E. and Rao, S. (1992), 'US travellers' perception of selected European destinations', *European Journal of Marketing*, **26**(7), pp. 45–64.

Lasn, K. (1999), *Culture Jam, The Uncooling of America*, New York: Eagle Brook.

Loch, R. (2003), Involvement Branding: Offering the Best of Both Worlds. Retrieved 18 November 2004 from www.marketingvox.com/archives/2003/05/14/

Moran, W. (1990), 'Brand preference and the perceptual frame', *Journal of Advertising Research*, October/November, pp. 9–16.

Robinson, P.J., Faris, C.W. and Wind, Y. (1967), *Industrial Buying and Creative Marketing*, Boston, Mass.: Allyn & Bacon.

Rossiter, J.R. and Percy, L. (1987), *Advertising and Promotion Management*, Lexington, Mass.: McGraw-Hill.

Rossiter, J.R., Percy, L. and Donovan, R.J. (1991), 'A better advertising planning grid', *Journal of Advertising Research*, October/November, pp. 11–21.

Settle, R.B. and Alreck, P. (1989), 'Reducing buyers' sense of risk', *Marketing Communications*, January, pp. 34–40.

Smith, P. (2004), 'Dotcom video star rises', *Sunday Times*, 11 July, p. 15.

Stone, R.N. and Gronhaug, K. (1993), 'Perceived risk: further considerations for the marketing discipline', *European Journal of Marketing*, **27**(3), pp. 39–50.

Sweney, M. (2004), '*Times* lines up stars for £4m umbrella activity', *Marketing*, 2 September, p. 3.

Webster, F.E. and Wind, Y. (1972), *Organizational Buying Behavior*, Englewood Cliffs, NJ: Prentice-Hall.

Part 1 summary

Review

This opening part of the book has explored the nature and diversity of marketing communications. It considers the role, nature and tasks of marketing communications and explores the increasing significance and importance of this aspect of marketing management.

Emphasis has been placed on the fundamental premise that marketing communications is an audience-centred activity. From that standpoint the tasks (in terms of DRIP) and role of marketing communications (to engage audiences) should be clear. Each of the tools of the mix is considered and readers should be aware of their different characteristics and their ability to achieve different communication effects. Therefore, mixing the tools (and media) in particular ways to meet the needs of different audiences can have a critical impact on campaign success. The tools are therefore an important aspect of marketing communications and constitute a major factor in the way marketing communications resources are used by organisations in order to communicate with their target audiences.

The successful development and maintenance of brands is mainly the result of successful marketing communications. Brands are about making promises and customers learn, through marketing communications, particular brand-related associations.

The second chapter considered some of the theories and methods associated with the ways in which communication is thought to work. From the simple, linear models to the multi-step and more multifaceted, interactional and relational approaches, readers are introduced to the depth and complexity of communication theory. In addition, time was given to the influence both people and technology have on the marketing communications process. These influences are important and need to be understood if effective marketing communications campaigns are to be implemented.

As marketing communications is an audience-centred activity it is crucial to comprehend the fundamental issues concerning information processing and buyer behaviour. The third and final chapter of this opening part explores some of these important elements, as they are the basis upon which marketing communications plans and messages, in particular, are rooted. Buyer behaviour needs to be understood in terms of the way target audience buyers process information (perception and attitudes), and the processes used to make purchase decisions. Attention was given to the level of involvement buyers feel, the risks they perceive when making such decisions and the role marketing communications can play in influencing these various elements. Readers should not forget that audience behaviour can be very different in consumer rather than organisational situations.

Questions and exercises

1. Explain the role of marketing communications and highlight the key tasks that it can be expected to undertake.

2. Discuss the view that word-of-mouth communications provides richer and more effective communication than that provided through mass media.

3. Explain why the promotional mix used by a snack food producer should be configured differently when dealing with major retailers rather than consumers.

4. Compare and contrast the ways in which marketing communications might be used by a charity and a profit-oriented commercial organisation.

5. Examine the ways in which marketing communications can be used to change attitudes towards products and services. Use a market or brand with which you are familiar to illustrate your points.

MINI CASE STUDY
adidas Originals training shoes

This mini case study was written by Lynn Sudbury, Senior Lecturer, Liverpool John Moores University, and Anthony Byrne, Senior Lecturer, Liverpool John Moores University.

I currently own around 140 pairs of old school training shoes, 100 of which are adidas. I tend to buy these from eBay or from outlets like size? and Aspecto. I don't just collect the shoes, I also collect adidas memorabilia, information, magazines, anything really historical to do with adidas. Yes, I do get asked about training shoes quite a bit! (Graham K. – opinion leader)

'Old school' or 'classic' are terms commonly used to describe sports training shoes originally produced and retailed between 1960 and 1980. adidas, Nike, Reebok and Puma have all reproduced models from this era that are now positioned as leisurewear, and are available on most major high streets. While the market for old school training shoes is small in comparison to the training shoes market overall, there are several benefits to producing back-catalogue products. These include a reduction in resources and expenditure on research and development, because the designs, patents and manufacturing capabilities are already owned. Additionally, a back catalogue of shoes that are considered 'classics' adds to brand equity and builds or maintains consumer franchise.

adidas has maintained a high profile in sport over the last five decades, resulting in becoming a global household brand. The adidas Originals line is identifiable by the adidas trefoil logo, and is an addition to the adidas portfolio that, in a market where brand differentiation is paramount, aims to reinforce brand values and steer consumers away from price considerations through leveraging the heritage and history of the brand. Sometimes, this reaches areas outside sport. For example, the adidas Superstar shoe was the footwear of choice during the formative era of

EXHIBIT 3.3 adidas Originals
adidas, the trefoil logo and the 3-stripe trademark are registered trademarks of the adidas–Salomon group, used with permission

hip-hop culture. Leading American hip-hop artists Run DMC even performed a song, entitled 'My adidas', in the brand's honour. This was reciprocated by adidas, which produced a model named in honour of deceased Run DMC member Jam Master Jay.

The overall creative strategy of the marketing communications for Originals is the authenticity and history of the brand. There has been relatively little advertising of the range, with the small amount that has been employed using the theme 'Every adidas has a story'. These ads draw on the history of the product by using people who may be of interest to the Originals target audience reminiscing about their first experience with the product at the time of its launch.

Contemporary magazines, positioned at the leading edge of fashion, art and culture, have also played a part in the communications mix through publicity. The adidas Originals range has received sizeable coverage in magazines such as *The Face*, *Wallpaper*

and *I-D*. For example, *The Face* dedicated a full page to espousing the virtues of the denim adidas Italia shoe, as well as coverage to Jay Kay of the band Jamiroquai, who was endorsing the Oregon shoe. adidas Originals products have also been given to Liam Gallagher, Robbie Williams and Madonna. Celebrities also played a large part in the launch of the Originals 83-C tracksuit top, which was not initially advertised. Rather, celebrities were given the garment and then 'captured' wearing it by the style press. Demand for the limited product resulted in it being offered only through selected retailers who skimmed the market with a price tag in excess of £300.

In another creative move, adidas Originals leveraged the authenticity of the brand through the opening of a store in Central London. The store, named SET, was open for two weeks only, and did not sell anything. Rather, it contained an exhibition of adidas tennis shoes dating back to the 1920s. In addition to generating considerable publicity, it also created a buzz with adidas enthusiasts, fuelling word of mouth communications via interpersonal sources and the Web. Indeed, for an increasing number of people the traditional social circle of friends and family is growing to include people with similar interests from around the world via specialist groups and e-forums. An example of a website where word-of-mouth marketing is prevalent is Terrace Retro, an e-forum dedicated to football-terrace culture and fashions of the 1980s and early 1990s. Here, among other topics, visitors swap information about classic training shoes, including where certain models can be purchased, and delve into the history of the shoe with regard to terrace culture.

Questions

1. Identify the different opinion leaders and opinion formers in the case study.

2. Explain the different ways in which adidas Originals use opinion leaders and opinion formers to generate word-of-mouth communications.

3. Why is word-of-mouth communication so important to adidas Originals?

4. Suggest ways in which adidas can further encourage word-of-mouth communications about the Originals brand.

5. In what ways could adidas monitor word-of-mouth communications?

MINI CASE STUDY
Crème

Market research has shown that the pharmaceutically developed shampoo market was at an immature stage of market development. This was characterised by consumers' apparent ignorance about the role and use of these products. They considered that these products should only by consumed if and when the need arose; in other words, the market was cause-driven. Prescription brands, of which Styloz held a substantial market share, accounted for 90 per cent of the total market. In contrast, manufacturers had not developed the OTC market, where HiPi held 37 per cent market share and total adspend was just €900,000.

Crème was launched at the end of 2002 and targeted AB and C1 men and women aged 25–54. Its positioning was 'the food your hair needs' and 'a successful product now available for you'. Legislation required that these products be distributed through pharmacies.

In 2002, the goal of all Crème promotional activities was to educate the public regarding the benefits of pharmaceutically developed shampoos containing vitamins, encouraging them to reconsider whether their way of living influenced the quality and quantity of their hair. Crème's marketing communications strategy was tailored for each of the three different target groups: end-users, pharmacists and doctors.

During 2003, communication with the selected consumer segment sought to achieve maximum publicity and included public relations activities, TV commercials and inserts in magazines. Additionally, as far as doctors were concerned, a relevant newsletter was created and mailed, sales representatives were hired and a sampling programme was developed to create awareness, encourage trial and through experience develop trust for the new product. Pharmacists were approached, informed and gradually convinced through a launch presentation, constant briefing by the sales force and an attractive sales policy.

In 2003, the total cost of media expenditure in the category reached €2 million, an increase of 222 per cent over the previous year. Crème's SOV was 20 per cent and by the end of 2003, Styloz's market share fell by 11 per cent. The OTC market in the nutrient shampoo category increased its volume

of sales by 143 per cent, with Crème becoming number two with 22 per cent market share. Among consumers, 23 per cent had come to believe that Crème was a good, benefit-giving product, and 11 per cent had either switched from another brand or were persuaded to try Crème.

In 2004, the brand continued to reach all three target groups:

● *end-users* by a TV campaign, inserts in health and lifestyle magazines, outdoor posters and sponsorships of various events;

● *pharmacists* were offered innovative POP material, educational leaflets for customers, window stickers and incentives to recommend the product;

● *doctors* were further informed through Crème's participation at medical conferences and the periodical edition of a newsletter on hair-health issues.

TV advertising continued to have a strong educational message, informing consumers of the benefits of hair products containing vitamins. Crème also started to build concern about people's hair health. Crème's message was differentiated from competitive brands, which only really focused on shine and beauty.

During 2004, the market changed dramatically, with Styloz losing 47 per cent of its sales and Crème doubling its sales. The OTC hair category showed a significant increase, reaching 51 per cent of the total market, while sales in the prescription category fell by 50 per cent.

Attitudes were gradually changing towards better hair protection and care. More OTC companies were attracted to the growing market. Five new products were launched, and by the end of 2004 it was obvious that competition was increasing and that different OTC brands were starting to defend their market share by increasing marketing expenditure. Total market media expenditure rose by 185 per cent, with Crème's SOV being 24 per cent, mainly allocated to TV. Research into pharmacists' attitudes at the end of 2004 showed that 55 per cent of them were already well aware of the brand and had a good perception of it. Of these, 15 per cent were persuaded to recommend it to their customers. The brand commanded 10 per cent brand loyalty.

In 2005, there were already 20 OTC brands in the market. Media expenditure remained high. Crème continued to have a high SOV. The TV ad became more aggressive, stressing the number one position of the brand in many countries and the benefits the product gives to the health of hair. The overall market increased by 14 per cent and at the same time the only prescription brand, Styloz, fell by another 22 per cent. The OTC category reached 65 per cent of the total market sales. In 2005 the Crème brand was completed with the introduction of 'Crème Men', which was developed for the special needs of young men aged 18–30.

In the same year, marketing communications activities were aimed mostly at end-users, to increase spontaneous brand awareness and brand loyalty. Apart from the TV campaign, many tailored activities were addressed to different target groups, involving inserts in trendy magazines, outdoor work, pharmacy posters and indoor ads in sports centres. In pharmacies and doctors' surgeries educational leaflets were distributed and innovative stands were used. Crème's leader image was further imprinted through a visual presence at pharmaceutical and medical conferences.

By 2006, the market had been radically transformed. People appreciated and used pharmaceutically developed shampoos containing vitamins as a pre-emptive measure to keep hair healthy. The number of users had dramatically increased and Crème became market leader with 27 per cent volume share.

Note: The information provided in this mini case is not intended to reflect on any single company or brand. All brands and companies have been disguised and the case does not reflect good or bad management practice.

Questions

1. Explain how management of the Crème brand demonstrates how consumer attitudes can be effectively changed.

2. To what extent does this mini case study demonstrate the role of attributes in the way consumers perceive brands?

3. What is the role of marketing communications at Crème?

4. How might the Crème brand be developed in the future?

5. To what extent might the impact of significant others affect the development of the vitamin-enriched shampoo market?

Managing marketing communications

Part

2

Strategy: approaches, integration and planning

4

Aims and objectives

The aim of this chapter is to explore marketing communications from a strategic perspective. There are three primary topics in this chapter:

Strategy, Integration, Planning

The learning objectives are to enable readers to:

1. explain the three main marketing communications strategies: pull, push and profile;

2. introduce ideas concerning integrated marketing communications;

3. describe the key elements associated with developing marketing communications plans;

4. draw and present a framework for developing marketing communications plans;

5. understand the linkages and interaction between the different elements of the plan.

Introduction

This chapter considers issues associated with marketing communications strategy. It looks not only at the overall direction of marketing communications activities but also examines aspects of integration and planning for marketing communications. For a long time marketing communications strategy was thought to be the combination of activities in the communications mix. However, marketing communications is an audience-centred activity so strategy should be guided in the first place by the nature of the audience, not tools or media. Three main types of audience can be identified: target customers, channel intermediaries (such as wholesalers and added-value resellers) and all of an organisation's stakeholders.

Marketing communications is an audience-centred activity.

The 3Ps of marketing communications strategy

Traditionally, strategy has been interpreted to be a mix of the marketing communications tools used to support a particular campaign: in other words, how the communications resources of an organisation are used. This inward-looking perspective is essentially production-oriented or resource-driven and constitutes what is referred to as an inside-out form of strategy. However, a strategy that is market-oriented requires a consideration of the needs of the audience first and then a determination of the various messages, media and disciplines to accomplish the strategy, an outside-in approach.

We also know that different audiences have different characteristics that necessitate different marketing communications messages and the use of different media mixes to reach them. As a result, it is possible to identify three main marketing communications strategies based on audiences:

- pull strategies – to influence end-user customers (consumers and b2b);
- push strategies – to influence marketing (trade) channel buyers;
- profile strategies – to influence a range of stakeholders.

The 3Ps of marketing communications strategy.

These can be referred to as the 3Ps of marketing communications strategy. Push and pull relate to the direction of the communication to the marketing channel: pushing communications down through the marketing channel or pulling consumers/buyers into the channel via retailers, as a result of receiving the communications. They do not relate to the intensity of communication and only refer to the overall approach. Profile refers to the presentation of the organisation as a whole and therefore the identity is said to be 'profiled' to various other target stakeholder audiences, which may well include consumers, trade buyers, business-to-business customers and a range of other influential stakeholders. Normally, profile strategies do not contain or make reference to specific products or services that the organisation offers. See Table 4.1.

This demarcation may be blurred where the name of a company is the name of its primary (only) product, as is often the case with many retail brands and many business-to-business organisations. For example, messages about B&Q are very often designed to convey meaning about the quality and the low prices of its consumer products and services; however, they often reflect on the organisation itself, especially when its

TABLE 4.1 Marketing communications strategy options

Strategy	Target audience	Message focus	Communications goal
Pull	Consumers	Product/service	Purchase
	End-user b2b customers	Product/service	Purchase
Push	Channel intermediaries	Product/service	Developing relationships and distribution network
Profile	All relevant stakeholders	The organisation	Building reputation

advertising shows members of staff in work-wear, doing their work or speaking highly about the organisation.

Within each of these overall strategies, individual approaches should be formulated to reflect the needs of each particular case. So, for example, the launch of a new shampoo product will involve a push strategy to get the product on the shelves of the appropriate retailers. The strategy would be to gain retailer acceptance of the new brand and to position it as a profitable new brand to gain consumer interest. Personal selling supported by trade sales promotions will be the main marketing communications tools. A pull strategy to develop awareness about the brand will need to be created, accompanied by appropriate public relations activities. The next step will be to create particular brand associations and thereby position the brand in the minds of the target consumer audience. Messages may be functional or expressive but they will endeavour to convey a brand promise. This may be accompanied or followed by the use of incentives to encourage consumers to trial the product. To support the brand, care lines and a website will need to be put in place to provide credibility as well as a buyer reference point. In order that these strategies are implemented, it is normal procedure to develop a marketing communications plan. The degree to which these plans are developed varies across organisations and many rely on their agencies to undertake this work for them. However, there can be major benefits as a result of developing these plans in-house, for example by involving and discussing issues internally and developing a sense of ownership.

A pull strategy

If messages are to be directed at targeted end-user customers, then the intention is often to generate increased levels of awareness, change and/or reinforce attitudes, reduce risk, encourage involvement and ultimately influence customer behaviour. The motivation is to stimulate action so that the target audience can expect the offering to be available to them when they decide to enquire, experiment or make a repeat purchase. This approach is known as a *pull* strategy and is aimed at encouraging customers to 'pull' products through the channel network. See Figure 4.1. This usually means that consumers go into retail outlets (shops) to enquire about a particular product and/or buy it, or to enter a similar transaction direct with the manufacturer or intermediary through direct mail or the Internet. B2b customers are encouraged to buy from dealers and distributors, while both groups of consumers and b2b customers have opportunities to buy through direct-marketing channels where there is no intermediary.

To accomplish and deliver a pull strategy, the traditional approach in the grocery sector has been to deliver mass-media advertising supported by below-the-line communications, most notably sales promotions. There has been greater use of direct marketing

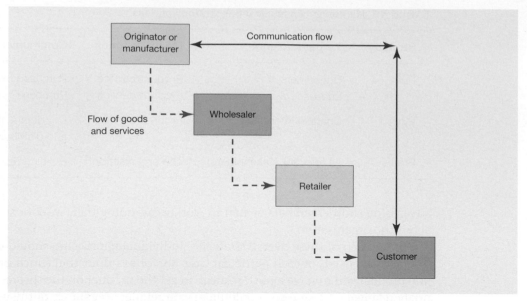

FIGURE 4.1 The direction of a pull strategy

in non-FMCG sectors, and use of the Internet presents opportunities to reach audiences in new ways and so reduce any reliance on the old formulaic approach to pull-based strategies. The decision to use a pull strategy has to be supported by a core-message proposition. This will vary according to the outcomes of the context analysis and the needs of the target audience. However, it is probable that the core message will seek to differentiate (position), remind or reassure, inform or persuade the audience to think, feel or behave in a particular way. Agencies and clients have their own approach to labelling this activity: one way might be to term a communication strategy pull/remind or pull/position, as this describes the audience and what the strategy seeks to achieve.

ViewPoint 4.1   Pull strategies

The mobile company 3 changed its business strategy to one based on driving sales of 3G by offering the lowest call tariffs on standard voice products. A pull strategy based on comparative advertising was used to demonstrate the low-cost/high-spec phones offering.

Asda-Walmart has developed a strong market share in the UK based mainly on price competition or on what is referred to as everyday low pricing (EDLP) (pull/price). Tesco runs everyday low pricing but uses sales promotions as a form of complementary positioning (pull/price/promotions). In their wake, Sainsbury's and Safeway have used differing pull strategies to try to regain lost share, increase profitability and stave off takeover threats. Sainsbury's has yet to recover and Safeway has been bought by Morrisons.

Although Sainsbury's uses EDLP on 1,000 selected lines, it has adopted a classic branding campaign, based around the celebrity chef Jamie Oliver. Making heavy use of television, the brand is positioned around a quality proposition emphasised by the personality and the associated redesign of major stores (pull/quality/repositioning).

The level and degree of customer involvement (see Chapter 3), has some implications for pull strategies. Some marketing communications messages can be considered to be a stimulus that in some situations will have a strong impact on the level of involvement enjoyed by the target audience. A strategic response to this would be to adapt marketing communications messages so that they are effective at different levels of involvement, a form of differentiation.

Use communications to turn low-involvement into high-involvement decisions.

Another approach would be to use communications to turn low-involvement into high-involvement decisions, by encouraging members of the target audience to reconsider their perception of a brand or of the competition. Again, this represents a form of differentiation. A third approach is to segment the market in terms of the level of involvement experienced by each group and according to situational or personality factors, and then shape the marketing communications messages to suit each group.

A pull strategy, therefore, refers to messages targeted at particular customer audiences and to the overall task that a campaign might seek to achieve.

A pull strategy, therefore, refers to messages targeted at particular customer audiences and to the overall task that a campaign might seek to achieve. This might be to differentiate or position a brand (e.g. by reference to specific attributes), remind/reassure, inform (by raising awareness) or persuade (stimulate action). To accomplish this, a functional or expressive positioning policy needs to be agreed and understood by all relevant parties. See Chapter 8.

A push strategy

A second type of target audience can be identified, one that is based on their contribution to the marketing channel. These organisations do not consume the products and services they buy, but add value before moving the product on to others in the demand chain. The previous strategy was targeted at customers who make purchase decisions related largely to their personal (or organisational) consumption of products and services. This second group buys products and services, performs some added-value activity and moves the product through the marketing channel network.

The degree of cooperation between organisations will vary and part of the role of marketing communications is to develop and support the relationships that are regarded as important.

Trade-channel organisations, and indeed all b2b organisations, are actively involved in the development and maintenance of interorganisational relationships. The degree of cooperation between organisations will vary and part of the role of marketing communications is to develop and support the relationships that are regarded as important.

The 'trade' channel has received increased attention in recent years as the strategic value of intermediaries has become both more visible and questioned in light of the Internet. As the channel networks have developed, so has their complexity, which impacts upon the marketing communications strategies and tools used to help reach marketing goals. The expectations of buyers in these networks have risen in parallel with the significance attached to them by manufacturers. The power of multiple retailers, such as Tesco, Sainsbury's, Morrisons and Asda-Walmart, is such that they are able to dictate terms (including the marketing communications) to many manufacturers of branded goods.

A *push* communication strategy involves the presentation of information in order to influence other trade-channel organisations and, as a result, encourage them to take stock, to allocate resources (e.g. shelf space) and to help them to become fully aware of the key attributes and benefits associated with each product with a view to adding value prior to further channel transactions. This strategy is designed to encourage resale to other members of the network and contribute to the achievement of their own objectives. This approach is known as a *push* strategy, as it is aimed at pushing the product down through the channel towards the end-users for consumption. See Figure 4.2.

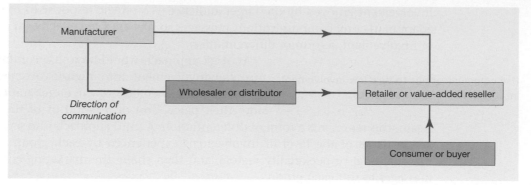

FIGURE 4.2 The direction of a push strategy

ViewPoint 4.2   Makita uses below-the-line branding

Black & Decker discovered that it was losing sales in the trade sector because its products were perceived to be more suitable for consumers and the do-it-yourself market. Its response was to develop a separate brand for this particular trade sector. It used a new name, 'Makita', identified the product range through the colour blue and made it available through different trade channels. The promotional materials and support documentation needed a different 'tone of voice' to reflect a more rugged and stronger position. The messages were integrated in order to reinforce the desired positioning.

EXHIBIT 4.1 Trade advertisement for Makita

The channel network (see Chapter 13) consists of those organisations with whom others must cooperate directly to achieve their own objectives. By accepting that there is interdependence, usually dispersed unequally throughout the network, it is possible to identify organisations that have a stronger/weaker position within a network. Communication must travel not only between the different levels of dependence and role ('up and down' in a linear channel context) and so represent vertical flows, but also across similar levels of dependence and role, that is, horizontal flows; these may be from retailer to retailer or wholesaler to wholesaler.

Marketing communications targeted at people involved in organisational buying decisions are characterised by an emphasis on personal selling. Trade advertising, trade sales promotions and public relations all have an important yet secondary role to play. Direct marketing has become increasingly important, and the development of the Internet has had a profound impact on b2b communications and interorganisational relationships. However, personal selling has traditionally been the most significant part of the promotional mix where a push strategy has been instigated.

Finally, just as it was suggested that the essence of a pull strategy could be articulated in brief format, a push strategy could be treated in a similar way. The need to consider the core message is paramount as it conveys information about the essence of the strategy. Push/inform, push/position or push/key accounts/discount might be examples of possible terminology. Whether or not this form of expression is used, it is important that marketing communications strategy refers to more than just push; what is to be achieved also needs to be understood.

A profile strategy

The strategies considered so far concern the need for interaction and dialogue with customers (pull) and trade-channel intermediaries (push). However, there is a whole range of other stakeholders, many of whom need to know about and understand the organisation rather than actually purchase its products and services. See Figure 4.3. This group of stakeholders may include financial analysts, trade unions, government

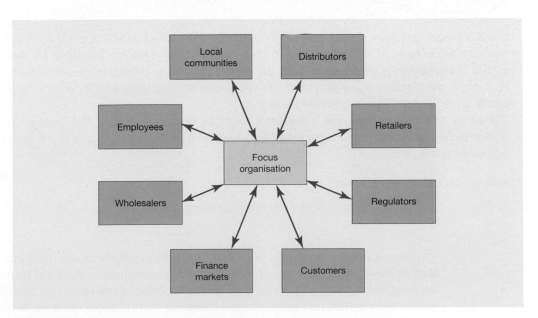

FIGURE 4.3 The direction of a profile strategy

bodies, employees or the local community. These different stakeholder groups have the potential to influence the organisation in various ways and, in doing so, need to receive (and respond to) different types of messages. So, the financial analysts need to know about financial and trading performance and expectations, and the local community may be interested in employment and the impact of the organisation on the local environment, whereas the government may be interested in the way the organisation applies health and safety regulations and pays corporation, VAT and other taxes. It should also be remembered that consumers and business-to-business customers may also be more interested in the organisation itself and so help initiate an umbrella branding strategy.

Traditionally, these organisation-oriented activities have been referred to as corporate communications, as they deal more or less exclusively with the corporate entity or organisation. Products, services and other offerings are not normally the focus of these communications. It is the organisation and its role in the context of the particular stakeholders' activities that is important. However, it should be noted that as more corporate brands appear, the distinction between corporate and marketing communications begins to become much less clear. Indeed, when considered in the light of the development and interest in internal marketing (and communications), it may be of greater advantage to consider corporate communications as part of an organisation's overall marketing communications activities.

> As more corporate brands appear, the distinction between corporate and marketing communications begins to become much less clear.

The awareness, perception and attitudes held by stakeholders towards an organisation need to be understood, shaped and acted upon. This can be accomplished through continual dialogue, which will normally lead to the development of trust and commitment and enable relationships to grow. This is necessary in order that stakeholders act favourably towards an organisation and enable strategies to flourish and objectives to be achieved.

ViewPoint 4.3   H. Samuel raising its profile

In 2003 the UK jewellery market became increasingly competitive as stores such as Argos and Asda-Walmart began to exert control over much of the bottom end of the market, while De Beers launched a chain of shops in a joint venture with the fashion company LVMH. In response to this squeeze, H. Samuel, the high street jewellery chain owned by Signet, attempted to differentiate itself by trying to create a destination lifestyle brand for its stores.

Part of this strategy required a rejuvenation of its corporate image. The goal was to enhance H. Samuel's profile and at the same time try to position it as more of a luxury brand than it has been perceived in the past.

Source: Adapted from Sweney (2003)

To build corporate brands, organisations must develop communications programmes that involve all of their key stakeholder groups. Audiences demand transparency and accountability, and instant online access to news, developments, research and networks means that inconsistent or misleading information must be avoided. As if to reinforce this, a survey reported by Gray (2000) found that CEOs rated the reputation of their organisations as more important than that of their products. However, the leading contributor to the strength of the corporate brand is seen to be its products and services, followed by a strong management team, internal communications, PR, social accountability, change management and the personal reputation of the CEO.

However, it would be incorrect to perceive corporate communications as just a means of shaping or influencing the attitudes and behaviour of other stakeholders. Organisations exist within a variety of networks that provide a context for the roles and actions of member organisations. Bidirectional communication flows exist and organisations adapt themselves to the actions and behaviour of others in the network. Therefore, corporate communications provides a mechanism by which it can learn about the context(s) in which it exists and is shaped and influenced by the other stakeholders with whom it shares communications. Reference is made to the work of Grunig and Hunt (1984).

A *profile* strategy is one that focuses an organisation's communications upon the development of corporate image, reputation and relationships, whether they be internal, external or both. To accomplish and deliver a profile strategy public relations, including sponsorship and corporate advertising, becomes the pivotal tool of the marketing communications mix, though personal selling may remain a vital element delivering both product/service and corporate messages.

Finally, readers are encouraged to use the 3Ps in combination and not to treat them as mutually exclusive units. Indeed, in most organisations it is possible to identify an element of each strategy at any one time. In reality, most organisations are structured in such a way that those responsible for communications with each of these three main audiences do so without reference to or coordination with each other. This is an example of how integrated marketing communications, which is examined later, needs to have one senior person responsible for all organisational communications. Only through a single point of reference is it realistically possible to develop and communicate a set of brand values that is consistent and credible. Recognising these limitations that organisations often place on themselves, the 3Ps should be considered as part of a total communications approach.

The role of each element of the marketing communications mix is important in promotional strategy. Each tool has different strengths and should be used accordingly. For example, direct marketing and sales promotion are more likely to be effective in persuading consumer audiences, while personal selling is likely to be more effective in b2b situations. A profile strategy designed to change the perception and understanding of an organisation is more likely to utilise public relations and corporate advertising.

Integrated marketing communications

Original thinking held that clients were able to achieve impacts or effects *on* audiences and buyers. These impacts were achieved through the autonomous use of each promotional tool. Consequently, clients were required to deal with a variety of functionally different and independent organisations in order to communicate with their various audiences. As a result, clients and suppliers of the promotional tools saw specialisation as the principal means to achieve communication effectiveness. This resulted in a proliferation of advertising and public-relations agencies plus the development of sales-promotion houses and direct-marketing agencies.

IMC has emerged partially as a reaction to these structural inadequacies of the industry and the realisation by clients that their communication needs can (and should) be achieved more efficiently and effectively than previously. In other words, just as power has moved from brand manufacturers to multiple retailers and now to consumers, so power is moving from agencies to clients.

There has also been a trend away from the use of traditional communications strategies, based largely on mass communications, delivering generalised messages, to one based more on personalised, customer-oriented and technology-driven approaches, referred to as integrated marketing communications. For many, integration is about orchestrating the tools of the promotional mix; indeed, Duncan and Everett (1993) recall that this new, largely media-oriented approach, has been referred to variously as *orchestration*, *whole egg* and *seamless communication*. Since this time many authors have expanded upon ideas concerning IMC and most recently Duncan (2002) and Gronroos (2004) have provided valuable insights into this dimension of IMC, one that Kitchen et al. (2004) refer to as the 'outside-in' IMC approach. For our purposes the following definition is offered:

> *IMC is a strategic approach to the planned management of an organisation's communications. IMC requires that organisations coordinate their various strategies, resources and messages in order that it engage coherently and meaningfully with target audiences. The main purpose is to develop relationships with audiences that are of mutual value.*

This definition serves to link IMC with business-level strategies and the importance of coherence within the organisation-wide use of resources and messages. Implicit is the underpinning notion that IMC is necessary for the development of effective relationships and that not all relationships need be collaborative and fully relational, as they are so often assumed to be in many contemporary interpretations. See also Cornelissen (2003).

What is to be integrated?

The notion that some aspects of marketing communications should be integrated has received widespread and popular support over the past decade. However, defining what integration actually means and what should be integrated is far from universal agreement, especially as there is an absence of any empirical evidence or definitive research in the area. While the origins of IMC might be found in the prevailing structural conditions and the needs of particular industry participants, an understanding of what elements should be integrated in order to achieve IMC needs to be established.

The origins of IMC might be found in the prevailing structural conditions.

The problem with answering this question is that unless there is agreement about what IMC is then identifying appropriate elements is far from easy, practical or in anyone's best interests. At one level the harmonisation of the tools of the promotional mix represents the key integration factors but as these represent a resource-driven view then perhaps a more strategic (audience-centred) perspective, one driven by the market and the objectives of the organisation, might be more realistic. Between these two extremes it is possible to identify messages, media, employees (especially in service-based environments), communication-planning processes, client/agency relationships and operations, and the elements of the marketing mix, all of which need to be involved and be a part of the integration process.

ViewPoint 4.4   Inside-out chocolate?

UK chocolate manufacturer Cadbury used an 'integrated' campaign that encouraged consumers to send in special wrappers in return for free sports-related goods. The tools of the mix were coordinated – advertising, sales promotions, packaging, sponsorship and marketing public relations.

The problems with the campaign concerned links between chocolate and sporting ability and between child-related obesity issues and chocolate consumption. Had the campaign been considered from an audience perspective then a different campaign strategy might have been developed.

For a more detailed review of what should be integrated see Fill (2006), and for a debate about the validity of the IMC concept readers should read Kitchen et al. (2004), Swain (2004) and Cornelissen (2003). However, two issues need to be raised at this point. The first concerns technology and the second concerns branding.

Technology the enabler

The use of technology, and in particular database technologies, has enabled marketing managers to obtain a vastly improved view of customer behaviour, attitudes and feelings towards brands. This has facilitated more precise and insightful communications, and the subsequent feedback and measurement facilities have further developed the overall quality of customer communications. However, the mere presence of technology does not result in effective marketing communications. Technology needs to be integrated into not just the overall information systems strategy but also the marketing strategies of organisations. Technology is an enabler and to use it effectively requires integration. The effective use of technology can touch a number of areas within the IMC orbit – for example, technology can be used to develop effective websites, extranets and intranets, customer contact centres, databases, advertising campaigns, fulfilment processes, CRM and sales-force automation. If each of these applications are deployed independently of each other then their impact will be limited. If they are developed within an integrated framework the potential for marketing and customer service can be tremendous.

> Associated with the use of technology are issues concerning the measurement and evaluation of IMC activities.

Associated with the use of technology are issues concerning the measurement and evaluation of IMC activities. One of the criticisms of IMC is that no evaluation system has yet been proposed or implemented so that the claims made about IMC delivering superior returns can be validated (Swain, 2004). This is, of course, part of the planning process and so integration of all aspects of the campaign planning process is necessary.

Branding

Among other things, brands represent the outcome of marketing communications activities over a period of time. Strong brands represent successful integration activities over a period of time. This means that internally, organisations need to be sufficiently coordinated so that the brand is perceived externally as consistent and uniform. However, this proposition is based on the view that a brand is prepared and delivered for a single target audience, but audience and media fragmentation make this task more challenging. Audience sizes are shrinking, which means that in many situations a single audience is no longer economically viable. Brands therefore need to appeal to a number of different audiences (White, 2000) and to do this it is necessary to develop brands that appeal to diverse consumer groups. For example, a top-of-the-range music system may be regarded by the owner as prestigious and technically superb, by a guest at a party as ostentatiously outrageous and overpriced, and by a friend as a product of clever design and marketing. All three might have developed their attitudes through different sources (e.g. different print media, exhibitions, the Internet, retail stores, word of mouth) but all agree that the brand has a common set of values and associations that are important to each of them.

A further dimension of the branding factor concerns the role of corporate brands and issues of corporate communications. Should these be integrated with product brand communications, and if so what are the branding strategies that should be followed?

Once the internal reorientation has begun (but not completed), it is possible to take the message to external audiences. As long as they can see that employees are starting to act in different ways, that they do care about them as customers and do know what they are talking about in support of the products and services offered, then it is likely that customers (and other stakeholders) will be supportive. IMC should be concerned with blending internal and external messages so that there is clarity, consistency and reinforcement of the organisation's (or brand's) core proposition.

> **IMC should be concerned with blending internal and external messages so that there is clarity, consistency and reinforcement of the organisation's (or brand's) core proposition.**

ViewPoint 4.5   Integrated ice cream

Media investment of £7.5 million in the market-leading Magnum ice cream was designed to provide support for an integrated promotional programme across television, press, outdoor (posters) and marketing public relations. This sum represented a 65 per cent share of voice and nearly 5,000 TVRs (television ratings) (see Chapter 8). In addition, in-store support was increased to provide for improved visibility and to cut through the own-brand imitations. Also, at a time when ideas about brand 'experiences' were becoming central, Magnum became associated with the UK's first triple-loop roller coaster 'Magnum Force'.

The public-relations programme sought to build on the visibility of the brand and the coverage that the Magnum Girl gained. For example, Magnum became the first brand ever to appear on the front cover of the *Sunday Mail* magazine supplement, which has the second-highest circulation of Sunday newspapers. The Magnum Girl became the central point of the campaign, featuring on posters, television, in-store and press work. Each year a competition is held to find a new Magnum Girl to front the brand, in itself a positive means of securing good public relations for the brand.

With thanks to Eileen Buckwald and Wall's Ice Cream for the original material.

EXHIBIT 4.2 Magnum
The Magnum brand has achieved market leadership through strong, consistent branding and positioning. Picture reproduced with the kind permission of Bird's Eye Walls

Integration – coordination or just exemplary marketing communications?

Although IMC has yet to become an established marketing theory, the original ideas (Schultz, 1993) inherent in the overall approach are intuitively appealing and appear to be of value. However, what is integration to one person may be coordination to another, and until there is a theoretical base upon which to build IMC practice the phrase will continue to be misused, misunderstood and employed in a haphazard and inconsistent way.

Viewed holistically, integration is a strategic concept that strikes at the heart of an organisation's marketing and business orientation.

Viewed holistically, integration is a strategic concept that strikes at the heart of an organisation's marketing and business orientation. The word integration has been used in various ways and it is the interpretation of the word that determines whether integrated marketing communications is real, achievable or even practised. In many ways, reality suggests that the claims many organisations and the communications industry make in the name of IMC are simply a reflection of improved management and coordination of the communications tools.

Reasons for the developing interest in IMC

The explosion of interest in IMC has resulted from a variety of drivers. They can generally be grouped into three main categories: those drivers (or opportunities) that are market-based, those that arise from changing communications, and those that are driven from opportunities arising from within the organisation itself. These are set out in Table 4.2.

The opportunities offered to organisations that contemplate moving to IMC are considerable and it is somewhat surprising that so few organisations have been either willing or able to embrace the approach. One of the main organisational drivers for IMC is the need to become increasingly efficient. Driving down the cost base enables managers to improve profits and levels of productivity. By seeking synergistic advantages through its communications and associated activities and by expecting managers to be able to account for the ways in which they consume marketing communication resources, so integrated marketing communications becomes increasingly attractive. At the same time, organisation structures are changing more frequently and the need to integrate across functional areas reflects the efficiency drive.

The predominant driver is the reorientation from transaction-based marketing to relationship marketing.

From a market perspective, the predominant driver is the reorientation from transaction-based marketing to relationship marketing. The extension of the brand personality concept into brand relationships (Hutton, 1996) requires a customer consideration in terms of asking not only 'What do our customers want?' but also 'What are their values, do they trust us and are we loyal to them?' By adopting a position designed to enhance trust and commitment an organisation's external communications need to be consistent and coordinated, if only to avoid information overload and misunderstanding.

From a communications perspective, the key driver is to provide a series of triggers by which buyers can understand the values a brand stands for and a means by which they can use certain messages to influence their activities within the relationships they wish to develop. By differentiating the marketing communications, often by providing clarity and simplicity, advantages can be attained.

TABLE 4.2 Drivers for IMC

Organisational drivers for IMC
- Increasing profits through improved efficiency
- Increasing need for greater levels of accountability
- Rapid move towards cross-border marketing and the need for changing structures and communications
- Coordinated brand development and competitive advantage
- Opportunities to utilise management time more productively
- Provide direction and purpose for employees

Market-based drivers for IMC
- Greater levels of audience communications literacy
- Media-cost inflation
- Media and audience fragmentation
- Stakeholders' need for increasing amounts and diversity of information
- Greater amounts of message clutter
- Competitor activity and low levels of brand differentiation
- Move towards relationship marketing from transaction-based marketing
- Development of networks, collaboration and alliances

Communications-based drivers for IMC
- Technological advances (Internet, databases, segmentation techniques)
- Increased message effectiveness through consistency and reinforcement of core messages
- More effective triggers for brand and message recall
- More-consistent and less-confusing brand images
- Need to build brand reputations and to provide clear identity cues

ViewPoint 4.6   Coordinated Bratz

The Bratz doll brand used a mix of TV and marketing PR to get coverage in 'tween' magazines, advertorials, in-store displays and gondola positions, sponsorship (with Nickleodeon) and incorporated a competition. Bratz was also linked with an established brand targeted at 4-to-7-year-olds.

The advertising was run in three phases, each reflecting a different stage of the Nickleodeon-based competition. Typically this is referred to as an integrated campaign, and although very successful in terms of market share (up from 16 per cent to over 45 per cent and outstripping Barbie's 30 per cent share) the question remains – is this really an integrated marketing communications programme?

> An integrated approach should attempt to provide a uniform or consistent set of messages.

An integrated approach should attempt to provide a uniform or consistent set of messages. These should be relatively easy to interpret and to assign meaning. This enables target audiences to think about and perceive brands within a relational context and so encourage behaviour as expected by the source. Those organisations that try to practise IMC understand that buyers refer to and receive messages about brands and companies from a wide range of information sources. Harnessing this knowledge is a fundamental step towards enhancing marketing communications.

The advantages and disadvantages associated with IMC are set out in Table 4.3.

TABLE 4.3 Advantages and disadvantages of IMC

Advantages of IMC

Provides opportunities to cut communications costs and/or reassign budgets

Has the potential to produce synergistic and more-effective communications

Can deliver competitive advantage through clearer positioning

Encourages coordinated brand development with internal and external participants

Provides for increased employee participation and motivation

Has the potential to cause management to review its communications strategy

Requires a change in culture and fosters a customer focus

Provides a benchmark for the development of communications activities

Can lead to a cut in the number of agencies supporting a brand

Disadvantages of IMC

Encourages centralisation and formal/bureaucratic procedures

Can require increased management time seeking agreement from all involved parties

Suggests uniformity and single message

Tendency to standardisation might negate or dilute creative opportunities

Global brands restricted in terms of local adaptation

Normally requires cultural change from employees and encourages resistance

Has the potential to severely damage a brand's reputation if incorrectly managed

Can lead to mediocrity as no single agency network has access to all sources of communications

General opinion suggests that the advantages far outweigh the disadvantages and that increasing numbers of organisations are seeking to improve their IMC resource. As stated earlier, database technology and the Internet have provided great impetus for organisations to review their communications and to implement moves to install a more integrated communications strategy.

Resistance to integration

The development and establishment of IMC by organisations has not been as widespread as the amount of discussion around the subject. Recent technological advances and the benefits of the Internet and related technologies have meant that organisations have had a reason to reconsider their marketing communications and have re-evaluated their approach. Whatever route taken, the development of IMC requires change, a change in thinking, actions and expectations. The changes required to achieve IMC are large and the barriers are strong. What can be observed in practice are formative approaches to IMC, organisational experiments undertaken within their resource and cultural contexts.

As with many aspects of change, there is nearly always resistance to the incorporation of IMC and, if sanctioned, only partial integration has been achieved. This is not to say that integration is not possible or has not been achieved, but the path to IMC is far from easy and the outcomes are difficult to gauge with great confidence. However, it is the expectation (what level of IMC) that really matters, as it signals the degree of change that is required.

Resistance to change is partly a reflection of the experiences and needs of individuals for stability and the understanding of their environments. However, it is also a reflection, again, of the structural conditions in organisations and industry that have helped determine the expectations of managers and employees.

Eagle and Kitchen (2000) set out four principal areas or themes concerned with barriers to IMC programmes:

- power, coordination and control issues;
- client skills, centralisation/organisation and cultural issues;
- agency skills/talent and overall time/resource issues;
- flexibility/modification issues.

Although these provide a useful general overview, the following represent some of the more common, more focused reasons for resistance to the incorporation of IMC.

Financial structures and frameworks

Resistance through finance-led corporate goals, which have dominated industry performance and expectations, has been particularly significant. The parameters set around it and the extent to which marketing communications are often perceived as a cost rather than an investment have provided a corporate environment where the act of preparing for and establishing integrative activities is disapproved of at worst or room for manoeuvre restricted at best. Furthermore, the period in which promotion activities are expected to generate returns works against the principles of IMC and the time needed for the effects to take place.

Opposition/reluctance to change

The attitudes and opinions of staff are often predictable, in the sense that any move away from tried and proven methods to areas that are unknown and potentially threatening is usually rejected. Change has for a long time been regarded with hostility and fear, and as such is normally resisted. Our apparent need for stability and general security has been a potent form of resistance to the introduction of IMC. This is changing as change itself becomes a familiar aspect of working life. Any move towards IMC therefore represents a significantly different approach to work, as not only are the expectations of employees changed but so also are the working practices and the associated roles with internal customers and, more importantly, those providing outsourcing facilities.

Change has for a long time been regarded with hostility and fear.

Traditional hierarchical and brand-management structures

Part of the reluctance to change is linked with the structure and systems inherent in many organisations. Traditional hierarchical structures and systems are inflexible and slow to cope with developments in their fast-adapting environments. These structures stifle the use of individual initiative, slow the decision-making process and encourage inertia. The brand management system, so popular and appropriate in the 1970s and early 1980s, focuses upon functional specialism, which is reflected in the horizontally and vertically specialised areas of responsibility. Brands now need to be managed by flexible teams of specialists, who are charged with responsibilities and the resources necessary to coordinate activities across organisations in the name of integration.

Attitudes and structure of suppliers and agencies

One of the principal reasons often cited as a barrier to integration is the relationship that clients have with their agencies, and in particular their advertising agencies. Generally, advertising agencies have maintained their traditional structures and methods of operating, whereas their clients have begun to adapt and reform themselves. The

Advertising agencies have tried to maintain their dominance of mass-media advertising as the principal means of brand development.

thinking behind this is that advertising agencies have tried to maintain their dominance of mass-media advertising as the principal means of brand development. In doing so they seek to retain the largest proportion of agency fee income, rather than having these fees diluted as work is allocated below the line (to other organisations). The establishment of IMC threatens the current role of the main advertising agencies. This is not to say that all agencies think and act in this way – they do not, as witnessed by the innovative approaches to restructuring and the provision of integrated resources for their clients by agencies such as St Lukes. So, while clients have seen the benefits of integrated marketing communications, their attempts to achieve them have often been thwarted by the structures of the agencies they need to work with and by the attitudes of their main agencies.

Perceived complexity of planning and coordination

The complexity associated with integrating any combination of activities is often cited as a means for delaying or postponing action. Of greater significance are the difficulties associated with coordinating actions across departments and geographic boundaries. IMC requires the cooperation and coordination of internal and external stakeholder groups. Each group has an agenda that contains goals that may well differ from or conflict with those of other participants.

For example, an advertising agency might propose the use of mass media to address a client's needs, if only because that is where its specialist skills lie. However, direct marketing might be a more appropriate approach to solving the client's problem, but because there is no established mechanism to coordinate and discuss openly the problem/solution, the lead agency is likely to have its approach adopted in preference to others.

Implementing IMC

The restraints that prevent the development of IMC need to be overcome. Indeed, many organisations that have made significant progress in developing IMC have done so by instigating approaches and measures that aim to reduce or negate the impact of the barriers that people put up to prevent change. The main approaches to overcoming the barriers are as follows.

Adopting a customer-focused philosophy

The adoption of a customer-focused approach is quite well established within marketing departments. However, this approach needs to be adopted as an organisation-wide approach, a philosophy that spans all departments and that results in unified cues to all stakeholders. In many cases, agencies need to adopt a more customer-oriented approach and be able and willing to work with other agencies, including those below the line.

Training and staff-development programmes

A move towards IMC cannot be made without changes in the expectations held by employees within the client and agency sectors. Some of the key processes that have been identified as important to successful change management need to be used. For example, the involvement and participation of all staff in the process is in itself a step to providing motivation and acceptance of change when it is agreed and delivered.

Appointing change agents

The use of change agents, people who can positively affect the reception and implementation of change programmes, is important. As IMC should span an entire organisation, the change agent should be a senior manager, or preferably director, in order to signal the importance and speed at which the new perspective is to be adopted. Some organisations have experimented with the appointment of a single senior manager who is responsible for all internal and external communications.

Planning to achieve sustainable competitive advantage

In order to develop competitive advantage, some organisations have restructured by removing levels of management, introducing business-reprocessing procedures and even setting up outsourcing in order that they achieve cost-efficiencies and -effectiveness targets. Prior to the implementation of these delayering processes, many organisations were (and many still are) organised hierarchically.

Back in 1997 Brown rightly stated that the emergence and establishment of IMC will only have a real chance of success once the industry matures, becomes market-oriented and leaves behind issues concerning client–agency complications and in many cases traditional brand-management systems, most designed to prevent the development of synergies or shared knowledge. These issues have not yet been resolved and IMC in practice remains ill defined, and superficial. What is required therefore is a restructuring and redesignation of who manages communications, and this requires a planned approach. It is evident that many of the current systems, processes, procedures and structures are not suitable to support and sustain a planned approach to enable the full development and delivery of IMC.

> Many of the current systems, processes, procedures and structures are not suitable to support and sustain a planned approach to enable the full development and delivery of IMC.

Finally, *total* IMC (integration of all marketing and corporate communications) is achieved when all external agencies, outsourcing providers and partners work with the organisation in such a way that customers perceive consistency in the promises and actions the organisation makes, and are satisfied with the organisation's attempts to anticipate and satisfy customer needs and the results that they seek from their relationships with the brand or organisation.

Planning for marketing communications

Having established the need for strategy and the principles associated with integrated communications, the remaining task is to plan for the development, delivery and evaluation of marketing communications activities. For many reasons, planning is an essential management activity, and if marketing communications are to be developed in an orderly and efficient way planning should be developed around a suitable framework. First, the principal tasks facing marketing communications managers need to be established. These are to decide:

1. who should receive the messages;
2. what the messages should say;
3. what image of the organisation/brand receivers are expected to retain;
4. how much is to be spent establishing this new image;
5. how the messages are to be delivered;
6. what actions the receivers should take;
7. how to control the whole process once implemented;
8. what was achieved.

Note that more than one message is transmitted and that there is more than one target audience. This is important, as recognition of the need to communicate with multiple audiences and their different information requirements, often simultaneously, lies at the heart of marketing communications. The aim is to generate and transmit messages that present the organisation and its offerings to its various target audiences, encouraging them to think, behave or respond in particular ways. It is the skill and responsibility of those charged with marketing communications to blend the communications tools and to create a satisfactory mix.

A framework for integrated marketing communications plans

The MCPF (Figure 4.4) seeks to bring together the various elements into a logical sequence of activities where the rationale for marketing communications decisions is built upon information generated at a previous level in the framework. Another advantage of using the MCPF is that it provides a suitable checklist of activities that need to be considered.

The MCPF represents a sequence of decisions that marketing managers undertake when preparing, implementing and evaluating communications strategies and plans.

The MCPF represents a sequence of decisions that marketing managers undertake when preparing, implementing and evaluating communications strategies and plans. It does not mean that this sequence reflects reality; indeed, many marketing decisions are made outside any recognisable framework. However, as a means of understanding the different elements, appreciating the ways in which they relate to one another and bringing together various aspects for work or for answering examination questions such as those offered by the Chartered Institute of Marketing, this approach has many advantages and has been used by a number of local, national and international organisations.

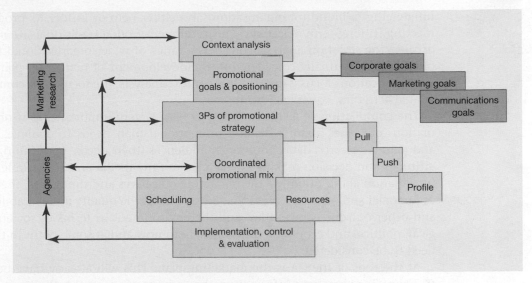

FIGURE 4.4 The marketing communications planning framework

Marketing communications requires the satisfaction of promotional objectives through the explicit and deliberate development of communications strategy. The MCPF will be used to show first the key elements, second some of the linkages and third the integrated approach that is required.

This framework reflects the deliberate or planned approach to strategic marketing communications. The process of marketing communications, however, is not linear, as depicted in this framework, but integrative and interdependent. The MCPF approach presented here is not intended to solve all the problems associated with the formulation of such plans, but it is robust enough to meet the needs of employers and examiners.

> The process of marketing communications, however, is not linear, as depicted in this framework, but integrative and interdependent.

Elements of the plan

Marketing communications plans consist of the following elements, which will be considered in turn:

- context analysis
- promotional objectives
- marketing communications strategy
- coordinated promotional mix (methods, tools and media)
- scheduling and implementation
- resources (human and financial)
- evaluation and control
- feedback.

Context analysis

Analysing the context in which marketing communications episodes occur is a necessary, indeed vital, first step in the planning process. The purpose is to understand the key market and communication drivers that are likely to influence (or already are influencing) a brand (or organisation) and either help or hinder its progress towards meeting its long-term objectives. This is different from a traditional situation analysis, because the situation analysis considers a range of wider organisational factors, most of which are normally considered in the development of marketing plans (while the communications focus is lost). In this context analysis, the focus is on communication-related activities, issues and events.

The compilation of a context analysis (CA) is very important, as it presents information and clues about what the promotional plan needs to achieve. Information and market-research data about target audiences (their needs, perception, motivation, attitudes and decision-making characteristics), the media and the people they use for information about offerings, the marketing objectives and timescales, the overall level of financial and other resources that are available, the quality and suitability of agency and other outsourced activities, and the environment in terms of societal, technological, political and economic conditions, both now and at some point in the future, all need to be considered.

At the root of the CA is the marketing plan. This will already have been prepared and contains important information about the target segment, the business and marketing goals, competitors and the timescales on which the goals are to be achieved.

The rest of the CA seeks to elaborate and build upon this information so as to provide the detail in order that the plan can be developed and justified.

The CA provides the rationale for the plan that follows. It is from the CA that the marketing objectives (from the marketing plan) and the marketing communications objectives are derived. The type, form and style of the message are rooted in the characteristics of the target audience, and the media selected to convey messages can be based upon the nature of the tasks, the media habits of the audience and the resources available. The main components of the context analysis are set out in Table 4.4.

TABLE 4.4 The main elements of the context analysis

Context element	Dimensions
The customer context	Segment characteristics Levels of awareness, perception and attitudes towards the brand/organisation Level of involvement Types of perceived risk DMU characteristics and issues
The business context	Corporate and marketing strategy and plans Brand/organisation analysis Competitor analysis
The internal context	Financial constraints Organisation identity Culture, values and beliefs Marketing expertise Agency availability and suitability
The external context	Who are the key stakeholders and why are they important? What are their communications needs? Social, political, economic and technological restraints and opportunities

Promotional objectives

The role of promotional objectives in the planning process is important for a number of reasons. The first is that they provide a balance to the plan and take away the sole emphasis on sales that inevitably arises. Second, they indicate positioning issues; third, they highlight the required balance of the promotional mix; fourth, they provide time parameters for campaigns; and fifth, they provide a crucial means by which particular marketing communication activities are evaluated.

Ideally, promotional objectives should consist of three main elements:

1. *Corporate objectives*
   These are derived from the business or marketing plan. They refer to the mission and the business area that the organisation believes it should be in.

2. *Marketing objectives*
   These are derived from the marketing plan and are output-oriented. Normally these can be considered as sales-related objectives, such as market share, sales revenues, volumes, ROI (return on investment) and profitability indicators.

3. *Marketing communication objectives*
   These are derived from an understanding of the current context in which a brand exists and the future context in the form of where the brand is expected to be at some point in the future. These will be presented as awareness levels, perception, comprehension/knowledge, attitudes towards and overall degree of preference for the brand. The choice of communication goal depends upon the tasks that need to be accomplished. In addition, most brands need either to maintain their current brand position or to reposition themselves in the light of changing contextual conditions.

These three elements constitute the promotional objectives and they all need to be set out in SMART terminology (see Chapter 5). What also emerges is a refinement to the positioning that managers see as important for success. Obviously, not all plans require express attention to positioning (e.g. government information campaigns) but most commercial and brand-oriented communications programmes need to communicate a clear position in their market. So at this point the positioning intentions are developed, and these will be related to the market, the customers or some other dimension. The justification for this will have been identified in the CA.

Marketing communications strategy

Communications strategy should be audience- not method/media-oriented.

The communications strategy should be audience- not method/media-oriented. The strategy therefore depends upon whether the target audience is a consumer segment, a distributor or dealer network or whether all stakeholders need to be reached. In addition, it is imperative that the strategy be geared to the communication needs of the target audience that is revealed during the customer and business-context analyses. This will show what the task is that marketing communications needs to achieve. Having established who the audience is, push-, pull- or profile-dominated strategies can be identified. The next step is to determine the task that needs to be accomplished. This will have been articulated previously in the marketing communications objectives but the approach at this stage is less quantitative and softer. The DRIP roles of marketing communications can be used to suggest the strategy being pursued. For example, if a new brand is being launched, the first task will be to inform and differentiate the brand for members of the trade before using a pull strategy to inform and differentiate the brand for the target end-user customers. An organisation wishing to signal a change of strategy and/or a change of name following a merger or acquisition may choose to use a profile strategy and the primary task will be to inform of the name change. An organisation experiencing declining sales may choose to remind customers of a need or it may choose to improve sales through persuasion.

Promotional methods

Having formulated, stated and justified the required position, the next step is to present the basic form and style of the key message that is to be conveyed. Is there to be a lot of copy or just a little? Is there to be a rational or emotional approach or some weighting between the two? What should be the tone of the visual messages? Is there to be a media blitz (the domination of a set of media in order to create attention when (re)launching a brand)? It is at this point that those responsible for the development of these plans can be imaginative and try some new ideas. Trying to tie in the message to the strategic orientation is the important part, as the advertising agency will refine and redefine the message and the positioning.

From this the promotional mixes need to be considered for *each* of the strategies proposed, that is, a mix for the consumer strategy, a mix for the trade strategy and a distinct mix for the communications to reach the wider array of stakeholders.

The choice of promotional methods should clearly state the methods and the media to be used. A short paragraph justifying the selection is very important, as the use of media in particular is to a large extent dependent upon the nature of the goals, the target audience and the resources. The key is to provide message consistency and a measure of integration.

> The key is to provide message consistency and a measure of integration.

The schedule

The next step is to schedule the deployment of the methods and the media. This is best achieved by the production of a Gantt chart.

Events should be scheduled according to the goals and the strategic thrust. So, if it is necessary to communicate with the trade prior to a public launch, those activities tied into the push strategy should be scheduled prior to those calculated to support the pull strategy.

Similarly, if awareness is a goal then, if funds permit, it may be best to use television and posters first before sales promotions (unless sampling is used), direct marketing, point of purchase and personal selling.

Resources

This is a vitally important part of the plan, one that is often avoided or forgotten about. The resources necessary to support the plan need to be determined, and these refer not only to the financial issues but to the quality of available marketing expertise and the time that is available to achieve the required outcomes.

Gantt charts and other project-planning aids are best used to support this part of the plan. The cost of the media and methods can either be allocated in a right-hand column of the chart, or a new chart can be prepared. Preferably, actual costs should be assigned, although percentages can be allocated if examination time is at a premium. What is of importance is the relative weighting of the costs and that there is a recognition and understanding of the general costs associated with the proposed individual activities.

It must be understood that a national television campaign cannot be run for less than £1.5 million and that the overall cost of the strategy should be in proportion to the size of the client organisation, its (probable) level of profitability and the size and dynamics of the market in which it operates.

Control and evaluation

Unless there is some form of evaluation, there will be no dialogue and no true marketing communications. There are numerous methods to evaluate the individual performance of the tools and the media used, and for examination purposes these should be stated. In addition, and perhaps more meaningfully, the most important measures are the promotional objectives set in the first place. The success of a promotional strategy and the associated plan is the degree to which the objectives set are achieved.

Feedback

The planning process is completed when feedback is provided. Not only should information regarding the overall outcome of a campaign be considered, but so should individual aspects of the activity. For example, the performance of the individual tools used within the campaign, whether sufficient resources were invested, the appropriateness of the strategy in the first place, any problems encountered during implementation and the relative ease with which the objectives were accomplished are aspects that need to be fed back to all internal and external parties associated with the planning process.

Feedback is vitally important because it provides information for the context analysis that anchors the next campaign.

This feedback is vitally important because it provides information for the context analysis that anchors the next campaign. Information fed back in a formal and systematic manner constitutes an opportunity for organisations to learn from their previous campaign activities, a point often overlooked and neglected.

Links and essential points

It was mentioned earlier that there are a number of linkages associated with different parts of the marketing communications plan. It is important to understand the nature of these links as they represent the interconnections between different parts of the plan and the rationale for undertaking the contextual analysis in particular. The contextual analysis feeds the items shown in Table 4.5. The promotional objectives derived from the CA feed decisions concerning strategy, tools and media, scheduling and evaluation.

TABLE 4.5 Linkages within the MCPF

Objectives	From the marketing plan, from the customer, stakeholder network and competitor analysis and from an internal marketing review
Strategic balance between push, pull and profile	From an understanding of the brand, the needs of the target audiences, including employees and all other stakeholders, and the marketing goals
Brand positioning	From users' and non-users' perceptions, motivations, attitudes and understanding about the brand and its direct and indirect competitors
Message content and style	From an understanding about the level of involvement, perceived risk, DMU analysis, information-processing styles and the positioning intentions
Promotional tools and media	From the target-audience analysis of media habits, involvement and preferences, from knowledge about product suitability and media compatibility, from a competitor analysis and from the resource analysis

The marketing communications strategy is derived from an overall appreciation of the needs of the target audience (and stakeholders) regarding the brand and its competitive position in the market. The promotional mix is influenced by the previous elements and the budget that follows. However, the nature of the tools and the capacity and characteristics of the media influence scheduling, implementation and evaluation activities.

Summary of key points

1. The development of a marketing communications strategy is important if an organisation is to support its marketing strategy and communicate effectively with its various target audiences. Unlike planning, which is normally an articulation of strategy, marketing communications should be rooted in its target audiences and the tasks that need to be completed.

2. Push, pull and profile strategies can be combined in different ways to meet the needs of different communication tasks. In addition to the broad target, it is important to express strategy in terms of the differentiation (positioning), reminding/reassuring, informing and persuading of audiences.

3. A pull strategy is aimed at encouraging customers, consumers and end-user business customers to think, feel or act in a particular way, usually towards an organisation's products and services.

4. A push communications strategy involves the presentation of information in order to influence other trade-channel organisations and, as a result, encourage them to take stock, to allocate resources (e.g. shelf space) and to help them to become fully aware of the key attributes and benefits associated with each product with a view to adding value prior to further channel transactions. This strategy is designed to encourage resale to other members of the network and contribute to the achievement of their own objectives.

5. A profile strategy is one that focuses an organisation's communications upon the development of its corporate image and reputation, whether that is internal, external or both. To accomplish and deliver a profile strategy public relations, including sponsorship and corporate advertising, becomes the pivotal tool of the marketing communications mix. Personal selling may remain a vital element delivering both product/service and corporate messages.

6. IMC represents a strategic approach to marketing communications but, although the concept is attractive, the development of the approach in practical terms has to date not been very encouraging. There has been a great deal of debate about the meaning and value of an integrated approach and some attempt to coordinate the content and delivery of marketing communications messages. Most organisations have yet to achieve totally integrated marketing communications; only partial or coordinated levels of activity have so far been achieved.

7. The marketing communications planning framework is itself a form of integration and offers a sequential format for the development of marketing communications plans. In real life such plans are developed in parallel and involve different individuals and stakeholders in varying degrees. The framework presented here is practical and robust, yet the linear approach should not be accepted without question.

8. The key elements of marketing communications plans are: the context analysis, communication objectives, marketing communications strategy, coordinated communications mix (methods, tools and media), scheduling and implementation, resources (human and financial), evaluation and control and feedback.

Review questions

1. What are the 3Ps of marketing communications strategy? Explain the differences between each of them.

2. Draw two diagrams depicting the direction of communications in both the push and the pull strategies.

3. What are the reasons for interest in IMC and is it a valid concept?

4. Appraise the main reasons offered for the failure of organisations to develop IMC.

5. Sketch the marketing communications planning framework – from memory.

6. Following on from the previous question, check your version of the MCPF with the original and then prepare some bullet-point notes, highlighting the critical linkages between the main parts of the framework.

References

Brown, J. (1997), 'Impossible dream or inevitable revolution: an exploration of integrated marketing communications', *Journal of Communication Management*, **12**(1), pp. 70–81.

Cornelissen, J.P. (2003), 'Change, continuity and progress: the concept of integrated marketing communications and marketing communications practice', *Journal of Strategic Marketing*, **11** (December), pp. 217–34.

Cornelissen, J.P. and Lock, A.R. (2000), 'Theoretical concept or management fashion? Examining the significance of IMC', *Journal of Advertising Research*, **50**(5), pp. 7–15.

Duncan, T. (2002), *IMC: Using Advertising and Promotion to Build Brand*, international edn, New York: McGraw-Hill.

Duncan, T. and Everett, S. (1993), 'Client perceptions of integrated marketing communications', *Journal of Advertising Research*, **3**(3), pp. 30–9.

Eagle, L. and Kitchen, P. (2000), 'IMC, brand communications, and corporate cultures', *European Journal of Marketing*, **34**(5/6), pp. 667–86.

Fill, C. (2006), *Marketing Communications: engagement, strategies and practice*, 4th edn, Harlow: FT Prentice Hall.

Gray, R. (2000), 'The chief encounter', *PR Week*, 8 September, pp. 13–16.

Gronroos, C. (2004), 'The relationship marketing process: communication, interaction, dialogue, value', *Journal of Business and Industrial Marketing*, **19**(2), pp. 99–113.

Grunig, J. and Hunt, T. (1984), *Managing Public Relations*, New York: Holt, Rinehart & Winston.

Hutton, J.G. (1996), 'Integrated relationship-marketing communications: a key opportunity for IMC', *Journal of Marketing Communications*, **2**, pp. 191–9.

Kitchen, P., Brignell, J., Li, T. and Spickett Jones, G. (2004), 'The emergence of IMC: a theoretical perspective', *Journal of Advertising Research*, **44** (March) pp. 19–30.

Schultz, D. (1993), *Integrated Marketing Communications: Putting It Together and Making It Work*, Lincolnwood, Ill.: NTC Business Books.

Swain, W.N. (2004), 'Perceptions of IMC after a decade of development: who's at the wheel, and how can we measure success?', *Journal of Advertising Research*, March, pp. 46–65.

Sweney, M. (2003), 'Samuel aims to raise profile with BMP hiring', *Campaign*, 14 February, p. 5.

White, R. (2000), 'Chameleon brands: tailoring brand messages to consumers', *Admap*, July/August, pp. 38–40.

Targeting audiences: segmentation, targeting, positioning and objectives

5

Aims and objectives

The aims of this chapter are, first, to explore how segmentation, targeting and positioning contribute to the development of effective marketing communications. The second aim is to consider issues associated with the setting of appropriate and meaningful campaign objectives. There are four primary topics in this chapter:

Segmentation, Targeting, Positioning, Objectives

The learning objectives are to enable readers to:

1. describe the key elements associated with the target market process;
2. explain how each element of the STP process contributes to marketing communications;
3. discuss various ways in which brands might be positioned in the minds of target audiences;
4. introduce ideas concerning the realistic use of marketing communications objectives;
5. understand how to write SMART objectives.

Introduction

Setting strategy and devising marketing communications plans are essential top-level marketing-management activities. However, the context analysis, part of the planning process, requires inputs from the segmentation, targeting and positioning (STP) process. This important part of marketing-strategy development is concerned with the identification of the various segments in a market, the determination of the potential of each of the market segments and the selection of the particular markets that become target markets for the organisation. Segmentation and targeting is followed by positioning. This involves determining the most advantageous position for a brand relative to competitors. The positioning component concerns the communication of information about the brand such that it is perceived by the target audience to be differentiated from the competition and to occupy a particular space in the market. According to Dibb et al. (2006, p. 247) 'Target customers must perceive the product to have a distinct image and positioning, vis-à-vis its competitors.'

> The positioning component concerns the communication of information about the brand such that it is perceived by the target audience to be differentiated from the competition and to occupy a particular space in the market.

The positioning intent needs to be supported by a set of viable marketing communication objectives. There are many different opinions about what it is that marketing communications seeks to achieve. There is much agreement that the task is complex, and it is probable that this perceived complexity has led a large number of managers to fail to set appropriate marketing communications objectives. For example, the most common promotional objectives are sales related whereas the most useful are those that create a communications impact. Therefore, setting objectives for changes in awareness levels, learning, perception or attitudes, for example, are of more use because they relate to marketing communication activities rather than any other influence. Communication related objectives can also provide a practical measure of campaign performance. This issue is considered in more detail later in this chapter.

Segmentation

The process of market analysis and evaluation leading to planned strategies designed to meet prescribed and measurable goals is well established. It is argued that this approach enables finite resources to be used more efficiently as they can be directed towards markets that hold, potentially, greater value than other markets. Market segmentation is a part of this approach and is both a functional and competitive-level strategy. More importantly, the process of market segmentation is the means by which organisations define the broad context within which their strategic business units (SBUs) and products are offered.

> The process of market segmentation is the means by which organisations define the broad context within which their strategic business units (SBUs) and products are offered.

Market segmentation is the division of a mass market into identifiable and distinct groups or segments, each of which have common characteristics and needs and display similar responses to marketing actions. Through this process specific target segments can be selected and marketing plans developed to satisfy the individual needs of the potential buyers in these chosen segments. The development, or rather identification, of segments can be perceived as opportunities and, as Beane and Ennis (1987) suggest,

ViewPoint 5.1   Segments galore

United Airlines segments its global markets using psychographic data about its customers. Among its categories are:

- Schedule optimisers: must reach their destination by a certain time and select their flights accordingly.
- Mile accumulators: go out of their way to take flights that will build up their air miles entitlement.
- Quality vacationers: treat the travel as part of the holiday experience and so fly with carriers that provide superior services.
- Frugal flyers: seek out the lowest-cost carriers, but still expect their flight experience to be a good one.

Source: http://www.thetimes100.co.uk/case_study

According to T-Mobile's website it targets four key market segments:

- personal
- small businesses
- medium businesses
- corporate.

The segments identified for a women's portal include the following groups:

- Pillars: characterised by their family orientation, high income and broad range of interests.
- Explorers: notable for being single, thirty-something, outgoing and more social- than career-oriented.
- Free spirits: the youngest segment, typically unmarried, Internet savvy, and not yet committed to careers or raising a family.

Source: www.debmcdonald.com/

'A company with limited resources needs to pick only the best opportunities to pursue.' The most common bases upon which markets can be segmented are set out in Table 5.1.

This process of segmentation is necessary because a single product is unlikely to meet the needs of all customers in a mass market. If it did, then a single type of toothpaste, chocolate bar or car would meet all our needs. This is not so, and there are a host of products and brands seeking to satisfy particular buyer needs. For example, ask yourself the question, 'Why do I use toothpaste?' The answer, most probably, is one of the following:

1. You want dental hygiene.
2. You like fresh breath and you don't want to offend others.
3. You want white, shining teeth.
4. You like the fresh oral sensation.
5. Other products (e.g. water, soap) do not taste very good.

TABLE 5.1 Bases for segmenting markets

Segmentation base	Explanation
Demographic	Key variables concern age, sex, occupation, level of education, religion, social class and income characteristics, many of which determine, to a large extent, a potential buyer's ability to enter into an exchange relationship or transaction.
Geographic	In many situations the needs of potential customers in one geographic area are different from those in another area. For example, it is often said that Scottish beer drinkers prefer heavy bitters, northerners in England prefer mild, drinkers in the West prefer cider, and in the South lager is the preferred drink.
Geodemographic	This type of segmentation is based on the assumption that there is a relationship between the type of housing people live in and their purchasing behaviours. At the root of this approach is the ability to use postcodes to send similar messages to similar groups of households, on the basis that where we live determines how we live. The most well-known commercial applications are Acorn (a classification of residential neighbourhoods), Mosaic and Pinpoint.
Psychographic	Through an analysis of consumers' activities, interests and opinions (AIO) it is possible to determine lifestyles or patterns of behaviour. These are a synthesis of the motivations, personality and core values held by individuals. These AIO patterns are reflected in the buying behaviour and decision-making processes of individuals. By identifying and clustering common lifestyles, a correlation with a consumer's product and/or media-usage patterns becomes possible.
Behaviouristic	Usage and lifestage segments are derived from analysing markets on the basis of customer behaviour. Usage of soft drinks can be considered in terms of purchase patterns (two bottles per week), usage situations (parties, picnics or as an alcohol substitute) or purchase location (supermarket, convenience store or wine merchant). Lifestage analysis is based on the principle that people have varying amounts of disposable income and different needs at different stages in their lives. Their priorities for spending change at different trigger points and these points or lifestages do not occur at the same time.

Whatever the reason, it is unlikely that given a choice everyone would choose the same product. In what is now regarded as a classic study, Russell Haley (1968) undertook some pioneering research in this field and from it established four distinct types of customer. Nearly 40 years later this typology remains a potent practical example of market segmentation: those who bought toothpaste for white teeth (sociables), those who wished to prevent decay (worriers), those who liked the taste and refreshment properties (sensors) and finally those who bought on a price basis (independents). Each of these groups has particular demographic, behaviouristic and psychographic characteristics.

It is not surprising that a range of toothpaste products has been developed that attempts to satisfy the needs of different buyers, for example Macleans for fresh breath, Crest for dental hygiene, Sensodyne for those sensitive to hot and cold drinks and numerous others promoted on special offers for those independent buyers looking for a low price. There are others who are not very interested in the product and have continued using a brand that others in their current or past households are comfortable

Target segments constitute the environment and the context for the marketing communications strategy and activities.

with. Therefore, target segments constitute the environment and the context for the marketing communications strategy and activities. It is the characteristics of the target segment, therefore, that are the focus of an audience-centred marketing communication strategy.

Targeting

The next task is to decide which, if any, of the segments discovered should be the focus of the marketing programme. The following criteria need to be present:

- All segments should be *measurable* – is the segment easy to identify and measure?
- All segments should be *substantial* – is the segment sufficiently large to provide a stream of profits?
- All segments should be *accessible* – can the buyers be reached with promotional programmes?
- All segments should be *differentiable* – is each segment clearly different from other segments so that different marketing mixes are necessary?
- All segments should be *actionable* – has the organisation the capability to reach the segment?

Decisions need to be made about whether a single product is to be offered to a range of segments, whether a range of products should be offered to multiple segments or a single segment, or whether one product should be offered to a single segment. Whatever the decision, a marketing mix should be developed to meet the needs of the segment and reflect the organisation's available resources.

A segmentation exercise will have been undertaken previously as part of the development of the marketing strategy. Marketing communications managers do not necessarily need to repeat the exercise. However, work is often necessary to provide current information about such factors as perception, attitudes, volumes, intentions and usage, among others. It is the accessibility question that is paramount: how can the defined group be reached with suitable communications? What is the media consumption pattern of the target audience?

Positioning

Positioning is the third and final part of the STP process and is an important aspect of marketing communications.

Positioning is the third and final part of the STP process and is an important aspect of marketing communications. Positioning is not about the product but what the buyer thinks about the product or organisation. As Ries and Trout (1972) first claimed, it is not the physical nature of the product that is important for positioning, but how the product is perceived that matters. This is why part of the context analysis requires a consideration of perception and attitudes and the way stakeholders see and regard brands and organisations. Of course, this may not be the same as the way brand managers intend their brands to be seen or how they believe the brand is perceived.

ViewPoint 5.2   Drink positioning

Slinky A white wine crush called Slinky, launched by Blue Nun, was positioned as a stepping stone from ready-to-drinks (RTDs) to wine. Analysis showed that there were two wine-based RTDs on the market (Bliss and Comira Coast) but they had not been marketed as a natural progression from RTDs to wine. The launch strategy was based first on a push strategy, using the trade press, which was designed to get distribution into bars. This was followed by a pull strategy, using press and broadcast media, aimed at 20–24-year-old women. The campaign spend was over £1 million and focused on advertising and PR, media promotions and product sampling.

Pernod Following a television-based campaign to position the Pernod brand for the 18–24-year-old market, attitude research revealed that the brand would be better suited to an older demographic group. McCawley (2001) reports that a campaign in 2001 was designed to reposition the brand so that it appealed to professionals in their late 20s to mid-30s and complemented their attitude set.

In the consumer market, established brands from washing powders (Ariel, Daz, Persil) and hair shampoos (such as Wash & Go, Timotei) to cars (for example, Peugeot, Saab, Nissan) and grocery multiples (Sainsbury's, Tesco) each carry communications that enable receivers to position them (consistently) in their respective markets.

The positioning concept is not the sole preserve of branded or consumer-oriented offerings or indeed those of the business-to-business market. Organisations are also positioned relative to one another, mainly as a consequence of their corporate identities, whether they are deliberately managed or not. The position an organisation takes in the mind of stakeholders may be the only means of differentiating one product from another. Given the advancements in technology, the high level of physical and functional similarity of products in the same class, and the increasing emphasis on ethical, corporate and social responsibilities, it is not surprising that many consumers make purchase decisions on their assessment of the company they are dealing with. Therefore, it is important to position organisations as brands in the minds of actual and potential customers.

The positioning concept

All products and all organisations have a position. The position held by each stakeholder can be managed or it can be allowed to drift. An increasing number of organisations are trying to manage the positions occupied by their brands and are using positioning strategies to move to new positions in buyers' minds and so generate an advantage over their competitors. This is particularly important in markets that are very competitive and where mobility barriers (ease of entry and exit to a market, e.g. plant and production costs) are relatively low.

Positioning is about visibility and recognition of what a product/service represents for a buyer. In markets where rivalry and competition are increasing and buyers have greater choice, the identification and understanding of a product's intrinsic values become critical. Network members have limited capacities,

Positioning is about visibility and recognition of what a product/service represents for a buyer.

whether this be the level or range of stock they can carry or the amount of available shelf space that can be allocated. An offering with a clear identity and orientation to a particular target segment's needs will not only be stocked and purchased but can warrant a larger margin through increased added value.

ViewPoint 5.3   Functional positioning

Marketing communications in the consumer and trade adhesives market places heavy reliance on demonstrating the performance of the individual brands. Solvite, for example, presents a man glued to a board and suspended in dangerous situations (above sharks, towed into the sky and at a theme park on a 'vertical-drop ride'). Another brand, No More Nails, uses a similar functional approach – one advertisement shows a man sitting on a chair that has been glued halfway up a wall inside a house.

Adhesives provoke low-involvement decision-making and there is generally little consumer interest in the properties of each brand. The essential information that consumers require is that the brand has strong performance characteristics. This sets up umbrella-brand credibility so that sub-brands for different types of glue are perceived to have the same properties as the umbrella brand and will do the 'job'.

Advertising needs to have dramatic qualities in order to attract attention and to build up a store of images that enable people to recall a brand of adhesives that do actually stick.

EXHIBIT 5.1 Solvite press ad. Used to demonstrate the functional attributes of the product

Positioning, therefore, is the natural conclusion to the sequence of activities that constitute a core part of the marketing strategy. Market segmentation and target marketing are prerequisites to successful positioning. From the research data and the marketing strategy, it is necessary to formulate a positioning statement that is in tune with the promotional objectives.

One of the roles of marketing communications is to convey information so that the target audience can understand what a brand stands for and differentiate it from other competitor brands. Clear, consistent positioning is an important aspect of integrated marketing communications, so the way in which a brand is presented to its audience determines the way it is going to be perceived. Therefore, accepting that there are extraneous reasons why a brand's perception might not be the same as that intended, it seems important that managers approach the task of positioning in an attentive and considered manner.

Generally, there are two main ways in which a brand can be positioned: functional and expressive (or symbolic). Functionally positioned brands stress the features and benefits, and expressive brands emphasise the ego, social and hedonic satisfactions that a brand can bring. Both approaches make a promise, a promise to deliver a whiter, cleaner and brighter soap powder (functional) or clothes that we are confident to hang on the washing line (for all to see), dress our children in and send to school and not feel guilty, or dress ourselves in and complete a major business deal (symbolic).

ViewPoint 5.4   Expressive positioning

In 2004 British Airways developed the tagline 'The way to fly' in an attempt to build on the successful 'The world's favourite airline' tag that was dropped in 1999. The aim of BA's first corporate branding campaign since 2000 was that it should become an overarching brand-positioning vehicle. It enables BA to communicate a diverse range of related offerings, such as food and service, use of primary airports, promotions, loyalty programmes and the Club World 'sleeper service', among many others.

For a while BA used rational messages based on product-led ads in the long-haul market. Campaigns that focused on flat beds in Club World and price discounts on short-haul flights ('Look how small our prices are') have in part been a reaction to the crisis of 11 September 2001 and the aggression of low-cost competitors.

'The way to fly' represents an emotional message and gives flyers a reason to choose the BA brand simply because it encapsulates the brand promise of reassurance and reliability.

Developing and managing a position

To develop a position, managers should be guided by the following process:

1. Which positions are held by which competitors? This will almost certainly require consumer research to determine attitudes and perceptions and possibly the key attributes that consumers perceive as important. Use perceptual mapping.

2. From the above, will it be possible to determine which position, if any, is already held by the focus brand?

3. From the information gathered so far, will it be possible to determine a positioning strategy, that is, what is the desired position for the brand?

4. Is the strategy feasible in view of the competitors and any budgetary constraints? A long-term perspective is required, as the selected position has to be sustained.

5. Implement a programme to establish the desired position.

6. Monitor the perception held by consumers of the brand, and of their changing tastes and requirements, on a regular basis.

Positioning strategies

Positioning is the communications element of the segmentation process and is concerned with influencing the way target audiences perceive the product or brand. This should be achieved through communications that present the product so that it occupies a particular position in the mind of each (potential) buyer, relative to the offerings of competitive products. In essence, the position adopted is a statement about what the brand is, what it stands for and the values and beliefs that customers (hopefully) will come to associate with the particular brand. The visual images or the position statement represented in the strapline may be a significant trigger that buyers use to recall images and associations of the brand.

> The position adopted is a statement about what the brand is, what it stands for and the values and beliefs that customers (hopefully) will come to associate with the particular brand.

There are a number of overall positioning strategies that can be implemented. The list that follows is not intended to be comprehensive or to convey the opinion that these strategies are discrete. They are presented here as means of conveying the strategic style, but in reality a number of hybrid strategies are often used.

Product features

This is one of the easier concepts and one that is more commonly adopted. The brand is set apart from the competition on the basis of the attributes, features or benefits that the brand has relative to the competition. For example, Volvos are safe; Weetabix contains most of the vitamins needed each day; and the Royal Bank of Scotland promotes its credit card by extolling the benefits of its interest rate compared with those of its competitors.

Price/quality

This strategy is more effectively managed than others because price itself can be a strong communicator of quality. A high price denotes high quality, just as a low price can deceive buyers into thinking a product to be of low quality and poor value. Retail outlets such as Harrods and Aspreys use high prices to signal high quality and exclusivity. At the other end of the retail spectrum, Matalan, BHS and Woolworths position themselves to attract those with less disposable income and to whom convenience is of greater importance. The price/quality appeal used to be best observed in Sainsbury's, 'where good food costs less', before it was changed, and with the alcoholic lager Stella Artois, which is positioned as 'refreshingly expensive'.

Use

A position can be created in the minds of the buyers by informing markets of when or how a product can be used. For example, Kellogg's, the breakfast-cereal manufacturer, has repositioned itself as a snack-food provider. Its marketing strategy of moving into new markets was founded on its overdependence on breakfast consumption. By becoming associated with snacks, not only is usage increased but the opportunity to develop new products becomes feasible. The launch of Pop Tarts is a testimony to this strategy. Milky Way, 'The sweet you can eat between meals', informs just when it is permissible to eat chocolate; and After Eight chocolate mints clearly indicate when they should be eaten. The hair shampoo Wash & Go positions the brand as a quick and easy-to-use (convenience) product for those whose lifestyles are full and demanding.

Product-class dissociation

Some markets are essentially uninteresting and others have no obvious available positions as they have been adopted by competitors. A strategy used by margarine manufacturers is to disassociate themselves from other margarines and associate themselves with what was commonly regarded as a superior product, butter. The Alliance & Leicester Building Society used to proclaim that 'Not all building societies are the same'. The suggestion was that they were different from the rest and hence offered better services and customer care. The moisturising bar Dove is positioned as 'not a soap'.

User

A sensible extension of the target marketing process is to position openly so that the target user can be clearly identified. Flora margarine was for men, and then it became 'for all the family'. American Express has used several prominent business celebrities, such as Anita Roddick, and has recently used the Chelsea football club manager, José Mourinho, to suggest that users can have a lifestyle profile that complements those who use and endorse the Amex card. Some hotels position themselves as places for weekend breaks, as leisure centres or as conference centres.

Competitor

For a long time, positioning oneself against a main competitor was regarded as dangerous and to be avoided. Avis, however, performed very successfully 'trying even harder' against Hertz, the industry number one. Saab contested the 'safest car' position with Volvo and Qualcast took on its new rival, the hover mower, by informing everyone that 'It's a lot less bovver than a hover', because its product collected the grass cuttings and produced the manicured lawn finish that rollerless mowers cannot reproduce.

Benefit

Positions can also be established by proclaiming the benefits that usage confers on those who consume. Sensodyne toothpaste appeals to all those who suffer from sensitive teeth, and a vast number of pain-relief formulations claim to smooth away headaches or relieve aching limbs, sore throats or some offending part of the anatomy. Daewoo entered the UK offering car buyers convenience by removing dealerships and the inherent difficulties associated with buying and maintaining cars.

Heritage or cultural symbol

An appeal to cultural heritage and tradition, symbolised by age, particular heraldic devices or visual cues, has been used by many organisations to convey quality, experience and knowledge. Kronenbourg 1664, 'Established since 1803', and the use of coats of arms by many universities to represent depth of experience and a sense of permanence, are just some of the historical themes used to position organisations. Trinity College Dublin, for example, makes prominent use in its marketing communications that it was first established in 1592.

Whatever the position adopted by a brand or organisation, both the marketing and promotional mixes must endorse and support the position so that there is consistency throughout all communications. For example, if a high-quality position is taken, such as that of the Ritz Carlton Hotel Group, then the product quality must be relatively high compared with competitors, the price must be correspondingly excessive and distribution synonymous with quality and exclusivity. Sales-promotion activity will be minimal so as not to convey a touch of inexpensiveness, and advertising messages should be visually affluent and rich in tone and copy, with public relations and personal-selling approaches transmitting high-quality, complementary cues.

Promotional mixes must endorse and support the position so that there is consistency throughout all communications.

The dimensions used to position brands must be relevant and important to the target audience, and the image cues used must be believable and consistently credible. Positioning strategies should be developed over the long term if they are to prove effective, although minor adaptations to the position can be carried out in order to reflect changing environmental conditions.

Repositioning

Technology is developing quickly, consumer tastes evolve and new offerings and substitute products enter the market. This dynamic perspective of markets means that the relative positions occupied by offerings in the minds of consumers will be challenged and shifted on a frequent basis. If the position adopted by an offering is strong, if it was the first to claim the position and the position is being continually reinforced with clear, simple messages, then there may be little need to alter the position originally adopted.

However, there are occasions when offerings need to be repositioned in the minds of consumers/stakeholders. This may be because of market opportunities and development, mergers and acquisitions or changing buyer preferences, which may be manifested in declining sales. Research may reveal that the current position is either inappropriate or superseded by a competitor, or that attitudes have changed or preferences have been surpassed; whatever the reason, repositioning is required if past success is to be maintained. However, repositioning is difficult to accomplish, often because of the entrenched perceptions and attitudes held by buyers towards brands and the vast (media) resources required to make the changes.

Repositioning is difficult to accomplish, often because of the entrenched perceptions and attitudes held by buyers.

ViewPoint 5.5   Repositioning Green & Black's

Green & Black's, the UK's fastest-growing confectionery brand, launched a £1.2 million national advertising campaign – *'Green & Black's . . . it deserves a little respect'* – as part of its programme to consolidate its repositioning from an organic to a luxury chocolate brand. Green & Black's has almost trebled its value since repositioning two years ago.

This campaign, timed to run during the key chocolate months of October and November, aims to give consumers a clear understanding of the Green & Black's taste and how it fits into their chocolate repertoire. Last year a £500,000 sampling and sponsorship programme enabled over 300,000 people to taste Green & Black's chocolate and ice cream at various high-profile English Heritage summer picnic concerts.

The new *'it deserves a little respect'* campaign highlighted the special nature of the Green & Black's brand and cues a number of usage occasions.

The advertising campaign ran nationally in food titles and Sunday supplements and was supported by London Underground posters and a commuter press schedule. An in-store sampling programme in key grocery accounts was also implemented.

Source: Green & Black's. Used with permission

EXHIBIT 5.2 Green & Black's

In an attempt to thwart the competitive threats of both rail (Channel Tunnel) and low-cost airlines (e.g. easyJet), the ferry operator P&O repositioned itself as the way to 'cruise across the Channel'. By presenting the cross-Channel experience as an integral part of the holiday/travel experience, it enabled P&O to provide added value that could not be copied, and a reason to be used.

The Defence Establishment and Research Agency (DERA) was required to change its name when it ceased being a government-owned organisation and was privatised. Although the new name QinetiQ represented a radical change, the agency needed to reflect its new position in a new commercial market.

The need to reposition a brand may be stimulated because of the actions of a major competitor. The United Kingdom's car recovery and driver support service market is dominated by two mainstream organisations, the AA and the RAC. In the early 1990s the AA tried to reposition itself away from the RAC as the market became increasingly cluttered, more competitive and depressed as consumer spending became constricted with the recession. The RAC then positioned itself as the 'knights of the road', with all the heroic rescue overtones that a knight confers, while the AA, having tried to be seen as a 'a very, very nice man', portrayed itself as highly professional and demanding high standards, since a vehicle breakdown was regarded as an emergency similar in scale to that requiring the assistance of the fire, police or ambulance services. The AA's new position, 'To our members we are the fourth emergency service', is an attempt to be pre-eminent and gain 'top of mind' awareness by conveying a rational benefit approach against the more emotive imagery suggested by the 'knight'. Then, in an attempt to challenge drivers with regard to the range of services provided by the AA, it changed its strapline to 'Just AAsk'.

Marketing communications objectives

Having established the target segments to be approached and the desired positioning within each of them, the next key task is to formulate, agree and establish the campaign objectives. Marketing communications objectives are an important and often abused part of marketing communications activities.

The most common promotional objectives set by managers are sales-related. These include increases in market share, return on investment, sales-volume increases and improvements in the value of sales made after accounting for the rate of inflation. Such a general perspective ignores the influence of the other elements of the marketing mix and implicitly places the entire responsibility for sales performance with the promotional mix. This is not an accurate reflection of the way in which businesses and organisations work. In addition, because sales tests are too general, they would be an insufficiently rigorous test of promotional activity and there would be no real evaluation of promotional activities. Sales volumes vary for a wide variety of reasons:

● Competitors change their prices.
● Buyers' needs change.
● Changes in legislation may favour the strategies of particular organisations.
● Favourable third-party communications become known to significant buyers.
● General economic conditions change.
● Technological advances facilitate improved production processes, economies of scale, experience effects and, for some organisations, the opportunity to reduce costs.
● The entry and exit of different competitors.

FIGURE 5.1 Three streams of objectives

The notion that marketing communications is entirely responsible for the sales of an offering is clearly unacceptable, unrealistic and incorrect.

These are a few of the many reasons why sales might increase and, conversely, why sales might decrease. Thus, the notion that marketing communications is entirely responsible for the sales of an offering is clearly unacceptable, unrealistic and incorrect.

Marketing communication objectives should consist of three main components. The first component concerns issues relating to sales volume, market share, profitability and revenue. The second concerns issues relating to the communication impact on the target audience, and the third stream relates to the image, reputation and preferences that other stakeholders have towards the organisation. See Figure 5.1.

The sales school

Many managers see sales as the only meaningful objective for marketing communications plans. Their view is that the only reason an organisation spends money on such communications is to sell its product or service, so the only meaningful measure of the effectiveness of the promotional spend is in the sales results.

These results can be measured in a number of different ways. Sales turnover is the first and most obvious factor, particularly in business-to-business markets. In consumer markets and the fast-moving consumer goods sector, market-share movement is measured regularly and is used as a more sensitive barometer of performance. Over the longer term, return on investment measures are used to calculate success and failure. In some sectors the number of products (or cases) sold, or volume of product shifted, relative to other periods of activity, is a common measure. There are a number of difficulties with this view. One is that *sales result from a variety of influences*, such as the other marketing-mix elements, competitor actions and wider environmental effects, for example the strength of the currency, changing social preferences or the level of interest rates.

A second difficulty rests with the concept of *adstock* or *carryover*. The impact of promotional expenditure may not be immediately apparent, as the receiver may not enter the market until some later date, but the effects of the promotional programme may influence the eventual purchase decision. This means that, when measuring the effectiveness of a campaign, sales results will not always reflect its full impact.

Sales objectives *do little to assist the media planner, copywriters and creative team* associated with the development of the communications programme, despite their inclusion in campaign documents such as media briefs.

Sales-oriented objectives are, however, applicable in particular situations. For example, where direct action is required by the receiver in response to exposure to a message, measurement of sales is justifiable. Such an action, a behavioural response, can be solicited in direct-response advertising. This occurs where the sole communication is through a particular medium, such as television or print.

The retail sector can also use sales measures, and it has been suggested that packaged-goods organisations, operating in markets that are mature with established pricing and distribution structures, can build a databank from which it is possible to isolate the advertising effect through sales. For example, Sainsbury's is able to monitor the stock movements of particular ingredients used in its 'celebrity recipe' commercials, which enables it to evaluate the success of particular campaigns and particular celebrities. Its use of celebrity chef Jamie Oliver is so successful that it can stock ingredients in anticipation of particular advertisements being screened. However, despite this cause-and-effect relationship, it can be argued that this may ignore the impact of changes in competitor actions and changes in the overall environment. Furthermore, the effects of the organisation's own corporate advertising, adstock effects and other family brand promotions need to be accounted for if a meaningful sales effect is to be generated.

The sales school advocates sales measures on the grounds of simplicity.

The sales school advocates sales measures on the grounds of simplicity. Any manager can utilise the tool, and senior management does not wish to be concerned with information that is complex or unfamiliar, especially when working to short lead times and accounting periods. It is a self-consistent theory, but one that may misrepresent consumer behaviour and the purchase process (perhaps unintentionally), and to that extent may result in less than optimal expenditure on marketing communications.

The communications school

There are many situations, however, where the aim of a communications campaign is to enhance the image or reputation of an organisation or product. Sales are not regarded as the only goal. Consequently, promotional efforts are seen as communications tasks,

Promotional efforts are seen as communications tasks, such as the creation of awareness or positive attitudes towards the organisation or product.

such as the creation of awareness or positive attitudes towards the organisation or product. To facilitate this process, receivers have to be given relevant information before the appropriate decision processes can develop and purchase activities established as a long-run behaviour.

Various models have been developed to assist our understanding about how these promotional tasks should be segregated and organised effectively. AIDA and other hierarchy-of-effects models such as Dagmar (defining advertising goals for measured advertising results) have been popular models in the past (Colley, 1961). Typically, the communications task is based on a sequential model of the communications process: awareness – comprehension – conviction – action. It was once thought that marketing communications succeeds or fails depending on how well it communicates the desired information and attitudes to the right people at the right time and at the right cost. See Table 5.2.

A more contemporary view holds that success should be based on the degree to which audience behaviour is influenced, but campaigns designed to develop awareness and establish brand-name familiarity are still necessary. Indeed, many brands seek to

TABLE 5.2 Hierarchy of communications

Stage	Explanation
Awareness	Awareness of the existence of a product or brand is necessary before any purchase will be made.
Comprehension	Audiences need information and knowledge about the product and its specific attributes. Often the audience needs to be educated and shown either how to use the product or how changes (in attributes) might affect their use of the product.
Conviction	By developing beliefs that a product is superior to others in a category or can confer particular rewards through use, audiences can be convinced to trial the product at the next purchase opportunity.
Action	Potential buyers need help and encouragement to transfer thoughts into behaviour. Providing call-free numbers, website addresses, reply cards, coupons and sales people helps people act upon their convictions.

Source: After Colley (1961)

establish 'top-of-mind awareness' as one of their primary objectives for their commun ications (advertising) spend.

The hierarchical approach has been subject to much debate and among the arguments against the use of communication objectives the following are prevalent.

Sales orientation

This criticism is levelled by those who regard sales as the only valid measure of campaign effectiveness. The sole purpose of communications activities, and advertising in particular, is to generate sales. So, as the completion of communications tasks may not result in purchases, the only measure that need be undertaken is that of sales.

Restrictions upon creativity

The creative flair can be lost as attention passes from looking for the big idea to concentration upon the numbers game, of focusing on measures of recall, attitude change and awareness. It is agreed that creative personnel are held to be more accountable under this approach and this may well inhibit some of their work. Perhaps the benefits of providing direction and purpose offsets the negative aspects of a slight loss in creativity.

Short-term accountability

To the above should be added the time period during which management and associated agencies are required to account for their performance. With accounting periods being reduced to as little as 12 weeks, the communications approach is impractical for two reasons. The first is that the period is not long enough for all of the communications tasks to be progressed or completed. Sales measures present a much more readily digestible benchmark of performance.

The second concerns the unit of performance itself. With the drive to be efficient and to be able to account for every communications pound spent, managers themselves need to use measures that they can understand and which they can interpret from published data. Sales data and communications-spend data are consistent measures and make no further demands on managers. Managers do not have enough time to spend analysing levels of comprehension or preference and to convert them into formats that are going to be of direct benefit to them and their organisations. Having said that, those organisations that are prepared to invest in a more advanced management information system will enable a more sophisticated view to be taken.

The communications school approach is not accepted by some, who argue that it is too difficult and impractical to translate a sales objective into a series of specific communications objectives. Furthermore, what actually constitute adequate levels of awareness and comprehension, and how can it be determined which stage the majority of the target audience has reached at any one point in time? Details of measurement, therefore, throw a veil over the simplicity and precision of the approach taken by the communications-orientation school.

From a practical perspective, it should be appreciated that most successful marketing organisations do not see the sales and communications schools as mutually exclusive.

> **Most successful marketing organisations do not see the sales and communications schools as mutually exclusive.**

They incorporate both views and weight them according to the needs of the current task, their overall experience, the culture and style of the organisation and the agencies with which they operate.

Derivation of promotional objectives

So, if specific marketing communications objectives need to be set up, from where are they derived in the first place? The answer is that they originate from a number of sources, but essentially they are derived from an understanding of the overall context in which the communications will operate. Comprehending the contexts of the buyer and the organisation allows the objectives of the planned communications to be identified: the *what* that is to be achieved. For example, objectives concerning the perception that different target customers have of a brand, the perception that members of a performance network have of the organisation's offerings, the reactions of key stakeholders to previous communications and the requirements of the current marketing plan all impact upon the objectives of the communication plan. Therefore, promotional objectives evolve principally from a systematic audit and analysis of the key communications contexts, the positioning intentions and specifically from the marketing plan and stakeholder analysis.

> **Promotional objectives evolve principally from a systematic audit and analysis of the key communications contexts, the positioning intentions and specifically from the marketing plan and stakeholder analysis.**

All three types of objectives are derived from an analysis of the current context. The marketing communications brief that flows from this analysis should specify the sales-related objectives to be achieved, as these can be determined from the marketing plan. Sales-related objectives might concern issues such as market share and sales volume.

Customer-related objectives concern issues such as awareness, perception, attitude, feelings and intentions towards a brand or product. The exact issue to be addressed in the plan is calculated by analysing the contextual information driven by the audit.

Issues related to the perception of the organisation are often left unattended or, worse, ignored. Research may indicate that the perception of particular stakeholders, in either the performance or the support network, does not complement the current level of corporate performance or may be misplaced or confused. Objectives will need to be established to correct or reinforce the perception held of the organisation. The degree of urgency may be directly related to the level of confusion or misunderstanding or be related to competitive or strategic actions initiated by competitors and other members of the network. Corporate strategy may have changed and, as identified earlier, any new strategy will need to be communicated to all stakeholders.

Promotional objectives need to be set that reflect the communications and sales tasks that the product or organisation needs to accomplish. It should be appreciated that promotional objectives are vitally important, as they provide the basis for a string of decisions that are to be taken at subsequent stages in the development of the communications plan.

ViewPoint 5.6　Norwich Union flood maps

Early in 2004 Norwich Union launched its flood maps, a digital method of gauging the flood danger to individual properties. This new system sought to replace the previous postcode approach to risk evaluation, which failed to discriminate potential flood-risk properties from high-rise flats.

The launch of the new product aimed to achieve two different objectives. The first was communications-related and geared to raising awareness of the maps to property owners, especially in high-risk parts of the country. The second was sales-related, as Norwich Union wanted to sell more property insurance policies.

Sources: Various

SMART objectives

To assist managers in their need to develop suitable objectives a set of guidelines has been developed, commonly referred to as SMART objectives. This acronym stands for specific, measurable, achievable, relevant, targeted and timed.

The process of making objectives SMART requires management to consider exactly what is to be achieved, when, where, and with which audience. This clarifies thinking, sorts out the logic of the proposed activities and provides a clear measure for evaluation at the end of the campaign:

- *Specific*
  What is the actual variable that is to be influenced in the campaign? Is it awareness, perception, attitudes, or some other element that is to be influenced? Whatever the variable, it must be clearly defined and must enable precise outcomes to be determined.

- *Measurable*
  Set a measure of activity against which performance can be assessed; this may be a percentage level of desired prompted awareness in the target audience.

- *Achievable*
  Objectives need to be attainable, otherwise those responsible for their achievement will lack motivation and a desire to succeed.

- *Realistic*

  The actions must be founded in reality and be relevant to the brand and the context in which they are set.

- *Targeted and timed*

  Which target audience is the campaign targeted at, how precisely is the audience defined and over what period are the results to be generated?

Having determined what levels of awareness, comprehension or preference are necessary or how attitudes need to be developed, the establishment or positioning of these objectives as a task for the organisation to accomplish should be seen as a primary communications objective. The attitude held or what individuals in the target market perceive, comprehend or prefer is a focus for campaign activity and subsequent evaluation.

Summary of key points

1. The development of a marketing strategy requires that general markets be segmented into particular groups of customers who share similar traits or characteristics. The overall process is referred to as the 'target market process' and consists of three main phases: segmenting markets, targeting particular markets and then positioning within each of the target markets that have been selected. This is simply referred to as the STP process.

2. Once a market has been segmented, each segment should be scrutinised in order to determine which should be highlighted and targeted for particular commercial (and marketing) activities. This is necessary for the development of effective marketing communications.

3. The target audience provides a context within which marketing communications attempts to convey meaningful messages and in some cases sustain a viable dialogue with selected stakeholders.

4. Part of the information generated during the marketing communications planning stage is intended to inform organisations how buyers and stakeholders position their brand relative to the other players in the target market. This information can help organisations devise suitable positions for their brands. There are a number of different positioning strategies available to organisations, ranging from positions based on use, user and benefits to others, which focus on heritage, features and price.

5. The way in which an organisation decides to position itself and/or its offerings determines the form, intensity and nature of the messages transmitted through its marketing communications.

6. The use of objectives in the marketing communications planning process is clearly vital, and these should be linked closely with the organisation's other functional and higher-level strategies if the desired outcomes are to be achieved. They are all interlinked, interdependent, multiple and often conflicting.

7. Marketing communications objectives are derived from an initial review of the current context and the requirements of the marketing plan. They are not a replication of the marketing objectives but a distillation of the research activities that have been undertaken subsequently. Such objectives consist of two main elements: sales-oriented and communications-oriented. A balance between the two will be determined by the situation facing the organisation, but may be a mixture of product and corporate tasks. These objectives, once quantified, need to be ranked and weighted in order that other components of the plan can be developed.

8. The use of the SMART approach to setting marketing communications objectives provides for good coverage, attention to detail and a more successful outcome to a campaign.

Review questions

1. Identify in note form the main characteristics of four main bases of segmenting markets.
2. Write a brief report arguing the case both for and against the use of an increase in sales as the major objective of all communications activities.
3. Repeat the exercise as for the previous question, but this time focus upon communications-based objectives.
4. Why is positioning an important part of marketing communications?
5. Explain, with examples, the main positioning strategies.
6. How and from where are communication objectives derived?

References

Beane, T.P. and Ennis, D.M. (1987), 'Market segmentation: a review', *European Journal of Marketing*, **21**(5), pp. 20–42.

Colley, R. (1961), *Defining Advertising Goals for Measured Advertising Results*, New York: Association of National Advertisers.

Dibb, S., Simkin, L., Pride, W.M. and Ferrell, O.C. (2006), *Marketing Concepts and Strategies*, 5th European edition, New York: Houghton Mifflin.

Haley, Russell I. (1968), 'Benefit segmentation: a decision-oriented research tool', *Journal of Marketing*, **32** (July), pp. 30–5.

McCawley, I. (2001), 'Pernod to rebrand in pursuit of older people', *Marketing Week*, 25 January, p. 8.

Ries, A. and Trout, J. (1972), 'The positioning era cometh', *Advertising Age*, 24 April, pp. 35–8.

Using technology: scope, applications and websites

6

Aims and objectives

The aims of this chapter are to consider the nature and key characteristics of new technology and then to consider their influence on marketing communications. There are four primary topics in this chapter:

Technology, Applications, Websites, Online tools

The learning objectives are to enable readers to:

1. explain the nature of some of the key developments in new technology;
2. understand how new technology has influenced marketing communications;
3. discuss the nature of ecommerce, CRM and multichannel activities;
4. describe the key characteristics associated with the design and use of customer-oriented websites.
5. explain how websites contribute to an organisation's marketing communications;
6. examine some of the issues concerning the management of websites and in particular discuss issues concerning visitor behaviour and online communities;
7. understand the way in which the promotional tools can be used online.

Introduction

The phrase 'information systems and technology' (IST) is used in this book to embrace the wide variety of new technologies that have been developed to improve the quality of life for the people who use IST and for those who benefit from their deployment. Ryssel et al. (2004) consider IST to be a term that embraces 'all forms of technology utilized to create, capture, manipulate, communicate, exchange, present and use information in its various forms (business data, voice conversations, still images, motion pictures, multimedia presentations and other forms, including those not yet conceived)'. They conceptualise the range of IST in terms of where the IST are used (internal or external) and across which broad functions, namely information, communication and decision support. However, it is not our intention to provide a detailed examination of each of these systems or of the various technologies as that is beyond the scope of this book. The intention here is threefold: first, to consider the breadth of new technology and to set out ways in which it has influenced marketing communications; second, to consider the nature of ecommerce and its impact on relationships and marketing communications; and third, consideration is given to the nature, characteristics and issues associated with websites and their role within marketing communications.

The breadth of technological applications

The breadth and range of developments in technology have been enormous over recent years. The Internet alone represents a gigantic step forward in the way we communicate, similar, for example, to the invention of the printing press, the telephone and radio in terms of the step change that each brought about.

The Internet impacts upon marketing in two main ways: distribution and communication. The first concerns distribution and marketing channels. The Internet provides a new, more direct route to customers, which can either replace or supplement current distribution/channel arrangements. The second element concerns the Internet as a communications medium. It provides a means of reaching huge new audiences and enabling the provision of vast amounts of information. These two elements, distribution and communication, combine as ebusiness and ecommerce to provide benefits for both buyers and sellers.

> The Internet provides a new, more direct route to customers, which can either replace or supplement current distribution/channel arrangements.

Other developments include email, mobile phones (incorporating SMS and 3G technologies), interactive television, videoconferencing, kiosks, databases, multimedia and a whole raft of applications specific to front- and back-end business functions. Brief details of these are set out in Table 6.1. (For further information see Fill, 2006.)

TABLE 6.1 Key developments in communications-related technology

Element of technology	Explanation
The Internet	Electronic mail, global information access and retrieval systems, discussion groups, multiplayer games and file-transfer facilities.
Database technologies	A marketing database is a collection of records that can be related to one another in multiple ways and from which information, usually customer-related, can be obtained in a variety of formats.
Mobile phones and WAP technologies	Wireless application protocol (WAP) phones possess the usual email and text-information services but they also have an Internet browser facility. General Packet Radio Service (GPRS) and third-generation (3G) services enable sound and image transfers, and underpin m-commerce.
Short-message services (SMS)	Using the Global System for Mobile Communication (GSM), SMS (texting) has become a standard protocol for users to send and receive messages across geographic boundaries. Apart from pure text other simple applications consist of games, email notifications, and information-delivery services such as sports and stock market updates.
Multimedia	Refers to the presentation of information or material that uses two or more media and often involves the integration of text, audio and images in order to enhance the user interface with computer-based applications. Typically, the 'streaming' of video and audio over the Internet typifies multimedia applications.
Digital and interactive television	These offer high-quality sound and picture formats, fast channel and picture/text 'hopping', plus opportunities to select and view programmes regardless of the time of delivery. Interactivity offers high levels of personal programming, entertainment and shopping facilities.
Kiosks	Electronic kiosks are terminals that can be accessed by the public for information and services. Very often kiosks are operated via touch screens and card readers that activate video displays, coupon printers and other devices specific to their application. Increasingly, electronic kiosks provide not only multimedia facilities but also enable access to the Internet.
Videoconferencing	Both room-based and desk-top systems enable users to communicate with speed and convenience and help reduce message ambiguity and travel costs.
Business applications	A wide range of computer-based applications designed to manage not only an organisation's internal processes and procedures but also the direct transmission between different companies' computer systems of data relating to business transactions and the coordination of supply-chain activities (ecollaboration). Customer relationship management systems have grown considerably.

The influence of technology on marketing communications

The various technologically driven facilities referred to above can influence an organisation's marketing communications in many different ways. The implementation and benefits derived from technology will vary across organisations. This is because of the level of strategic significance afforded to these investments, the culture, managerial skills, resources and degree to which the organisation has a true customer orientation differ widely. Table 6.2 summarises some of the key influences on marketing communications arising from new technology.

TABLE 6.2 The impact of technology on marketing communications

Benefit for marketing communications	Explanation
Multichannel marketing	Rather than use a single marketing channel organisations now use a variety of channels to reflect the access needs of different target audiences. For organisations, this has reduced message wastage, used media more efficiently and, in doing so, reduced costs and improved communications effectiveness.
Personalisation	Digital technology has empowered organisations to personalise messages and communicate with stakeholders on a one-to-one basis, on a scale that is commercially viable.
Mobility	Mobile commerce (or m-commerce) refers to the use of wireless devices such as mobile phones that enable transactions to be undertaken in real time and at any location. This gives organisations improved opportunities to keep in touch and provide increased convenience, localisation and personalisation opportunities. This in turn will allow, theoretically, the chance to track people to particular locations to then deliver personalised and pertinent information plus inducements and promotional offers.
Speed	Marketing communications can be conducted at very fast, electronic speeds. Draft documents, film and video clips, contracts, address lists and research and feedback reports and proposals, for example, can all now be transmitted electronically, saving processing time and reducing the elapsed production time necessary to create and implement marketing communications activities and events.
Efficiency	Through narrow casting, that is, targeting messages at specific audiences, communications costs and message wastage can be drastically reduced. The relative costs may be higher but these richer communications facilitate interactive opportunities with a greater percentage of the target audience than previously experienced in the mass broadcast era. Marketing communications can be used to deliver product information, specifications and service details, contracts, designs, drawings and development briefs when customising to meet customer needs.
Relationships	Many b2c and b2b relationships have been improved through new technology. For example, through the automation of various procurement and payment functions, trust and commitment can be increased – e.g. many financial services organisations are able to inform customers of their bank balances automatically without human intervention.

The impact of technology has been very significant and there is every reason to believe that these changes will continue to occur with increasing frequency. From the changes to date the development of multichannel marketing, CRM systems, ecommerce and the role of websites have been particularly significant in terms of marketing communications and have touched most people in developed economies. Before considering these in more detail, a review of the ways in which technology has assisted the sales force is considered.

Sales-force automation (SFA)

The use of technology to assist field-force selling has grown substantially, and the advent of 3G technology is likely to accelerate usage of digital technology in the sales and selling context. There are a number of reasons for this interest, most notably the attraction of lower selling costs, improved communication effectiveness and enhanced market and customer information. Various forms of technology have been employed (Engle and Barnes, 2000). What constitutes sales-force automation is questionable, simply because of the breadth of internal and external activities undertaken in the name of selling. One perspective is that such technology embraces sales-force automation, communication technology and customer-relationship management (Widmier et al., 2002).

What constitutes sales-force automation is questionable, simply because of the breadth of internal and external activities undertaken in the name of selling.

These authors identify six main sales-related functions, namely organising, presenting, reporting, communicating, informing and supporting transactions. These are set out in Table 6.3.

Research by these authors shows that technology is used extensively to assist all of the selling functions but is used least by salespersons when in the field for actually supporting transactions (e.g. order status and stock enquiries and qualifying customers). It also indicates that technology is more likely to be used by salespersons in the office (preparing presentations, proposals, route planning, scheduling and reporting) than the field.

The deployment of SFA varies among organisations and its effectiveness will, to a large extent, be dependent upon appropriate implementation, proper utilisation by the

TABLE 6.3 The use of technology in sales

Sales function	Use of technology
Organising	Call schedules, route plans, contacts, sales plans
Presenting with	Portable multimedia presentations, customised proposals
Reporting on	Call reports, expense claims, monthly performance
Informing about	Prospecting, product performance and product configuration information
Communicating via	Mobile phones, pagers, the Internet, email, personal organisers, fax machines
Supporting transactions	Order status and tracking, stock control, stock availability

Source: Adapted from Widmier et al. (2002)

sales force and suitable support processes. Indeed, Morgan and Inks (2001) report SFA failure rates between 25 and 60 per cent, a large proportion of which can be accredited to poor management and sales-force resistance to change. The factors that relate to the successful implementation of SFA will vary according to industry and organisation and perhaps even to individual salespeople. Research by Morgan and Inks identified four main elements associated with the successful implementation of SFA: management commitment, training, user involvement and accurate expectation-setting. They also determined that implementation will be less than satisfactory when there are fears of technology, of interference in an individual's selling activities or a loss of power (over the information they have on their customers), and where there is a general resistance to change.

It would appear reasonable to suggest that the adoption of SFA should lead to substantial productivity gains. However, high implementation costs, sales-force resistance and underutilisation have been cited as some of the key reasons for the failure to substantially increase productivity. This apparent conflict of views should be considered in the light of varying industry characteristics, operational circumstances and different definitions of SFA and technology. To date, there is little research evidence to show the impact of SFA on relationships.

> The adoption of SFA should lead to substantial productivity gains.

There can be little doubt that most salespeople use technology much more in their work than their counterparts of 15 years ago. However, it may be that technology is used by sales-force personnel to engage with internal colleagues more than their customers. The greater adoption of SFA will only come through appropriate management leadership, training, accurate expectations and the influence and encouragement of users themselves (Morgan and Inks, 2001).

Multichannel marketing

Although not entirely responsible, new technology has enabled organisations to reach new markets and different segments using more than a single marketing channel. Database-generated telemarketing, direct mail, email and Internet channels now complement field sales, retail and catalogue selling and in doing so have allowed organisations to determine which customers prefer which channels and which (customers and channels) are the most profitable. This in turn enables organisations to allocate resources far more effectively and to spread the customer base upon which profits are developed. At the same time, customers benefit because they perceive increased value as they have improved opportunities to access the products and services they prefer. So a multichannel strategy should accommodate customers' channel preferences, their usage patterns, needs, price sensitivities and preferred point of product and service access. As Stone and Shan (2002) put it, the goal is to manage each channel profitably while optimising the attributes of each channel so that they deliver value for each type of customer.

> New technology has enabled organisations to reach new markets and different segments using more than a single marketing channel.

> A multichannel strategy should accommodate customers' channel preferences, their usage patterns, needs, price sensitivities and preferred point of product and service access.

Multichannel strategies have added new marketing opportunities and enabled audiences to access products and services in ways that best meet their own lifestyle and behavioural needs. For organisations, this has reduced message wastage, used media more efficiently and in doing so reduced costs and improved communication effectiveness.

ViewPoint 6.1   Multichannel banking in the UK

UK commercial banks are trying to develop new channels in a market where current distribution channels (branches, call centres and echannels) are the largest operating expense. In the UK, the majority of customers use physical branches, partly because they represent the banking experience. Even for customers who rarely use them for transactions, branches are still seen as the embodiment of the bank, and often the place at which significant changes in the relationship take place (e.g. account openings, complex financial products bought or at least investigated, serious problems resolved).

Many banks have pursued strategies based on Internet, wireless and call-centre facilities while closing branches and removing the physical presence and customer experience of branch-based banking. Branch-based delivery has moved through a number of significant phases, namely the old 'bricks and personal service only', through the introduction of self-service branches, to sales branches with transactions handled in other channels. Some banks have changed strategy and are planning to increase the number of branches, often as part of a joint venture with retailers or as a franchise. However, Stone and Shan (2002) suggest that some banks may move towards the use of branch portals, which seek to combine the best of all approaches yet are still clearly centred on the branch. Such a move will re-emphasise the personal branch service facility but recognises that some customers will prefer a remote technological service based on e-banking that abandons all personal contact with a branch.

Source: Adapted from Stone and Shan (2002)

Customer-relationship management

Customer-relationship management (CRM) is about the delivery of customer value through the strategic integration of business functions and processes, using customer data and information systems and technology.

Early CRM applications were designed for supplier organisations to enable them to manage their end-user customers, and hence they became regarded as a front-end application. Originally developed as sales-force support systems (mainly sales-force automation) they have subsequently evolved as a more sophisticated means of managing customers, using real-time customer information.

CRM applications typically consist of call management, lead management, customer record, sales support and payment systems.

CRM applications typically consist of call management, lead management, customer record, sales support and payment systems. These are necessary in order to respond to questions from customers (e.g. about products, deliveries, prices and order status) and questions from internal stakeholders about issues such as strategy, processes and sales forecasts.

These systems should be used at each stage of the customer life cycle, in order to develop an understanding about customer attitudes and behaviour that the organisation desires. CRM should be used to assist decisions about whom to target, which customer differences should be taken into account and what impact this will have on profitability. It is this aspect of profitability, or relative profitability, of individual customers that is important and which is a core aspect of relationship marketing. As Nancarrow and Rees (2003) suggest, only by understanding the actual, potential, current and lifetime forms of individual customer profitability can different strategies be developed for different profit segments. Low-profit-generating customers may need to be treated differently from those customers that are highly profitable, and those customers that incur losses for the organisation may need to be dropped.

TABLE 6.4 Reasons for CRM disappointment

Author	Reasons for CRM underachievement
Wightman, 2000	Failure to adopt CRM within a strategic orientation
Stone, 2002	CRM is regarded as a mere add-on application that is expected to resolve all customer-interface difficulties
Sood, 2002	Failure of systems to accommodate the wide array of relationships that organisations seek to manage
O'Malley and Mitussis, 2002	Internal political issues concerning ownership of systems, data and budgets

However, many client organisations have voiced disappointment and even criticism when such systems fail to meet their expectations, while Rigby et al. (2002) report that very few CRM investments have proved to be successful. Table 6.4 lists some of the more prominent reasons.

Most of the reasons cited in Table 6.4 are based on the failure of a large number of organisations, both clients and vendors, to understand the central tenets of a customer-focused business philosophy. If CRM systems are to work then a central business strategy, one based on the importance of trust, commitment and customer satisfaction, has to be agreed and led by the senior managers. Only within this context can it be expected that the installation of databases, data warehouses and associated software will help influence the quality of an organisation's relationships with its customers and stakeholders. Good customer management requires attention to an organisation's culture, training, strategy and propositions and processes. Regretfully, too many organisations focus on the interface or fail to understand the broader picture.

> Good customer management requires attention to an organisation's culture, training, strategy and propositions and processes.

Customer contact centres

Originally customer contact centres (CCCs) were designed for in-house use to handle a large volume of telephone calls. They became a largely outsourced facility and manage high volumes of incoming calls through automatic call distribution (ACD) technology. ACDs distribute incoming calls to predetermined groups of agents. An ACD can hold calls in queues if necessary and play music and make announcements. Now CCCs are Internet-enabled communication solutions, designed to process and integrate a variety of media using voice messaging, interactive voice response, outbound calling and fax.

Whereas CCCs were once in-house and then outsourced, they are viewed by many as a core business activity, mainly because they are a critical component when delivering customer satisfaction and driving efficiency.

In the near future, CCCs will not be tied to a particular physical location and agents will work either from home or in various offices around the globe, each connected through a voice-over IP network (Bocklund, 2003). CRM software will be integrated with computer–telephone integration (CTI), which means that each interaction is immediately reported (to the database) so that updated information is available to agents right away.

ViewPoint 6.2   Aetna's contact-centre partnership

Using phone, fax or email and the Internet-based Web chat and Web call-back features, Aetna provides its customers and insurance agents with a 24-hour service. The development of the centre was characterised by Aetna's decision to select three partner organisations that each brought a unique technology to the customer contact centre.

1. CTIL, a leading Hong Kong-based customer interaction and ebusiness solution provider, brought implementation skills.

2. Interactive Intelligence provides an interaction management solution that combines the functionality of a digital PBX, ACD, IVR, voicemail system, fax server, Web gateway and computer telephony system all on a single software platform.

3. Alliance Systems provided the advanced, standards-based communication platform that enables the contact centre's multiple applications and functions to run on a single system.

As a result, Aetna has used customer-contact and CRM technologies to create a multimedia-based, interactive system not only to provide superior levels of customer service but in doing so have remained competitive.

Source: Adapted from www.alliancesystems.com/about/news/casestudies/aetna.asp, accessed 28 November 2003; used with kind permission

ecommerce

From the vast and increasing range of advances in technology, ecommerce, the electronic buying and selling of goods and services, has had a significant impact on businesses, organisations and consumers. The essential attraction for sellers is that a global market becomes available and transaction costs are reduced. For buyers, search convenience combined with lower prices make ecommerce a compelling business channel. There are a number of ecommerce or business models that can be identified operating over the www. The range of business models is shown in Table 6.5.

TABLE 6.5 ecommerce business models

Model	Explanation
eauction	Demand- and supply-oriented bidding processes for both consumers and organisations
ecollaboration	Demand and supply orientation for mutual benefit
emalls	Demand-led collection of eretail 'shops' that seek common synergies
epurchase	Demand-led buying and selling for businesses
eprocurement	Supply-led services for the purchase of materials and equipment
eretail	Demand-led buying opportunities for the public
eservice providers	Supply-led provision of speciality business services

Other dot-com models include what are known colloquially as 'clicks' (or pure play) and 'bricks and clicks' operations. 'Bricks and clicks' operations refer to organisations that retain a physical presence (high street or business park) and online facilities are added either to reach discrete segments/new markets or as a supplement to the current distribution and communication facilities. The 'clicks' model refers to dedicated Internet brands (e.g. Amazon.com, Lastminute.com) that have only a virtual presence. However, long-established businesses have added dot-com facilities to their business and promotional activities. There are two types of Internet operations. One concerns inter-organisational communications and associated transaction activities, referred to as business-to-business (b2b). The other concerns activities with consumers and is referred to as business-to-consumer (b2c).

Business-to-business ecommerce

In b2b markets organisational buying behaviour is more complex than that observed in consumer markets. This is because of the increased number of people involved in the decision-making process and the nature of the relationships between individuals and organisations. As a result of this and other factors, marketing communications in the b2b market are traditionally characterised by the predominance of personal selling and relatively little use of advertising. In fact, it is the complete reversal of consumer-based promotional activity (b2c) where mass-media-based communications have tended to be the most important route through to the target audience.

One of the principal reasons for using the Internet as a distribution channel and communication medium between organisations is that it can drastically improve effectiveness and productivity. Electronic commerce saves transaction time, lowers costs and shortens the time between order and delivery. Digitally based communications can improve the accuracy of the information provided and so give a good measure of the effectiveness of marketing communications activities. However, offline communications are still going to be important and these new communication formats should be considered as an addition to rather than a substitute for current marketing communications. For example, the collection of data for use through on- and offline sources can be deployed to improve direct-marketing activities, to target sales promotions so as to provide real and valued incentives and even benefit public-relations activities by placing suitable material on the web pages. Therefore, productivity measures apply to marketing communications on- and offline.

Communications costs can also be considerably reduced. Just as sales literature and demonstration packs take time to prepare, even longer to change/update and are quite expensive with a great deal of wastage, brochureware on a website is fast, easily accessible and adaptable at any time. One step further into website development is the collection of names and addresses, response to email questions and the provision of rich data for the sales force. If developed further, transactional websites enable routine orders to be processed quickly and at a lower cost. This can free up the sales force to visit established customers more often, open more new accounts and manage more attentively those accounts that are strategically important.

The propensity of organisations to share information and to provide higher rather than lower volumes of information is perceived as an indicator of high-quality (and therefore satisfying) communication. The Internet is an ideal resource for enabling this to happen and in doing so bind partner organisations closer to each other.

Business-to-consumer ecommerce

Using the Internet to communicate and engage directly with consumers and encourage them to enter into financial exchanges has been an enticing goal for most businesses operating in this sector. The speed at which this sector has grown (outside the United States) has not been as rapid or as profitable as first thought, evidenced by commentator predictions in 1999 and the failure of most dot-com brands to achieve profitability and some that have collapsed. Indeed there are a number of far-ranging b2c issues, beyond the scope of this text, concerning fraud, morality, education, family life and the nature and purpose of the current and future retail environments (e.g. the configuration and use of the high street).

Books, music, travel and computer products make up a large percentage of the main online purchase categories. Books and music represent low-involvement purchases and low perceived risk, so the distribution (and price) advantages of the www dominate. Travel and computer equipment represent high involvement and high perceived risk so the search (and price) facilities of the www dominate buyers' use and selection.

An important issue associated with ecommerce is fulfilment. Fulfilment of customer orders is absolutely imperative if a repeat visit to an ecommerce website is to be encouraged. There used to be some uncertainty as to what constitutes an acceptable delivery period, but now expectations have moved from three weeks to three days. Fulfilment expectations are also raised because the online experience of placing the order is characteristically convenient, quick and efficient, and this is then projected by consumers on to all consequent order-processing activities. Email is often used to acknowledge orders and to advise of despatch. If this should be delayed, however, consumers may perceive this as a failure of part of the fulfilment exercise.

However, order fulfilment often requires the cooperation of outsourcing suppliers as stock may not be stored on site but in a warehouse at a distant location. According to Gray (2000), this is a key decision for organisations moving from a conventional trading environment to a multichannel approach. Should warehousing and fulfilment be outsourced or kept in-house? Even if the decision is to undertake fulfilment in-house, slim stocking still requires suitable systems to enable suppliers to replenish stock quickly.

ViewPoint 6.3   Fulfilling food and wine

When Asda-Walmart first developed its home shopping service two independent, purpose-designed depots were built. However, this approach proved less than successful and the company soon migrated to a store-based service, the model used so successfully by Tesco. The in-store approach allows for the full range of products to be offered online so customers get a better service in terms of the range of products available.

In-store pickers use hand-held systems devices to help them fulfil a number of orders simultaneously. Asda's systems are integrated with its parent company Wal-Mart, which not only assists in terms of IST and fulfilment developments in North America but also provides leading-edge technologies to integrate fulfilment with a range of corporate functions.

For Direct Wines Ltd, one of the world's largest mail-order suppliers of wines, efficient fulfilment is a key competitive factor, as even the best wines in the world need to be delivered promptly and accurately. Through the use of appropriate systems, planning and stock control Direct Wines has had to make fewer substitutions, thus improving customer service, while at the same time reducing the overall amount of stock held as working capital by around 10 per cent.

Websites

Websites are the cornerstone of Internet activity for organisations, regardless of whether they are operating in the b2b, b2c or not-for-profit sectors and whether the purpose is merely to offer information or to provide fully developed embedded ecommerce (transactional) facilities. The characteristics of a website can be crucial in determining the length of stay, activities undertaken and the propensity for a visitor to return to the site at a later time. When the experience is satisfactory, then both the visitor and the website owner might begin to take on some of the characteristics associated with relationship marketing.

To understand the characteristics associated with website interaction, consideration will first be given to their strengths and weaknesses, then the issues associated with the development of a website will be identified and finally the processes involved in attracting and managing website activity will be examined.

Websites can be used for a variety of purposes, but essentially they are either product-oriented or corporate-oriented. Product-oriented websites aim to provide product-based information such as brochureware, sales-based enquiries, demonstrations and endorsements through to online transactions and ongoing technical support as the main activities.

Corporate-oriented websites aim to provide information about the performance, size, prospects, financial data and job opportunities relating to the organisation.

Corporate-oriented websites aim to provide information about the performance, size, prospects, financial data and job opportunities relating to the organisation. They also need to relate to issues concerning the ethical expectations and degree of social responsibility accepted by the company, if only to meet the needs of prospective investors and employees. The demarcation is not necessarily as clear cut as this might suggest but the essence of a site's orientation is to a large extent derived from the organisation's approach to branding.

The strengths and weaknesses of website facilities are set out in Table 6.6; however, it should be remembered that these are generalised comments and that some

TABLE 6.6 Strengths and weaknesses of website-based communications

Strengths	Weaknesses
Quick to set up and easy to maintain	Slow access and page downloading speeds
Flexibility	Huge variability in website design and user friendliness
Variety of information	
High level of user involvement	Unsolicited email
Potentially high level of user convenience (and satisfaction)	Security and transaction-privacy issues
Range of service facilities	Relatively poor Internet penetration across UK households
Global reach and equal-access opportunities	
Open all hours – reduced employment costs	Inconsistent fulfilment standards (information to online transactions only)
Very low relative costs (per person reached)	Variability and speed of technology provision
Can provide cost efficiencies in terms of marketing research	Lack of regulation concerning content and distribution
	Online search-time costs prohibitive for many users

organisations have attended to these issues and have been able to develop the strengths and negate some of the weaknesses such that their websites are particularly attractive, user-friendly and encourage repeat visits.

Strengths

Any www user can create a website, consisting of a home page and a number of linked pages. Business pages can carry advertising, product catalogues, descriptions, pricing, special offers, press releases – all forms of promotional material. They can link to online order pages, so that potential customers can order directly, or to email facilities for requesting further information or providing feedback. Consumer interest and activity can be monitored easily, allowing for timely market research, rapid feedback and strategy adaptation.

Barriers to entry are low, it is relatively inexpensive to create/maintain a site, and share of voice is theoretically equal for all participants, although in practice this is clearly not the case. Large organisations can buy banner ads and have a better chance of appearing in the first few results presented by search engines. Good design can add to brand appeal and recognition. Potential customers actively seek products and services, which is both time- and cost-effective from a company's point of view, and indicative of positive attitudes, perception and involvement. Channel communications can also be swift and supportive. Coverage is global, without the need for huge investment or expensive staff to be employed around the clock. Savings can be made in advertising budgets, travel, postage and telephone costs. Different time zones no longer matter in the virtual environment, and language barriers are less of an issue. However, it has been suggested that cultural and language issues have been partly responsible for the relatively slow take-up of the Internet through PCs, which is in essence a geographic and cultural variance in the process of diffusion (Curtis, 2000).

Weaknesses

Some of the disadvantages are that the speed of access, page location and loading are still too slow for many users, especially from home PCs. Potential customers are easily put off by slow or unreliable connections and this frustration can result in negative images of the company or product. Poorly designed websites, which confuse rather than clarify, also leave a lasting poor impression, one that deters a return visit.

Unsolicited email is extremely annoying to many users and may be counter-productive. The worries over the security of financial details and transactions online, although not discouraging people from seeking information, may still be a barrier to full ecommerce. Fulfilment issues, principally delivery problems (such as long delays), wrong items, incorrect billing, plus the associated inconvenience of returning products or otherwise seeking resolution, may deter repeat purchase.

It is interesting to note that the UK supermarket chain Somerfield announced in June 2000 that it was closing the online shopping-facility site and three associated distribution centres. A spokesman said on the radio that this operation had been 'a distraction'. Although this is potentially true, consideration must be given to the marketing strategy and the overall context, internal resources, audience requirements, available computing and telecommunications facilities, prior to the design and build of any marketing website. Interestingly, Somerfield now offer a home-delivery service for goods bought in-store. This negates the need for a car when shopping and reflects the urban (rather than retail park) location of many of their stores.

Some regard ecommerce as transactional websites or extended enterprises but it is more to do with information/communication management and the impact on relationships. Ecommerce should be aimed at building new relationships with established customers and providing potential customers with a reason to change. The idea that ecommerce provides process efficiencies is correct but these features need to be transformed into benefits for customers.

Ecommerce should be aimed at building new relationships with established customers and providing potential customers with a reason to change.

Website design

The design and functionality of a website is now recognised as an important and integral aspect of an organisation's communication strategy. What constitutes a suitable website has also been the subject of much debate and speculation, marked by a lack of substantial empirical work to determine a common framework. Many best-practice frameworks have been offered, some of the more notable ones by Rayport and Jaworski (2004) who offer a 7Cs framework that they subsequently develop into a map that can be used to analyse sites and to design sites more effectively (see also Fill, 2006).

Karayanni and Baltas (2003) suggest that websites have four main characteristics. These are set out in Table 6.7 and were presented in the context of b2b markets. This breakdown is useful because it indicates the main facilities that a successful site should provide. However, what it does not provide is a depth of insight and balance that would help organisations design their sites more appropriately.

Chaffey et al. (2003) suggest that there should be a set of standards regarding website design, especially when sites have several staff working on different parts or site sections, as is the case with many large corporate sites. However, the principles apply to all other sites as a means of working within a common framework or template. See Table 6.8.

TABLE 6.7 Four aspects of website design

Website characteristic	Explanation	
Interactivity	The provision of solutions in response to the provision of personal information and the ability of users to customise preferences. This can be delivered through memory storage/organisation and response to individual needs.	
Navigability	The structure and organisation of the site combined with the ease with which information can be retrieved.	
Multimedia design	The Internet offers all the facilities that each of the other media provide individually. This provides opportunities for stimulation as well as flexibility and visitor involvement with a site.	
Content	Company content	Information relating to the organisation, its markets, culture and values are important to establish credibility and reduce risk.
	Customer content	This concerns both the provision of information (for example, a *frequently asked questions* facility) and the collection of information about customers and the market.

Source: Karayanni and Baltas (2003)

TABLE 6.8 Website standards

Standard	Details	Applies to
Site structure	Will specify the main areas of the site, for example products, customer service, press releases, how to place content and who is responsible for each area.	Content developers
Navigation	May specify, for instance, that the main menu must always be on the left of the screen with nested (sub-) menus at the foot of the screen. The home button should be accessible from every screen at the top left corner of the screen. See Lynch and Horton (1999) for guidelines on navigation and site design.	Website designer/webmaster usually achieves these through site templates
Copy style	General guidelines, for example reminding those writing copy that web copy needs to be briefer than its paper equivalent. Where detail is required, perhaps with product specifications, it should be broken up into chunks that are digestible on-screen.	Individual content developers
Testing standards	Check site functions for: ● different browser types and versions ● plug-ins ● invalid links ● speed of download of graphics ● spellcheck each page See text for details.	Website designer/webmaster
Corporate branding and graphic design	Specifies the appearance of company logos and the colours and typefaces used to convey the brand message.	Website designer/webmaster
Process	The sequence of events for publishing a new web page or updating an existing page. Who is responsible for reviewing and updating?	All
Performance	Availability and download speed figures.	

Source: Chaffey et al. (2003)

To conclude this section it should be noted that there is little empirical research that shows how different website design features impact on visitor responsiveness. However, it is generally recognised that websites are poorly used dialogic tools, and that the actual design of a website can have a strong impact on the way in which visitors perceive the organisation and hence influence its relationship-building potential.

Websites – visitor behaviour

It is possible to deconstruct users' website behaviour into a number of discrete activities, but the resultant list would be far too complex to be of any practical assistance. However, several authors have tried to discriminate among Internet users and segment

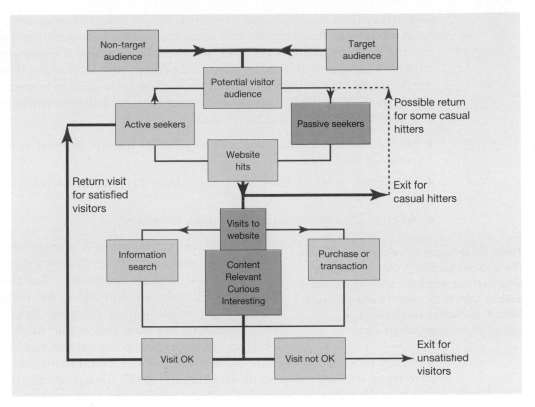

FIGURE 6.1 A framework depicting website visitor behaviour

the market accordingly. For example, Lewis and Lewis (1997) have segmented the Internet on the basis of people who use the Internet, and Forsyth et al. (2002) on the basis of those who are active online consumers, a behavioural approach to segmentation.

The design of websites should account for the needs of different types of users and also the different stages each has reached in terms of their experience in using the Internet.

The design of websites should account for the needs of different types of users and also the different stages each has reached in terms of their experience in using the Internet, their stage in the adoption process (see Chapter 2) and the different stages users have reached in the buying process. For the purposes of the rest of this text, reference is made to two broad categories, active (goal-directed) and passive (experiential) information-seekers. Figure 6.1 depicts a process framework that describes the path visitors follow when visiting a website.

The initial goal is to generate awareness of the website, and this needs to be understood in the knowledge that there are many Web users who have no interest in a particular (your) website and that those who do are said to have a potential interest. The task is therefore to drive awareness levels among those who might find the site useful.

The second phase is to encourage the potential segment to actually visit the site. The problem is that there are two types of information-seeker, passive and active. Passive seekers have no intention of hitting any particular site, whereas active seekers do have the express intention of visiting a particular site. Part of the communication strategy must therefore be geared to facilitating active seekers and attracting passive information-seekers.

The next phase is to ensure that active seekers, once on the website, are able to find the information they need quickly and efficiently so that they are inclined to revisit. This entails good site access and, once found, good site design so that navigation is easy, simple and fast. This normally means that the design of the site is simple and is user, rather than technologically, oriented. Passive information-seekers, on the other hand, need to be made curious and stimulated to want to know more about the site and the products and services available. Here the objective is to convert hitters into visitors. A site-registration book, supported perhaps with sales-promotion devices, or a site design that is sufficiently intriguing may allow these goals to be met. Research suggests that there are three main elements that strongly influence the perceived quality of a website visit (Oxley and Miller, 2000):

- all are content-oriented and refer to whether the site material is relevant to the needs of the visitor;
- the degree to which the content (and design) encourages curiosity to explore the site;
- whether the content is presented in an interesting way.

These three points correlate strongly with the idea of 'likeability', that advertising effectiveness improves when an individual assigns significant value to any particular form of marketing communication discipline but often advertising.

These three points correlate strongly with the idea of 'likeability', that advertising effectiveness improves when an individual assigns significant value (represented by relevance, curiosity and interest) to any particular form of marketing communication discipline but often advertising. Therefore, the main factors that might influence the way an individual perceives a website may be similar to the way they process and evaluate other marketing communications and, in particular, advertising messages. Goldsmith and Lafferty (2002) have made similar observations and consider theories concerning attitudes towards the ad as developed by Lutz et al. (1983) and Bruner and Kumar (2000). Attitudes developed towards advertisements can also impact on attitudes towards the brand and hence are better indicators of purchase intentions (see Chapter 3). Goldsmith and Lafferty also refer to advertisement-brand recall and the fact that those consumers who have strong emotional feelings towards a brand (a positive attitude) are more likely to be able to recall it. Therefore, investment in marketing communications that seeks to establish top-of-mind awareness of a brand and also create positive attitudes may be more likely to be successful.

Online communities

Armstrong and Hagel (1996) were two of the first to propose the benefits of virtual communities, and the development of these communities is one of the key elements that differentiates interactive from traditional media. Through communities people who share a common interest(s) interact, share information, develop understanding, build relationships and add value through their contribution to others involved with the website. In a sense user groups and special-interest groups are similar facilities but the key to all these variations is the opportunity to share information electronically, often in real time.

Chaffey et al. (2003) refer to Durlacher (1999), who argues that there are four main types of community defined by their purpose, position, interest and profession. See Table 6.9.

Communities are characterised by several determining elements. Muniz and O'Guinn (2001) identify three core components:

- consciousness of kind: an intrinsic connection that members feel towards one another;

TABLE 6.9 Four types of virtual community

Type of community	Explanation
Purpose	Those attempting to achieve the same goal or who are experiencing a similar process.
Position	Those experiencing particular circumstances. These might be to do with lifestage issues (the old or the young), health issues or perhaps career-development opportunities.
Interest	Those sharing a hobby or pastime, or who are passionately involved with, for example, sport, music, dance, family trees, jigsaws, gardening, film, etc.
Profession	Those involved with the provision of b2b services. Often created by publishers these portals provide information about jobs, company news, industry issues and trading facilities (e.g. auctions).

Source: After Durlacher (1999)

- the presence of shared rituals and traditions that perpetuate the community's history, culture and consciousness;
- a sense of moral responsibility, duty or obligation to the community as a whole and its individual members.

Within virtual communities five particular characteristics can be identified.

Within virtual communities five particular characteristics can be identified. The first concerns the model of communication, which is essentially visitor to visitor and in some cases customer to customer. Secondly, communities create an identity that arises from each individual's involvement and sense of membership and belonging. The more frequent and intense the interaction the stronger the identity. Thirdly, relationships, even friendships, develop among members, which facilitate mutual help and support. The fourth characteristic concerns the language that the community adopts. Very often specialised languages or codes of (electronic) behaviour emerge that have particular meaning to members. The fifth and final characteristic refers to the methods used to regulate and control the behaviour and operations of the community. Self-regulation is important in order to establish acceptable modes of conduct and interaction among the membership.

The role that members assume within these communities and the degree to which they participate also varies. There are members who attend but contribute little to those who create topics, lead discussion, summarise or perform brokerage or intermediary roles among other members.

Affiliate marketing

Associated with the concepts of communities and networks, affiliate marketing has become an essential aspect of online marketing communications and ecommerce. Affiliate schemes are based on a network of websites on which advertisements or text

Affiliate schemes are based on a network of websites on which advertisements or text links are placed.

links are placed. Those who click on them are taken directly to the host site. If this results in a sale, only then will the affiliate receive a commission (payment for the ad). Cookies are used to track, monitor and record transactions and pay commission plus any agreed charges. As with many online marketing schemes management can be undertaken in-house or outsourced. If the latter approach is adopted then many of the relationship issues discussed earlier need to be considered and managed.

Affiliate schemes are popular because they are low-cost operations, paid on a results-only basis and generating very favourable returns on investment. Rigby (2004) reports that the low-cost airline Flybe has an affiliate network of over 1,450 websites, which generates 10 per cent of sales, an ROI twice as big as that earned through direct-response press activity and all at zero risk.

The next section considers the role of each of the main tools of the promotional mix, when used in an online context.

The marketing communications mix – online

All marketing communications activity on the Internet needs to be planned and managed in just the same way as if the context was offline using traditional media. Setting suitable goals is part of this process and Cartellieri et al. (1997) provide a useful set of objectives in this context:

- *delivering content:* click through to a corporate site that provides more detailed information (e.g. health advice);
- *enabling transactions:* a direct response that leads to a sale (e.g. easyJet);
- *shaping attitudes:* development of brand awareness (e.g. start-up situations);
- *soliciting response:* encouraging interaction with new visitors (building market share);
- *improving retention:* reminding visitors and seekers of the organisation (developing reputation and loyalty).

Before considering online advertising it is necessary to clarify what constitutes Internet advertising. According to Goldsmith and Lafferty (2002), Internet advertising should be considered as one of two main forms. One concerns all offline media that are used to drive traffic to a website. The second form concerns advertising that only appears in an online environment. Both need to be used together in a coordinated way as they are complementary forms of advertising that are necessary if a website is to be successful.

Online advertising

Online advertising is not confined to an organisation's website. Traffic needs to be directed from other sites, so advertisements need to be placed on other websites where it is thought the target audience is most likely (or known) to visit. Therefore, advertisements are bought and placed on other websites, and through careful analysis it is possible to place the ads on sites where it is thought that members of the target

Advertisements are bought and placed on other websites, and through careful analysis it is possible to place the ads on sites where it is thought that members of the target market will pass.

market will pass and not only see the advertisements but also be prompted to click the banner and be taken to the advertiser's own corporate site.

The most common form of ads are referred to as banner ads (see below), but as technology and marketing knowledge improve so more sophisticated versions of the banner ad have evolved. Some of these are outlined below.

Banner ads

These are the dominant form of paid-for communication on the Web. Some 55 per cent of all Web ads are banner ads, which are responsible for 96 per cent of all Internet ad awareness. Banner ads use a link through to an advertiser's chosen destination and therefore can act as a gateway to other websites but are also effective in their own right. Banner ads are linked to key words submitted by a seeker into a search engine. The ad should therefore be strategically positioned to catch the optimum, or even greatest, traffic flow. Certain product groups such as computer-related products represent 56 per cent of all banner ads, whereas financial products account for only 7 per cent. An extension of the banner concept is e*banners. These allow for media-rich content that enables a depth of material and even ecommerce transactions. Therefore banners are said to signpost and e*banners provide action.

The aim of the banner ad is to attract attention and stimulate interest.

The aim of the banner ad is to attract attention and stimulate interest but the problem is that click-through rates are low (some reports suggest just 4 per cent), which leads to the question about whether banner ads are worthwhile.

Pop-ups

Instead of transferring users to an orthodox website, banner ads can also be used to transfer users to an interactive site based upon product information, games or a competition. These games provide entertainment and seek to develop user involvement and an incentive to return to the site at a later date. In addition, data can be captured about the user in order to refine future marketing offers. These ads can be saved for later use and are therefore more adaptable and convenient than interstitial ads that appear as users move between websites and cannot be controlled by the user.

Superstitials or interstitials

Also known as transitional online ads, these appear during the time when pages are being downloaded. They are intended to appear as a relief to the boredom that might set in when downloading can take a long time. In that sense they are not regarded as intrusive but supportive. One of the first of these was run by British Airways with a three-second media-rich advertisement that was triggered when users clicked on either the travel or the business link on the the *Times* home page. In turn, there was a link to the British Airways website.

Micro sites

This type of site is normally product- or promotion-specific and is often run as a joint promotion with other advertisers. Creating a separate site avoids the difficulty of directing traffic to either of the joint partners' sites. Micro sites are much less expensive to set up

Micro sites are particularly adept at building awareness as click-throughs to micro sites are higher than through just banners.

than the traditional site and are particularly adept at building awareness as click-throughs to micro sites are higher than through just banners.

Email

Email can be used with high levels of frequency, which is important when building awareness. Email communications are easily customised, enabling tailored messages for different segments, and are inexpensive. Email is also a part of direct marketing (see below).

ViewPoint 6.4   Houses by email

One of the problems encountered by estate agents (and house buyers and sellers) is the inordinate amount of time it takes to complete the cycle of transactions necessary to sell and buy a house. Paul Smith, an established estate agent, developed email systems in order to shorten the cycle.

As soon as a property came on the market his agency would email the particulars to preselected target buyers. Customers appreciated the promptness, detail and personal attention (sales rose 11 per cent), while Smith slashed his mailing and copying costs (by £729,000).

Now he uses SMS and texts his customers at 8 in the morning and queues often form outside some of his 250 nationwide branches.

Source: Armistead (2002); used with permission

The use of email to attract and retain customers has become a main feature of many organisations' marketing communications programmes. Using appropriate email lists is a fast, efficient and effective way to communicate regularly with a market. Email-based marketing enables organisations to send a variety of messages concerning public-relations-based announcements, newsletters and sales promotions, to distribute online catalogues and to start and manage permission-based contact lists. Many organisations build their own lists using data collected from their CRM system. By acquiring email responses and other contact mechanisms, addresses and contact details can be captured for the database and then accessed by all customer-support staff.

The use of viral marketing, that is, email messages conveyed to a small part of the target audience where the content is sufficiently humorous, interesting or persuasive that the receiver is compelled to send it on to a friend, is limited in the b2b market. However, apart from just preparing lists and messages, organisations must be equally prepared to manage responses. The majority of responses are likely to be received within a day of transmission, and organisations must be prepared to act upon the requests of those responding by at least acknowledging their message. The next step may require the activation of some form of internal processing and fulfilment, very often offline and outsourced.

Another approach is to identify affinity groups, such as those used within the financial services industry. Given the increasingly goal-directed nature of much Web activity, communicating to people through an affinity site can be more cost-effective than trying to bring people to a site.

The use of the Internet should not be restricted to a series of independent, isolated communication activities. Through coordination with other tools and media the influence of the Internet can be considerably enhanced. The website lies at the heart of an organisation's Internet activities, but it is necessary to use other tools and media to drive traffic to the site. Direct mail to generate leads and permission-based email lists plus print advertising for product and company awareness are effective at directing potential visitors and customers to a website. Once at the website the quality and relevance of the content will be paramount for retaining and developing interest.

> The website lies at the heart of an organisation's Internet activities, but it is necessary to use other tools and media to drive traffic to the site.

Email strategies require a central creative proposition around which all communications are linked. This might be related to particular attributes such as product features – for example, colour, size or speed of service. The benefits of the attributes might also be used – no production downtime or improved staff efficiency might be valid claims. In contrast, an emotional feeling might be generated through the use of a tag line, gimmick, slogan, music or perhaps a mood. In other words, some form of branding needs to be used to differentiate the website and create longer-lasting memories that can be easily recalled through the mention of the brand name or perhaps an attribute or central theme.

Rich-media banner ads

The essential difference between regular and rich-media banner ads is that the latter allow for significantly more detailed and enhanced messages to be communicated to the target audience. Video, and other more visitor-engaging material, provide depth and interest. Gluck and Bruner (2005) argue that media-rich banner ads are highly effective mainly because the medium enhances the message.

Online sales promotions

In principle, these have been used either to attract and retain customers or as a way of providing interest and involvement with the brand by encouraging return visits. In reality, price deals and competitions have been the main tools used. Bol.com used a viral campaign to announce a three-hour window in which it offered spectacular discounts. The information spread quickly, thousands of new customers registered and Bol had a huge number of new names and addresses on its database.

Virtual sales promotions are generally cheaper than hard-copy versions but to date it appears that www sales promotions have not been used to develop brand differentiation or added value. The issue is, of course, that sales promotions are normally used to bring forward future sales, to provide a reason to buy now. On the Internet this motivation does not exist in the same way, and for many people the only reason to use the Internet is to find information and to compare prices. However, digital media is being used increasingly to deliver sales-promotion activity. Indeed, there has been a decline in the use of traditional on-pack promotions (Barrand, 2004) and a significant growth in the use of SMS, email and the Internet as means of delivering sales-promotion activity. Whereas traditional forms of sales promotion are in need of innovation, the use of the Internet to deliver promotions and the use of text-to-win strategies are signs of the industry adapting and reinventing itself.

McLuhan (2000) refers to Amazon, which emails occasional users offering them a £3 voucher that is instantly redeemable and of immediate value. Beenz is a cyber currency that can be collected at a number of sites and then 'cashed in' for goods at other sites. Honda used Beenz to encourage test drives, but the real value of Beenz collection is questioned by McLuhan as all that is involved is site registration. iPoints works in much the same way, but the major difference is that these points can only be accessed at one appointed trader in each sector. This offers competitive advantage and the benefit of horizontal cooperation between iPoints traders (e.g. database knowledge). However, these currency-collection devices (similar to old-fashioned Green Shield Stamps) serves only to foster 'site grazing' for Web points and are hardly a suitable way to develop brand value. They are also in danger of being abused through the development of automated software designed to scan and collect points by cheating.

Online direct marketing

The most obvious form of direct marketing on the Internet is email. However, direct marketing has an important part to play offline to drive site traffic. Interestingly, advertising was the primary offline tool used to drive traffic but, following the reassessment and consolidation of dot-com growth at the beginning of 2000, direct marketing (and direct mail in particular) appears to have taken on the mantle as primary traffic generator. It does this in one of two main ways. The first way is to launch a teaser campaign appealing to people's innate curiosity or, secondly, the direct-mail piece is part of a sales promotion campaign where the promise of a reward lures people to the website.

In order to utilise this potency, by far the most influential aspect of email is what is referred to as viral marketing. This works on the principle that brand-based email messages are conveyed to a small part of the target audience and the content is sufficiently humorous, interesting or persuasive that the receiver is compelled to send it on to a friend. Felix pet food used this approach so that recipients ended up with cartoon cats walking around their screens. This is effectively word-of-mouth (word-of-mouse) communication and as such has very high credibility and penetration.

> Word-of-mouth (word-of-mouse) communication has very high credibility and penetration.

ViewPoint 6.5 Viral Crystal

The use of a viral campaign backed up by an offline direct-mail activity can only be really successful if there is a large database. Crystal Holidays, which offers action-based holidays and is part of the TUI Group, holds both email and postal-address details of its customers so this combined approach was perfectly feasible.

In addition to a personalised message about Crystal, the email contained an Mpeg movie about a hang-glider that appears to fly out of the film and knock over items on the recipient's desk top. This was followed up by an oversized postcard with images of the various holiday options.

Another approach is to identify affinity groups. Given the increasingly goal-directed nature of much Web use, communicating to people through an affinity site can be more cost-effective than trying to bring people to your site. Many online retailers sell via other sites, using the visitors of that site and the relationship that those visitors have with the site content. Although the potential through email advertising and communications is high and often quite legitimate when a user has registered his/her email address at a particular site, the risk of being accused of sending spam or junk mail is equally high, as it is perceived as unethical and intrusive. The development of permission marketing has brought about a change in perspective as contemporary approaches are now based upon communication with people who have already agreed to receive such marketing communications, very often agreed when registering at a site.

Online public relations

The use of public relations on the Internet, and extranets in particular, is claimed by many as a viable and active part of the promotional mix. The claim is that website hosts become media owners in the sense that they are free to publish materials and information without recourse to the origin. The problem is that the information they present or convey (on behalf of themselves) has not been influenced by an independent third party, such as an opinion former, and may be no more than brochureware. However, the role is more complex because the website assumes the role of the fax machine, with press releases posted so that those interested can view (at their discretion and initiative) and then enter into a dialogue in order to expand on the information provided.

Online and new media developments have been instrumental in assisting public relations to move from a predominantly one-way model of communication to a two-way model. Hurme (2001) suggests that public relations practitioners can be divided into two main groups: those that use traditional media and those that adopt online communications. Since that paper was written an increasing number of practitioners will have moved over to online communications, but the realisation of the potential to develop true dialogue with stakeholders remains unfilled in most cases. Thus opportunities for interactivity and dialogue have increased, even if websites are not being designed to fulfil this requirement completely.

Sponsorship activity is an important part of online marketing communications. Other forms of public relations are more easily observable. Sponsorship activity is an important part of online marketing communications, whether it be a partnership deal or direct sponsorship of a site. Websites can also play an important role in terms of crisis management. In the event of an organisational crisis or disaster, up-to-date information can be posted quickly either providing pertinent information or directing visitors to offline facilities should it be appropriate.

Online personal selling

Face-to-face personal communications over the Internet for the purposes of buying and selling remain the one part of the promotional mix that the Internet cannot address. Increasingly, videoconferencing (see later) provides this facility but costs and logistics limit the practical application of this tool to conferencing and non-sales meetings. The Internet is an impersonal medium and as such does not allow for direct personal communication. The recognition of this limitation should direct management attention to the use of the Internet as a complementary role within the promotional mix. However, it has been determined that the Internet can impact upon sales performance indirectly through sales-management activities (Avlonitis and Karayanni, 2000). They describe how managing and analysing data can refine segmentation and customer-classification schemes, allowing salespeople to spend more time on core activities.

ViewPoint 6.6   Website to build sales

Zyrotech Project Management (ZPM) provides design/build services, engineering, validation and compliance solutions that are customised for companies in the biotech and pharmaceutical industries.

Its original website was little more than brochureware and limited the perception visitors had of the company. There were several goals attached to the new site design. First, it should display ZPM's expertise, flexibility and technological ability; second, it needed to convey credibility such that large pharmaceutical organisations would be comfortable dealing with the company; and finally it also had to have a strong sales presence and be capable of delivering good-quality sales leads.

The result was a site designed using content management, interactive flash movies, flash animation, custom-designed banners and database-driven content. To launch the site a multimedia campaign was used. This was an interactive programme that incorporated print brochures with ecards, a multimedia trade show and presentation plus an Internet marketing campaign.

The results suggest that the new design was extremely successful. In essence the new site changed the way the company approached its business. Site visitors rose 52 per cent, the number of new clients increased by a record 43 per cent, including a deal with a major pharmaceuticals company, and page views doubled to 32,000 per month.

Sales leads are now handled very quickly on the basis that it is far better to contact potential clients as soon as possible after they visit the site, so the marketing department relays potential leads to the sales department at the close of each day. Closely monitoring the behaviour of the Web visitors has sparked ZPM to create an entirely new marketing strategy for 2004.

The website remains at the core of Internet marketing and ecommerce activities and therefore it is important to attempt to evaluate a site's overall effectiveness if progress and goals are to be achieved. Many researchers have formulated methodologies and techniques to achieve this (e.g. Dreze and Zurfryden, 1997; Evans and King, 1999; Scharl, Dickenger and Murphy, 2005). However, a website does appear to have particular general parameters that need to be in position if the site is to be successful. These parameters concern access to the page (and ease of initial location), the technical specification of the page (e.g. page loading times) and the design and content in order that seekers can complete their visit goals as quickly and efficiently as possible, yet be stimulated in order to want to return another time.

Summary of key points

1. The growth of information systems and technology has been astonishing in recent years and has had a defining impact on many aspects of marketing communications. Through the Internet and Web-enabled devices and software applications, organisations have, at varying speeds, attempted to harness and adapt new technologies in order to find a competitive advantage and drive improved added value for their stakeholders.

2. Among the many benefits of IST, interactivity has had a strong impact on the shape and nature of marketing communications. Interactivity through machines with people is now complemented with interactivity with machines. The Internet has two main elements, distribution and communication, and when these are applied together ecommerce opportunities, along with Internet marketing, provide opportunities to transform the way business is conducted, shape the relationships between organisations and provide consumers with increased search convenience, lower prices and access to a wealth of information.

3. New technologies are changing the way marketing communications is used by organisations, witnessed by an increased use of below-the-line tools and a renewed interest in using communications to influence customer behaviour. The establishment of the Internet has led many organisations to reconsider the pattern and format of their marketing communications strategies, and some have not only taken the opportunity to reconfigure the way they communicate with their target audiences but also enabled their customers to reconfigure the way they interact with their preferred suppliers.

4. The characteristics of a website can be crucial in determining the length of stay, activities undertaken and the propensity for a visitor to return to the site at a later time. When the experience is satisfactory, then both the visitor and the website owner might begin to take on some of the characteristics associated with relationship marketing. Websites can be used for a variety of purposes but essentially they are either product-oriented or corporate-oriented.

5. Through online communities people who share a common interest(s) can interact, share information, develop understanding, build relationships and add value through their contribution to others involved with the website. There are four main types of community defined by their purpose, position, interest and profession.

6. In addition to an offline marketing communications mix, consideration now needs to be given to an online version. Each of the disciplines can be used in an online context, offering audiences new opportunities to engage with brands and organisations of their choice.

7. All online marketing communications activity needs to be planned and managed in just the same way as if the context was offline using traditional media. Setting suitable goals is part of this process: delivering content, enabling transaction, shaping attitudes, soliciting responses, improving retention.

8. Perhaps above all else, advances in technology have provided a catalyst for greater degrees of personalisation and one-to-one communications. It has also challenged the balance of the marketing communications mix and made IMC a more feasible strategy.

Review questions

1. Discuss ways in which use of the Internet has assisted organisations to develop their marketing communications.
2. What is multichannel marketing? Explain its key characteristics.
3. Find three examples of customer contact centres and identify ways in which they might contribute to the relationships between a brand and its customers.
4. Explain CRM and identify three reasons why it appears not to have satisfied many client organisations.
5. Discuss the nature of customer contact centres and consider how these might develop in the future.
6. Write brief notes exploring the extent to which online marketing communications needs the support of offline marketing communications.

References

Armistead, L. (2002), 'Forms sold short by bad sales technique', *Sunday Times*, 20 October, p. 17.

Armstrong, A. and Hagel III, J. (1996), 'The real value of online communities', *Harvard Business Review*, **74**(3) (May/June), pp. 134–41.

Avlonitis, G.J. and Karayanni, D. (2000), 'The impact of Internet use on business-to-business marketing', *Industrial Marketing Management*, **29**, pp. 441–59.

Barrand, D. (2004), 'Promoting change', *Marketing*, 6 October, pp. 43–5.

Bocklund, L. (2003), 'Building the next-generation customer contact center', *Network World*. Retrieved from www.nwfusion.com/auddev/pop/ 25 August 2004.

Bruner, G.C. and Kumar, A. (2000), 'Web commercials and advertising hierarchy of effects', *Journal of Advertising Research*, January/April, pp. 35–42.

Cartellieri, C., Parsons, A., Rao, V. and Zeisser, M. (1997), 'The real impact of Internet advertising', *McKinsey Quarterly*, **3**, pp. 44–63.

Chaffey, D., Mayer, R., Johnston, K. and Ellis-Chadwick, F. (2003), *Internet Marketing Strategy, Implementation and Practice*, 2nd edn, Harlow: Pearson Education.

Curtis, J. (2000), 'Not taking luxury for granted', *Marketing*, 24 August, pp. 26–7.

Dreze, X. and Zurfryden, F. (1997), 'Testing web site design and promotional content', *Journal of Advertising Research*, **39**(4) (March/April), pp. 77–91.

Durlacher (1999), 'UK online community', *Durlacher Quarterly Internet Report*, Q3, 7–11, London.

Engle, R.L. and Barnes, M.L. (2000), 'Sales-force automation usage, effectiveness and cost benefit in Germany, England and the United States', *Journal of Business and Industrial Marketing*, **15**(4), pp. 216–42.

Evans, J.R. and King, V.E. (1999), 'Business-to-business marketing and the world wide web: planning, managing and assessing web sites', *Industrial Marketing Management*, **28**, pp. 343–58.

Fill, C. (2006), *Marketing Communications: engagement, strategies and practice*, 4th edn, Harlow: FT Prentice Hall.

Forsyth, J.E., Lavoie, J. and McGuire, T. (2002), 'Segmenting the e-market', *McKinsey Quarterly*, **4**. Retrieved 10 November 2004 from www.mckinseyquarterly.com/article.

Gluck, M. and Bruner, R.E. (2005), 'The evolution of media rich advertising'. Retrieved 1 February, 2006 from http://www.doubleclick.com/us/knowledge_central/documents/RESEARCH/.

Goldsmith, R.E. and Lafferty, B.A. (2002), 'Consumer response to websites and their influence on advertising effectiveness', *Internet Research: Electronic Networking Applications and Policy*, **12**(4), pp. 318–28.

Gray, R. (2000), 'The chief encounter', *PR Week*, 8 September.

Hurme, P. (2001), 'On-line PR: emerging organisational practice', *Corporate Communications: an International Journal*, **6**(2), pp. 71–5.

Karayanni, D.A. and Baltas, G.A. (2003), 'Web site characteristics and business performance: some evidence from international business-to-business organisations', *Marketing Intelligence and Planning*, **21**(2), pp. 105–14.

Lewis, H. and Lewis, R. (1997), 'Give your customers what they want'. Cited in Chaffey et al. (2003) and Fill (2006).

Lutz, J., Mackensie, S.B. and Belch, G.E. (1983), 'Altitude toward the ad as a mediator of advertising effectiveness', *Advances in Consumer Research X*, Ann Arbor, Mich.: Association for Consumer Research.

McLuhan, R. (2000), 'A lesson in online brand promotion', *Marketing*, 23 March, pp. 31–2.

Morgan, A.J. and Inks, S.A. (2001), 'Technology and the sales-force: increasing acceptance of sales force automation', *Industrial Marketing Management*, **30**(5) (July), pp. 463–72.

Muniz, A.M. Jr and O'Guinn, T.C. (2001), 'Brand community', *Journal of Consumer Research*, **27**(4), pp. 412–32.

Nancarrow, C. and Rees, S. (2003), 'Market research and CRM'. Retrieved 21 August 2004 from http://www.wnim.com/issue21/pages/crm.htm.

O'Malley, L. and Mitussis, D. (2002), 'Relationships and technology: strategic implications', *Journal of Strategic Marketing*, **10**(3) (September), pp. 225–38.

Oxley, M. and Miller, J. (2000), 'Capturing the consumer: ensuring website stickiness', *Admap*, July/August, pp. 21–4.

Rayport, J.F. and Jaworski, B.J. (2004), *Introduction to E-commerce*, 2nd edn, New York: McGraw-Hill.

Rigby, D.K., Reichheld, F.F. and Schefter, P. (2002), 'Avoid the four perils of CRM', *Harvard Business Review*, February, pp. 101–9.

Rigby, E. (2004), 'E-tail affiliate marketing', *Revolution*, October, pp. 66–9.

Ryssel, R., Ritter, T. and Gemunden H.G. (2004), 'The impact of information technology deployment on trust, commitment and value creation in business relationships', *Journal of Business and Industrial Marketing*, **19**(3), pp. 197–207.

Scharl, A., Dickenger, A. and Murphy, J. (2005), 'Diffusion and success factors of mobile marketing', *Electronic Commerce Research and Applications*, **4**, pp. 159–73.

Sood, B. (2002), 'CRM in B2B: Developing customer-centric practices for partner and supplier relationships'. Online. Retrieved 28 April 2003 from http://www.intelligentcrm.com/020509/508feat2_2.shtml.

Stone, M. (2002), 'Managing public sector customers', *What's New in Marketing*, October. Retrieved October 2002 from www.wnim.com/.

Stone, M. and Shan, P. (2002), 'Transforming the bank branch experience for customers', *What's New in Marketing*, issue 10, September. Retrieved 23 August 2004 from http://www.wnim.com/archive/issue1003/CRM%20in%20Finance.htm.

Widmier, S.M., Jackson Jr, D.W. and McCabe, D.B. (2002), 'Infusing technology into personal selling', *Journal of Personal Selling and Sales Management*, **22**(3) (Summer), pp. 189–99.

Wightman, T. (2000), 'e-CRM: the critical dot.com discipline', *Admap*, April, pp. 46–8.

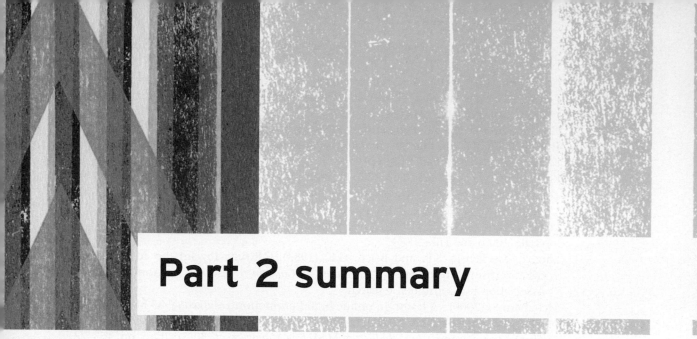

Part 2 summary

Review

This part of the book has considered some of the key issues associated with managing marketing communications. In order to use marketing communications effectively and to use scarce resources efficiently it is necessary to set strategies and to plan marketing communications activities. This part examined integration and planning, issues associated with the segmentation, targeting and positioning requirements before concluding with a view of the way in which technology has influenced the use of and dynamics associated with marketing communications.

The first chapter in this part explored ideas associated with strategy, integrated marketing communications and planning. If marketing communications strategy is to be effective it should reflect the audience-centred perspective discussed previously. Marketing communications needs to be rooted in its target audiences and the tasks that need to be completed. Hence, three main strategic approaches can be identified: push, pull and profile.

Integrated Marketing Communications (IMC) is a popular if misunderstood concept, as IMC lacks agreement about its status and definition. There is little or no empirical data to support it, yet IMC is an intuitively appealing concept. Some argue that it represents a strategic approach to marketing communications but others view it merely as good, coordinated management practice. It seems fair to say that most organisations have yet to achieve totally integrated marketing communications. At best only partial or coordinated levels of activity have so far been attained.

Planning can be regarded as different from strategy. Planning is more often concerned with the articulation of strategy. The marketing communications planning framework is itself a form of integration and offers a sequential format for the development of marketing communications plans.

The segmentation, targeting and positioning process (STP) requires that markets (audiences) be selected in order that marketing strategies and communications be directed at particular audiences to achieve particular, predetermined and measurable goals. The positioning component is a crucial aspect of marketing communications, as it is the ways audiences perceive brand messages that largely determine whether a brand is purchased.

The final chapter in this part explored the impact that technology has on marketing communications. There can be no disagreement with the notion that advances in technology have provided a catalyst for major change in the way in which marketing communications works. In particular, organisations can now personalise their communications and enter into one-to-one communications with individual customers. Indeed, the increasing use and development of methods and ideas concerning interactive communications has become a central and defining change within the world of marketing communications.

By using websites, developing online communities and adapting the traditional tools of the communications mix to work in an online environment, marketing communications has changed radically from its previous mass-media, mass-audience perspective.

Questions and exercises

1. Consider the differences between the outside-in and inside-out approach to marketing communications. What impact do these two approaches have on the management of marketing communications?

2. Identify the different types of positioning strategy and find contemporary examples of each, from a country or region of your choice.

3. Draw the marketing communications planning framework and identify the linkages between the major sections.

4. Compare and contrast the use of marketing communications in online and offline environments. Find practical examples to demonstrate your points.

5. Find examples of online communities that can be defined by their purpose, position, interest and profession. Is this a realistic way of determining online communities?

MINI CASE STUDY
Polder Locks

Polder Locks manufactures and distributes mechanical locks and anti-theft devices for a number of different markets. Of these the car market is the largest, but others include bicycles, motorcycles, lorries and various types of personal equipment.

Some 65 per cent of the $24m turnover is generated through sales of steering-wheel and pedal-based clamps. These mechanical-based products are made of carbonised steel that helps to deter thieves and criminals because they cannot be cut or drilled. In the last few years the company has developed search equipment and devices that enable stolen objects to be located and tracked using new technology such as satellite and Internet facilities. This development is referred to internally as Project Alfa. The development of a mixed-technology group

of products has been an important business strategy move for the organisation, and for marketing communications it represents a major opportunity.

Consumer-oriented promotional activities for the mechanical-based products have been based on communicating their ease of use and their role has been to inform and persuade. Black-and-white ads in newspapers and specialist-interest magazines aim to reach the target audience who are characterised by their emotional involvement with cars and their strong fear of having them stolen. Transport advertising, especially on taxis and city buses, is used extensively. In addition, attention is given to packaging and providing a distinctive difference at the point of purchase.

Garages, direct-mail catalogues and high street motor and bicycle accessory shops are the principal distribution channels. To reach these channel members, attendance at certain key exhibitions and trade fairs is regarded as an important part of the mix. Personal selling is seen as important to encourage and support these resellers and the consumer advertising campaigns are also perceived as an important part of the overall communication process. Some public-relations work is undertaken but the focus of the effort is on corporate hospitality and events for members of the marketing channel. However, the lack of any real coordination between the elements of the promotional mix and a failure to set objectives, other than those based on sales targets, appears to be a significant weakness.

The introduction of a range of products that utilise new technology has promoted an internal review about the role, nature and volume of Polder Locks' marketing communications activities. Although the finance director acknowledges the need for marketing communications to help the launch of new products, she has indicated that she wishes to see a proportional reduction in the size of the budget. She believes that, as current expenditure is not measured in a meaningful way, the promotional budget should be reduced from 7 per cent of sales to around 5 per cent. The sales director wants to recruit more specialist salespeople in order to reach new target corporate audiences, while the marketing director wants to develop a brand and this requires increased investment in promotional activities.

Project Alfa is intended for a more affluent market, people who are prepared to buy products not only to deter thieves taking their cars but to help secure their return. The marketing plan suggests that these customers are unlikely to be reached using the established distribution channels and that more specialist facilities will be required. Their higher incomes and education, and their liking for new technology, combined with their ability and willingness to spend a greater proportion of their personal wealth, suggests that a new marketing communications mix will be necessary to reach this audience. The complexity of the Project Alfa products suggests that simply making the products available on retailers' shelves and entertaining intermediaries once or twice a year will not be sufficient to penetrate the market. In addition to the consumer market it is recognised that alliances with insurance companies, fleet managers and particular car manufacturers will be required in order to maximise the growth potential of this new type of product.

Note: Fleet – a number of cars owned by a single company.

The materials used in this case study have been drawn from a variety of sources. Polder Locks is a fictitious organisation and the case is to be used for teaching and learning purposes only.

Questions

As marketing communications manager responsible to the marketing director at Polder Locks, prepare a report which answers the following questions.

1. Explain why sales-based targets may not be a suitable objective for Polder Locks' marketing communications activities. What other goals might they use?

2. Devise and justify a promotional mix for the strategy you outlined in answer to the second part of question 1.

3. Prepare brief notes explaining the communication strategies used by Polder Locks.

4. If Polder Locks were to embark on an IMC strategy, what would need to be integrated?

5. Discuss ways in which technology might be used to assist the marketing communications at Polder Locks. What might be the benefits for their audiences?

MINI CASE STUDY
Flowersbypost.com

This mini case study was written by Mike Molesworth, Senior Lecturer, Bournemouth University.

Flowersbypost (FBP) is an internet-based florist and gift retailer operating from a warehouse in Hampshire, UK. It has been trading for 18 months. The company is run by partners Daisy Campbell and Harvey McCraken. Daisy has over 15 years' experience as a florist and Harvey gave up his highly paid job in the computer industry to start FBP. Neither have any real marketing experience.

FBP specialises in next-day delivery of bouquets of flowers, but also offers other gifts: chocolate, muffins, cuddly toys and up-market food hampers through a 'sister' website, Giftsbypost (GBP). Flowers account for 89 per cent of sales by value. FBP uses the Royal Mail for deliveries and each day goods are collected from its warehouse, where orders are also made up. Delivery is 'guaranteed' next day, or the Royal Mail will refund the full cost. In the event of a failed delivery, FBP will refund the full cost of the order. Currently failed deliveries happen in fewer than one in 200 orders.

Competition is fierce in this market and currently FBP is one of over 200 firms offering online flower purchase in the UK. Many of its competitors are also small specialists, but it also competes against large florist chains, Interflora and the major supermarkets. The large players always get the top slots on the major search engines and the rest of the competitors, including FBP, fight for the next spaces through search-engine optimisation. Daisy and Harvey feel

that they are doing pretty much all they can with search-engine optimisation and have also made regular use of expensive paid-for links. Like many of their competitors, FBP also makes extensive use of affiliate sites and directories, but this too is very expensive. The advantage of affiliate programmes is that they are paid on commission and therefore only have to be paid if they produce a sale. However, most affiliates promote several online florists and gift retailers and it seems clear that when a customer uses an affiliate, loyalty to the retailer is likely to be much lower. Overall, Harvey and Daisy feel that it is something of a 'lottery' as to whether a potential customer clicks on to a particular retailer's site. They are therefore putting most of their effort into ensuring that the experience of a visitor once they arrive at FBP is as good as possible. This means that they have invested heavily in the site. They pay for studio photography of the flowers and gifts, for example, and employ an external Web design company to help build the site. They also use a third-party secure payment service. Harvey feels that, together, all these things give the impression that the company is a lot bigger than it really is. Sales since the start of trading are given in Table 1.

Although sales in the second year of trading are showing healthy increases and the company is in profit, both Daisy and Harvey are aware that, with so much competition, they need to grow the company

TABLE 1 FBP/GBP sales data by source

Quarter	Flower sales (£)				Gift sales (£)				Total (3)
	Total flowers	Direct (new)	Affiliate	Repeat	Total gifts	Direct (new)	Affiliate	Repeat	
2005 1st	69,100	31,871	29,876	7,353	9,100	4,337	2,798	1,965	78,200
2004 4th	339,100	297,899	10,178	31,023	47,900	23,433	14,867	9,600	387,000
2004 3rd	86,800	44,190	36,634	5,976	13,500	7,867	3,780	1,853	100,300
2004 2nd	128,000	68,815	52,642	6,543	9,000	5,034	2,254	1,712	137,000
2004 1st	40,300	20,842	17,982	1,476	6,400	4,457	1,476	467	46,700
2003 4th	176,300	105,263	70,675	362	21,800	17,117	4,531	152	198,100

as fast as possible. As a result they have employed an external marketing consultant. The consultant, Lily Chalk, quickly identified several key aspects of the operation that may inform further strategies for growth.

Firstly, Lily notes that FBP, and almost all their competitors offer a very similar product – simple gifts and bouquets – although GBP is more innovative than many others in the way it packages and combines gifts. Daisy explains that the similarity in offerings is because none of them use trained florists, but rather rely on casual labour. This is necessary because business is highly seasonal and because the cost of recruiting and retaining qualified staff would be too high. Experienced florists would almost certainly prefer to work in a shop where they get to talk with customers. Bouquets are therefore simple tied bunches designed by Daisy. Daisy is confident, however, that her years of experience means that FBP use the very best-quality flowers and comparisons suggest that their gifts are at least as good as their main competitors and in many ways better. Harvey also points out that over 95 per cent of orders are delivered to an address different from the billing address. As gifts are received by a third party, they are less likely to question value for money. Again, this suggests that as long as quality is acceptable, the focus should be on promoting the company and on developing the site itself. But Lily notes that, despite its professional appearance and the recognition of the importance of the user experience by Daisy and Harvey, the site lacks innovative interactive functions. It is simply presented as an online catalogue. She further observes that the same is true of almost all the competitors. Currently few, if any, offer competitive advantage through the use of interactive functions such as personal choice helpers, personalised pages, chat with a florist, or special event reminders.

Secondly, Lily also observes that a large proportion of sales seem to be coming from expensive affiliate sites, and that there is relatively little repeat business. The customer database currently holds 30,630 unique entries (total customers over the 18 months of trading). Less that 5,000 of these have ordered more than once. Lily further notes that a high proportion of repeat business is from business addresses and a significant number of the direct sales come from overseas addresses. Currently the site has a very English feel and focuses on private buyers. Daisy and Harvey confess that they have done little to encourage repeat business, or overseas business, although they do get customers to click a box allowing future communication from FBP and GBP in line with the Data Protection Act. They also confirm that a problem with affiliate business is that net profits from sales are reduced by about a half where business comes through an affiliate.

Lastly, Lily reviewed existing marketing communications. Other than the expensive affiliate links and paid-for search results, FBP and GBP have done almost no promotion. They were lucky enough to get good PR coverage in a major Sunday newspaper in the run up to Christmas 2004, but this was not planned. However, budgets for marketing communications are very low. It is unlikely that the company could afford more than about £20,000 in total on marketing in the next year and this would include any major additions to the existing website.

Lily feels that there are several key issues that need to be addressed. Firstly the company needs to consider ways in which it can differentiate itself from other retailers. In particular, this might be through the way gifts are presented on the site and the overall experience of using the site. Daisy and Harvey might also consider a focus on specific markets. Secondly, the company needs to consider ways of gaining more repeat business. Lastly, the company needs to consider ways of gaining new customers that do not rely on expensive affiliate programmes that produce little loyalty. Lily considers it important that the brands FBP and GBP are built so that consumers seek out the specific stores rather than stumble on them via searches or affiliates. Lily now sits down with Harvey and Daisy to discuss options for the future.

Questions

1. Do you agree with Lily's analysis? Are there any other issues that you think might be important?

2. Consider the issue of site development and differentiation. Should the company focus on just some sections of the gift market, and if so what? How might this be reflected in site development? Which specific interactive functions should be included and why?

3. What can be done to encourage more repeat business?

4. Given the very limited budget, what approaches might be taken to drive new customers to the site?

5. How might the various online developments be integrated with offline marketing communications approaches?

Elements of
the marketing
communications
mix

Advertising: frameworks, messages and evaluation

7

Aims and objectives

The aims of this chapter are, first, to consider different ideas about how advertising works, second, to explore some of the ways in which advertising messages can be created, and lastly, to review some of the main ways in which advertising campaigns can be measured and evaluated. There are three primary topics in this chapter:

Advertising frameworks, Messages, Measurement

The learning objectives are to enable readers to:

1. describe the principal frameworks by which advertising is thought to influence individuals;

2. evaluate the strong and the weak theories of advertising;

3. examine the use of emotions and feelings in advertising messages;

4. identify and explain the different ways in which messages can be presented to audiences;

5. explore the advantages and disadvantages of using spokespersons in message presentation;

6. explain the value and methods of pre-testing and post-testing advertisements.

Introduction

The role of advertising in marketing communications is an important one. Advertising, whether it be on an international, national, local or direct basis, is important, as it can influence audiences by informing or reminding them of the existence of a brand, or alternatively by persuading or helping them differentiate a product or organisation from others in the market.

Advertising can reach huge audiences with simple messages that present opportunities to allow receivers to understand what a product is, what its primary function is and how it relates to all the other similar products. This is the main function of advertising: to communicate with specific audiences. These may be consumer or business audiences but whatever their nature the prime objective is to build or maintain awareness of a product or an organisation.

Advertising does not have a single role, as it can be used to achieve a number of outcomes.

Advertising does not have a single role, as it can be used to achieve a number of outcomes. In DRIP terminology it can be used to differentiate and position brands, it can be used to reinforce brand messages, and it can easily inform and even persuade audiences to think and behave about and around products, services, brands and organisations. However, apart from its ability to reach large audiences, the key strengths of advertising have been to develop brand awareness, values and associations.

Management's control over advertising messages is strong; indeed, of all the elements in the promotional mix, advertising has the greatest level of control. The message, once generated and signed off by the client, can be transmitted in an agreed manner and style and at times that match management's requirements. This means that, should the environment change unexpectedly, advertising messages can be 'pulled' immediately. For example, a campaign to encourage train passengers to make more frequent journeys would have to be 'pulled' (stopped) if there was a major train accident immediately before the campaign broke. Difficulties associated with clearing the line and restoring rail services, plus the ensuing debate concerning the nature of the accident, the appropriateness of unmanned crossings or rail repairs, and the potential of further 'accidents', would prevent promotional messages from being received and processed in an unbiased and objective manner. It is more likely that there would have been a negative effect had the planned advertising been allowed to proceed.

Absolute costs can be enormous, and they impact directly on cash flow. For example, the rate-card cost of a full-page (mono) advertisement in the *Daily Mail* was £32,508 (March 2006) and a single 30-second spot, each day for one week, in the Odeon Cinema, Leicester Square in London, cost £1,160 (March 2006).

Advertising costs can be regarded in one of two ways. On the one hand, there are the absolute costs, which are the costs of buying space in magazines or newspapers or the time on television, cinema or radio. Absolute costs can be enormous, and they impact directly on cash flow. For example, the rate-card cost of a full-page (mono) advertisement in the *Daily Mail* was £32,508 (March 2006) and a single 30-second spot, each day for one week, in the Odeon Cinema, Leicester Square in London, cost £1,160 (March 2006).

On the other hand, there are the relative costs, which are those costs incurred to reach a member of the target audience with the key message. So, if an audience is measured in hundreds of thousands, or even millions on television, the cost of the advertisement spread across each member of the target audience reduces the cost per contact significantly.

The main roles of advertising are to build awareness, induce an engagement and to (re)position brands, by changing either perception or attitudes. The regular use of

ViewPoint 7.1   easyAdvertising

Rather than concentrate on differentiation or the development of brand awareness, the role of advertising at easyJet appears to be essentially about reinforcement. The airline undertakes substantial levels of in-house public relations. This is used to drive awareness levels, and is accomplished by the successful television docu-soap called *Airline*. This fly-on the-wall-type programme, which draws audiences of over 8 million, is about the everyday working life of easyJet's staff and customers at Luton airport.

All tickets are booked online so advertising's role is partly to drive site traffic. This is typified by the use of sales promotions, which are all linked to the Internet. This means customers must go online if they wish to take advantage of promotional fares.

The advertising strategy, therefore, is intended to reinforce the easyJet brand values that are based around the idea of 'consumer champion' and to drive customers to its website. The advertising also serves to position the easyJet brand based slightly on anarchy as well as price and value for money. Interestingly, the media used are essentially press, outdoor and radio plus use of its own aircraft as flying billboards. Television is not used partly because of the exposure generated by the docu-soap, partly because of the targeting and costs, and partly because of the effectiveness of the media used.

advertising, in cooperation with the other elements of the communications mix, can be important to the creation and maintenance of a brand personality. Indeed, advertising has a significant role to play in the development of competitive advantage. In some consumer markets advertising is the dominant form of communication for many organisations. Advertising can become a mobility barrier, deterring exit and, more importantly, deterring entry to a market by organisations attracted by the profits of the industry. Many people feel that some brands sustain their large market share by sheer weight of advertising – for example, the washing powder brands of Procter & Gamble and Unilever.

Advertising can also be regarded as an anchor for many integrated campaigns.

Advertising can also be regarded as an anchor for many integrated campaigns. Normally, it is necessary to use advertising to build awareness and to develop brands. Indeed, the explosion in the number of dot-com businesses and the flurry of stock-market flotations that many sought in 1999 were largely driven by the use of some television and print advertising but also by a huge amount of outdoor 48- and 96-sheet poster work, trying to raise awareness of the dot-com brands and drive traffic to their websites. In addition, public relations and sales promotions are more effective when advertising is used to raise initial awareness and shape attitudes respectively.

Advertising in the business-to-business market is geared, primarily, to providing relevant factual information upon which 'rational' decisions can be made. Regardless of the target audience, all advertising requires a message and a carrier to deliver the message to the receiver.

Emotion in advertising

The preceding material, if taken at face value, suggests that advertising only works by people responding to advertising in a logical, rational and cognitive manner. It also suggests that people only take out the utilitarian aspect of advertising messages (cleans better, smells fresher). This is obviously not true and there is certainly a strong case for the use of emotion in advertising in order to influence and change attitudes through the affective component of the attitudinal dimensions (Chapter 3).

ViewPoint 7.2   Emotion-led Tesco

Emotion in advertising can be expressed in many different ways. From 1995 to 2004 Tesco used the actresses Prunella Scales and Jane Horrocks as a slightly zany and demanding mother (called Dotty) and forbearing daughter respectively. The emotion is displayed through the various scenes where the 'mother of all shoppers' is depicted demanding more and more from Tesco employees. The message was invariably about communicating low prices, a wide range of goods, and excellent customer service despite the provocation.

In one of the many ads, Dotty was shown hauling her pregnant daughter out of ante-natal classes just to register for a Tesco Clubcard. In another she buys large carrots simply to plant in her own garden to impress a visitor. The ads had a sit-com feel to them that involved and entertained viewers while developing trust and goodwill.

It should also be remembered that advertised brands are not normally new to consumers as they have some experience of the brand, whether that be through use or just through communications. This experience affects their interpretation of advertising as memories have already been formed.

The role of feelings in the way advertisements work suggests a consumerist interpretation of how advertising works rather than the rational, which is much more a researchers' interpretation (Ambler, 1998). Consumers view advertising in the context of their experience of the category and memories of the brand. Aligned with this approach is the concept of likeability, where the feelings evoked by advertising trigger and shape attitudes to the brand and attitudes to the advertisement (Vakratsas and Ambler, 1999). Feelings and emotions play an important role in advertising especially when advertising is used to build awareness levels and brand strength.

> Consumers view advertising in the context of their experience of the category and memories of the brand.

Advertising models and concepts

Early ideas about how advertising worked were based on the logic of mirroring the purchase-decision sequence. One such model, AIDA (Strong, 1925), typifies this thinking; advertising is used to create awareness, which leads to interest, which in turn drives desire and which finally leads to action. A further model, developed most notably by Lavidge and Steiner (1961), is called the hierarchy of effects approach, assumes that there are a series of steps a prospect must pass through, in succession, from unawareness to actual purchase. Advertising, it is assumed, cannot induce immediate behavioural responses; rather, a series of mental effects must occur with fulfilment at each stage necessary before progress to the next stage is possible. Both of these, and scores of similar frameworks, are neat, simple, easy to remember and, if creating advertising materials, provide a broad template to follow.

Although intuitively attractive, this approach is essentially flawed for several reasons. Questions arise concerning what actually constitute adequate levels of awareness, comprehension and conviction, how it can be known at which stage the majority of the target audience has reached at any one point in time, and whether this purchase sequence is applicable to all consumers for all purchases? Each of the stages from the different models can be grouped in such a way that they are a representation of the three attitude components, these being cognitive (learn), affective (feel) and conative (do) orientations. The learn, feel and do approach is not applicable to all buying situations and therefore advertising cannot be assumed to work in only one particular way. These hierarchy of effects models are no longer significant and cannot logically be used as appropriate interpretations of how all advertising works.

The learn, feel and do approach is not applicable to all buying situations.

In their place a number of new frameworks and explanations have arisen, all of which claim to reflect practice and the different situations that buyers experience. In other words, these new theories about how advertising works are a reflection of practice, of the way advertising is considered to work, or at least used by advertising agencies and interpreted by marketing research agencies. The first to be considered here were developed by Hall (1992) and O'Malley (1991) and they suggest that there are four main advertising frameworks. See Table 7.1 and Exhibit 7.1.

TABLE 7.1 Advertising frameworks

Framework	Explanation
The sales framework	Based on the premise that the level of sales is the only factor that is worth considering when measuring the effectiveness of an advertising campaign. Advertising is considered to have a short-term direct and measurable impact on sales.
The persuasion framework	Persuasion is effected by gradually moving buyers through a number of sequential steps. These hierarchy of effects models (e.g. AIDA) assume that buyer decision-making is rational and can be accurately predicted.
The involvement framework	These ads work by drawing members of the target audience into the advertisement and eliciting a largely emotional response. Involvement with the product develops as a consequence of involvement with the advertisement. For example, a Yellow Pages campaign centred upon a fictional elderly gentleman called J.R. Hartley who was shown using Yellow Pages as a means of resolving a number of problems, and served to provide warmth and character that involved people not only with J.R. Hartley but also helped establish brand values. See also Exhibit 7.1.
The salience framework	Based upon the premise that advertising works by standing out, by being different from all other advertisements in the product class. The launch of Radion, a soap powder that used the twin propositions of cleaning and removing odours, was remarkable because of the advertising that was designed to 'shout' at the audience. This was achieved through the use of very bright and lurid-coloured packaging, the orange clothes worn by the presenters and the strong, dominating tone of voice. This technique was very different from the established routines used by competing brands. Tango (a canned drink) was repositioned using strikingly different, zany (and interactive) messages.

EXHIBIT 7.1 No More Nails
This ad for No More Nails is an example of the salience approach, one that seeks to stand out and be different from other ads in the category. Used with permission

Acceptance of the persuasion and salience frameworks is based on the assumption that the audience are active, rational problem-solvers and that they are perfectly capable of discriminating among brands and advertisements. Furthermore, the models bring to attention two important points about people and advertising. Advertisements are capable of generating two very clear types of response: a response to the featured product and a response to the advertisement itself. Advertising, therefore, should strive

> Advertising, therefore, should strive to communicate clear product-related information and simultaneously generate an emotional response to the ad itself.

to communicate clear product-related information and simultaneously generate an emotional response to the ad itself. For some audiences advertising creativity may be more important than the delivery of product-related information so advertising works by understanding the motivations of the target audience.

The strong and the weak theories of advertising

The explanations offered to date are all based on the premise that advertising is a potent marketing force, one that is persuasive and is done *to* people. More recent views of advertising theory question this fundamental perspective. Prominent among the theorists are Jones, McDonald and Ehrenberg, some of whose views will now be presented. Jones (1991) presented these new views as the strong theory of advertising and the weak theory of advertising.

The strong theory of advertising

All the models presented so far are assumed to work on the basis that they are capable of effecting a degree of change in the knowledge, attitudes, beliefs or behaviour of target audiences. Jones refers to this as the strong theory of advertising, and it appears to have been universally adopted as a foundation for commercial activity.

According to Jones, exponents of this theory hold that advertising can persuade someone to buy a product that they have never previously purchased. Furthermore, continual long-run purchase behaviour can also be generated. Under the strong theory, advertising is believed to be capable of increasing sales at the brand and class levels. These upward shifts are achieved through the use of manipulative and psychological techniques, which are deployed against consumers who are passive, possibly because of apathy, and are generally incapable of processing information intelligently. The most appropriate theory would appear to be the hierarchy of effects model, where sequential steps move buyers forward to a purchase, stimulated by timely and suitable promotional messages.

The weak theory of advertising

Increasing numbers of European writers argue that the strong theory does not reflect practice. Most notable of these writers is Ehrenberg (1988, 1997), who believes that a consumer's pattern of brand purchases is driven more by habit than by exposure to promotional messages.

The framework proposed by Ehrenberg is the awareness–trial–reinforcement (ATR) framework. Awareness is required before any purchase can be made, although the elapsed time between awareness and action may be very short or very long. For the few people intrigued enough to want to try a product, a trial purchase constitutes the next phase. This may be stimulated by retail availability as much as by advertising, word of mouth or personal selling stimuli. Reinforcement follows to maintain awareness and provide reassurance to help the customer to repeat the pattern of thinking and behaviour and to cement the brand in the repertoire for occasional purchase activity. Advertising's role is to breed brand familiarity and identification (Ehrenberg, 1997).

Following on from the original ATR model (Ehrenberg, 1974), various enhancements have been suggested. However, Ehrenberg added a further stage in 1997, referred to as the nudge. He argues that some consumers can 'be nudged into buying the brand more frequently (still as part of their split-loyalty repertoires) or to favour it more than the other brands in their consideration sets'. Advertising need not be any different from before; it just provides more reinforcement that stimulates particular habitual buyers into more frequent selections of the brand from their repertoire.

Advertising provides more reinforcement that stimulates particular habitual buyers into more frequent selections of the brand from their repertoire.

ViewPoint 7.3   **Nudging chocolate**

Our choice of preferred chocolate brands is fairly clear cut and considering that the amount we eat each year is so large it is difficult to see how the volume of purchases or the frequency of consumption could be improved. The role of advertising in this market is not to inform or improve awareness, as these are high enough already. The real task in this market is to assist those who are lapsed brand users to try the brand again, in other words to nudge them back to the brand.

So, rather than build brand values the focus is on consolidating or changing behaviour. Consumer buying of chocolate has also changed as impulse buying has declined and been replaced by mass purchasing at supermarkets. Consumers get cost savings and control consumption through a single weekly purchase. This pressurises advertising into helping to secure the trade listings necessary to get the product on to the supermarket shelves.

According to the weak theory, advertising is capable of improving people's knowledge, and so is in agreement with the strong theory. In contrast, however, consumers are regarded as selective in determining which advertisements they observe and only perceive those that promote products they either use or of which they have some prior knowledge. This means that they already have some awareness of the characteristics of the advertised product, so it follows that the amount of information actually communicated is limited. Advertising, Jones continues, is not potent enough to convert people who hold reasonably strong beliefs that are counter to those portrayed in an advertisement. The time available (30 seconds in television advertising) is not enough to bring about conversion and, when combined with people's ability to switch off their cognitive involvement, there may be no effective communication. Advertising is employed as a defence, to retain customers and to increase product or brand usage. Advertising is used to reinforce existing attitudes, not necessarily to drastically change them.

Unlike the strong theory, this perspective accepts that when people say that they are not influenced by advertising they are in the main correct. It also assumes that people are not apathetic or even stupid, but capable of high levels of cognitive processing.

In summary, the strong theory suggests that advertising can be persuasive, can generate long-run purchasing behaviour, can increase sales and regards consumers as passive.

The strong theory suggests that advertising can be persuasive, can generate long-run purchasing behaviour, can increase sales and regards consumers as passive.

The weak theory suggests that purchase behaviour is based on habit and that advertising can improve knowledge and reinforce existing attitudes. It views consumers as active problem-solvers.

These two perspectives serve to illustrate the dichotomy of views that has emerged about this subject. They are important because they are both right and they are both wrong. The answer to the question 'How does advertising work?' lies somewhere between the two views and is dependent upon the particular situation facing each advertiser. Where elaboration is likely to be high if advertising is to work, then it is most likely to work under the strong theory. For example, consumer durables and financial products require that advertising urges prospective customers into some form of trial behaviour. This may be a call for more information from a sales representative or perhaps a visit to a showroom. The vast majority of product purchases, however, involve low levels of elaboration, where involvement is low and where people select, often unconsciously, brands from an evoked set.

New products require people to convert or change their purchasing patterns. It is evident that the strong theory must prevail in these circumstances. Where products become established their markets generally mature, so that real growth is non-existent. Under these circumstances, advertising works by protecting the consumer franchise and by allowing users to have their product choices confirmed and reinforced. The other objective of this form of advertising is to increase the rate at which customers reselect and consume products. If the strong theory were the only acceptable approach, then theoretically advertising would be capable of continually increasing the size of each market, until everyone had been converted. There would be no 'stationary' markets.

Considering the vast sums that are allocated to advertising budgets, not only to launch new products but also to pursue market share targets aggressively, the popularity and continued implicit acceptance of the power of advertising suggest that a large proportion of resources are wasted in the pursuit of advertising-driven brand performance. Indeed, it is noticeable that organisations have been switching resources out of advertising into sales-promotion activities. There are many reasons for this (Chapter 9), but one of them concerns the failure of advertising to produce the expected levels of performance: to produce market share. The strong theory fails to deliver the expected results, and the weak theory does not apply to all circumstances. Reality is probably a mixture of the two.

Advertising to engage

Advertising has traditionally been used to develop brand identities by stimulating awareness and perception. Marketing communications has evolved such that identity and values are no longer sufficient. The growth of direct marketing and one-to-one, preferably interactive, communications have become paramount and marketing budgets have swung more towards establishing a call to action, encouraging a behaviour rather than attitudinal response. The issues that remain regard the role for advertising and the strategies that should be used. One approach would be to maintain current advertising strategies on the grounds that awareness and perception are always going to be key factors. The other extreme approach would be to call for advertising to be used solely for direct-response work. Neither of these two options seems appropriate or viable in the twenty-first century.

In an age where values and response are both necessary ingredients for effective overall communication, advertising strategy in the future will need to be based on

Many customers will choose to engage with the values offered by a brand that are significant to them individually.

engagement. Many customers will choose to engage with the values offered by a brand that are significant to them individually. However, there will also be a need to engage with them at a behavioural level and to encourage audiences to respond to the messages within advertising. Advertising strategy, indeed marketing communications strategy, should therefore reflect a brand's context and be adjusted according to the required level of engagement regarding the relationship needs of the audience, identity and image development and the required level of behavioural response. Advertising will no longer be able to rightly assume the lead role in a campaign and should be used according to the engagement needs of, first, the audience, second, the brand, and third, the communication industry, in that order.

Cohen (2003) refers to the gap between advertising used to develop brand identity and the need to encourage audience responses. He develops an OPC model where O refers to the offer, P to the product and C to the call-to-action. Advertising, therefore, should attempt to bring these elements together in a single, significant presentation. Key to his model is the brand/response (B/R) ratio, which relates to the relative levels of emphasis on the brand and response elements. The ratio refers to a line or spectrum of effects between these two elements. Traditional brand-based advertising equates with a B/R of 100/0 and direct response has a B/R of 0/100 where the sole intention is to maximise the likelihood of a response. The strategic claim behind this approach may be in need of elaboration to be operationally robust, but the principle of moving the focus of advertising strategy to one that recognises the need to incorporate brand experiences is sound.

Advertising messages

Whether advertising converts people into becoming brand-loyal customers or acts as a defensive shield to reassure current buyers, and whether central or peripheral cues are required, there still remains the decision about the nature and form of the message to be conveyed: the creative strategy. Messages (and media) are the means by which engagement can be encouraged, so attention to the construction of advertising messages is important.

In practice, the generation of suitable messages is derived from the creative brief. For the sake of discussion and analysis, consideration is given here to the *balance*, *structure* and *presentation of the message* itself to the target audience.

Message balance

It is evident from previous discussions that the effectiveness of any single message is dependent upon a variety of issues. From a receiver's perspective, two elements appear to be significant: first, the amount and quality of the information that is communicated and, second, the overall judgement that each individual makes about the way a message is communicated.

The style of a message should reflect a balance between the need for information and the need for pleasure or enjoyment in consuming the message.

This suggests that the style of a message should reflect a balance between the need for information and the need for pleasure or enjoyment in consuming the message. Messages can be product-oriented and rational or customer-oriented and based upon feelings and emotions.

There are two main factors associated with the presentation. Is the message to be dominated by the need to transmit product-oriented information or is there a need to transmit a message that appeals predominantly to the emotional senses of the receiver? The main choice of presentation style, therefore, concerns the degree of factual information transmitted in a message against the level of imagery thought necessary to make sufficient impact for the message to command attention and then be processed. It is clear that when dealing with high-involvement decisions the emphasis of the message should be on the information content, in particular the key attributes and associated benefits. This style is often factual and product-oriented. If low-involvement decision-making is present, then the message should concentrate upon the images that are created within the mind of the message recipient. This style seeks to elicit an emotional response from receivers. There are, of course, many situations where both rational and emotional messages are needed by buyers in order to make purchasing decisions.

> If low-involvement decision-making is present, then the message should concentrate upon the images that are created within the mind of the message recipient.

ViewPoint 7.4   Salon brand messages

Salon brands of haircare products, such as Toni & Guy, Paul Mitchell, Fudge and Tigi, are distributed through hair salons and use the credibility that consumers bestow upon their 'regular' hairdressers as an important means to judge salon brands. Consumers delegate decision responsibilities to their professional.

Decisions about salon brands are made as a result of interpreting both rational and emotional messages. Rational messages are driven by the superior quality of the product, the strength of the relationship held with their hairdresser and the diagnosis that hairdressers provide. Emotional messages are derived from the packaging, the quality of the relationship with the hairdresser and the imagery associated with the relative exclusivity that salon brands afford. Younger buyers perceive increased 'shower cred' and older customers perceive indulgence and a treat factor.

Message structure

An important part of message strategy is the consideration of the best way of communicating the key points, or core message, to the target audience without encountering objections and opposing points of view. The structural features of an ad message are how a message should be concluded, whether a one- or two-sided message should be used and the order in which key messages are presented. These are set out in Table 7.2.

ViewPoint 7.5   Sure conclusion

The deodorant brand Sure used screen icons Steve McQueen, Elvis and James Dean to promote its Crystal for Men range. The message was that this simple antiperspirant product minimises the white marks on clothes, and to convey this it used doctored pictures of the celebrities showing white stains on their clothes.

The message drew a conclusion for the audience whose low involvement required a clear one-sided message: white stains are bad, so use this product and you will avoid such problems.

TABLE 7.2 Message features

Structural element	Explanation	Issues
Conclusion drawing	Should the message draw a firm conclusion for the audience or should people be allowed to draw their own conclusions from the content?	● The complexity of the issue ● The level of education possessed by the receiver ● Whether immediate action is required ● The level of involvement
One- and two-sided messages	Should the case both for and against an issue or just that in favour be presented to an audience?	
Order of presentation	At what point in a message should the argument be placed for maximum influence?	Primacy effects Recency effects

Message presentation

The presentation of the message requires that an appeal be made to the target audience. The appeal is important, because unless the execution of the message appeal (the creative) is appropriate to the target audience's perception and expectations, the chances of successful communication are reduced.

There are numerous presentational or executional techniques, but the following are some of the more commonly used appeals.

Appeals based upon the provision of information

Factual

Sometimes referred to as the 'hard sell', the dominant objective of these appeals is to provide information. This type of appeal is commonly associated with high-involvement decisions where receivers are sufficiently motivated and able to process information. Persuasion is undertaken through the central processing route. This means that advertisements should be rational and contain logically reasoned arguments and information in order that receivers are able to complete their decision-making processes.

Slice of life

As noted earlier, the establishment of credibility is vital if any message is to be accepted. One of the ways in which this can be achieved is to present the message in such a way that the receiver can identify immediately with the scenario being presented. This process of creating similarity is used a great deal in advertising and is referred to as slice-of-life advertising. For example, many washing powder advertisers use a routine that depicts two ordinary women (assumed to be similar to the target receiver), invariably in a kitchen or garden, discussing the poor results achieved by one of their washing powders. Following the advice of one of the women, the stubborn stains are seen to be overcome by the focus brand.

The overall effect of this appeal is for the receiver to conclude the following: that person is like me; I have had the same problem as that person; he or she is satisfied using brand X; therefore I, too, will use brand X. This technique is simple, well tried, well liked and successful, despite its sexist overtones. It is also interesting to note that a number of surveys have found that a majority of women feel that advertisers use inappropriate stereotyping to portray female roles, these being predominantly house-wife and mother roles.

Demonstration

A similar technique is to present the problem to the audience as a demonstration. The focus brand is depicted as instrumental in the resolution of a problem. Headache remedies, floor cleaners and tyre commercials have traditionally demonstrated the pain, the dirt and the danger respectively, and then shown how the focus brand relieves the pain (Panadol), removes the stubborn dirt (Flash) or stops in the wet on a coin (or the edge of a rooftop – Continental tyres). Whether the execution is believable is a function of the credibility and the degree of lifelike dialogue or copy that is used.

> Whether the execution is believable is a function of the credibility and the degree of lifelike dialogue or copy that is used.

Comparative advertising

Comparative advertising is a popular means of positioning brands. Messages are based upon the comparison of the focus brand with either a main competitor brand or all competing brands, with the aim of establishing and maintaining superiority. The comparison may centre upon one or two key attributes and can be a good way of entering new markets. Entrants keen to establish a presence in a market have little to lose by comparing themselves with market leaders. However, market leaders have a great deal to lose and little to gain by comparing themselves with minor competitors. See ViewPoint 7.6.

ViewPoint 7.6   Duracell uses comparative bunnies

Duracell has established itself as the leading battery manufacturer in many markets, including the UK. Its advertising messages are information-based and use the strength and longevity of its batteries as the key attribute upon which it wants to be evaluated. Independent tests verify the Duracell attribute claims and prevent any counterclaim by competitors. Its positioning, with regard to ordinary zinc carbon batteries, is emphasised through the use of the strapline 'Duracell . . . lasts longer, much longer'.

One of the interesting aspects of Duracell's approach is its use of pink bunnies to symbolise the attribute. From a consumer perspective, batteries evoke little enthusiasm or engagement, yet the use of the bunnies enables consumers to connect with the Duracell brand, provides standout in the category and enables consumers to remember the key brand messages.

EXHIBIT 7.2 Duracell using bunnies in order to compare brand attributes. Used with permission © Duracell 2004 . . . 'Lasts longer, much longer*.'
* versus ordinary zinc carbon batteries.

Appeals based upon emotions and feelings

Appeals based on logic and reason are necessary in particular situations. However, as products become similar and as consumers become more aware of the range of available products, so the need to differentiate becomes more important. Increasing numbers of advertisers are using messages that seek to appeal to the target's emotions and feelings, a 'soft sell'. Cars, toothpaste, toilet tissue and mineral water often use emotion-based messages to differentiate their products.

There are a number of appeals that can be used to solicit an emotional response from the receiver. Of the many techniques available, the main ones that are observed are fear, humour, animation, sex, music, and fantasy and surrealism.

Fear

Fear is used in one of two ways. The first type demonstrates the negative aspects or physical dangers associated with a particular behaviour or improper product usage.

Drink-driving, life assurance and toothpaste advertising typify this form of appeal. The second approach is the threat of social rejection or disapproval if the focus product is not used. This type of fear is used frequently in advertisements for such products as anti-dandruff shampoos and deodorants and is used to support consumers' needs for social acceptance and approval.

Humour

The use of humour as an emotional appeal is attractive because it can draw attention and stimulate interest.

The use of humour as an emotional appeal is attractive because it can draw attention and stimulate interest. A further reason to use humour is that it can put the receiver in a positive mood. Mood can also be important, as receivers in a positive mood are likely to process advertising messages with little cognitive elaboration (Batra and Stayman, 1990). This can occur because there is less effort involved with peripheral rather than central cognitive processing, and this helps to mood protect. In other words, the positive mood state is more likely to be maintained if cognitive effort is avoided. Yellow Pages has used humour quietly to help convey the essence of its brand and to help differentiate it from the competition.

It is also argued that humour is effective because argument quality is likely to be high. That is, the level of counter-argument can be substantially reduced. Arguments against the use of humour concern distraction from the focus brand, so that although attention is drawn, the message itself is lost. With the move to global branding and standardisation of advertising messages, humour does not travel well. Whereas the level and type of humour are difficult to gauge in the context of the processing abilities of a domestic target audience, cultural differences seriously impede the transfer of jokes around the world. Visual humour (lavatorial, Benny Hill-type approaches) is more universally acceptable (Archer, 1994) than word-based humour, as the latter can get lost in translation without local references to provide clues to decipher the joke. Humour, therefore, is a potentially powerful yet dangerous form of appeal.

Animation

Animation techniques have advanced considerably in recent years, with children as the prime target audience. However, animation has been successfully used in many adult-targeted advertisements, such as those by Schweppes, Compaq, Tetley Tea, Direct Line Insurance and the Electricity Board. The main reason for using animation is that potentially boring and low-interest/involvement decisions or products can be made visually interesting and provide a means of gaining attention. A further reason for the use of animation is that it is easier to convey complex products in a way that does not patronise the viewer.

Sex

Sexual innuendo and the use of sex as a means of promoting products and services are both common and controversial. Using sex as an appeal in messages is excellent for gaining the attention of buyers. Research shows, however, that it often achieves little else, particularly when the product is unrelated. Therefore, sex appeals normally work well for products such as perfume, clothing and jewellery but provide for poor effectiveness when the product is unrelated, such as cars, photocopiers and furniture. Häagen-Dazs premium ice cream entered the UK market using pleasure as central to the message appeal. This approach was novel to the product class and the direct, natural relationship between the product and the theme contributed to the campaign's success.

The use of sex in advertising messages is mainly restricted to getting the attention of the audience and, in some circumstances, sustaining interest. It can be used openly, as in various lingerie, fragrance and perfume advertisements, such as Wonderbra and Escape; sensually, as in the Häagen-Dazs and Cointreau campaigns; and humorously in the Locketts brand.

Music

Music can provide continuity between a series of advertisements. A jingle, melody or tune, if repeated sufficiently, can become associated with the advertisement. Processing and attitudes towards the advertisement may be directly influenced by the music. Music has the potential to gain attention and assist product differentiation. Braithwaite and Ware (1997) found that music in advertising messages is used primarily either to create a mood or to send a branded message. In addition, music can also be used to signal a lifestyle and so communicate a brand identity through the style of music used.

Many advertisements for cars use music, partly because it is difficult to find a point of differentiation.

Many advertisements for cars use music, partly because it is difficult to find a point of differentiation (*Independent*, 18 October 1996), and music is able to draw attention, generate mood and express brand personality (e.g. BMW, Nissan, Peugeot and Renault).

Some luxury and executive cars are advertised using commanding background music to create an aura of power, prestige and affluence, which is combined with strong visual images in order that an association be made between the car and the environment in which it is positioned.

Fantasy and surrealism

The use of fantasy and surrealism in advertising has grown partly as a result of the increased clutter and legal constraints imposed on some product classes. By using fantasy appeals, associations with certain images and symbols allow the advertiser to focus attention on the product. The receiver can be distracted from the overall purpose of the communication and become involved with the execution of the advertisement. If this is a rewarding experience it may be possible to affect the receiver's attitudes peripherally. Readers may notice that this links to the earlier discussion on 'liking the advertisement'.

The surrealist approach does not provide or allow for closure. The conformist approach, by contrast, does require closure in order to avoid any possible counter-arguing and message rejection. Parker and Churchill argue that, by leaving questions unanswered, receivers can become involved in both the product and the execution of the advertisement. Indeed, most advertisements contain a measure of rational and emotional elements. A blend of the two elements is necessary and the right mixture is dependent upon the perceived risk and motivation that the target audience has at any one particular moment.

Evaluating advertising

One of management's prime responsibilities is to manage the organisation's resources to achieve optimum efficiency and effectiveness. The use of advertising (and, indeed, all the tools and media used in the name of marketing communications) is no exception and management must ensure that the advertising campaign used is effective. In an age where integrated marketing communications is considered good practice, questions arise about what it is that should be measured. If advertising is just one part of a campaign then surely it makes sense to measure the effectiveness of the campaign rather than the individual tools. However, it can also be argued that it is important to understand the degree to which each individual communication tools contributed to the success of a campaign. Time is spent here, and the remaining chapters in this part of the book, in considering ways in which the effectiveness of each tool of the mix can be determined. For those interested in these issues of campaign measurement, see Chapter 17 in Fill (2006).

Advertising can be considered to be a very complex business.

At one level, advertising is a relatively simple business. Understand the client's problem, design an ad and arrange for it to be placed in suitable media. At another level advertising can be considered to be a very complex business. Understanding the client's actual business problem may be far from easy (sometimes because even the client does not fully understand it), designing ads with messages that relate to an audience's various buying criteria, abilities to learn, attitudes and attention spans plus having to account for the host of variables that impact on message reception, for example perception and comprehension, render the advertising business process far from predictable or straightforward. In addition to these difficulties it is important to understand how advertising in the past was successful in order to learn how to reduce wastage and costs for future campaigns. Therefore, measuring advertising effectiveness is an important, if often underutilised, aspect of the business.

What is to be measured?

An important question is, of course, what is to be measured? Many will respond to this question with the emphatic response, sales results. This is a common measure and will be discussed later. However, it is necessary to consider two main elements, both of which should be part of the advertising objectives, namely communication and behavioural goals.

Communication goals

Advertising is used to communicate and engage with audiences, therefore measurement should be in terms of the impact advertising has had in terms of its success in communicating particular messages to target audiences.

Measurement should be in terms of the impact advertising has had in terms of its success in communicating particular messages to target audiences.

The communication effectiveness of advertising can best be observed in terms of the hierarchy of effects models referred to earlier. So, if the intention was to create awareness then measurement should be in terms of the increased number of people who are aware of the product/message as a result of the advertising campaign. Other communication-related goals are perception, understanding, comprehension, attitude and preference, and they should be measured in a similar way.

Behavioural goals

For many people, often quite senior managers, sales is the only meaningful way of measuring advertising effectiveness. In certain circumstances this may well be quite correct (for example, direct-response ads) but advertising campaigns can set out to change peoples' behaviour in other ways. For example, encouraging people to visit a website, call for a brochure, visit a store or test a product (e.g. take a test drive) are all examples of behavioural changes and it is these elements that should be measured.

Therefore, issues concerning measurement of advertising effectiveness must take into account the goals or objectives that were set for the advertising to accomplish. Readers are referred to Chapter 5 for more detail on this topic. These objectives should consist of both communications and behavioural-related elements. However, as most advertising campaigns set out to accomplish a mixture of both communications and behavioural-related changes, both should be measured.

Methods used to evaluate advertising effectiveness

Following on from the communication/behaviour issues there are of course many different approaches used to measure these different goals. The choice of method is also dependent upon the point at which measurement is to take place. Is it important to measure the effectiveness of an ad at the design stage, or is it really only worthwhile once the ad is released into the market? The first refers to pre-testing and the latter to post-testing. Table 7.3 contains a summary of the various tests that can be used at different stages in the advertising process. Emphasis here is given to post-testing.

Pre-testing

The primary purpose of testing advertisements during the developmental process is to ensure that the final creative will meet the advertising and campaign goals. The practical objective of pre-testing unfinished and finished creative work is that it is more effective for an advertiser to terminate an advertisement before costs become so large and commitment too final. The main methods used are: concept testing, focus groups, consumer juries, dummy vehicles, readability, theatre and physiological tests.

Post-testing

Testing advertisements that have been released is generally more time-consuming and involves greater expense than pre-testing. However, the big advantage with post-testing is that advertisements are evaluated in their proper environment, or at least the environment in which they are intended to be successful. The main methods used are: enquiry, recall, recognition and sales-based tests.

Inquiry tests (behavioural)

These tests are designed to measure behaviour; in particular, the number of enquiries or direct responses stimulated by advertisements. Enquiries can take the form of returned coupons and response cards, requests for further literature or actual orders, perhaps

TABLE 7.3 Methods used to evaluate advertising effectiveness

Method	Explanation
Pre-testing	Used to shape the creative aspect of an ad prior to its release. The most common methods used to pre-test advertisements are concept testing, focus groups, consumer juries, dummy vehicles, readability, theatre and physiological tests. Focus groups are the main qualitative method used and theatre or hall tests the main quantitative test.
Post-testing	Used to evaluate the effectiveness of such advertisements, once released. The most prominent techniques used are inquiry, recall, recognition and sales-based tests.
Tracking studies	A tracking study involves interviewing a large number of people on a regular basis, weekly or monthly, with the purpose of collecting data about buyers' perceptions of marketing communications messages, not just advertisements and how these messages might be affecting buyers' perceptions of the brand. By measuring and evaluating the impact of a campaign when it is running, adjustments can be made quickly. The most common elements that are monitored, or tracked, are the awareness levels of an advertisement and the brand, image ratings of the brand and the focus organisation, and attributes and preferences.
Likeability	The degree to which people enjoy an ad has the strongest correlation with future sales. This is a multifaceted concept, so that ads that are perceived as personally meaningful, relevant, informative, true to life, believable, convincing, and that stimulate interest about the brand while generating warm feelings through enjoyment of the advertisement, are regarded as reliable indicators of ad effectiveness.
Enquiry tests	These tests are designed to measure the number of enquiries or direct responses stimulated by advertisements. Enquiries can take the form of returned coupons and response cards, requests for further literature or actual orders.

An increase in the use of direct response media will normally lead to an increase in sales and leads generated by enquiry-stimulating messages.

from websites. They were originally used to test print messages, but an increasing number of television ads now carry 0870 (free) telephone numbers. An increase in the use of direct response media will normally lead to an increase in sales and leads generated by enquiry-stimulating messages, so this type of testing will become more prevalent.

Enquiry tests can be used to test single advertisements or a campaign in which responses are accumulated. Using a split run, an advertiser can use two different advertisements and run them in the same print vehicle. This allows measurement of the attention-getting properties of alternative messages. If identical messages are run in different media then the effect of the media vehicles can be tested.

Sales tests (behavioural)

If the effectiveness of advertisements could be measured by the level of sales that occurs during and after a campaign, then the usefulness of measuring sales as a testing procedure would not be in doubt. However, the practical difficulties associated with market tests are so large that these tests have little purpose. Counting the number of direct-response returns and the number of enquiries received are the only sales-based tests that have any validity.

Practitioners have been reluctant to use market-based tests because they are not only expensive to conduct but they are also historical by definition. Sales occur partly as a consequence of past actions, including past communication strategies, and the costs (production, agency and media) have already been sunk. There may be occasions where it makes little political and career sense to investigate an event unless it has been a success, or at the very least reached minimal acceptable expectations.

For these reasons and others, advertisers have used test markets to gauge the impact their campaigns have on representative samples of the national market.

Recall tests (communication)

Recall tests are designed to assess the impression that particular advertisements have made on the memory of the target audience. Interviewers, therefore, do not use a copy of the advertisement as a stimulus, as the tests are intended to measure impressions and perception, not behaviour, opinions, attitudes or the advertising effect.

ViewPoint 7.7	Swedish Printpanel

Printpanel is a Swedish-based research project supported by 126 Swedish newspapers, and conducted by TNS-Gallup set up to measure print audiences. Using a panel of 2,300 respondents, the goal is to differentiate between the performance of the media and the performance of the ad itself. Media performance refers to the delivery of a message to an 'eyes open' audience in front of the page, as opposed to how readers react to specific print messages.

Panel members report their daily reading via mobile phones, with SMS advertisement recognition questions asked via the Internet. Each panel member reports daily for 30 days, then is replaced. Since Internet and mobile phone/SMS penetration is around 80 per cent in Sweden the panel is considered reasonably representative of the adult population.

Agencies and advertisers can therefore monitor day by day how their campaigns are performing, in terms of net coverage, gross coverage and frequency. Adjustments to the campaign can be made, if necessary, while the campaign is still running.

Printpanel represents a major change in syndicated print media research, simply because it eliminates two main flaws in other systems. Firstly, it reports media exposure within a few hours, and secondly, it separates media exposure from how well the ad itself performs.

Source: Adapted from Randrup (2004). See also www.fipp.com/sadmin/1421

Recognition tests (communication)

Rather than test people's memory a different way of determining advertising effectiveness is to ask respondents if they recognise an advertisement. This is the most common of the post-testing procedures for print advertisements. One of the main methods used to measure the readership of magazines is based on frequency of reading, and generally there are three main approaches:

● *recency:* reading any issue during the last publishing interval (e.g. within the last seven days, for a weekly magazine);

- *specific issue:* reading of a specific issue of a publication;
- *frequency of reading:* how many issues a reader has read in a stated period (such as a month, in respect of a weekly magazine).

Online advertising

Most of the material so far has been developed with regard to offline, or traditional, advertising. Advertising has moved into the online and digital environments and its deployment needs to evaluated for all of the same reasons as offline communications.

The amount invested on online advertising is growing.

The amount invested on online advertising is growing; indeed, it is growing faster than any other medium. However, it should be noted that although growing at rates of 60 per cent in some quarters, online ads only account for approximately 3.9 per cent of the total amount of ad spend in the UK (IAB, 2005). Unsurprisingly, the amount, quality and impact of ad research has grown as the Internet population has soared, and the measures used have developed through trial and experience.

Online ads are predominantly banners and they are available in many shapes and sizes. Other types of ads include interstitials, pop-ups, skyscrapers, buttons, tiles and, more recently, keyword placement searches.

Banner ads

Not surprisingly, there is disagreement about whether it is possible to measure effectively online advertising. Dreze and Zurfryden (1998) rightly point out that, as a viable advertising medium, Internet advertising must be subject to suitable measurement standards to gauge the effectiveness of the medium. Web servers can indicate how many pages have been requested, the time spent on each page and even the type of computers that were used to request the page. However, this type of information is largely superficial and fails to provide insight into the user, their motivation to visit the site or the behavioural or attitudinal outcomes as a result of the interaction. Traditional measurement techniques of reach, frequency and target audience impressions are not capable of being readily transferred to the Internet.

Others argue that it is possible to measure online tools. For example, Briggs and Hollis (1997) point out that one of the more common measures used (and still is) is the click-through rate. They indicate, however, that this normally only measures behaviour, whereas what is needed is an indicator of the user's attitudes. They claim to have developed a technique to measure attitudes (online) and show that banner advertising can be one of the most effective forms of advertising and brand development.

Website effectiveness

Good marketing management practice suggests that evaluation of any management activity should always include a consideration of the degree to which the objectives have been satisfied. However, the reasons organisations have for setting up a website are many and varied. These might be to establish a Web presence, to move to new methods of commercial activity, to enter new markets, to adhere to parent-company demands or to supplement current distribution channels. Consequently, it is not practicable to set up a definitive checklist to use as a measure of website effectiveness, although certain principles need to be followed.

One of the basic approaches is to develop profiles of website visitors built up by presenting every tenth visitor with a questionnaire. The next stage will be to provide media planners with these data to optimise banner ad placement.

Dreze and Zurfryden (1998) were apprehensive of the difficulties associated with measuring the number of unique site visitors, mainly because of various technology-related factors and the difficulties of isolating who is a unique visitor. Rather than just measure click-through, it is the sales that are generated that are regarded as a more pertinent figure. These are referred to as conversions (Gordon, 2005). She also refers to a combination of immediate (click-through) and longer-term responses (view-throughs), both of which determine the actual campaign conversion rate. Therefore, just as a print ad does not result in an immediate sale and several exposures of several months are required for a print campaign to fully realise its potential, so too with online ads. A single click-through reveals very little, but view-through in time suggests interest, relevance and positive attitudes, intentions, or, to put it another way, engagement. Different types of online ads work in different ways and generate different responses. In addition, it is hard to isolate the impact of offline ads, used to drive site traffic. By monitoring both click-through and view-through conversions it becomes easier to determine when a campaign has reached its potential (and that is unlikely to be when click-through has peaked).

> The use of technology will help the measurement and evaluation of both behavioural and communication goals related to both on- and offline aspects of advertising.

In the future, the use of technology will help the measurement and evaluation of both behavioural and communication goals related to both on- and offline aspects of advertising. The technology is now in place to meter what people are watching, by appending meters not just to sets, but to people as well. Strapped-on mobile people meters can pick up signals indicating which poster site, TV or radio programme is being walked past, seen or heard respectively.

Summary of key points

1. The early sequential models, such as AIDA and the hierarchy of effects approaches, are now regarded by most researchers as too general and inadequate explanations about how advertising works and how advertising campaigns should be developed.

2. Advertising is now considered to work in other ways, two of which are to persuade audiences to behave in particular ways and to reinforce brand messages. The strong theory of advertising reflects the persuasion concept, and has high credibility when applied to new brand and product introductions. The weak theory suggests that advertising should be regarded as a means of defending customers' purchase decisions and for protecting markets, not building them. Reality suggests that the strong and the weak theories are equally applicable but not at the same time and not in the same context.

3. A more current perspective of advertising (and marketing communications) suggests that advertising should become more connected with the customer's experience of the brand and not be rooted just in the development of brand values. By engaging the audience and by using a combination of brand value and behavioural approaches, a more effective use of advertising might be achieved.

4. Only by appreciating the underlying informational and emotional needs of the target buyer, and the motivations that drive attitudes and purchase intentions, can effective advertising messages be developed.

5. The measurement and evaluation of advertising campaigns is an essential part of the management and planning process.

6. Sales measurement is the most used measurement approach, but because sales can be influenced by many variables it is not a sound approach. Both the communication and behavioural goals attached to a campaign should be considered.

7. Online and digital-based advertising should be evaluated although it is often difficult to isolate the influence of offline ads used to generate traffic to a website.

8. Online ads are measured mainly through behavioural elements, and both click-through and view-through rates should be monitored as these combine to generate conversions (sales).

Review questions

1. Write a short presentation explaining the differences between the strong and weak theories of advertising.

2. Select an organisation of your choice and find three ads it has used recently. Are the ads predominantly trying to persuade audiences or are they designed to reinforce brand values?

3. Select five print advertisements and comment on the balance of emotional and informational content. What would you do to change the balance in each?

4. What is pre- and post-testing? Write a brief report comparing recall and recognition tests.

5. What are the techniques used to measure website effectiveness? Are they any good?

6. Explain why advertising should be considered as a means of engaging audiences, and how it differs from previous ideas.

References

Ambler, T. (1998), 'Myths about the mind: time to end some popular beliefs about how advertising works', *International Journal of Advertising*, **17**, pp. 501–9.

Archer, B. (1994), 'Does humour cross borders?', *Campaign*, 17 June, pp. 32–3.

Batra, R. and Stayman, D.M. (1990), 'The role of mood in advertising effectiveness', *Journal of Consumer Research*, **17** (September), pp. 203–14.

Braithwaite, A. and Ware, R. (1997), 'The role of music in advertising', *Admap*, July/August, pp. 44–7.

Briggs, R. and Hollis, N. (1997), 'Advertising on the Web: is there response before click-through?, *Journal of Advertising Research*, **37**(2), pp. 33–46.

Cohen, A. (2003), 'Closing the brand/response gap', *Admap*, **38** (September), pp. 20–2.

Dreze, X. and Zurfryden, F. (1998), 'Is Internet advertising ready for prime time?', *Journal of Advertising Research*, May/June, pp. 7–18.

Ehrenberg, A.S.C. (1974), 'Repetitive advertising and the consumer', *Journal of Advertising Research*, **14** (April), pp. 25–34.

Ehrenberg, A.S.C. (1988), *Repeat Buying*, 2nd edn, London: Charles Griffin.

Ehrenberg, A.S.C. (1997), 'How do consumers come to buy a new brand?', *Admap*, **32** (March), pp. 20–4.

Fill, C. (2006), *Marketing Communications: engagement, strategies and practice*, 4th edn, Harlow: FT Prentice Hall.

Gordon, K. (2005), '3 Tips for Measuring Online Success'. Retrieved from www.newsletter.interland.com, 30 May 2005.

Hall, M. (1992), 'Using advertising frameworks', *Admap*, **27** (March), pp. 17–21.

IAB (2005), '2004: Online Adspend leaps 60%'. Retrieved from www.iabuk.net/ knowledgebank/, 30 May 2005.

Jones, J.P. (1991), 'Over-promise and under-delivery', *Marketing and Research Today*, November, pp. 195–203.

Lavidge, R.J. and Steiner, G.A. (1961), 'A model for predictive measurements of advertising effectiveness', *Journal of Marketing*, October, p. 61.

O'Malley, D. (1991), 'Sales without salience?', *Admap*, **26** (September), pp. 36–9.

Parker, R. and Churchill, L. (1986), 'Positioning by opening the consumer's mind', *International Journal of Advertising*, **5**, pp. 1–13.

Randrup R. (2004), 'Why newspaper ads are effective', *Admap*, **39**(6) June, pp. 47–9.

Strong, E.K. (1925) *The Psychology of Selling*, New York: McGraw-Hill.

Vakratsas, D. and Ambler, T. (1999), 'How advertising works: what do we really know?', *Journal of Marketing*, **63** (January), pp. 26–43.

Media: traditional, digital and planning

8

Aims and objectives

The aims of this chapter are, first, to consider the characteristics of traditional and digital media, and second, to explore some of the principal issues and concepts associated with media planning. There are three primary topics in this chapter:

Types of media, Media planning, Measurement

The learning objectives are to enable readers to:

1. describe the different types and characteristics of the main media;
2. explain the impact of media and audience fragmentation;
3. describe the main tasks associated with media planning;
4. explain some of the key concepts used in media selection;
5. discuss some of the issues associated with media planning;
6. consider media source effects as an important factor in their selection;
7. set out the different ways in which campaigns can be scheduled.

Introduction

This chapter explains the main characteristics associated with each of the primary traditional and digital media. It also considers issues relating to media planning.

Organisations use the services of a variety of media in order that they can deliver their planned messages to target audiences. Of the many available media, six main classes can be identified. These are broadcast, print, outdoor, new, in-store and other media classes. Within each of these classes there are particular media types. For example, within the broadcast class there are television and radio, and within the print class there are newspapers and magazines.

Of the many available media, six main classes can be identified.

Within each type of medium there are a huge number of different media vehicles that can be selected to carry an advertiser's message. For example, within UK television there are terrestrial networks (Independent Television Network, Channel 4 and Channel 5) and the satellite (BSkyB) and cable (e.g. NTL) networks. In print, there are consumer and business-oriented magazines, and the number of specialist magazines is expanding rapidly. These specialist magazines are targeted at particular activity and interest groups, such as *Amateur Photographer*, *Golf World* and the infamous *Potato Storage Monthly*. This provides opportunities for advertisers to send messages to well-defined homogeneous groups, which improves effectiveness and reduces wastage in communication spend. There are, therefore, three forms of media: classes, types and vehicles. See Table 8.1.

TABLE 8.1 A summary chart of the main forms of media

Class	Type	Vehicles
Broadcast	Television	*Coronation Street*, *Big Brother*
	Radio	Virgin 1215, Classic FM
Print	Newspapers	The *Sunday Times*, the *Daily Mirror*, the *Daily Telegraph*
	Magazines: Consumer	*Cosmopolitan*, *FHM*, *Woman*
	Business	*The Grocer*, *Plumbing News*
Outdoor	Billboards	96- and 48-sheet
	Street furniture	Adshel
	Transit	London Underground, taxis, hot-air balloons
New media	Internet	Websites, email, intranet
	Digital television	Teletext, SkyText, Ceefax
	CD-ROM	Various: music, educational, entertainment
In-store	Point of purchase	Bins, signs and displays
	Packaging	The Coca-Cola contour bottle
Other	Cinema	Pearl & Dean
	Exhibitions	Ideal Home, the Motor Show
	Product placement	Films, TV, books
	Ambient	Litter bins, golf holes, petrol pumps, washrooms
	Guerrilla	Flyposting

Evaluative criteria

One of the key marketing tasks is to decide which combination of (media) vehicles should be selected to carry a client's message to the target audience. This type of decision can only be made once an understanding of the fundamental characteristics of the available media has been achieved. The fundamental characteristics concern the costs, delivery and audience profile associated with a communication event.

Costs

There are two types of cost: absolute and relative.

One of the important characteristics concerns the costs that are incurred using each type of medium. There are two types of cost: absolute and relative. *Absolute costs* are the costs of the time or space bought in a particular media vehicle. For example, the cost of a full-page, single-insertion black-and-white advertisement, booked for a firm date in the *Sunday Times*, is £56,150 (November 2004). Cash flow is affected by absolute costs.

Relative costs are the costs incurred when making contact with each member of the target audience and is calculated by taking the absolute cost (of a media buy) and dividing it by the total number of individuals reached with the message. Television, as will be seen later, has a high absolute cost but, because messages are delivered to a mass audience, the relative cost is very low.

Communication (of the message)

The way in which an advertiser's message is delivered to the target audience varies across media. Certain media, such as television, are able to use many communication dimensions, and through the use of sight, sound and movement can generate great impact with a message. Other types of media have only one dimension, such as the audio capacity of radio. The number of communication dimensions that a media type has will influence the choice of media mix. This is because certain products, at particular points in their development, require the use of different media in order that the right message is conveyed and understood. A new product, for example, may require demonstration in order that the audience understands the product concept. The use of television may be a good way of achieving this. Once understood, the audience does not need to be educated in this way again and future messages need to convey different types of information that may not require demonstration, so radio or magazine advertising may suffice.

Audience profile

The profile of the target audience (male, female, young or old) and the number of people

The profile of the target audience (male, female, young or old) and the number of people within each audience that a medium can reach are also significant factors in media decisions.

within each audience that a medium can reach are also significant factors in media decisions. For example, 30 per cent of adults in the socio-economic group A read the *Sunday Times*. Only 4 per cent of the C2 group also read this paper. Messages appropriate to the A group would be best placed in the *Sunday Times* and those for the C2 group transmitted through the *News of the World*, which 34 per cent of the C2 group read. It is important that advertisers use media vehicles that convey their messages to their target markets with as little waste as possible. Newspapers enable geographically based target audiences to be reached. The tone of their content can be controlled, but the cost per target reached is high. Each issue has a short lifespan, so for positive learning to occur in the target audience a number of insertions may be required.

A large number of magazines contain specialised material that appeals to particular target groups. These special-interest magazines (SIMs) enable certain sponsors to reach interested targets with reduced wastage. General-interest magazines (GIMs) appeal to a much wider cross-section of society, to larger generalised target groups. The life of these media vehicles is generally long and their 'pass along' readership high. It should not be forgotten, however, that noise levels can also be high owing to the intermittent manner in which magazines are often read and the number of competing messages from rival organisations.

ViewPoint 8.1 Glamorous Guardians

In September 2005, *The Guardian* newspaper relaunched itself in a new format. Officially known as a *Berliner*, the redesigned paper reaches the news-stands folded smaller than a tabloid. Reacting to falling sales and competitors such as *The Independent* and *The Times*, which had already moved to a tabloid format, *The Guardian* used substantial television and poster campaigns to reach both current and lapsed readers. The campaign sought to inform and retain current readers of the change and to reach lapsed readers in an attempt to persuade them to return to the paper.

When *Glamour* was launched in March 2001 the new publication from Condé Nast also received huge marketing communications support. This included a £4.5 million campaign featuring television, print, outdoor and cinema. In addition, public relations generated a huge amount of publicity about the A5 'handbag-sized' format.

Part of the rationale for the radically different size was not only the success experienced in the United States and Italy, where the format has been successful for over seven years, but also the trend towards miniaturisation (Walkmans, mobile phones) and the fashion appeal that the smaller size might represent. In addition, however, is the high impact the smaller size has in standing out on the shelves of newsagents among the clutter of the established, larger, heavyweight competitors.

Television reaches the greatest number of people, but although advertisers can reach general groups, such as men aged 16–24 or housewives, it is not capable of reaching specific groups and incurs high levels of wastage. This blanket coverage offers opportunities for cable and satellite entrepreneurs to offer more precise targeting, but for now television is a tool for those who wish to talk to mass audiences. Television is expensive from a cash-flow perspective but not in terms of the costs per target reached.

> Television is expensive from a cash-flow perspective but not in terms of the costs per target reached.

Radio offers a more reasonable costing structure than television and can be utilised to reach particular geographic audiences. For a long time, however, this was seen as its only real strength, particularly when its poor attention span and non-visual dimensions are considered. Research in the 1990s, however, indicated that it is not destined to remain the poor relation to television, as radio has been shown to be capable of generating a much closer personal relationship with listeners, witnessed partly by the success of Classic FM and Virgin 1215, than is possible through posters, television or print.

The use of direct marketing has grown in recent years, as technology has developed and awareness has increased. The precise targeting potential of direct mail and its ability to communicate personally with target audiences is impressive. In addition, the control over the total process, including the costs, remains firmly with the sponsor.

Print media

Of the total amount spent on advertising, across all media, most is spent on the printed word. Newspapers and magazines are the two main types of media in this class. They attract advertisers for a variety of reasons, but the most important is that print media are very effective at delivering a message to the target audience.

Most people have access to either a newspaper or a magazine. They read in order to keep up to date with news and events or to provide themselves with a source of entertainment. People tend to have consistent reading habits and buy or borrow the same media vehicles regularly. For example, most people read the same type of newspaper(s) each day and their regular choice of magazine reflects either their business or leisure interests, which are normally quite stable. This means that advertisers, through marketing research, are able to build a database of the main characteristics of their readers. This in turn allows advertisers to buy space in those media vehicles that will be read by the sort of people they think will benefit from their product or service.

> The printed word provides advertisers with the opportunity to explain their message in a way that most other traditional media cannot.

The printed word provides advertisers with the opportunity to explain their message in a way that most other traditional media cannot. Such explanations can be in the form of either a picture or a photograph, perhaps demonstrating how a product is to be used. Alternatively, the written word can be used to argue why a product should be used and detail the advantages and benefits that consumption will provide the user. In reality, advertisers use a combination of these two forms of communication.

The print media are most suitable for messages designed when high involvement is present in the target market. These readers not only control the pace at which they read a magazine or newspaper but also expend effort to read advertisements because they care about particular issues. Where elaboration is high and the central processing route is preferred, messages that provide a large amount of information are best presented in the printed form.

Magazines are able to reach quite specialised audiences and tend to be selective in terms of the messages they carry. In contrast, newspapers reach a high percentage of the population and can be referred to as a mass medium. The messages that newspapers carry are usually for products and services that have a general appeal.

Newspapers

Expenditure on newspaper advertising increased steadily in the 1980s, fell back sharply with the recession in the early 1990s, and has since slowly redeveloped its position. Since 1986 newspaper readership has fallen, but the biggest shift has been away from the popular press with some movement towards the quality press. In 2004 expenditure on national newspaper advertising reached £1.9 billion or 13 per cent of the total UK advertising spend (Advertising Association, 2005).

Readers have a positive view of newspaper advertisements because they are in control of the speed and depth of reading the newspaper.

Readers have a positive view of newspaper advertisements because they are in control of the speed and depth of reading the newspaper. This means that they choose which advertisements to read. Statistics show that newspaper circulation has fallen behind population growth; furthermore, there is a declining trend in the number of teenagers and young adults who read newspapers.

Printing technologies advanced considerably during the last two decades but the relatively poor quality of reproduction, compared with magazines, means that the impact of advertisements can often be lost.

Magazines

In a market that is extremely competitive, the overall trend is that the number of monthly consumer magazines has grown, mainly at the expense of weekly magazines. Advertising revenue, at around £819 million, rose slightly in 2004 after a couple of years of no growth (Advertising Association, 2005). This slight increase was reflected in business magazines advertising, which rose by 3.2 per cent. Business magazines attract nearly a third as much advertising revenue as the consumer sector, despite being highly fragmented and complex. The fastest growing part of the consumer magazine market has been the men's lifestyle sector, where titles such as *Loaded*, *FHM* and *Men's Health* established themselves quickly. However, circulation and advertising revenues have started to fall.

The visual quality of magazines is normally very high, a result of using top-class materials and technologies. This provides advertisers with greater flexibility in the way in which the visual dimension is used to present their messages, which can be used to create impact and demand the attention of the reader.

Magazines are often passed along to others to read once the original user has finished reading it. However, magazine audience growth rates have fallen behind the growth in advertising rates, so the value of advertising in magazines has declined relative to some other types of media. The long period of time necessary to book space in advance of publication dates and to provide suitable artwork means that management has little flexibility once it has agreed to use magazines as part of the media schedule.

Customer magazines differ from consumer magazines because they are sent to customers direct, often without charge, and contain highly targeted and significant brand-related material. These have made a big impact in recent years and, partly because of high production values, have become a significant aspect of many direct-marketing activities.

ViewPoint 8.2   Parenting-based customer titles

The number of customer magazines has grown in recent years across a variety of sectors. *M&S Magazine*, Waitrose's *Food Illustrated*, Honda's *Dream* and Boots' *Health and Beauty* are just some of the more prevalent titles. In spring 2005 the NSPCC, in a co-branding alliance with Woolworths, launched *Your Family*. This is a quarterly magazine and is part of the charity's positive parenting campaign. Distributed free through Woolworths' stores, the magazine will be funded through advertising and compete against paid-for consumer magazine titles, *Practical Parenting* and *BBC Parenting*.

One final form of print media yet to be discussed concerns directories. Advertising expenditure on directories has continued to increase. One of the largest consumer directories is Yellow Pages, or Yell as it is now called as it has diversified across new media (e.g. Yell.com). Directories account for 12 per cent of press advertising and 25 per cent of classified advertising revenues.

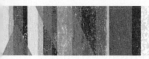

Broadcast media

Broadcast media are quite young in comparison with the printed word. Fundamentally, there are two main forms of broadcast – television and radio – to which attention will be given here. Advertisers use these classes of media because they can reach mass audiences with their messages at a relatively low cost per target reached.

The majority of viewers use television passively.

The majority of viewers use television passively, as a form of entertainment; however, new technological applications, such as digitalisation, indicate that television will be used proactively for a range of services, such as banking and shopping. Radio demands active participation, but can reach people who are out of the home environment.

Broadcast media allow advertisers to add visual and/or sound dimensions to their messages. The opportunity to demonstrate or to show the benefits or results that a particular product can bring give life and energy to an advertiser's message. Television uses sight, sound and movement, whereas radio can only use its audio capacity to convey meaning. Both media have the potential to tell stories and to appeal to people's emotions when transmitting a message. These are dimensions that the printed media find difficulty in achieving effectively within the time allocations that advertisers can afford.

Advertising messages transmitted through the broadcast media use a small period of time, normally 60, 30 or 20 seconds, that the owners of the media are prepared to sell. The cost of the different time slots varies throughout a single transmission day and with the popularity of individual programmes. The more listeners or viewers that a programme attracts, the greater the price charged for a slice of time to transmit an advertising message. This impacts upon the costs associated with such advertising. The time-based costs for television can be extremely large. For example, as at 4 November 2005, the rate-card cost of a nationwide 30-second spot in the middle of *Coronation Street* was £82,932 (www.itvsales.com). However, this large cost needs to be put in perspective. The actual cost of reaching individual members of the target audience is quite low, simply because all of the costs associated with the production of the message and the purchase of time to transmit the message can be spread across a mass of individuals, as discussed earlier.

The costs associated with radio transmissions are relatively low when compared with television.

The costs associated with radio transmissions are relatively low when compared with television. This reflects the lack of prestige that radio has and the pervasiveness of television. People are normally unable, and usually unwilling, to become actively involved with broadcast advertising messages. They cannot control the pace at which they consume such advertising and as time is expensive and short, so advertisers do not have the opportunity to present detailed information. The result is that this medium is most suitable for low-involvement messages, where the need for detailed information processing and consideration of the purchase itself is low. Messages transmitted through electronic media should seek to draw attention, create awareness and improve levels of interest.

As the television and radio industries become increasingly fragmented, so the ability to reach particular market segments improves. This means that the potential effectiveness of advertising through these media increases. These media are used a great deal by consumer markets, mainly because of their ability to reach mass audiences. Messages targeted at other organisations need to be delivered by other media that are more selective and controlled more effectively.

Television

For a number of years there was above inflation growth in television advertising expenditure but when the dot-com bubble burst in 2000, revenue growth stopped abruptly and station average prices have been falling by anything up to 30 per cent, causing major difficulties for the various television-company owners. Annual growth in 2003 was just 1 per cent, but this increased to 5.4 per cent in 2004.

The number of households connected to cable networks represented 13.2 per cent of all homes by December 2003. More importantly, the percentage of homes connected as a percentage of the number of homes that could be connected rose from 21 per cent in 1996 to 26.6 per cent in 2003.

From a creative point of view, this medium is very flexible and the impact generated by the combination of sight and sound should not be underestimated. The prestige and status associated with television advertising is higher than that of other media: in some cases, the credibility and status of a product or organisation can be enhanced significantly just by being seen to be advertising on television. However, because the length of any single exposure is short, messages have to be repeated in order to enhance learning and memory. This increases the absolute costs of producing and transmitting television commercials, which can be large, making this medium the most expensive form of advertising.

Radio

Advertising expenditure on radio reached £604 million in 2004, a growth of 3.4 per cent on the previous year. Interest in radio has continued over a number of years recently, possibly due to changing lifestyles and a recognition of the versatility of what is often regarded as a secondary medium.

Radio permits specialised programming, which in turn attracts selective audiences.

Radio permits specialised programming, which in turn attracts selective audiences. Radio is a mobile medium (that is, one that can travel with audiences), so that messages can be relayed to them, for example, even when shoppers are parking their cars near to a shopping precinct. The production costs are low and radio has great flexibility, which management can use to meet changing environmental and customer needs. If it is raining in the morning, an advertiser can implement a promotional campaign for umbrellas in the afternoon.

From a creative point of view the medium needs the active imagination of the listener. Radio has a high level of passive acceptance and the messages that are received are more likely to be retained than if they were delivered via a different medium. This combination of features makes radio an excellent support medium. However, because there is an absence of visual stimuli, the medium lacks impact and the ability to hold and enthuse an audience. Levels of inattentiveness can be high, which means that a large number of messages are invariably ignored or missed. When this is combined with low average audiences, high levels of frequency are required to achieve acceptable levels of reach.

Outdoor media

The range of outdoor media encompasses a large number of different media, each characterised by two elements. First, they are observed by their target audiences at locations away from home. Secondly, they are normally used to support messages that are transmitted through the primary media: broadcast and print. Outdoor media can, therefore, be seen to be a secondary but important support media for a complementary and effective media mix.

Outdoor media consist of three main formats: street furniture (such as bus shelters); billboards (which consist primarily of 96-, 48- and 6-sheet poster sites); and Transit (which covers the underground, buses and taxis). Outdoor media revenues, which reached £986 million in 2004, accounted for approximately 5.4 per cent of total advertising expenditure and have steadily been taking an increasing percentage of organisations' media spend.

Other reasons for the growth in outdoor expenditure are that it can reinforce messages transmitted through primary media, act as a substitute media when primary media are unavailable, and provide novelty and interest (electronic, inflatable and three-dimensional billboards), which can help avoid the clutter caused by the volume of advertising activity.

Billboards and street furniture

These are static displays and, as with outdoor media generally, are unable to convey a great deal of information in the short period of time available that people can attend to the messages. However, advances in technology permit precise targeting of poster campaigns on a national, regional or individual audience basis, or by their proximity to specific outlets, such as banks, CTNs (confectioner, tobacconist and newsagent) and off-licences.

One of the main advantages of this medium springs from its ability to reach a large audience. This means that most members of a target audience are likely to have an opportunity to see the message, so the cost per contact is very low. It has become recognised that outdoor media can provide tremendous support to other tools in the media mix, particularly at product launch, as back-up and when attempting to build brand-name recognition.

> Outdoor media can provide tremendous support to other tools in the media mix.

The medium is characterised by its strong placement flexibility. Messages can be placed geographically, demographically or by activity, such as on the main routes to work or shopping. The potential impact is high, as good sites can draw the eye and make an impression. However, messages transmitted by this medium do not allow for the provision of detailed information. Posters are passed very quickly and the potential attention span is therefore brief. This means that the message must be short, have a high visual impact and be capable of selling an idea or concept very quickly.

Transit

Transit or transport advertising is best represented by the names and signs that are painted on the sides of lorries. These moving posters, which travel around the country, serve to communicate names of organisations and products to all those who are in the vicinity of the vehicle. Indeed, transport advertising includes all those vehicles that are used for commercial purposes. In addition to lorries, transport media include buses, the Underground (trains, escalators and walkways), taxis, planes, blimps and balloons, ferries and trains, plus the terminals and buildings associated with the means of transport, such as airports and railway stations.

The exposure time given to messages delivered via transport media can be high, but is dependent upon the journey time of the reader. The high readership scores that are recorded are due, possibly, to the boredom levels of travellers. The cost is relatively low, mainly because no extra equipment is necessary to transmit the message. Local advertisers tend to benefit most from transport advertising, as it can remind buyers of particular restaurants, theatres and shops. However, the medium fails to cover all market segments, as only particular groups use transportation systems. In comparison with other media it lacks status, is difficult to read (particularly in the rush hour) and suffers from the high level of clutter associated with inside cards.

Cinema

There has been a revival in the level of expenditure on cinema advertising, reflecting the trends in audience sizes. In 2004 cinema advertising was worth £192 million, or approximately 1 per cent of total advertising spend. The number of people visiting cinemas in the United Kingdom has grown considerably in recent years and attendances reached 171 million in 2004 (CAA/EDI). This growth is linked to the increase in multiplex cinemas (multiple screens at each site). With customer satisfaction levels improving, advertisers have consistently increased the adspend in this medium. Advertising messages transmitted in a cinema have all the advantages of television-based messages. Audio and visual dimensions combine to provide high impact. However, the audience is more attentive because the main film has yet to be shown and there are fewer distractions or noise in the communication system.

Cinema advertising has greater power than television advertisements.

This means that cinema advertising has greater power than television advertisements. This power can be used to heighten levels of attention and, as the screen images are larger than life and because they appear in a darkened room that is largely unfamiliar to the audience, the potential to communicate effectively with the target audience is strong.

The mood of the audience is generally positive, particularly at the start of a show. This mood can be carried over into the commercials. Furthermore, the production quality of cinema messages is usually very high and transmission is often assisted by high-quality audio (digital surround-sound systems) that is being installed in the new multiplex arenas.

The production and transmission costs are quite low, which makes this an attractive media vehicle. However, if an advertiser wishes to reach a national audience, the costs can be much higher than those for television.

The audience profile for UK cinema admissions indicates that approximately 80 per cent of visitors are aged 15–34. With an increasing proportion of the population aged over 55 (the grey market), cinema advertising is limited by the audience profile and the type of products and services that can be realistically promoted.

ViewPoint 8.3	Kidman turns heads in cinemas

Cinema advertising was boosted by the debut of Chanel No. 5's new ad in the premiere of *Bridget Jones: The Edge of Reason*. The production costs of the ad, at £18 million, were reputed to be the most expensive ad made to date and the decision to show the ad in the cinema before breaking it on television was greeted as a positive endorsement for the medium.

The celebrity star was Nicole Kidman, who at the time was reputedly considering the role as Coco Chanel in a film to be made about the fashion designer's life. The only reference to the brand appears at the end of the ad when Kidman is shown wearing a pendant saying No. 5.

In-store media

As an increasing number of brand-choice decisions are made during the shopping experience, advertisers have become aware of the need to provide suitable in-store communications. The primary objective of using in-store media is to direct the attention of shoppers and to stimulate them to make purchases. The content of messages can be easily controlled by either the retailer or the manufacturer. In addition, the timing and the exact placement of in-store messages can be equally well controlled.

Of the two main forms of in-store media, point-of-purchase displays and packaging, retailers control the former and manufacturers the latter. Increasingly there is recognition of the huge potential of retail stores becoming an integrated media centre, with retailers selling and managing media space and time.

Point of purchase

There are a number of POP techniques, but the most used are window displays, floor and wall racks to display merchandise, posters and information cards, plus counter and checkout displays. Supermarket trolleys with a video screen attached have been trialled

ViewPoint 8.4	Out of the home and into the community

The use of new technology to reach targeted audiences outside the home is a reflection of the breakdown in the use of traditional media. With audiences fragmenting, clients are searching for new ways and techniques of reaching customers. One of these approaches involves using outdoor media where communities or naturally forming groups of people gather outside the home.

One such group forms in stores and supermarkets, and the rapid development of in-store media (see below) is a sign of the media industry's search for pull rather than push-based media. Another approach has been to use media in order to engage audiences. For example, Yahoo used the 22-storey-high Reuters giant screen in New York to display a public virtual car-racing game, in order to promote its motoring pages at the time of the New York motor show.

Source: Silverman (2004)

by a number of stores. As soon as the trolley passes a particular infrared beam a short video is activated, promoting brands available in the immediate vicinity of the shopper. Other advances include electronic overhead signs, in-store videos at selected sites around the store and coupons for certain competitive products dispensed at the checkout once the purchased items have been scanned.

End-of-row bins and cards displaying special offers are POP media that aim to stimulate impulse buying. Point-of-purchase media are good at attracting attention and providing information, while the absolute and relative costs of POP advertisements are low. However, these messages are usually directed at customers who are already committed, at least partly, to purchasing the product or one from their evoked set. POP messages certainly fail to reach those not actively engaged in the shopping activity.

> Point-of-purchase media are good at attracting attention and providing information, while the absolute and relative costs of POP advertisements are low.

Packaging

Apart from its core role to protect and preserve products, packaging has become a significant contributor to the way consumers make brand-choice decisions. Low-involvement decision-making requires peripheral cues to stimulate buyers into action. It has already been noted that decisions made at the point of purchase, especially those in the FMCG sector, often require buyers to build awareness through recognition. The design of packages and wrappers is important, as continuity of design in combination with the power to attract and hold the attention of prospective buyers is a vital part of point-of-purchase activity.

There are a number of dimensions that can affect the power and utility of a package. Colour is influential and should be appropriate to the product class, to the brand and to the prevailing culture if marketing overseas. The shape of the package may reflect a physical attribute of the product itself and can be a strong form of persuasion. Verebelyi (2000) suggests that this influence may be due to the decorative impact of some brands. Various domestic lavatory cleaners have a twist in the neck or a trigger action, facilitating directable and easier application. The shape may also provide information about how to open and use the product, while some packages can be used after the product has been consumed for other purposes. For example, some jars can be reused as food containers, so providing a means of continual communication for the original brand in the home.

Packaging can also be used as a means of brand identification, as a cue by which buyers recognise and differentiate a brand. The supreme example of this is the Coca-Cola contour bottle, with its unique shape and immediate power for brand recognition at the point of purchase.

Retail media centres

Supermarkets have begun to recognise the media potential that lies within their stores. For example, Tesco and Asda-Walmart have installed various in-store plasma television screens and are selling television time according to product category, some of which equates directly with particular aisles and store space. In addition, Asda-Walmart has created its own media (or sales) centre through which media activities are to be coordinated. Based on its own publishing facilities this change may impact on media planning and change the way established media houses account for the new retail media environment.

TABLE 8.2 Ambient media categories

Ambient category	Explanation
Standard posters	Washrooms, shopping trolleys, phone boxes
Distribution	Tickets, receipts, carrier bags
Digital	Video screens, projections, LED screens
Sponsorships	Playgrounds, golf holes, petrol pump nozzles
Mobile posters	Lorries, barges, sandwich boards
Aerials	Balloons, blimps, towed banners

Source: Advertising Association's *Advertising Statistics Yearbook*, published by the World Advertising
Research Centre, 2004

Ambient media

Ambient media are a fairly recent innovation and represent a non-traditional alternative to outdoor media. Ambient media are regarded as out-of-home media that fail to fit any of the established outdoor categories. Ambient-driven advertising revenue, although relatively small, grew from £101 million in 2001 to £113 million in 2002. Ambient media can be classified according to a variety of factors. See Table 8.2. Of these, standard posters account for the vast majority of ambient activity (59 per cent) with distribution accounting for 24 per cent and the four remaining categories just 17 per cent.

> Ambient-driven advertising revenue, although relatively small, grew from £101 million in 2001 to £113 million in 2002.

Direct-response media

The principal use of the media is to convey one of two types of message: one is oriented towards the development of brand values and attitudes; the other is aimed at provoking a physical (and mental) response. It follows that attitude- and response-based communications require different media.

Conventional media (television, print or radio), once used just to develop brands and attitudes, are now used as a mechanism or device to provoke a response through which consumers/buyers can follow up a message, enter into an immediate dialogue and either request further information or purchase goods. The main difference with new media is the time delay or response pause between receiving a message and acting upon it. Through direct-response mechanisms the response may be delayed for as long as it takes to make a telephone call, press a button or fill out a reply coupon. However, the response pause and the use of a separate form of communication highlight the essential differences.

Estimates vary, but somewhere between 30 per cent and 40 per cent of all television advertisements now carry a telephone number or Web address. Direct-response television (DRTV) is attractive to those promoting service-based offerings, and increasingly FMCG brands such as Tango, Pond's face creams and Pepperami have used it.

One aspect that is crucial to the success of a direct-response campaign is not the number of responses but the conversion of leads into sales.

One aspect that is crucial to the success of a direct-response campaign is not the number of responses but the conversion of leads into sales. This means that the infrastructure to support these promotional activities must be thought through and put in place, otherwise the work and resources put into the visible level will be wasted if customers are unable to get the information they require.

The provision of the infrastructure itself is not sufficient. The totality of the campaign should support the brand. Indeed, this is an opportunity to extend brand opportunities and provide increased brand experiences. For example, many brands use direct response to involve consumers in the brand and to encourage greater identification with the brand's values. Telemarketing programmes require that the tone of voice and the content the respondents hear provide opportunities for entertainment, added value and an extension of the advertisement that drives the behaviour. This opportunity to extend the brand experience has to be adapted in different ways when texting is the format. Whatever is offered, the brand must give something back in order that interaction occurs.

Digital media

In comparison with traditional media, the Internet and digital media facilities provide an interesting contrast. See Table 8.3. Space (or time) within traditional media is limited and costs rise as demand for the limited space/time increases. On the Internet, space is unlimited so absolute costs remain very low and static, while relative costs plummet as more visitors are recorded as having been to a site. Another aspect concerns the focus of the advertising message. Traditionally, advertisers tend to emphasise the emotional rather than the information aspect, particularly within low-involvement categories. Digital media allow focus on the provision of information and so the emotional aspect of advertising messages tends to have a lower significance. As branding becomes a more important aspect of Internet activity, it is probable that there will be a greater use of emotions, especially when the goal is to keep people at a website rather than driving them to it.

Digital media allow focus on the provision of information and so the emotional aspect of advertising messages tends to have a lower significance.

TABLE 8.3 A comparison of new and traditional media

Traditional media	New media
One-to-many	One-to-one and many-to-many
Greater monologue	Greater dialogue
Active provision	Passive provision
Mass marketing	Individualised marketing
General need	Personalised
Branding	Information
Segmentation	Communities

Apart from the obvious factor that digital media and the Internet in particular provide interactive opportunities that traditional media cannot provide, it is important to remember that opportunities to see are generally driven by customers rather than by the advertiser that interrupts viewing or reading activities. People drive the interaction at a speed that is convenient to them; they are not driven by others.

ViewPoint 8.5   Getting the kit digitised

The increasing use of digital print highlights one of the areas where new technology can enhance conventional direct-response media. Digital print allows for high colour quality and huge creative opportunities, such as different imagery for male and female customers or geographic variations to reflect local markets and offers. However, the biggest advantages are the speed at which materials can be produced (in comparison with litho printing) and the high level of personalisation that is possible. Just knowing a child's name and birthday enabled the Early Learning Centre to personalise storybooks by making the child the hero in the book and then sending it to them on their birthday.

The Carphone Warehouse sends a unique, personalised welcome pack to each new customer. In each pack are guides to the key features of their handset plus tariff details and accessories that are particular to each individual. From this the company can better cross-sell other Carphone Warehouse products and services.

Source: Adapted from Blyth (2005)

Management control over Internet-based marketing communications is relatively high as not only are there greater opportunities to control the position and placement of advertisements, promotions and press releases but it is possible to change the content of these activities much more quickly than is possible with traditional media. The goals outlined above indicate the framework within which advertising needs to be managed.

In addition to considering the attributes of the two different forms of media it is also worth considering the content of the information that each is capable of delivering. These are set out in Table 8.4.

As mentioned earlier, digital media are superior at providing rational, product-based information whereas traditional media are much better at conveying emotional brand values. The former has a dominant cognition orientation and the latter an emotional one. There are other differences but the predominant message is that these types of media are, to a large extent, complementary, suggesting that they should be used together, not one independently of the other.

Interactive television

Digital television and interactive services are two related but different facilities. Digital television is now a reality, but full interactivity has yet to be delivered to the majority of the population. Potential advantages are consumer familiarity, the full-screen, high-quality sound and picture format, fast channel and picture/text 'hopping', combining entertainment and shopping. The disadvantages include the current high cost of the sets to consumers and of broadcasting for companies. In addition, it cannot deal with

TABLE 8.4 A comparison of information content

Websites/Internet	Traditional media
Good at providing rational, product-based information	Better at conveying emotional brand values
More efficient as costs do not increase in proportion to the size of the target audience	Costs are related to usage
Better at prompting customer action	Less effective for calling to action except point of purchase and telemarketing
Effective for short-term, product-oriented brand action goals and long-term corporate identity objectives	Normally associated with building long-term values
Poor at generating awareness and attention	Strong builders of awareness
Poor at managing attitudes	Capable of changing and monitoring attitudes
Measures of effectiveness weak and/or in the process of development	Established methodologies, if misleading or superficial (mass media); direct-marketing techniques are superior
Dominant orientation – cognition	Dominant orientation – emotion

individual customers until TV-based email is widely established. Penetration rates will rise as analogue services in the UK are phased out.

Digital services provide many benefits for consumers, one of which will be the opportunity to screen out current intrusive advertising. Interactive advertising is often driven by consumers, who decide which advertisements they watch, when, and for how long they stay involved. The creative possibilities are far-ranging but in order to retain audiences it will become increasingly important to develop creative ideas based upon a sound understanding of the target audience and their interactive and buying patterns. Currently on UK teletext there are pages about holiday bargains that direct potential users to the Internet (www.teletext.co.uk/holidays) where they will find a searchable database, plus weather reports, resort reviews and advice. This service claims a choice of preferred operators, competitive pricing, confidence – full financial protection, up-to-date offers and human interaction at the point of sale. It states that, in the future, customers will be able to access the full functionality of the website via digital TV and/or mobile phone. The point is that digital television and interactive marketing communications are unlikely to thrive isolated from other methods of communication. Just as online facilities need offline drivers, and just as bricks and clicks appear to be a more profitable format than clicks only, so an integrated perspective is required if digital television and interactive advertising are to be successful.

To draw this part of the chapter together, Table 8.5 summarises the strengths and weaknesses of the main forms of media.

> Interactive advertising is often driven by consumers, who decide which advertisements they watch, when, and for how long they stay involved.

TABLE 8.5 A summary of media characteristics

Type of media	Strengths	Weaknesses
Print *Newspapers*	Wide reach High coverage Low costs Very flexible Short lead times Speed of consumption controlled by reader	Short lifespan Advertisements get little exposure Relatively poor reproduction, gives poor impact Low attention-getting properties
Magazines	High-quality reproduction that allows high impact Specific and specialised target audiences High readership levels Longevity High levels of information can be delivered	Long lead times Visual dimension only Slow build-up of impact Moderate costs
Television	Flexible format, uses sight, movement and sound High prestige High reach Mass coverage Low relative cost so very efficient	High level of repetition necessary Short message life High absolute costs Clutter Increasing level of fragmentation (potentially)
Radio	Selective audience, e.g. local Low costs (absolute, relative and production) Flexible Can involve listeners	Lacks impact Audio dimension only Difficult to get audience attention Low prestige
Outdoor	High reach High frequency Low relative costs Good coverage as a support medium Location oriented	Poor image (but improving) Long production time Difficult to measure
New media	High level of interaction Immediate response possible Tight targeting Low absolute and relative costs Flexible and easy to update Measurable	Segment-specific Slow development of infrastructure High user set-up costs Transaction-security issues
Transport	High length of exposure Low costs Local orientation	Poor coverage Segment-specific (travellers) Clutter
In-store POP	High attention-getting properties Persuasive Low costs Flexible	Segment-specific (shoppers) Prone to damage and confusion Clutter

Media planning

Once a message has been created and agreed, a media plan should be determined. The aim of the media plan is to devise an optimum route for the delivery of the message to the target audience. This function is normally undertaken by specialists, either as part of a full-service advertising agency or as a media house whose sole function is to buy air time or space from media owners (e.g. television contractors or magazine publishers) on behalf of their clients, the advertisers. This traditional role has changed since the mid-1990s, and many media independents now provide consultancy services, particularly at the strategic level, plus planning and media research and auditing services.

Media departments are responsible for two main functions. These are to 'plan' and to 'buy' time and space in appropriate media vehicles. There is a third task – to monitor a media schedule once it has been bought – but this is essentially a subfunction of buying. The planner chooses the target audience and the type of medium, while the buyer chooses programmes, frequency, spots and distribution, and assembles a multi-channel schedule (Armstrong, 1993).

Media planning is essentially a selection and scheduling exercise.

Media planning is essentially a selection and scheduling exercise. The selection refers to the choice of media vehicles to carry the message on behalf of the advertiser. Scheduling refers to the number of occasions, timing and duration that a message is exposed, in the selected vehicles, to the target audience. However, there are several factors that complicate these seemingly straightforward tasks. First, the variety of available media is huge and rapidly increasing. This is referred to as media fragmentation. Second, the characteristics of the target audience are changing equally quickly. This is referred to as audience fragmentation. The job of the media planner is complicated by one further element: money. Advertisers have restricted financial resources and require the media planner to create a plan that delivers their messages not only effectively but also efficiently.

The task of the media planner, therefore, is to deliver advertising messages through a selection of media that match the viewing and/or reading habits of the target audience at the lowest possible cost. In order for these tasks to be accomplished, three sets of decisions need to be made about the choice of media, vehicles and schedules.

Decisions about the choice of media are complex. Whereas choosing a single one is reasonably straightforward, choosing media in combination and attempting to generate synergistic effects is far from easy. Advances in IT have made media planning a much faster, more accurate process, one that is now more flexible and capable of adjusting to fast-changing market conditions.

Media planning concepts

Media planning involves certain key principles and concepts. These are set out in Table 8.6.

Reach

Building reach within a target audience is relatively easy as the planner needs to select a range of different media vehicles. This will enable different people in the target

TABLE 8.6 Media planning concepts

Planning concept	Explanation
Reach	The percentage of the target audience exposed to the message at least once during the relevant time period. Where 80 per cent of the target audience has been exposed to a message, the figure is expressed as an '80 reach'.
Frequency	Refers to the number of times a member of the target audience is exposed to a media vehicle (not the advertisement) during the relevant time period.
Opportunity to see (OTS)	Simply because a person has been exposed to a particular vehicle does not mean they have seen the ad. What it does mean is that they have had an OTS the ad and it is this element that is measured.
Duplication	Targets exposed to two or more advertisements carrying the same message are said to have been duplicated.
Gross rating points (GRPs)	GRPs are a measure of the total number of exposures (OTS) generated within a particular period of time. The calculation itself is simply reach × frequency = gross rating point
Effective frequency	Refers to the number of times an individual needs to be exposed to an advertisement before the communication is effective.

audience to have an opportunity to see the media vehicle. However, a point will be reached when it becomes more difficult to reach people who have not been exposed. As more vehicles are added, so repetition levels (the number of people who have seen the advertisement more than once) also increase.

Frequency

The number of times people are exposed to an ad should be a function of how many times planners believe targets need to see and learn about the ad.

The number of times people are exposed to an ad should be a function of how many times planners believe targets need to see and learn about the ad before acting in particular ways. This frequency, essentially a repetition level, will always be greater than the advertisement exposure rate. However, a high opportunity to see (OTS) might be generated by either, a large number of the target audience being exposed once (high reach), or a small number being exposed several times (high frequency).

This then raises the first major issue. As all campaigns are restricted by limitations of time and budget, advertisers have to trade off reach against frequency. It is impossible to maximise both elements within a fixed budget and set period of time.

All campaigns are restricted by limitations of time and budget.

To launch a new product, it has been established that a large number of people within the target audience need to become aware of the product's existence and its salient attributes or benefits. This means that reach is important but, as more and more people become aware, so more of them become exposed a second, third or fourth time, perhaps to different vehicles. At the outset, frequency is low and reach high, but as a campaign progresses so reach slows and frequency develops. Reach and frequency are

ViewPoint 8.6   Haier than the weather

Haier, the major Chinese global manufacturer of consumer durables, uses television in China to reach its main audiences. In a country where it is estimated that over 250 million Chinese families watch CCTV programmes, Haier sponsors the weather forecast, which is the highest-rated programme in China. Guaranteeing large audiences on a repeat basis ensures Haier achieves high OTS based on a large frequency.

Source: Adapted from unpublished student coursework and www.zaobao.com/

inversely related within any period of time, and media planners must know what the objective of any campaign might be: to build reach or frequency.

Gross rating point

The term gross rating point (GRP) is used to express the relationship between reach and frequency, which is a means of deciding which of the two concepts is important in a campaign: reach × frequency = GRP.

Media plans are often determined on the number of GRPs generated during a certain period. For example, the objective for a media plan could be to achieve 450 GRPs in a burst (usually four or five weeks). However, as suggested earlier, caution is required when interpreting a GRP, because 450 GRPs may be the result of 18 message exposures to just 25 per cent of the target market. It could also be an average of nine exposures to 50 per cent of the target market.

Effective frequency

Frequency refers to the number of times members of the target audience are exposed to the vehicle. Effective frequency refers to the number of times a message needs to be repeated for effective learning to occur. The level of effective frequency is generally unknown, but for a long time it was generally assumed to be three within any purchase period: the three-hit theory. The first exposure provokes a 'What is this?' reaction, the second reaction is 'What does this mean to me?' The reaction to the third is 'Oh I remember' (du Plessis, 1998).

Determining the average frequency partially solves the problem. This is the number of times a target reached by the schedule is exposed to the vehicle over a particular period of time. For example, a schedule may generate the following:

10 per cent of the audience is reached ten times ($10 \times 10 = 100$)

25 per cent of the audience is reached seven times ($25 \times 7 = 175$)

65 per cent of the audience is reached once ($65 \times 1 = 65$)

Total = 340 exposures

Average frequency = 340/100 = 3.4

However, this figure of average frequency is misleading because different groups of people have been reached with varying levels of frequency. In the example above, an

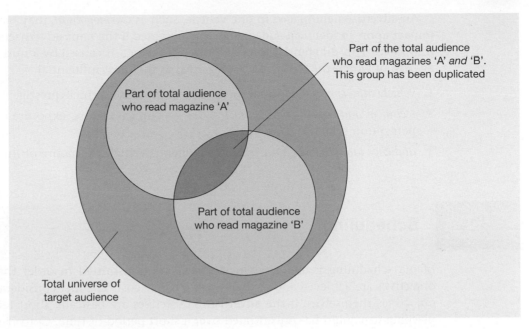

FIGURE 8.1 Duplication

average frequency of 3.4 is achieved but 65 per cent of the audience is reached only once. This means that the average frequency, in this example, may lead to an audience being underexposed.

Duplication

Members of the target audience do not buy and read just one magazine or watch a single television programme. Consumer media habits are complex, although distinct patterns can be observed, but it is likely that a certain percentage of the target audience will be exposed to an advertisement if it is placed in two or more media vehicles. Those who are exposed once constitute unduplicated reach. Those who are exposed to two or more advertisements carrying the same message are said to have been duplicated. Such overlapping of exposure, shown in Figure 8.1, is referred to as duplicated reach.

Those who are exposed to two or more advertisements carrying the same message are said to have been duplicated.

Duplication provides an indication of the levels of frequency likely in a particular schedule, so media plans need to specify levels of duplicated and unduplicated reach. Duplication also increases costs, so if the objective of the plan is unduplicated reach, duplication brings waste and inefficiency.

Media-source effects

So far attention has been given to the various quantitative elements associated with media planning. However, these all fail to account for the qualitative aspects associated with media vehicles. Before vehicles are selected, their qualitative aspects need to be considered on the basis that a vehicle's environment may affect the way in which a message is perceived, decoded and meaning is ascribed.

An advertisement placed in one vehicle, such as *Cosmopolitan*, may have a different impact upon an identical audience to that obtained if the same advertisement is placed in *Options*. This differential level of 'power of impact' is caused by a number of source factors, of which the following are regarded as the most influential:

1. *vehicle atmosphere* – editorial tone, vehicle expertise, vehicle prestige;
2. *technical and reproduction characteristics* – technical factors, exposure opportunities, perception opportunities;
3. *audience and product characteristics* – audience/vehicle fit, nature of the product.

Scheduling

Media scheduling is about when messages are transmitted in order that the media objectives are achieved and at the lowest possible cost. The first considerations are the objectives themselves. If the advertising objectives are basically short term, then the placements should be concentrated over a short period of time. Conversely, if awareness is to be built over a longer term, perhaps building a new brand, then the frequency of the placements need not be so intensive and can be spread over a period so that learning can occur incrementally.

The second consideration is the purchasing cycle.

The second consideration is the purchasing cycle. We have seen before that the optimum number of exposures is thought to be a minimum of three, and this should occur within each purchasing cycle. This, of course, is only really applicable to packaged goods, and is not as applicable to the business-to-business sector. However, as a principle, the longer the cycle, the less frequency is required.

The third consideration is the level of involvement. If the objective of the plan is to create awareness, then when there is high involvement few repetitions will be required compared with low-involvement decisions. This is because people who are highly involved actively seek information and need little assistance to digest relevant information. Likewise, when there is low involvement, attitudes develop from use of the product, so frequency is important to maintain awareness and to prompt trial.

Finally, the placement of an advertisement is influenced by the characteristics of the target audience and their preferred programmes. By selecting compatible 'spots' message delivery is likely to improve considerably.

Timing of advertisement placements

The timing of placements is dependent upon a number of factors. One of the overriding constraints is the size of the media budget and the impact that certain placement patterns can bring to an organisation's cash flow. Figure 8.2 represent a synthesis of the more common scheduling options.

Continuity patterns

Continuous patterns involve regular and uniform presentation of the message to the target audience. Over the long term, a continuous pattern is more appropriate for

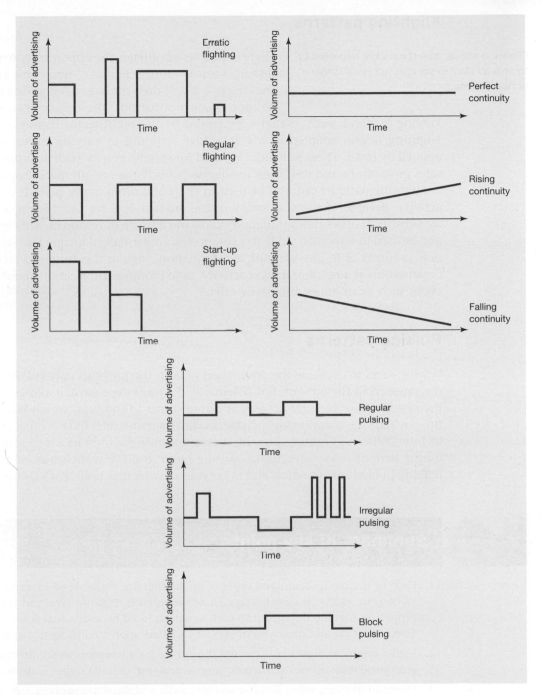

FIGURE 8.2 Scheduling

products and services where demand is crisis led, e.g. plumbing, or where there is a long purchase cycle. These continuous patterns are often used for mature products, where reminder advertising is appropriate. A rising pattern is used when activity centres around a particular event, such as the FA Cup Final, the Olympic Games or a general election. A fading pattern may follow an initial burst to launch a new product or to inform of a product modification.

Flighting patterns

Flighting allows advertisers the opportunity to spread their resources across a longer period of time.

Flighting allows advertisers the opportunity to spread their resources across a longer period of time. This may improve the effectiveness of their messages. A flighting pattern may be appropriate in situations where messages need to reflect varying demand, such as that experienced by the retail sector throughout the year. Flighting is also adopted as a competitive response to varying advertising weights applied by rivals. These schedules are used for specific events, such as support for major sales promotions and responses to adverse publicity or one-off market opportunities.

Flighting patterns can also be used in short and often heavy periods of investment activity. Because of the seasonality of the product (e.g. for inclusive tour operators), advertising at other times is inappropriate and a waste of resources. This approach can also be used to respond quickly to a competitor's potentially damaging actions, to launch new products or to provide unique information, such as the announcement of a new organisation as a result of merger activity, or to promote information about a particular event such as an impending share offer.

Pulsing patterns

Pulsing seeks to combine the advantages of both the previous patterns. As a result it is the safest of all the options, but potentially the most expensive. It allows advertisers to increase levels of message activity at certain times of the year, which is important for times when sales traditionally increase, as with fragrance sales in December and ice cream in June. Whereas flighting presents an opportunity for individuals to forget messages during periods of no advertising, pulsing helps to prevent the onset of forgetting, to build high levels of awareness and to provide a barrier that holds back competitor attack.

Summary of key points

1. Each of the main classes and types of media that are available to advertisers has its own strengths and weaknesses. In addition, each medium type and vehicle has properties that are important to each situation faced by individual advertisers. Their selection and deployment should be based upon a contingency approach.

2. Media fragmentation has increased the choice for advertisers in an attempt to customise messages for particular, precise and well-defined target audiences.

3. Direct marketing, using direct-response media and database support, permits the generation and feedback of messages for and from individual customers. The overarching objectives are to build and sustain a mutually rewarding relationship with each customer, reduce media costs and improve effectiveness and measurement.

4. The use of direct-response media will continue to grow, while for some organisations their whole marketing approach can be built around the concept (e.g. insurance and financial services) as changes in distribution drive whole strategic shifts.

5. Digital and interactive television services are beginning to provide new forms of entertainment, shopping and banking facilities as well as marketing communications opportunities. In the longer term fully interactive services will bring increased leisure and entertainment facilities to a greater number of people and new opportunities for advertisers through interactive advertisements.

6. Media planning is essentially about management making judgements about where best to place its client's messages to maximise their effectiveness and the efficiency of the spend.

7. The task of buying the time or space in media vehicles in order that an advertising message is carried to a target audience is complicated by a number of factors, ranging from the size and dispersion of the target audience to the increasing number and variety of available media. These factors are referred to as audience and media fragmentation, which bring both benefits to and difficulties for media planners and advertisers.

8. There are a number of media concepts that are used to help planners and buyers select the most efficient and most effective media for their clients.

9. It is generally accepted that three exposures to an ad are necessary for effective learning and action to occur.

10. Decisions regarding the media cannot be made in isolation from the qualitative factors associated with each vehicle. Known as vehicle source effects, these are concerned with the quality of the vehicle in terms of its atmosphere, technical aspects and audience/product fit.

11. Media scheduling calls for qualitative and quantitative measures to assist the decision concerning when and for how long ads should run in the media.

Review questions

1. Explain the differences between media classes, types and vehicles. Give two examples of each to support your answer.

2. Describe the main characteristics of both print and broadcast media. Find examples to illustrate your points.

3. Why are the relative costs of each medium different?

4. What are the main tasks facing media planners and why is it important that a media planner knows whether reach or frequency is the main objective of a media plan?

5. Why are frequency levels so important? Explain the concept of effective frequency.

6. What are the main ways in which media plans can be scheduled?

References

Advertising Association (2004), *Advertising Statistics Year Book*, Henley-on-Thames: NTC, and at www.adassoc.org.uk/inform/.

Advertising Association (2005), *Advertising Statistics Year Book*, Henley-on-Thames: NTC, and at www.adassoc.org.uk/inform/.

Armstrong, S. (1993), 'The business of buying: time, lads, please', *Media Week*, 3 September, pp. 26–7.

Blyth, A. (2005), 'Digital's rapid rise', *Marketing Direct*, October, pp. 55–6.

du Plessis, E. (1998), 'Memory and likeability: keys to understanding ad effects', *Admap*, **33** (July/August), pp. 42–6.

Silverman, G. (2004), 'Back to the future: advertisers get out of the living room and onto the street', *Financial Times*, 25 October, p. 15.

Verebelyi, N. (2000), 'The power of the pack', *Marketing*, 27 April, p. 37.

Sales promotion: principles, techniques and evaluation

9

Aims and objectives

The aims of this chapter are to consider the nature and role of sales promotion within the marketing communications mix and to consider the characteristics of the main sales promotion tools and techniques. There are three primary topics in this chapter:

Characteristics, Techniques, Measurement

The learning objectives are to enable readers to:

1. discuss the nature, role and impact of sales promotions in the communications mix;

2. explain how sales promotions can be used strategically;

3. clarify the particular objectives sales promotions seek to satisfy;

4. discuss the reasons for the increased use of sales promotions;

5. examine the way in which sales promotions are considered to work;

6. explain the various sales promotional techniques;

7. examine ways in which sales promotions can be evaluated.

Introduction

If advertising is used to create brand values then sales promotion delivers a call to action. These two tools complement each other as advertising seeks to work over the long term to create awareness and positive feelings, whereas sales promotion works in the shorter term to encourage people to behave in particular ways and to create sales.

Sales promotion offers buyers additional value, an inducement to generate an immediate sale.

Sales promotion offers buyers additional value, an inducement to generate an immediate sale. These inducements can be targeted at consumers, distributors, agents and members of the sales force. A whole range of stakeholders can benefit from the use of sales promotion.

This promotional tool is traditionally referred to as a form of below-the-line communication because, unlike advertising, agencies are not paid a commission by the media owners. The promotional costs are borne directly by the organisation initiating the activity, which in most cases is a manufacturer, producer or service provider.

Understanding the value of sales promotions

There are many sales-promotion techniques, but they all offer a direct inducement or an incentive to encourage receivers of these promotional messages to buy a product/service sooner rather than later. The inducement (for example, price deals, coupons, premiums) is presented as an added value to the basic product and is intended to encourage buyers to act 'now' rather than later. Sales promotion is used, therefore, principally as a means to accelerate sales. The acceleration represents the shortened period of time in which the transaction is completed relative to the time that would have elapsed had there not been a promotion. This action does not mean that an extra sale has been achieved, just that a potential future exchange is confirmed and transacted now.

Sales promotions consist of a wide range of tools and methods. These instruments are considered in more detail later, but consideration of what constitutes sales promotion methods is important. In many cases price is the determinant variable and can be used to distinguish between instruments. Sales promotions are often perceived purely as a price discounting mechanism through price deals and the use of coupons. This, however, is not the whole picture, as there are many other ways in which incentives can be offered to buyers.

Reference has already been made to the idea that sales promotions are a way of providing value and it is this value orientation that should be used when considering the nature and essential characteristics of sales promotion.

As a result of this diversity of sales-promotion instruments it should be of no surprise to learn that they are used for a wide range of reasons. Sales promotions can be targeted, with considerable precision, at particular audiences and there are three broad audiences at whom sales promotions can be targeted: consumers, members of the distribution or channel network, and the sales forces of both manufacturers and resellers. It should be remembered that the accuracy of these promotional tools means that many subgroups within these broad groups can be reached quickly and accurately. These are presented in Table 9.1.

Sales promotions can be targeted, with considerable precision, at particular audiences.

TABLE 9.1 Reasons for the use of sales promotions

Reach new customers	They are useful in securing trials for new products and in defending shelf space against anticipated and existing competition.
Reduce distributor risk	The funds that manufacturers dedicate to them lower the distributor's risk in stocking new brands.
Reward behaviour	They can provide rewards for previous purchase behaviour.
Retention	They can provide interest and attract potential customers and in doing so encourage them to provide personal details for further communications activity.
Add value	Can encourage sampling and repeat-purchase behaviour by providing extra value (superior to competitors' brands) and a reason to purchase.
Induce action	They can instil a sense of urgency among consumers to buy while a deal is available. They add excitement and interest at the point of purchase to the merchandising of mature and mundane products.
Preserve cash flow	Since sales-promotion costs are incurred on a pay-as-you-go basis, they can spell survival for smaller, regional brands that cannot afford big advertising programmes.
Improve efficiency	Sales promotions allow manufacturers to use idle capacity and to adjust to demand and supply imbalances or softness in raw material prices and other input costs, while maintaining the same list prices.
Integration	Provide a means of linking together other tools of the promotional mix.
Assist segmentation	They allow manufacturers to price discriminate among consumer segments that vary in price sensitivity. Most manufacturers believe that a high-list, high-deal policy is more profitable than offering a single price to all consumers. A portion of sales promotion expenditures, therefore, consists of reductions in list prices that are set for the least-price-sensitive segment of the market.

Lee (2002) suggests that the main reasons for the use of sales promotions can be reduced to four:

1. as a reaction to competitor activities;
2. as a form of inertia – this is what we have always done;
3. as a way of meeting short-term sales objectives;
4. as a way of meeting long-term objectives.

It appears that the first three are used widely and Lee comments that many brand owners use sales promotion as a panic measure when competitors threaten to lure customers away. Cutting prices is undoubtedly a way of prompting a short-term sales response but it can also undermine a longer-term brand strategy.

Not too many years ago sales promotions were regarded as a key way of developing sales. However, the use of sales promotions has stagnated and in particular the use of on-pack promotions, bonus packs, competitions and price deals have failed to maintain the growth of previous years. Reasons for the decline include changing consumer behaviour, the rise of new media and a distinct lack of innovation in the industry. Another important factor has been the expectations and drive of resellers, and the main supermarket chains in particular. They desire sales-promotion programmes that are exclusive to them as this is seen as a major way of developing their retail brands.

Supermarkets have become media owners and realise the value of their store space as a means of exposing other brands. Therefore, any form of sales-promotion activity within their environments should be exclusive and tied into their brand. Providing on-pack promotions for individual stores is normally too expensive and uneconomic, so this form of promotion has suffered a great deal.

New solutions have had to be found and, as Barrand (2004) suggests, the use of digital media and the integration of sales promotion within other campaigns has been successful. The use of SMS, email, viral campaigns and the Internet are being used increasingly to drive sales by providing the call to action, which for a long time was the province of sales-promotion activities.

> The use of SMS, email, viral campaigns and the Internet are being used increasingly to drive sales by providing the call to action.

The role of sales promotion

The role of sales promotion has changed significantly over recent years. At one time, the largest proportion of communications budgets was normally allocated to advertising. In many cases advertising no longer dominates the communications budget and sales promotion has assumed the focus of the communications investment, for reasons that are described below. This is particularly evident in consumer markets that are mature, have reached a level of stagnation, and where price and promotion work are the few ways of inducing brand-switching behaviour.

Short termism

The short-term financial focus of many industrialised economies has developed a managerial climate geared to short-term performance and evaluation, over periods as short as 12 weeks. To accomplish this, communications tools are required that work quickly and directly impact upon sales. Many see this as leading to an erosion of the brand franchise.

Managerial accountability

Following on from the previous reason is the increased pressure upon marketing managers to be accountable for their communications expenditure. The results of sales-promotion activities are more easily justified and understood than those associated with advertising. The number of coupons returned for redemption and the number of bonus packs purchased can be calculated quickly and easily, with little room for error or misjudgement. Advertising, however, cannot be measured so easily, in either the short or the long term. The impact of this is that managers can relate this type of investment in communications to the bottom line much more comfortably than with advertising.

Brand performance

Technological advances have enabled retailers to track brand performance more effectively. This in turn means that manufacturers can be drawn into agreements that promulgate in-store promotional activity at the expense of other more traditional forms of mass-media promotion. Barcode scanners, hand-held electronic shelf-checking equipment and computerised stock systems facilitate the tracking of merchandise. This means that brand managers can be held responsible much more quickly for below-par performance.

Brand expansion

As brand quality continues to improve and as brands proliferate on the shelves of increasingly larger supermarkets, so the number of decisions that a consumer has to make also increases. Faced with multiple-brand decisions and a reduced amount of time to complete the shopping expedition, the tension associated with the shopping experience has increased considerably over the last decade.

ViewPoint 9.1	Sales promotions in Boots

In August 2003 Boots, the high street chemist and retailer, announced that it had reviewed its use of sales promotions, which until then had been a central part of its marketing offer. In particular, its three-for-two product offers had been a prominent part of its communications.

Using the incentive of extra product in order to create store traffic was considered not to be a viable or compatible strategy with the desire to make Boots a must-visit high street destination.

Associated with this development was the evolution of its loyalty card scheme (Advantage card). Through improved data mining it hoped to better understand its customers and then create improved cross-selling opportunities. Boots wants to be perceived as more exclusive and to achieve that it needs to give consumers more powerful reasons for shopping there than those provided through traditional product promotions.

Source: Adapted from Kleinman (2003)

Promotions can make decision-making easier for consumers.

Promotions can make decision-making easier for consumers: they simplify a potentially difficult process. So, as brand choice increases, the level of shopping convenience falls. The conflict this causes can be resolved by the astute use of sales promotions. Some feel that the cognitive shopper selects brands that offer increased value, which makes decision-making easier and improves the level of convenience associated with the shopping experience. However, should there be promotions on two offerings from an individual's repertoire then the decision-making is not necessarily made easier.

Competition for shelf space

The continuing growth in the number of brands that are launched and the fragmentation of consumer markets mean that retailers have to be encouraged to make shelf space available. Sales promotions help manufacturers win valuable shelf space and assist retailers to attract increased levels of store traffic and higher utilisation of limited resources.

The credibility of this communication tool is low.

The credibility of this communication tool is low, as it is obvious to the receiver what the intention is of using sales promotion messages. However, because of the prominent and pervasive nature of the tool, consumers and members of the trade understand and largely accept the direct sales approach. Sales promotion is not a tool that hides its intentions, nor does it attempt to be devious (which is not allowed, by regulation).

The absolute costs of sales promotion are low, but the real costs need to be evaluated once a campaign has finished and all redemptions received and satisfied. The relative costs can be high, as not only do the costs of the premium or price discount need to be determined, but also the associated costs of additional transportation, lost profit, storage and additional time spent organising and administering a sales promotion campaign need to be accounted for.

In its favour, sales promotion allows for a high degree of control. Management is able to decide just when and where a sales promotion will occur and also estimate the sales effect. Sales promotions can be turned on and off quickly and adjusted to changed market conditions. The intended message is invariably the one that is received, as there is relatively little scope for it to be corrupted or damaged in transmission.

Sales promotion plans: the objectives

The objectives of using this tool are sales oriented and are geared to stimulating buyers either to use a product for the first time or to encourage use on a routine basis.

One objective of sales promotion activity is to prompt buyers into action, to initiate a series of behaviours that result in long-run purchase activity. These actions can be seen to reflect high or low involvement and they occur in the conative stage of the attitudinal set. If the marketing objectives include the introduction of a new product or intention to enter a new market, then the key objective associated with low-involvement decisions is to stimulate trial use as soon as possible. When high involvement decisions are present, then sales promotions need to be withheld until a suitable level of attitudinal development has been undertaken by public relations and advertising activities.

If a product is established in a market, then a key objective should be to use sales promotions to stimulate an increase in the number of purchases made by current customers and to attract users from competing products. See Figure 9.1. The objectives, therefore, are either to increase consumption for established products or to stimulate

	Involvement	
	High	Low
New product or market	Withhold sales promotion	Use sales promotion to stimulate trial
Established product or market	Non-loyals – use for switching Loyals – use carefully	Non-loyals – use sales promotion to attract for trial Loyals – use sales promotion to reward for increased usage

FIGURE 9.1 A sales promotion objectives grid

trial by encouraging new buyers to use a product. Once this has been agreed then the desired trial and usage levels need to be determined for each of the target audiences.

The strategic use of sales promotions

Sales promotions have been regarded as a short-term tactical tool whose prime purpose is to encourage customers to try a brand or to switch brands.

For a long time sales promotions have been regarded as a short-term tactical tool whose prime purpose is to encourage customers to try a brand or to switch brands (within their repertoire), attracted by the added value of the sales promotion. Indeed, Papatia and Krishnamurthi (1996) claim that coupons can actively promote switching behaviour and so reduce levels of loyalty. As discussed earlier, what happens after a sales-promotion activity finishes is debatable. Some claim that once a promotion is withdrawn satisfied customers will return to the brand unsupported by a sales promotion, but supported by other elements of the marketing communications mix: in particular advertising, to maintain awareness of the brand and its values; direct marketing, to provide personal attention and the opportunity to take immediate action; and public relations to sustain credibility and relevance.

By way of contrast it can be argued that sales promotion serves to discount a brand, either directly through price-based reductions or indirectly through coupons and premiums. Customer alignment is to the deal rather than to the brand itself. This serves to lower expectations of what a brand stands for and what it is capable of delivering. So, once a sales promotion is removed, the normal price is perceived as representing inferior value and so repeat purchase behaviour is deterred.

However, despite these less than positive views, some writers (Davis, 1992; O'Malley, 1998) argue that sales promotions have a strategic role to play in the communications mix. Traditionally, they have been viewed as short-term tactical tools that can be used offensively to induce the trial of new products, or defensively for established products to retain shelf space and consumers. Sales promotions that do not work as intended may have been used to support inappropriate products or may have been devised without adequate planning. An example of the latter issue may be the Hoover free-flights misjudgement and the associated oversubscription which followed the launch of that particular sales-promotion activity. There can be no doubt that sales promotions oriented to consumer deals and temporary price reductions (TPRs), in particular, do little to contribute to the overall strategy adopted for an organisation or even a product.

One of the consequences of competitive sales promotions, especially in consumer markets, is the spiral effect that retaliatory actions can have on each organisation. A sales promotion 'trap' develops when competitors start to imitate each other's activities, often based upon price reductions. This leads eventually to participants losing profitability and consumers losing value and possibly choice as some products are forced to drop out of the market.

With the development of relationship marketing and the move towards integrated marketing communications has been the realisation that employees are an important target audience. There is a strong need to motivate the workforce and sales-promotion activities have an important role to play. However, employee incentives need to be made accessible to everyone and not just a few (such as the sales force). This means that rewards need to be more broadly spread and there needs to be choice. Vouchers, for example, enable the prizewinner to make a choice based on their circumstances, and they are easier to administer than many of the other types of reward. Incentive schemes should be designed in such a way that they do not fall into the trap of creating winners and losers, which can be the case when, for example, the top 20 in a scheme win a prize, which effectively creates 80 losers out of every 100 employees.

Many schemes are based around product prizes, typically electrical goods. However, for many people these are no longer attractive (or sufficiently motivating) as rewards. Virgin vouchers provide activity-based rewards where there is an experience that gives the recipient a memory. Activities such as hot-air ballooning, sky diving, visits to the theatre or to health farms appeal to a wide cross-section of people.

> The true strategic effect of sales-promotion activities can only be achieved if they are coordinated with the other activities of the communications mix.

The true strategic effect of sales-promotion activities can only be achieved if they are coordinated with the other activities of the communications mix, and this requires planning. In particular, the complementary nature of sales promotion and advertising should be exploited through the use of common themes and messages, timing, targeting and allocation of resources (in particular budgets). Sales promotions that are planned as a sequence of predetermined activities, reflecting the promotional requirements of a product over the longer term, are more likely to be successful than those sales promotions that are simply reactions to competitors' moves and market developments.

The strategic impact of sales promotions is best observed when they are designed or built into a three- to four-year plan of promotional activities, coordinated with other promotional tools and integrated with the business strategy.

The manner in which many of the loyalty programmes are managed signals a move from pure sales promotion to direct marketing. The integration of these two approaches has become necessary in order that the advantages of both are realised. This raises an interesting conflict, in that sales promotion is essentially a short-term tool, and direct marketing needs to work over the long term. The former is product oriented (albeit giving added value to consumers) and often oriented to mass audiences, whereas the latter is based upon developing a personal dialogue (Curtis, 1996).

A further strategic issue concerns the use of joint promotions with other leading brands. With the intention of promoting the health aspects of its oil for frying purposes, Goldenfields rapeseed oil joined up with Morphy Richards to offer a two-tier campaign. The first involved 20 stainless steel fat fryer prizes in return for coupons from the oil bottle label and the second was a health farm prize and a further 20 fat fryers (Clarke, 2001). By twinning brand names increased

> By twinning brand names increased promotional impact can assist both partners.

promotional impact can assist both partners. However, there is a danger that such a pairing will be short lived, and hence the strategic perspective may be limited.

Finally, the huge sums of money involved in some of the mainstream loyalty or reward-based programmes suggest that these should be seen as longer-term promotional investments. As the return will spread over many years a medium-term perspective may be more appropriate, rather than a short-term view based on a sales 'blip'.

Sales promotion: methods

There are a variety of sales-promotion methods or techniques. These vary in their characteristics but they are essentially incentives, which are rewards for buyers behaving in particular ways. There are three main audiences for sales promotions: resellers, consumers and the sales forces of the manufacturers and resellers. These are considered in turn.

Sales promotions: manufacturers to resellers

Manufacturers and retailers see sales promotions as important devices to encourage trials among non-users and to stimulate repeat purchase among users. Retailers prefer in-store promotions (push) instead of promotions aimed at consumers (pull) strategies. This has implications for the communications mixes deployed by manufacturers. Essentially this represents sales promotions within a b2b context.

Allowances

The main type of sales promotion used to motivate trade customers is an *allowance*. Allowances can take many forms, some of the more common ones being buying, count and recount, buy-back allowances, merchandising and advertising allowances. See Table 9.2. Trade allowances are a means of achieving a short-term increase in sales. They can be used defensively to protect valuable shelf space from aggressive competitors. By offering to work with resellers and providing them with extra incentives, manufacturers can guard territory gained to date.

One of the main drawbacks concerns the cooperative aspect of the allowance arrangements. Resellers are able to assume control over the process and this can lead to circumstances where inappropriate messages and media are used. Furthermore, fraudulent claims have been submitted for advertising that either did not take place or duplicated a previous claim. This lack of control can lead to conflict, and the very scheme that was designed to foster collaborative behaviour can degenerate into a conflict of opinion and a deterioration in reseller/manufacturer relationships. It is interesting to observe that the organisations in the network that have the responsibility for distributing the manufacturer's products are the same ones that may (theoretically) be penalised by their supplier following abuse of sales promotions (Grey, as cited in Govoni et al., 1986).

TABLE 9.2 Allowance-based schemes between manufacturers and resellers

Allowance	Explanation
Buying allowances	Resellers are entitled to a refund or allowance of × per cent off the regular case or carton price, in return for specific orders between certain dates.
Count and recount allowances	Provides a reward (allowance) for each case shifted into the store during a specified period of time. Used to encourage clearance of old stock.
Buy-back allowances	Provides a reward on stock purchased when stores replenish their stocks after a count and recount scheme.
Merchandise allowances	Subject to terms and orders, this approach enables resellers to receive free stock rather than credit or cashback.
Advertising allowances	Used to stimulate product trial by stores, this allowance either discounts prices for purchases made during a particular campaign or a contribution is made by the manufacturer to the reseller's advertising campaign.

Other forms of sales promotions aimed at resellers

There are a number of other techniques that can be used to achieve sales-promotion objectives. These include dealer contests, which should be geared to stimulating increased usage. Dealer conventions and meetings are used extensively, often in conjunction with a dealer contest, to launch new products, develop relationships and provide new information.

Many manufacturers provide extensive training and support for their resellers. This is an important communications function, especially when products are complex or subject to rapid change, as in the IT markets. Such co-ordination means that a stronger relationship can be built and manufacturers have greater control over the messages that the reseller's representatives transmit. It also means that the switching costs of the reseller are increased, since the training and support costs will be incurred again if a different supplier is adopted. Coordination through training and support can be seen as a form of marketing communications.

Coordination means that a stronger relationship can be built.

Marketing communications between manufacturers and resellers is vitally important. Sales promotions play an increasingly important role in the coordination between the two parties. Resellers look for sales promotions to support their own marketing initiatives. Supplier selection decisions depend in part upon the volume and value of the communications support. In other words, will supplier X or Y provide the necessary level of communications support, either within the channel or direct to the consumer?

Sales promotions: manufacturers to consumers

Manufacturers use sales promotions to communicate with consumers mainly because they can be a cost-effective means of achieving short-term increases in sales. The objectives are twofold: first, to stimulate trial use by new users, or second, to increase the amount of product used by current customers. Methods relating to these two main tasks are now considered in turn.

ViewPoint 9.2	Sampling and SMS at Brylcreem

Brylcreem used sampling and SMS to launch its Next Generation Ultra Gel product. Samples of the brand were handed out to young males at welcome meetings at Club 18–30 holiday destinations. Each sample pack carried a code, encouraging recipients to text in for a chance to win prizes such as holidays and PlayStation games and consoles. They were also asked to text in their opinions on Brylcreem.

The simplicity of the campaign was intended to reflect Brylcreem's brand values and was designed to complement the fact that increasingly people are taking their phones on holiday and using SMS.

Increasing product trial

There are three main approaches to encouraging new customers to try a product for the first time: sampling, coupons and a range of consumer deals.

Sampling

When a product is introduced, whether it be into a new product category or an improved or modified product, sampling is one of the most effective sales-promotion techniques available. For decisions that evoke low involvement, attitudes are confirmed as a result of product experience. It makes sense, therefore, to provide a risk-free opportunity for consumers to test a product.

Sampling is one of the most effective sales-promotion techniques available.

Samples are very often free miniature versions of the actual product and can be used to win new customers and to protect a customer base. Samples can take the form of demonstrations, trial-size packs that have to be purchased or free use for a certain period of time. Car purchases can be incentivised through test drives at car experience centres, and the use of scented page folds in women's magazines to demonstrate new scents and perfumes is a way of making trial easier and more convenient than a visit to a high street store.

ViewPoint 9.3   Philips Softone samples

In order to introduce the new range of Softone light bulbs to a newer, younger audience, Philips Lighting used a two-stage sampling approach. Utilising a door-to-door approach, the first phase consisted of the delivery of a questionnaire to collect database material and to ask which colour of bulb the householder would like to receive. The following day, phase 2 kicked in with the collection of the questionnaire and the delivery of the appropriate colour bulb (so avoiding the problem of delivering a glass product through a letterbox too small to accept it).

Awareness rose to 82 per cent, 10 per cent of targeted households requested a sample and from the 1,100,000 questionnaires that were completed, Philips was able to pinpoint innovators, early adopters and early majority individuals and use these data to roll the campaign out nationwide. In doing so it substantially reduced its costs and improved its efficiency and effectiveness.

Sampling is expensive. Of all the available sales promotion techniques, the costs associated with sampling are the largest. To offset the high cost, the potential rewards can be equally dramatic, especially if the audience is familiar with or predisposed to the product class, and if the sample has some superior benefits. Sampling is best undertaken when the following apply:

1. Advertising alone is unable to communicate the key benefits.
2. The product has benefits that are superior to its competitors and that are clearly demonstrable.
3. Competitive attacks require loyal customers to be reminded of a product's advantages. A further use occasion of sampling is to introduce the product to customers of competitive products, in an effort to encourage them to switch.

Apart from the size, mass and degree of perishability associated with the physical characteristics, the main constraints concern the number of people who are required to receive the samples and when they are to receive them: the timing of the trial. Samples are often distributed to consumers free of charge, with the twin goals of introducing the product to new users and hopefully encouraging them to switch brands. In addition to this, sampling provides an ideal opportunity to gather valuable market-research data from the field.

Sampling provides an ideal opportunity to gather valuable market-research data from the field.

Coupons

Coupons are vouchers or certificates that entitle consumers to a price reduction on a particular product. The value of the reduction or discount is set and the coupon must be presented when purchasing the product. The objective, therefore, is to offer a price deal, a discount off the full price of the product. They may be distributed via resellers or directly to consumers and are a proven brand-switching device. Retailers and wholesalers act as agents for manufacturers by allowing consumers to redeem the value of coupons from them at the point of purchase. They in turn recover the cost of the deal, the value of the coupon, from the manufacturer.

Coupons provide precision targeting of price-sensitive customers, without harming those regular customers who are prepared to pay full price. In reality, however, some coupons are redeemed by regular product users, and their use reduces margins unnecessarily. The level of perceived risk experienced by new users can be reduced through the use of coupons. Users of competitive products can also be encouraged to try the product, so coupons can be effective for product introductions and established products in stable markets.

This form of sales promotion allows management to set a specific period of time in which a promotion is to run. This in turn allows the other elements of the promotional mix to be integrated. For example, advertising can be used to create awareness, and print media can then be used to display a coupon for the reader to cut out for redemption at the next purchase opportunity. When attempting to generate trial, advertising must be used to create awareness, since a coupon for an unknown product will be totally ineffective and usually discarded by consumers. Personal selling can be timed to inform resellers of a forthcoming coupon offer and give time for shelves to be fully stocked when the campaign breaks. Unfortunately, it is difficult to estimate when and how many coupons will be redeemed. There are certain guides developed through experience, and a redemption rate of between 3 per cent and 5 per cent can be considered good. The variance, however, can be marked, and the promotional cost of a stock-out can be considerable.

Couponing is an expensive activity. Not only has the face value of the coupons to be considered, but the production and distribution costs must also be accounted for. There are three primary ways in which coupons can be distributed. Coupons can be sent through the post, delivered on a door-to-door basis or delivered via a website. They may also be delivered as 'free-standing inserts' or printed directly into a newspaper or magazine. However, the redemption rates of this second approach are low because of the short life of such media vehicles, particularly newspapers, and the extra effort required by readers to cut out and store the coupon until the next purchase opportunity arises. On-page coupons can be found in magazines coupled with an advertisement. Pop-ups are coupons printed on card and bound into a magazine. Finally, tip-ins are coupons glued to the cover of a magazine. The final method of distribution refers to coupons printed on a package. This generates the highest redemption rates as they only reach current rather than competitive, lapsed or non-users.

Instant coupons are an effective point-of-purchase incentive, as they allow purchasers literally to rip the coupon off the package for redemption at the check-out. This can generate very high levels of redemption and is administratively easier to manage than price deals, as the latter require the active participation of the reseller.

Over 5 billion coupons were issued in the UK in 2002 (Advertising Association, 2004) and a 2 per cent redemption figure is considered good. In 2004 the value of the vouchers issued was £1.4 billion, and research by Mintel indicates that marketers are increasing their usage of coupons (Derrick, 2005). Approximately 75 per cent of coupons are distributed by direct mail. Fulfilment houses undertake the work for brand managers, acting as brokers for the issuers and retailers who accept them. Manufacturers outsource coupon work, if only because it is so labour-intensive. New software systems threaten to replace some of this work, especially the tracking of vouchers, which can be undertaken in-house.

Consumer deals

Consumer deals bring about a short-term increase in sales by moving the product from the shelves of the reseller to the homes of consumers. They can encourage trial behaviour by new users and also stimulate repurchase by existing users but they do little to build brands or associated franchisees. The techniques are as follows.

Price-offs

By far the simplest technique is to offer a direct reduction in the purchase price with the offer clearly labelled on the package or point-of-purchase display. These are simply referred to as 'price-offs'. A minimum reduction of 15 per cent appears to be required for optimal effect (Della Bitta and Monroe, 1980). Others suggest that this figure varies according to the store and the type of brand under consideration. Research indicates that consumers are sceptical of price deals, in particular those concerning price-offs. This may result in individuals discounting the discounts (Gupta and Cooper, 1992).

Bonus packs

Bonus packs offer more product for the regular pack price. They provide direct impact at the point of purchase, and this, combined with the lure of lower unit costs and extra value, means that this is a popular technique with consumers and manufacturers. However, resellers do not gain from bonus packs: there is no additional margin and extra shelf space is required.

Refunds and rebates

These are very effective in encouraging the trial of new products.

Refunds and rebates are used to invite consumers to send in a proof of purchase and in return receive a cash refund. These are very effective in encouraging the trial of new products and have proved exceptionally popular with consumer durables (rebate) as well as fast-moving consumer goods (refunds). The process of redeeming refunds may evoke negative feelings, as consumers do not like the trouble and inconvenience associated with claiming refunds and, when combined with the negative perception that consumers have of manufacturers that offer such rebates, the conclusion has to be that any redemption procedure should be clear, simple and easy to implement.

Increasing consumption

Organisations need to encourage consumers to repurchase products. In markets that are mature, sales growth can be achieved by encouraging users of competitive products to switch their allegiance, attracting non-users and finding new uses for the product.

There are two main ways in which sales promotions can be used to encourage increased usage: premiums, and contests and sweepstakes.

Premiums

Premiums are items of merchandise that are offered free or at a low cost in return for purchase of one or many products or services. Premiums are used as a direct incentive to motivate people to purchase a specific product. The premium merchandise is used to add value to the product and represent an advantage over competitor products. Premiums are used to increase sales by attracting repeat buyers, stimulating impulse purchase and brand-switching behaviour, and to offset competitor moves. There are two main forms of premium: direct and self-liquidating.

Premiums are used as a direct incentive to motivate people to purchase a specific product.

Direct premiums are provided at the point of purchase. They are free of charge and require the consumer to do nothing other than buy the package. In contrast, *self-liquidating* premiums require consumers to contribute to the cost of the incentive. Manufacturers seek only to cover their costs and, by buying the premium merchandise in volume, can offer the merchandise at prices considerably below the regular retail price. In many ways these can be referred to as delayed premiums, as proof of purchase needs to be sent through the mail (d'Astous and Jacob, 2002).

ViewPoint 9.4   Self-liquidating Cointreau is tops

A joint promotion with Classic FM sought to increase usage of the French liqueur Cointreau. Using a special collar in the shape of an orange on 300,000 bottles of the drink, consumers were invited to participate in two main activities. One was a set of recipes informing drinkers how to mix six different drinks with Cointreau as the key ingredient. The second urged consumers to send in the collar, the bottle cap and a 45p postal order, in order to receive a free Essential Violin Classics CD. Classic FM provided radio advertising support for the campaign and Cointreau sponsored live classical concerts that of course enabled members of the audiences to experience the brand through sampling.

Source: Adapted from Couldwell (2003)

The effectiveness of self-liquidating premiums is not as strong as that of direct premiums because they do not provide the same immediate impact, as the time delay between awareness of the offer and the reward can often be a number of weeks. Consequently, the redemption rate for these types of sales promotion is very low (0.1 per cent).

Contests and sweepstakes

A contest is a sales promotion whereby customers compete for prizes or money on the basis of skill or ability. Entry requires a proof of purchase and winners are judged against a set of predetermined criteria. A sweepstake is a sales-promotion technique where the winners are determined by chance and proof of purchase is not required. There is no judging and winners are drawn at random. A variant of the sweepstake is a game that also has odds of winning associated with it. Scratchcards have become very popular games, mainly because consumers like to participate and winners can be instantly identified.

Sweepstakes are more popular than contests because they are easier to enter.

Sweepstakes are more popular than contests because they are easier to enter and, because there is no judging, administration is less arduous and less expensive. Both contests and sweepstakes bring excitement and attention to campaigns, and if the contest or sweepstake is relevant, both approaches can bring about increased consumer involvement with the product.

Other forms of sales promotions

Sales promotions are used in other situations, although the volumes may not be as large as those experienced in the markets discussed so far.

Retailers use sales promotions to generate store traffic and to increase the number of people who become store (brand) loyal. These promotions are therefore targeted at store switchers and non-store users. They are also used to simply move stock (and associated costs) from the retailer's shelves to the cupboards and refrigerators of consumers. This increases usage, lowers profits and prepares shelves to receive new products.

Organisations also use sales promotions to incentivise members of either the manufacturer's or reseller's sales force. Incentives such as contests and sales meetings are two of the most-used motivators. Contests have been used a great deal, and if organised and planned properly can be very effective in raising the performance outcomes of sales teams. By appealing to their competitive nature, contests can bring about effective new-product introductions, revive falling sales, offset a rival's competitive moves and build a strong customer base. Sales meetings provide an opportunity for management to provide fresh information to the sales force about performance, stock positions, competitor activities, price deals, consumer or reseller promotions and new products. Sales-training exercises can be introduced and short product-training sessions can often be included. These formal agenda items are supplemented by the informal ones of peer reassurance and competitive stimulus, as well as information exchange and market analysis.

Finally, sales literature can be considered a form of sales promotion. Brochures can be used not only to impart factual information about a product or service, but also to stimulate purchase and guide decision-making. For service-based organisations, the brochure represents a temporary, tangible element of the product. Holiday companies (agents, operators, owners), for example, might entice people to book a holiday or short break, but consumption may take place several months in the future. The brochure acts as a temporary product substitute and can be used to refresh expectations during the gestation period and remind significant other people of the forthcoming event (Middleton, 1989). Just as holiday photographs provide opportunities to relive and share past experiences, so holiday brochures enable people to share and enjoy pre-holiday experiences and expectations with the brochure extending or adding value to the holiday experience.

For service-based organisations, the brochure represents a temporary, tangible element of the product.

Sales literature can trigger awareness of potential needs. As well as this, it can be useful in explaining technical and complex products. For example, leaflets distributed personally at DIY stores can draw attention to a double-glazing-manufacturer's products. Some prospective customers may create an initial impression about the manufacturer, based on past experiences triggered by the literature, the quality of the leaflet and the way it was presented. The leaflet acts as a cue for the receiver to review whether there is a current need and, if there is, then the leaflet may be kept longer, especially where high involvement is present; value is thus added to the purchase experience.

Financial services companies use sales literature at various stages in the sales process. Mailers are used to contact prospective customers, corporate brochures are used to provide source credibility, booklets about the overall marketplace are left with clients after an initial discussion and product guides and brochures are given to customers after a transaction has been agreed. To help prevent the onset of cognitive dissonance, a company magazine is sent soon after the sale and at intermediate points throughout the year to cement the relationship between client and company.

Evaluating sales-promotion activities

The measurement and evaluation of sales promotions are similar in principle to those conducted for advertising. The notion that some piloting should occur prior to launch in order that any wrinkles can be ironed out still holds strong, as does the need to balance qualitative with quantitative data. However, advertising seeks to influence awareness and image over the long term, whereas sales promotions seek to influence behaviour over the short term. As discussed earlier in this chapter, the evaluation of advertising can be imprecise and is subject to great debate. In the same way, the evaluation of sales promotions is subject to debate, but the means by which they are measured is not as ambiguous or as difficult as advertising (Shultz, 1987).

The use of quantitative methods as a testing tool leads to directly measurable and comparable outcomes, in comparison with the more subjective qualitative evaluations. Notionally, the balance in testing advertising is to use a greater proportion of qualitative than quantitative methods. The balance with sales promotions is shifted the other way. This is because the object being measured lends itself more to these kinds of measurement. If the purpose of sales promotion is to influence purchasing behaviour, then a measure of sales performance is necessary in addition to the evaluation of individual promotions.

Manufacturers to resellers

The main objectives are to stimulate the resellers to try new products and to encourage them to allocate increased shelf space for established products. If campaigns are devised to meet these objectives, then a pre- and post-test analysis of the amount of allocated shelf space and the number of new products taken into the reseller's portfolio needs to be completed. These processes are called retail audits (such as those undertaken by Nielsen Marketing Research), and although the information about changes in distribution and stock levels is not usually available until after the promotion has finished, it does provide accurate information concerning the effects that the event had on these variables.

Resellers to consumers

By generating higher levels of store traffic and moving stock from the store shelves to the consumers, sales promotions in this context require two main forms of evaluation. The first requires measures of the image held of the retailer, and this needs the use of tracking studies. The second requires measures of stock turnover per product category or brand against a predetermined planned level of turnover.

Manufacturers to consumers

The objectives are to encourage new users to try a product or to increase the amount that current users consume.

The objectives are to encourage new users to try a product or to increase the amount that current users consume. Targets can be set for the number of coupons to be redeemed, sales generated during and after a price deal, the volume of bonus packs sold, the speed and volume of premiums disposed of and other direct measures of activity. Consumer audits reveal changes in the penetration and usage patterns of consumers. Redemption levels give some indication of participation levels, but should not be considered as the sole method of evaluation, as there are many people who might be encouraged to purchase by the promotion but who then fail to participate for a variety of reasons.

Manufacturers to sales forces

The objectives of these activities are to build performance, morale and allegiance to the manufacturers and their products. Apart from measuring sales performance, the effectiveness of these activities can be expensive and difficult to measure. Attitude studies of the sales force can indicate the degree to which a contest has been influential, but it is hard to isolate the effects from those of other variables acting on them.

Through systematic tracking of sales and market share, products in mature markets can be evaluated in terms of their responsiveness to sales promotions. This type of information must be treated carefully, as the impact of other environmental factors has not been determined. Redemption rates allow for quantitative analysis that, through time, leads to the establishment of a database from which benchmarks for promotional measurement and achievement can be obtained.

Using technology to evaluate sales promotions

It was noted in a previous section on advertising that advances in IT have radically altered the way in which advertising and product purchases can be evaluated. The same applies to sales promotions. It is now possible to predict with a high level of accuracy the impact on sales of different combinations of in-store promotions and price deals. This permits greater understanding of the way in which different sales promotions work and when they are most effective. This has two main benefits: the first is to focus promotions on activities that are effective; the second is to help to target the communication spend on periods of the year, month and week that consumers are most responsive.

Homescan is an electronic household panel offered by ACNielsen that tracks day-to-day shopping patterns.

Homescan is an electronic household panel offered by ACNielsen that tracks day-to-day shopping patterns. It measures the household penetration and the retail distribution of a product. ACNielsen uses the system to analyse trial and repeat use and it provides data on consumer buying behaviour across most types of channel. These range from warehouse clubs and convenience stores to supermarkets, mass merchandisers, mail order and the Internet. It can measure the number of households that use the product once and it can then determine how many of these trialists adopt a product through repeat purchase activity. It follows that test promotions can be used in particular stores or geographic areas, and control promotions can be used to test impact and effectiveness. What might work in one area might be unsuccessful elsewhere.

Coupons can be distributed not only via products and media. Technology has been developed that allows coupons of competitive brands to be automatically dispensed at the checkout once a product has been scanned. This information, together with the demographics and psychographic details compiled for panel members, enables detailed profiles to be built up about the types, timing and value of sales promotions to which different consumers respond.

Sales promotions are a competitive tool that allows for swift reaction and placement. In that sense, they are not being used as part of an overall campaign, more as an ad hoc sales boost. This implies that the manageability of sales promotions is very high relative to the other elements of the promotions mix and that the opportunity to pre-test might not be as large in practice as is theoretically possible (Peattie and Peattie, 1993).

The evaluation of sales promotion is potentially fast, direct, precise and easily comprehended (Doyle and Saunders, 1985). However, evaluation is not necessarily that clear cut. The synergistic qualities of the communications mix inevitably lead to crossover effects where the impact of other communications influences responses to particular sales-promotion events. Promotions may also bring about increased awareness in addition to the trial, use and switching activities. Peattie and Peattie suggest that not only might brand and product substitution result from promotions, but store-loyalty patterns might also be affected.

Of all the tools in the communications mix, sales promotions lend themselves more easily to evaluation rather than to testing. Testing is not realistically possible in the time frames in which some organisations operate, particularly those in the FMCG sector. Activities should be planned and research built into campaigns, but it is the availability of improved IT that will continue to improve and accelerate the quality of information that management has about its sales.

Summary of key points

1. Sales promotion offers buyers additional value, as an inducement to generate an immediate sale. These inducements can be targeted at consumers, distributors, agents and members of the sales force.

2. Sales promotions represent a significant share of many organisations' promotional budget. This is because they can be a very effective means of increasing sales in the short term. However, there are growing doubts about the effectiveness and profitability associated with some sales promotions.

3. Sales promotions have a strategic role to play, particularly when they are used to complement the other activities in the promotional mix. By attempting to develop a consistent theme to a promotional plan, sales promotions can follow advertising's awareness-building activities with a series of messages that continue the theme already established.

4. Sales promotions used by manufacturers to communicate with resellers are aimed at encouraging resellers to either try new products or purchase more of the ones they currently stock. To do this, trade allowances, in various guises, are the principal means.

5. Sales promotions used by resellers (largely retailers) to influence consumers are normally driven by manufacturers, although some price deals and other techniques are used to generate store traffic.

6. The majority of sales promotions are those used by manufacturers to influence consumers. Again, the main tasks are to encourage trial or increase product purchase. A range of techniques, from sampling and coupons to premiums, contests and sweepstakes, are all used with varying levels of success, but there has been a distinct shift away from traditional promotional instruments to the use of digital media in order to reflect consumers' preferences and media behaviour.

7. In comparison with advertising and public relations, many of the sales-promotion techniques are easier to evaluate, if only because the number of variables is smaller and they are easier to isolate.

Review questions

1. Why do organisations use sales promotion and why has sales promotion assumed such a large share of promotional expenditure?

2. Write brief notes outlining some of the issues associated with loyalty programmes and customer-retention initiatives.

3. How might use of technology assist the development of loyalty and retention programmes?

4. List the main sales-promotion methods used by manufacturers and targeted at consumers. How can coupons be used to reduce levels of perceived risk?

5. Explain the objectives that manufacturers might have when encouraging resellers to take stock of more product.

6. How would you advise a newly appointed assistant brand manager on the expected outcomes of a sales-promotion programme? (Choose any sector/industry of your choice.) Suggest four ways in which sales promotions can be evaluated.

References

Advertising Association (2004), *Marketing Statistics*, Henley-on-Thames: NTC.

Barrand, D. (2004), 'Promoting change', *Marketing*, 6 October, pp. 43–5.

Clarke, A. (2001), 'Finger on the pulse', *Promotions and Incentives* (February), pp. 41–4.

Couldwell, C. (2003), 'Countdown to music', *Incentive Business*, November, pp. 45–6.

Curtis, J. (1996), 'Opposites attract', *Marketing*, 25 April, pp. 28–9.

d'Astous, A. and Jacob, I. (2002), 'Understanding consumer reactions to premium-based promotional offers', *European Journal of Marketing*, 36(11), pp. 1270–86.

Davis, M. (1992), 'Sales promotions as a competitive strategy', *Management Decision*, 30(7), pp. 5–10.

Della Bitta, A.J. and Monroe, K.B. (1980), 'A multivariate analysis of the perception of value from retail price advertisements', in *Advances in Consumer Research*, Vol. 8 (ed. K.B. Monroe), Ann Arbor, Mich.: Association for Consumer Research.

Derrick, S. (2005), 'The power of paper', *Marketing*, 1 May, pp. 39–40.

Doyle, P. and Saunders, J. (1985), 'The lead effect of marketing decisions', *Journal of Marketing Research*, 22(1), pp. 54–65.

Govoni, N., Eng, R. and Gaper, M. (1986), *Promotional Management*, Englewood Cliffs, NJ: Prentice-Hall.

Gupta, S. and Cooper, L.G. (1992), 'The discounting of discounts and promotion brands', *Journal of Consumer Research*, 19 (December), pp. 401–11.

Kleinman, M. (2003), 'Boots to overhaul loyalty strategy', *Marketing*, 28 August, p. 1.

Lee, C.H. (2002), 'Sales promotions as strategic communication: the case of Singapore', *Journal of Product and Brand Management*, **11**(2), pp. 103–14.

Middleton, V.T.C. (1989), *Marketing in Travel and Tourism*, Oxford: Heinemann.

O'Malley, L. (1998), 'Can loyalty schemes really build loyalty?', *Marketing Intelligence and Planning*, **16**(1), pp. 47–55.

Papatia, P. and Krishnamurthi, L. (1996), 'Measuring the dynamic effects of promotions on brand choice', *Journal of Marketing Research*, **33**(1) (February), pp. 20–35.

Peattie, K. and Peattie, S. (1993), 'Sales promotion: playing to win', *Journal of Marketing Management*, **9**, pp. 255–69.

Shultz, D.E. (1987), 'Above or below the line? Growth of sales promotion in the United States', *International Journal of Advertising*, **6**, pp. 17–27.

Public relations and sponsorship

10

Aims and objectives

The aims of this chapter are to explore public relations in the context of promoting organisations and their products, and to introduce and examine sponsorship as an increasingly significant and potent form of marketing communications. There are four primary topics in this chapter:

Public relations, Activities, Sponsorship, Evaluation

The learning objectives are to enable readers to:

1. discuss the role of public relations in the communications mix;
2. explain the main audiences at which public relations activities are directed;
3. understand the main methods, approaches and tools used to generate public relations;
4. discuss the ways in which public relations complements the other tools of the communications mix;
5. explain the variety and different forms of sponsorship activities;
6. provide an insight into the main characteristics of this form of communication;
7. explore ways in which the use of public relations and sponsorship can be best measured and evaluated.

Introduction

Increasingly, organisations are recognising the impact and influence that public relations can play in their external and internal communications. All organisations in the public, hybrid, not-for-profit and private sectors can use this tool to raise visibility, interest and goodwill.

Traditionally, public relations has been a tool that dealt with the manner and style with which an organisation interacted with its major 'publics'. It sought to influence other organisations and individuals by public relations, projecting an identity that would affect the image that different publics held of the organisation. By spreading information and improving the levels of knowledge that people held about particular issues, the organisation sought ways to advance itself in the eyes of those it saw as influential. This approach is reflected in the definition of public relations provided by the Institute

Public relations is concerned with the management of relationships between organisations and their stakeholders (publics).

of Public Relations: 'Public relations practice is the planned and sustained effort to establish and maintain goodwill and mutual understanding between an organisation and its publics'. An alternative definition from Bruning and Ledingham (2000) is that public relations is concerned with the management of relationships between organisations and their stakeholders (publics). This definition indicates the direction in which both public relations and marketing theory is moving.

For a long time public relations has been concerned with the development and communication of corporate and competitive strategies. Public relations provides visibility for an organisation, and this in turn, it is hoped, allows it to be properly identified, positioned and understood by all of its stakeholders. What some definitions do not emphasise or make apparent is that public relations should also be used by management as a means of understanding issues from a stakeholder perspective. Good relationships are developed by appreciating the views held by others and by 'putting oneself in their shoes'.

Through this sympathetic and patient approach to planned communication, a dialogue can be developed that is not frustrated by punctuated interruptions (anger, disbelief, ignorance and objections). Public relations is a management activity that attempts to shape the attitudes and opinions held by an organisation's stakeholders. It

Public relations is a management activity that attempts to shape the attitudes and opinions held by an organisation's stakeholders.

attempts to identify its own policies with the interests of its stakeholders and formulates and executes a programme of action to develop mutual goodwill and understanding. Through this process relationships are developed which are in the long-term interests of all parties.

Characteristics of public relations

There are a number of characteristics that single out this particular tool from the others in the communications mix. One of the most important points of difference is that public relations does not require the purchase of airtime or space in media vehicles, such as television or magazines. The decision on whether an organisation's public relations messages are transmitted or not rests therefore with those charged with managing the media resource, not the message sponsor. The outcome is that these messages usually carry greater perceived credibility than those messages transmitted through paid media, such as advertising.

The degree of trust and confidence generated by public relations singles out this tool from others in the communications mix as an important means of reducing buyers' perceived risk. However, while credibility may be high, the amount of control that management is able to bring to the transmission of the public relations message is very low. For example, a press release may have been carefully prepared in-house, but as soon as it is passed to the editor of a magazine or newspaper, a possible opinion former, all control is lost. The release may be destroyed (highly probable), printed as it stands (highly unlikely) or changed to fit the available space in the media vehicle (almost certain, if it is decided to use the material). This means that any changes to the message may not have been agreed with management, so the context and style of the original message may be lost or corrupted.

The costs associated with public relations also make this an important tool in the communications mix. The absolute costs are minimal, except for those organisations that retain an agency, but even then their costs are low compared with those of advertising. The relative costs (the proportional costs associated with reaching each member of the target audience) are also very low. The main costs associated with public relations are the time and opportunity costs associated with the preparation of press releases and associated literature. If these types of activity are organised properly, many small organisations could develop and shape their visibility in a relatively inexpensive way.

A further characteristic of this tool is that it can be used to reach specific audiences, in a way that paid media cannot. With increasing media fragmentation and finer segmentation (customisation) of markets, public relations represents a cost-effective way of reaching such markets and audiences.

New technology has played a key role in the development and practice of public relations. New technology has played a key role in the development and practice of public relations. Gregory (2004) refers to the Internet and electronic communication 'transforming public relations'. With regard to the use of the Internet by public relations practitioners she identifies two main schools. One refers to those who use the Internet as an extension to traditional or pre-Internet forms of communication. The second see opportunities through the Internet to develop two-way, enhanced communication. There can be little doubt that new technology has assisted communication management in terms of improving the transparency, speed and reach of public relations messages and at the same time enabling interactive communication between an organisation and its specific audiences.

Audiences

Mention has already been of stakeholders, those groups who influence or who are influenced by the actions of an organisation. Stakeholder groups are not static and new groups can emerge in response to changes in the environment. The main core groups, however, tend to be the following.

Employees (internal public relations)

The employees of an organisation are major stakeholders and represent a major opportunity to use word-of-mouth communications. It has long been established that employees need to be motivated, involved and stimulated to perform their tasks at a high level. Their work as external communicators is less well established, but their critical role is providing external cues as part of the corporate identity programme.

Financial groups (financial or investor relations)

Shareholders require regular information to maintain their continued confidence in the organisation and to prevent them changing their portfolios and reducing the value of the organisation.

In addition to the shareholders, there are those individuals who are either potential shareholders or who provide advice for shareholders and investors. These represent the wider financial community but nevertheless have a very strong influence on the stature, strength and value of an organisation. Financial analysts need to be supplied with information in order that they be up to date with the activities and performance outcomes of organisations, but also need to be advised of developments within the various markets that the organisation operates.

Customers (media relations)

The relationships that organisations develop with the media are extremely important in order that their messages reach their current and potential customers.

The relationships that organisations develop with the media are extremely important in order that their messages reach their current and potential customers. Customers represent a major stakeholder audience and are often the target

---

ViewPoint 10.1   Press for Dyson

When James Dyson launched his revolutionary upright vacuum cleaner he did not have the resources to fund an advertising campaign to support the launch. Although the design enabled the product to stand out in showrooms there was little to inform customers of the advantages of the product and to justify the starting price, which was double that of the competition.

One solution was to hang a brochure and a point-of-sales tag on the handle of each machine. The brochure folded out, provided basic information about each component and avoided any superlatives or attempts at persuasion. The sales tag, however, was used to tell the story about the experiences Dyson encountered trying to design and bring the new product to the market. People would be seen bending over avidly reading the Dyson story.

The second solution was to use press journalists to recall the same story because they could reach the target market and their messages would be highly credible in the eyes of the target audience. Rather than write press releases Dyson gave interviews to selected reporters, many of whom were from the quality press. The articles tended to be extremely positive about the product but concentrated more on the life experiences of James Dyson himself and reinforced the messages conveyed through the sales tags. The personalised account of the development process and the frequency with which these articles appeared provided readers with a way of identifying and becoming emotionally engaged with the whole Dyson experience. The language used and the repetition of the messages only served to increase the overall intensity of these marketing communications messages.

Source: Adapted from Boyle (2004); used with permission

of public relations activities, because although members of the public may not be current customers the potential they represent is important. The attitudes and preferences
towards the organisation and its products may be unfavourable, in which case it is
unlikely that they will wish to purchase the product or speak positively about the
organisation. By creating awareness and trust it is possible to create goodwill and interest, which may translate into purchase activity or favourable word-of-mouth communications. This is achieved through media relations.

Of all the media, the press is the most crucial, as it is always interested in newsworthy
items and depends to a large extent on information being fed to it by a variety of corporate press officers. Consequently, publicity can be generated for a range of organisational events, activities and developments.

Organisations and communities (corporate public relations)

There are a variety of public, private, commercial and not-for-profit organisations and
communities with whom organisations need to communicate and interact on a regular basis.

Corporate public relations (sometimes referred to as corporate communications) are
used to reach this wide spectrum of audiences and cover a range of activities. Each
audience and set of issues have particular characteristics that lead to individual forms
of public relations practice:

● *public affairs* – government and local authorities;
● *community relations* – members of local communities;
● *industry relations* – suppliers, associations and other trade stakeholders;
● *issues management* – various audiences concerning sensitive industries (e.g. tobacco
  or pharmaceuticals).

Organisations should seek to work with, rather than against, these stakeholder groups.
As a result, public relations should be aimed at informing audiences of their strategic
intentions and seeking ways in which the objectives of both parties can be satisfied.

A framework of public relations

Communications with such a wide variety of stakeholders need to vary to reflect different environmental conditions, organisational objectives and form of relationship.
Grunig and Hunt (1984) have attempted to capture the diversity of public relations
activities through a framework. They set out four models to reflect the different ways
in which public relations is, in their opinion, considered to work. These models, based
on their experiences as public relations practitioners, constitute a useful approach to
understanding the complexity of this form of communication. The four models are set
out in Figure 10.1.

The press agentry/publicity model

The essence of this approach is that communication is used as a form of propaganda.
That is, the communication flow is essentially one way, and the content is not bound

Characteristic	Model			
	Press agentry/publicity	Public information	Two-way asymmetric	Two-way symmetric
Purpose	Propaganda	Dissemination of information	Scientific persuasion	Mutual understanding
Nature of communication	One way; complete truth not essential	One way; truth important	Two way; imbalanced effects	Two way; balanced effects
Communication model	Source→Rec.*	Source→Rec.*	Source ⇌ Rec.* Feedback	Group ⇌ Group
Nature of research	Little; 'counting house'	Little; readability, readership	Formative; evaluative of attitudes	Formative; evaluative of understanding
Leading historical figures	P.T. Barnum	Ivy Lee	Edward L. Bernays	Bernays, educators, professional leaders
Where practised today	Sports, theatre, product promotion	Government, not-for-profit associations, business	Competitive business, agencies	Regulated business, agencies
Estimated percentage of organisations practising today	15%	50%	20%	15%

* Receiver.

FIGURE 10.1 Four models of public relations. From Grunig and Hunt (1984); used with kind permission

to be strictly truthful as the objective is to convince the receiver of a new idea or offering. This can be observed in the growing proliferation of media events and press releases.

The public information model

Unlike the first model, this approach seeks to disseminate truthful information. While the flow is again one way, there is little focus on persuasion, more on the provision of information. This can best be seen through public health campaigns and government advice communications in respect of crime, education and health.

The two-way asymmetric model

Two-way communication is a major element of this model. Feedback from receivers is important, but as power is not equally distributed between the various stakeholders and the organisation, the relationship has to be regarded as asymmetric. The purpose remains to influence attitude and behaviour through persuasion.

The two-way symmetric model

This represents the most acceptable and mutually rewarding form of communication. Power is seen to be dispersed equally between the organisation and its stakeholders,

The organisation and its respective publics
are prepared to adjust their positions.

and the intent of the communication flow is considered to be reciprocal. The organisation and its respective publics are prepared to adjust their positions (attitudes and behaviours) in the light of the information flow. A true dialogue emerges through this interpretation, unlike any of the other three models, which see an unbalanced flow of information and expectations.

The model has attracted a great deal of attention and has been reviewed and appraised by a number of commentators (Miller, 1989). As a result of this and a search for excellence in public relations, Grunig (1992) revised the model to reflect the dominance of the 'craft' and the 'professional' approaches to public relations practices. That is, those practitioners who utilise public relations merely as a tool to achieve media visibility can be regarded as 'craft'-oriented. Those organisations whose managers seek to utilise public relations as a means of mediating their relationships with their various stakeholders are seen as 'professional' practitioners. They are considered to be using public relations as a longer-term and proactive form of planned communication. The former see public relations as an instrument, the latter as a means of conducting a dialogue.

These models are not intended to suggest that communication planners should choose among them. Their use and interpretation depend upon the circumstances that prevail at any one time. Organisations use a number of these different approaches to manage the communication issues that exist between them and the variety of different stakeholder audiences with whom they interact. However, there is plenty of evidence to suggest that the press agentry/publicity model is the one most used by practitioners and that the two-way symmetrical model is harder to observe in practice.

Public relations and relationship management

In addition, it is important to remember that the shift to a relationship management perspective effectively alters the way public relations is perceived and practised by organisations. Ehling (1992) suggests that instead of trying to manipulate audience opinion so that the organisation is of primary importance, the challenge is to use symbolic visual communication messages with behaviour such that the organisation–audience relationship improves for all parties. Bruning and Ledingham (2000) and Kent and Taylor (2002) develop this theme by suggesting that it is the ability of organisations to encourage and practise dialogue that really enables truly symmetrical relationships to develop.

It is the ability of organisations to encourage and practise dialogue that really enables truly symmetrical relationships to develop.

What follows from this is a change in evaluation, from measuring the decimation of messages to one that measures audience influence and behavioural and attitudinal change and, of course, relationship dynamics. Bruning and Ledingham phrase this as a change from measuring outputs to outcomes.

In addition to this discernible shift in emphasis has been a change in the way public relations is used by organisations. Traditionally, public relations has been used as a means of managing communication between parties, whereas now communication is regarded as a means of managing relationships (Kent and Taylor, 2002). In order to use communication to develop the full potential within relationships many argue that dialogic interaction should be encouraged. At a practical level they argue that organisations should place email and Web addresses, 0800 telephone numbers and organisational addresses prominently in all forms of external communication, most notably advertisements and websites, just to enable dialogue to happen.

Corporate public relations and marketing public relations

Many writers and organisations are now challenging the traditional view of public relations. The marketing dimension of public relations has been developed considerably in recent years. This is a response to media rates increasing ahead of inflation, media and markets becoming increasingly fragmented and marketing managers seeking more effective communications mixes. Public relations has a distinct role within the marketing communications mix to influence perceptions of the organisation as well as the products and services offered.

> The development of integrated marketing communications has helped bring marketing and public relations closer together.

The development of integrated marketing communications has helped bring marketing and public relations closer together. The advantage of utilising a number of tools together is that, through coordination, message impact is improved. One of the best examples of this is the Wonderbra campaign by Playtex. It is estimated that the poster campaign was enhanced by £50 million worth of 'extra' media coverage based on the stories and publicity generated by the programme (Barrett, 1997).

Two main types of public relations have begun to emerge: corporate public relations and marketing public relations. According to Cutlip et al. (1985), corporate public relations is 'a function of management seeking to identify, establish and maintain mutually beneficial relationships between an organisation and the various publics on whom its success and failure depend'. They then define marketing public relations as 'not only concerned with organisational success and failure but also with specific publics: customers, consumers and clients with whom exchange transactions take place'.

This dichotomy is not intended to suggest that these are mutually exclusive forms of public relations, since they are not, and, as Kitchen and Proctor (1991) rightly point out, they are mutually interactive. The use of corporate communications has an effect similar to that of ink being injected into a bottle of water: the diffusion produced can assist all parts of an organisation and its stakeholders. Similarly, public relations at the product level can have an immediate effect upon the goodwill and perspective with which stakeholders perceive the whole organisation.

For example, for an airline opening a new route, its marketing PR activities focused on customers in the hinterland of each destination will impact on both the product and the airline as a whole. Further examples of MPR can be observed by companies installing 'carelines' that can be used by customers to contact them (to seek advice and complain) about aspects of the company's products and services. The telephone number, which can be made visible on posters, receipts, catalogues, advertisements, email, websites and shopping bags, serves to feed negative and positive aspects and through the use of data analysis can assist the development of new products and services. Indeed, both Burger King and McDonald's have used this to develop new menus and merchandising items.

The net impact of either approach has to be reflected in the performance of the organisation, and for many that is the profitability of the unit. The identification of these two forms of public relations does not mean that this approach is a widely used practice. Indeed, at this stage only a minority of organisations recognise the benefits that the approach can bring. However, as an increasing number of organisations, in a variety of sectors, are expanding their use of PR, so more sophisticated approaches are likely to emerge, aimed at improving product, corporate and overall performance and satisfaction levels.

The roles of public relations

It can be seen that the broad objectives of public relations activities are to provide visibility for the corporate body and support for the marketing agenda at the product level. The promotional objectives, established earlier in the plan, will have identified issues concerning the attitudes and relationships stakeholders have with an organisation and its products. Decisions will have been made to build awareness and to change perception, preferences or attitudes. The task of the public relations plan is to provide a series of coordinated programmes that complement the overall marketing communications strategy and which develop and enhance some of the identity cues used by stakeholders. The overall goal should be to develop relationships by engaging the organisation and its different audiences.

The overall goal should be to develop relationships by engaging the organisation and its different audiences.

Public relations has three major roles to play within the communications programme of an organisation. These are the development and maintenance of corporate goodwill, the continuity necessary for good product support and, through these, the development and maintenance of suitable relationships.

The first is the traditional role of creating goodwill and stimulating interest between the organisation and its various key stakeholders. Its task is to provide a series of cues by which the stakeholders can recognise, understand and position the organisation in such a way that the organisation builds a strong reputation. This role is closely allied to the corporate strategy and the communication of strategic intent.

EXHIBIT 10.1 HP invent

As part of the process of preparing for the future, Hewlett-Packard used corporate advertising to reaffirm corporate values, with staff and major stakeholders. Picture reproduced with the kind permission of Hewlett-Packard Ltd

The second role of public relations is to support the marketing of the organisation's products and services, and its task is to integrate with the other elements of the communications mix. Public relations and advertising have complementary roles. For example, the launch of a new product commences not with advertising to build awareness in target customers but with the use of public relations to inform editors and news broadcasters that a new product is about to be launched. This news material can be used within the trade and consumer press before advertising occurs and the target buyers become aware (when the news is no longer news). To some extent this role is tactical rather than strategic, but if planned, and if events are timed and coordinated with the other elements of the communications mix, then public relations can help build competitive advantage.

Public relations and advertising have complementary roles.

The third role is to provide the means by which relationships can be developed. To do this public relations has a responsibility to encourage interaction and dialogue to provide the means through which discourse and discussion can occur and to play a full part in the communications process and the messages that are conveyed, listened to, considered and acted upon.

Public relations methods and techniques

Public relations provides some of the deliberate cues that enable stakeholders to develop images and perceptions by which they recognise, understand and converse with organisations.

The range of public relations cues or methods available to organisations is immense. Different organisations use different permutations in order that they can communicate effectively with their various stakeholder audiences. For the purposes of this text a general outline is provided of the more commonly used methods.

Media relations

Media relations consists of a range of activities designed to provide media journalists and editors with information. The intention is that they relay the information, through their media, for consumption by their audiences. Of course, the original message may be changed and subject to information deviance as it is processed but audiences perceive much of this information as highly credible simply because opinion formers (Chapter 2) have bestowed their judgement on the item. Of the various forms of media relations, press releases, interviews, press kits and press conferences are most used.

Press releases

The press release is a common form of media relations activity. A written report concerning a change in the organisation is sent to various media houses for inclusion in the media vehicle as an item of news. The media house may cover a national area, but very often a local house will suffice. These written statements concern developments in the organisation, such as promotions, new products, awards, prizes, new contracts and customers. The statement is deliberately short and written in such a style that it attracts the attention of the editor. Further information can be obtained if it is to be included within the next publication or news broadcast.

Press conferences

Press conferences are used when a major event has occurred and where a press release cannot convey the appropriate tone or detail required by the organisation. Press conferences are mainly used by politicians, but organisations in crisis (e.g. accidents and mergers) and individuals appealing for help (e.g. police requesting assistance from the public with respect to a particular incident) can use this form of communication. Press kits containing a full reproduction of any statements, photographs and relevant background information should always be available.

Interviews

Interviews with representatives of an organisation enable news and the organisation's view of an issue or event to be conveyed. Other forms of media relations concern bylined articles (articles written by a member of an organisation about an issue related to the company and offered for publication), speeches, letters to the editor, and photographs and captions.

Media relations can be planned and controlled to the extent of what is sent to the media and when it is released. Although there is no control over what is actually used, media relations allow organisations to try to convey information concerning strategic issues and to reach particular stakeholders.

The quality of the relationship between an organisation and the media will dramatically affect the impact and dissemination of news and stories released by an organisation. The relationships referred to are those between an organisation's public relations manager and the editor and journalists associated with both the press and the broadcast media.

> The quality of the relationship between an organisation and the media will dramatically affect the impact and dissemination of news and stories released by an organisation.

Publicity and events

Control over public relations events is not as strong as that for media relations. Indeed, negative publicity can be generated by other parties, which can impact badly on an organisation by raising doubts about its financial status or perhaps the quality of its products.

Three main event activity areas can be distinguished: product, corporate and community events.

1. *Product events*
   Product-oriented events are normally focused upon increasing sales. Cookery demonstrations, celebrities autographing their books and the opening of a new store by the CEO or local MP are events aimed at generating attention, interest and sales of a particular product. Alternatively, events are designed to attract the attention of the media and, through stories and articles presented in the news, are able to reach a wide audience.

2. *Corporate events*
   Events designed to develop the corporate body are often held by an organisation with a view to providing some entertainment. These can generate a lot of local media coverage, which in turn facilitates awareness, goodwill and interest. For example, events such as open days, factory visits and donations of products to local events can be very beneficial.

3. *Community events*
   These are activities that contribute to the life of the local community. Sponsoring local fun runs and children's play areas, making contributions to local community

TABLE 10.1 Forms of public relations

Form of public relations	Explanation
Lobbying	Attempts by organisations to persuade and negotiate with government on matters of opportunity and/or threat. While legislation is being prepared, lobbyists can provide a flow of information into their organisations to keep them informed about events and also ensure that the views of the organisation are heard in order that legislation can be shaped appropriately, limiting any potential damage that new legislation might bring. Used a great deal by the pharmaceutical and tobacco industries.
Sponsorship	Sponsorship allows one organisation to reach the audience of another in order to develop new or established product- and service-based associations. See later in this chapter for more details.
Corporate advertising	The use of advertising to present managed messages about the organisation (not products) to a wide range of stakeholders, with a view to influencing the way the organisation is perceived and understood, either generally or on a specific issue.
Crisis management	Organisations are vulnerable to the impact of a crisis. These crises may be caused by uncontrollable events (e.g. climate change) or are potentially controllable but because of mismanagement an organisation suffers a temporary or even permanent failure. Crisis communications plans should be in position to avert or diminish the impact of both offline and online threats.

centres and the disabled are typical activities. The organisation attempts to become more involved with the local community as a good employer and good member of the community. This helps to develop goodwill and awareness in the community.

The choice of events an organisation becomes involved with is critical. The events should have a theme and be chosen to satisfy objectives established earlier in the communications plan.

In addition to these key activities there are several important variants of public relations. These are set out in Table 10.1. Readers interested in these topics are advised to see Fill (2006).

Sponsorship

Sponsorship is a relatively new marketing communications tool and has become an increasingly popular element of the mix because of the quality of the communication it generates. It is a cross between advertising, with its capacity for message control, and public relations with its potential for high levels of credibility and message diffusion, directed through or with a third party. In this sense sponsorship lacks the harshness of advertising and the total lack of control that characterises much of the work of public relations. A definition of sponsorship might be that it is a commercial activity whereby one party permits

> In this sense sponsorship lacks the harshness of advertising and the total lack of control that characterises much of the work of public relations.

another an opportunity to exploit an association with a target audience in return for funds, services or resources. In particular it allows:

1. Exposure to particular audiences that each event attracts in order to convey simple awareness-based brand messages.
2. To suggest to the target audiences that there is an association between the sponsored and the sponsor and that by implication this association may be of interest and/or value.
3. To allow members of the target audiences to perceive the sponsor indirectly through a third party and so diffuse any negative effects associated with traditional mass-media and direct persuasion.
4. Sponsorship provides sponsors with the opportunity to blend a variety of tools in the communications mix and use resources more efficiently and, arguably, more effectively.

Sponsorship is not usually used as a primary or lead promotional tool. Generally it is a secondary form of communication, used to support other communications activities. However, sponsorship can also play a major strategic role for organisations. For example, many companies and brands originating in south-east Asia and the Pacific regions have used sponsorship as a means of overseas market entry in order to develop name or brand awareness (e.g. Panasonic, JVC and Daihatsu).

Corporate sponsorships, according to Thwaites (1994), are intended to focus upon developing community involvement, public awareness, image, goodwill and staff relations. Product- or brand-based sponsorship activity is aimed at developing media coverage, sales leads, sales/market share, target-market awareness and guest hospitality. What is important is that sponsorship is not a tool that can be effective in a stand-alone capacity. The full potential of this tool is only realised when it is integrated with some (or all) of the other tools of the communications mix. As Tripodi (2001) comments, the implementation of integrated marketing communications is further encouraged and supported when sponsorship is an integral part of the mix in order to maximise the full impact of this communication tool.

Sponsorship objectives

There are both primary and secondary objectives associated with using sponsorship. The primary reasons are to build awareness, to develop customer loyalty and to improve the perception (image) held of the brand or organisation. Secondary reasons are more contentious, but generally they can be seen to be to attract new users, to support dealers and other intermediaries and to act as a form of staff motivation and morale building (Reed, 1994).

Sponsorship is normally regarded as a communications tool used to reach external stakeholders. However, if chosen appropriately sponsorship can also be used effectively to reach internal audiences. Care is required because different audiences transfer diverse values (Grimes and Meenaghan, 1998). According to Harverson (1998), one of the main reasons IT companies sponsor sports events is that this form of involvement provides opportunities to 'showcase' their products and technologies in context. Through application in an appropriate working environment, the efficacy of a sponsor's products can be demonstrated. The relationship between

Care is required because different audiences transfer diverse values.

sports organisers and IT companies becomes reciprocal as the organisers of sports events need technology in order for the events to run (e.g. swimming, athletics, Formula One).

Corporate hospitality opportunities are often taken in addition to the brand exposure that the media coverage provides. EDS claims that it uses sponsorship to reach two main audiences, customers (and potential customers) and potential future employees. The message it uses is that EDS involvement in sport is sexy and exciting.

Types of sponsorship

It is possible to identify particular areas within which sponsorship has been used. These areas are sports, programmes/broadcasts, the arts, and others that encompass activities such as wildlife/conservation and education. Of all of these, sport has attracted most attention and sponsorship money. See Table 10.2.

Sports sponsorship

Sports activities have been very attractive to sponsors, partly because of the high media coverage they attract. Sport is the leading type of sponsorship, mainly for the following reasons:

1. Sport has the propensity to attract large audiences, not only at each event but more importantly through the media that attach themselves to these activities.
2. Sport provides a simplistic measure of segmentation, so that as audiences fragment generally, sport provides an opportunity to identify and reach often large numbers of people who share particular characteristics.
3. Visibility opportunities for the sponsor are high in a number of sporting events because of the duration of each event (e.g. the Olympics or the FIFA World Cup).

Barclaycard's sponsorship of the football Premier League and Coca-Cola's sponsorship of the football Championship have been motivated partly by the attraction of large and specific target audiences with whom a degree of fit is considered to exist. The constant media attention enables the sponsors' names to be disseminated to distant audiences, many of them overseas.

TABLE 10.2 Long-term trends in the UK sponsorship market by sector, 1980–2003, in £m

	Sports	Arts	Broadcast	Other	Total
1980	30	3	–	2	35
1990	223	35	7	16	281
1995	285	83	75	35	478
2000	401	150	176	80	807
2002	429	111	193	58	791
2003	411	120	199*	63*	793*

* estimated

Source: Mintel, Ipsos

Marshall and Cook (1992) found that event sponsorship (e.g. the Olympics or World Championships) is the most popular form of sponsorship activity undertaken by organisations. This was followed by team, league and individual support.

Both football and golf have attracted a great deal of sponsorship money, mainly because they have global upmarket appeal and generate good television and press coverage. Golf clubs are also well suited for corporate entertainment and offer the chance of playing as well as watching. HSBC, one of the world's largest financial services organisations, are sponsors of the men's World Match Play Championship in England. In January 2005 they announced their financial support for the first and complementary individual match play championship for women. Agreeing to a five-year deal, HSBC claimed that there is a strong fit with sport, and with golf in particular, because of its global appeal. The bank believes that golf is well established in developed markets and is a booming and aspirational sport in regions like Asia, where the banking group was founded. More importantly, they believe the game mirrors HSBC's character and how they prefer to do business. Internationalism, inclusiveness and integrity are as much characteristics of the sport as they are of HSBC.

Before HSBC, Toyota used to support the men's World Match Play Championship at Wentworth, because the tournament fitted into a much wider promotion programme. Toyota dealers sponsored competitions at their local courses, with qualifiers going through to a final at Wentworth. The winner of that played in the pro-am before the World Match Play. Toyota incorporated the tournament into a range of incentive and promotional programmes and flew in top distributors and fleet customers from around the world. In addition, the environment was used to build customer relationships.

ViewPoint 10.2   Rugby World Cup

The Rugby World Cup finals held in Australia in 2003 attracted a number of different sponsors, termed official worldwide partners.

Heineken was the official beer and one of its goals was to add to the experience of the event for rugby fans and beer drinkers all over the world, regardless of whether they are at the game, at home or at their local bar or pub.

Visa's sponsorship was partly shaped by its desire to be associated with some of the world's most recognised brands. One brand in particular was Avis, with whom a competition was run.

British Airways and Qantas were the official airlines of the tournament and were responsible for flying teams, officials and international visitors into Australia and carrying Australian fans to matches around the country.

Peugeot was the official car of the tournament and it used the occasion to help launch its 307 Tourer model. This was used to transport players and officials between locations.

Sponsorship is used to reach specific target groups. Samsung signed a five-year, £50 million deal to sponsor Chelsea in the Premiership. The logo on the players' shirts is *Samsung Mobile*, which, according to Mawston, cited by Gray (2005), seeks to raise awareness and brand equity – and through Chelsea, target a younger and cooler market segment. He claims that sport and mobile telephony provide opportunities for strong sponsorship relationships and cites the Vodafone and Ferrari association to make the point.

Programme sponsorship

Although becoming established in North America in the 1980s, television programme sponsorship only began to receive serious attention in the UK in the late 1990s. The market was worth around £200 million (estimates vary) in 2003 and is growing, partly because of a relaxation by the Independent Television Commission in the regulations. However, the visibility that each sponsor is allowed has been strictly controlled to certain times, and before, during the break and after each programme with the credits. Allen (2000) reports that while it is still not intended that sponsors influence the content or scheduling of a programme so as to affect the editorial independence and responsibility of the broadcaster, it is now permissible to allow the sponsor's product to be seen along with the sponsor's name in bumper credits and to allow greater flexibility in terms of the use of straplines. There is a requirement on the broadcaster to ensure that the sponsored credit is depicted in such a way that it cannot be mistaken as a spot advertisement. So, Hedburg (2000) gives the example of Nescafé sponsoring *Friends* and shows a group of people sitting on a sofa and drinking coffee, and of *Coronation Street* sponsor Cadbury, which presents a whole chocolate street and chocolate characters.

Masthead programming, where the publisher of a magazine such as *Amateur Photographer* sponsors a programme in a related area, such as *Photography for Beginners*, is generally not permitted, although the regulations surrounding this type of activity are being relaxed.

It allows clients to avoid the clutter associated with spot advertising.

There are a number of reasons why programme sponsorship is appealing. First, it allows clients to avoid the clutter associated with spot advertising. In that sense it creates a space or mini-world in which the sponsor can create awareness and provide brand-identity cues unhindered by other brands. Second, it represents a cost-effective medium when compared with spot advertising. It is expected that the cost of programme sponsorship will increase as the value of this type of communication is appreciated by clients (Fry, 1997). Lastly, the use of credits around a programme offers opportunities for the target audience to make associations between the sponsor and the programme.

Research by the Bloxam Group suggests that for sponsorship to work there needs to be a linkage between the product and the programme. Links that are spurious, illogical or inappropriate are very often rejected by viewers. For example, soft drinks companies associated with youth programmes should be compatible but insurance companies linking with specialist film programmes or branded cheese with television dramas appear to be disconnected.

The same research suggests that viewers claim to own their favourite programmes, so sponsors should acknowledge this relationship and act accordingly, perhaps as a respectful guest, and not intrude too heavily on the programme. They should certainly resist any active participation in the programme. This suggests that the temptation to use the sponsor's products in the programme, either as props or within the copy or storyline, has to be resisted. To make the point memorable, Summers (1995) said that 'If Pop Larkin starts asking for a cup of Tetley, then that's not right'. Indeed, placement issues have been the subject of much recent debate. One report revealed some of the product placements used in some BBC programmes, where product placement is generally not permitted. Products such as Canon cameras, Sol beer, Belstaff jackets, Apple laptops, Kellogg's corn flakes, Dyson cleaners and even the soon-to-be-launched Reds beer had been spotted (Calvert and Walsh, 2005). The aim for the brands is to either avoid costly and, some would say, ineffective advertising or to have their products appear in natural settings and usage. Following successful placement and screening, public relations can be used to be build on the activity by proclaiming 'as seen on . . .'.

Programme sponsorship should not be regarded as a replacement for advertising.

Programme sponsorship should not be regarded as a replacement for advertising; indeed, the argument that sponsorship is not a part of advertising is demonstrated by the point that many sponsors continue with their spot advertising when running major sponsorships.

ViewPoint 10.3   Imperial Leather tops the Games

Imperial Leather undertook a leading sponsorship role within the Commonwealth Games in 2002. Rather than attempt to build a sports-performance association for the luxury soap brand and to adopt the normal serious tone of an official endorser the sponsorship was used to develop a set of fun values that matched the unofficial name 'The Friendly Games'.

This was implemented by a media-neutral approach aimed at the trade, consumers and employees. During the Games, three different TV advertisements were run featuring diving, athletics and gymnastics. In addition to normal public relations and sales promotions (including competitions and sampling events) the main media used were outdoor and press, signage, ambient plus online microsites. During the two weeks of the Games £880,000 worth of extra sales were found to be definitely related to the sponsorship. In direct comparison with many of the other leading sponsors, all of which spent far more on advertising prior to the Games than Imperial Leather, research showed that the soap brand recorded the highest spontaneous awareness of all the sponsors.

Source: Adapted from Hawtin (2004)

Cadbury's sponsorship of the major UK soap opera, *Coronation Street*, which began in 1996, is reported to have cost £10 million each year, when all the additional promotional activities and requirements are considered. The linkage established between the two parties (Cadbury's and *Coronation Street*) exemplifies the view about the relationship and the linkages.

Arts sponsorship

Arts sponsorship was very successful in the 1980s and 1990s, as responsibility for funding the arts in the UK has shifted from the government to the private sector and business in particular. Growth has slowed down, partly because of the increasing need to justify such investments, partly because of the increasing number of opportunities to reach target audiences and also because it is difficult to engage in these very visible activities when economic and financial performance is declining and when company restructuring activities are of greater concern to those being made redundant or being displaced.

Arts sponsorship, according to Thorncroft (1996), began as a philanthropic exercise, with business giving something back to the community. It was a means of developing corporate image and was used extensively by tobacco companies as they attempted to reach their customer base. It then began to be appreciated for its corporate hospitality opportunities: a cheaper, more civilised alternative to sports sponsorship, and one that appealed more to women.

Many organisations sponsor the arts as a means of enhancing their corporate status and as a means of clarifying their name. Another important reason why organisations use sponsorship is to establish and maintain favourable contact with key business people, often at board level, together with other significant public figures. Through related corporate hospitality, companies can reach substantial numbers of their targeted key people.

> Many organisations sponsor the arts as a means of enhancing their corporate status and as a means of clarifying their name.

Sponsorship of the arts has moved from being a means of supporting the community to a sophisticated means of targeting and positioning brands. Sponsorship, once part of corporate public relations, has developed skills that can assist marketing public relations.

These three main forms of sponsorship, sports, arts and programme, are not mutually exclusive and use of one does not necessarily prevent use of either of the others. NTL currently sponsor four major English and Scottish football teams to achieve brand awareness, particularly in areas where it seeks to develop cable services. NTL also undertakes programme sponsorship and work with *Who Wants to Be a Millionaire?* This helps to develop brand values and may be more cost-effective than spot advertising, especially at peak times. In addition to these two major sponsorships, NTL also supports the Macmillan Cancer Relief fund, perhaps to present a more caring or balanced identity for its various audiences. However, because of targeting issues many organisations find it more efficient to use one major form of sponsorship, supported by a range of secondary sponsorship activities.

Other forms of sponsorship

It has been argued that there is little opportunity to control messages delivered through sponsorship, and far less opportunity to encourage the target audiences to enter into a dialogue with sponsors. However, the awareness and image opportunities can be used by supporting either the local community or small-scale schemes. Whitbread has been involved in supporting school programmes, environmental developments and other locally oriented activities because that is where its customers are based. Volkswagen wanted to be associated with the motoring environment rather than just the motorist. To help achieve this goal it sponsored the jackets worn by road-crossing wardens (lollipop people) so that the local authority was free to use the money once spent on uniforms on other aspects of road safety (Walker, 1995).

A fresh form of sponsorship emerged in 1997 as brands sought to leverage each other and achieve greater efficiencies and impact through association with each other. For example, the Microsoft/NSPCC co-branding relationship has enabled the latter access to financial resources to fund bigger awareness and donor-appeal campaigns. Microsoft are able to tap into the caring and community associations that are linked to the charity. Similarly, Cable & Wireless (C&W) supported Barnardos in its campaign to increase awareness of current issues, generate funds and redefine the image held of the charity. C&W provided the funds for the TV campaign and in return had a credit at the end of the commercial.

The majority of sponsorships, regardless of type, are not the sole promotional activity undertaken by the sponsors. They may be secondary and used to support above-the-line work or they may be used as the primary form of communication but supported by a range of off-screen activities, such as sales promotions and (in particular) competitions.

The role of sponsorship in the communications mix

Whether sponsorship is a part of advertising, sales promotion or public relations has long been a source of debate. It is perhaps more natural and comfortable to align sponsorship with advertising. Since awareness is regarded as the principal objective of using sponsorship, advertising is a more complementary and accommodating part of the mix. Sales promotion from the sponsor's position is harder to justify, although from the perspective of the sponsored the value-added characteristic is interesting. The more traditional home for sponsorship is public relations (Witcher et al., 1991). The sponsored, such as a football team, a racing-car manufacturer or a theatre group, may be adjudged to perform the role of opinion former. Indirectly, therefore, messages are conveyed to the target audience with the support of significant participants who endorse and support the sponsor. This is akin to public relations activities.

Messages are conveyed to the target audience with the support of significant participants who endorse and support the sponsor.

ViewPoint 10.4   Golfing media

Sports events represent prime promotional opportunities, if only because of the television coverage. The picture at Exhibit 10.2 depicts a golf tournament at the Forest of Arden. Here on the final hole, British golfer David Howell is shown teeing off, surrounded by promotional media. The flowers on the bank remind audiences of the location, the perimeter boards reinforce messages from the main sponsors of the event, the clock and timing of the event is sponsored by Omega, the caddies' bibs carry advertising messages and even the bins receive financial support.

EXHIBIT 10.2 A variety of promotional messages communicated at an important golfing event

Hastings (1984) contests that advertising messages can be manipulated and adapted to changing circumstances much more easily than those associated with sponsorship. He suggests that the audience characteristics of both advertising and sponsorship are very different. For advertising there are viewers and non-viewers. For sponsorship there are three groups of people that can be identified. First there are those who are directly involved with the sponsor or the event, the active participants. The second is a much larger group, consisting of those who attend sponsored events, and these are referred to as personal spectators. The third group is normally the largest, and comprises all those who are involved with the event through various media channels; these are regarded as media followers.

As if to demonstrate the potential sizes of these groups, estimates suggest that in excess of four million people attend the Formula One Grand Prix championship races (active participants) and over half a billion people (media followers) watch the races on television.

Exploratory research undertaken by Hoek et al. (1997) suggests that sponsorship is

Sponsorship is better able to generate awareness and a wider set of product-related attributes than advertising when dealing with non-users of a product.

better able to generate awareness and a wider set of product-related attributes than advertising when dealing with non-users of a product, rather than users. There appears to be no discernible difference between the impact that these two promotional tools have with users.

The authors claim that sponsorship and advertising can be considered to work in approximately the same way if the ATR model developed by Ehrenberg (1974) is adopted (Chapter 7). Through the ATR model, purchase behaviour and beliefs are considered to be reinforced by advertising rather than new behaviour patterns being established. Advertising fulfils a means by which buyers can meaningfully defend their purchase patterns. Hoek et al. regard this approach as reasonably analogous to sponsorship. Sponsorship can create awareness and is more likely to confirm past behaviour than prompt new purchase behaviour. The implication, they conclude, is that, whereas awareness levels can be improved with sponsorship, other promotional tools are required to impact upon product experimentation or purchase intentions.

Evaluating the performance of public relations

Each of the two main forms of public relations, corporate and marketing, seeks to achieve different objectives and does so by employing different approaches and techniques. However, they are not mutually exclusive and the activities of one form of public relations impact upon the other; they are self-reinforcing.

ViewPoint 10.5   Free Cone Day

For a long time Ben & Jerry's has used public relations to position itself as a socially conscious and environmentally friendly brand. Of the many aspects of its communications work the organisation often tries to gauge its corporate reputation, in addition to message penetration of its commitment to social causes.

One of the brand's important events is its annual Free Cone Day, and when planning the 2003 event a competitive aspect was noticed through mentions in the media. Some of Ben & Jerry's competitors had started similar Free Cone Days and this was picked up through shared mentions in the media.

As a response, Ben & Jerry's teamed up with 'Rock the Vote and Apple for a campaign titled, *ETOV – Turn it Around* ("ETOV" being "vote" spelt backwards)'. The one-day event featured a grand prize from Apple, retained the tradition of giving away free ice-cream cones and drew 10,000 voters. As a result Ben & Jerry's secured the vast majority of the media coverage and overcame the shared mentions issue.

Source: Adapted from Iacono (2004)

Corporate public relations (CPR)

Much of the work of CPR is continuous, and therefore measurement should not be campaign oriented or time restricted but undertaken on a regular, ongoing basis. CPR is mainly responsible for the identity cues that are presented to the organisation's various stakeholders as part of a planned programme of communications. These cues signal the visibility and profile of the organisation and are used by stakeholders to shape the image that each has of the focus organisation.

Evaluation should, in the first instance, measure levels of awareness of the organisation. However, CPR can be focused upon a range of other communication activities, such as understanding, preference, interest and conviction. Attention should then focus upon the levels of interest, goodwill and attitudes held towards the organisation as a result of all the planned and unplanned cues used by the organisation.

Traditionally these levels were assumed to have been generated by public relations activities. The main method of measuring their contribution to the communications programme was to collect press cuttings and to record the number of mentions the organisation received in the electronic media. These were then collated in a cuttings book that would be presented to the client. However, the use of a cuttings book can do little more than provide a rough and ready way of appreciating the level of opportunities to see created by public relations activities.

The content of the cuttings book and the recorded media mentions can be converted into a different currency.

The content of the cuttings book and the recorded media mentions can be converted into a different currency. The exchange rate used is the cost of the media that would have been incurred had this volume of communication or awareness been generated by advertising activity. For example, a 30-second news item about an organisation's contribution to a charity event may be exchanged for a 30-second advertisement at rate-card cost. The temptation is clear, but the validity of the equation is misleading. By translating public relations into advertising currency, the client is expected not only to understand but also to approve of the enhanced credibility that advertising possesses. It is not surprising that the widely held notion that public relations is free advertising has grown so substantially when practitioners use this approach.

A further refinement of the cuttings book is to analyse the material covered. The coverage may be positive or negative, approving or disapproving, so the quality of the cuttings needs to be reviewed in order that the client organisation can make an informed judgement about its next set of decisions. This survey of the material in the cuttings book is referred to as a content analysis. Traditionally, content analyses have had to be undertaken qualitatively and were therefore subject to poor interpretation and reviewer bias, however well they approached their task. Today, increasingly sophisticated software is being used to produce a wealth of quantitative data reflecting the key variables that clients want evaluated.

Hauss (1993) suggests that key variables could include the type of publication, the favourability of the article, the name of the journalist, the audiences being reached and the type of coverage. All these and others can be built into programmes. The results can then be cross-tabulated so that it is possible to see in which part of the country the most favourable comments are being generated or observe which opinion formers are positively or negatively disposed.

Evaluation of corporate image, recruitment and crisis-management-based communications demand various adaptations to accommodate their subtle differences, but the main and overriding measurement should always be against the objectives set for the communication activity.

Marketing public relations (MPR)

Evaluating the contribution of MPR is problematic. Some practitioners believe that this can be overcome by coding press releases as a campaign, and with the use of particular software leads can be tracked and costed. With the right software, the actual cost of a press release can be input and the number of leads that come back can be measured against sales on the database.

The software can not only estimate sales but also work out the number of leads required to make quota. The formula used is based on the rule that 45 per cent of leads turn into sales for someone in the market within the year. The organisation's own conversion rate can be used to adjust the 45 per cent, and the quality of its lead-conversion process can also be input. One of the benefits of this approach is that quantitative outcomes provide a measure of effectiveness, but not necessarily the effectiveness of the MPR campaign.

Pre- and post-test measures of awareness, preference, comprehension and intentions are a better measure of the quality and impact that an MPR campaign might have on a target audience. Measuring the conversion ratio of leads to sales is not the only measure, as it fails to isolate the other forces that impact on market performance. In addition, tracking studies can be used to plot attitudes and opinions against which the timings of campaigns and MPR activities can be traced and evaluated.

Other measuring techniques

Of all the tools available to practitioners, Goften (1999) reports the following as the most common approaches to measuring public relations:

Set objectives and agree the criteria in advance of a campaign.

Press cuttings, radio and TV tapes, but this is a measure of volume and not quality of impact.

A media equivalent value is then applied.

Media evaluation through commercial systems such as CAMMA, Impact, Precis. Under this approach, panels of readers judge whether a mention is positive or negative and whether the client's key message has been communicated. Computer programmes then cut through the data.

Tracking studies are expensive but are important when changing a perception of a brand, etc.

Both CPR and MPR are difficult and elusive elements of the communications mix to test, measure and evaluate.

Both CPR and MPR are difficult and elusive elements of the communications mix to test, measure and evaluate. Practitioners use a variety of methods, but few provide the objectivity and validity that is necessary. For example, Comic Relief monitored the impact of media coverage on the organisation in the run-up to Red Nose Day. It was able to track which initiatives were failing to attract attention and which issues were attracting negative coverage. It evaluated coverage over six key areas: TV initiatives, education, grants (Africa and the UK), special projects, public fundraising and corporate fundraising.

The variety of measurement devices is increasing, especially as technology advances.

ViewPoint 10.6   Monitoring TeleTrax

TeleTrax is an electronic tagging system that can monitor broadcast use of its footage, anywhere in the world. Using an indelible code embedded within video material and through the use of approximately 100 listening posts across Europe, the company is alerted as soon as the tape is broadcast. It does not track the tone of the content but it does record every single time a video is broadcast and so enables organisations to identify the exact station and location where the video was used and, in addition, identify the length of the broadcast and even which parts of the overall footage were used.

Net.Cut was set up originally to provide early warning of unfavourable corporate comment on the Internet. It can monitor comment in Internet publications, UK newsgroups and the www by searching the www at night and saving company mentions. The cuttings are then reviewed the following morning for key messages prior to warning the client as necessary. It costs about £50 a month and each alert costs an extra £1.

Evaluating the performance of sponsorship

The measurement of sponsorship activities is problematic although the importance of doing so is accepted (Armstrong, 1998). The problem concerns the ability to separate the impact of the various elements of the communications mix, which can be expensive and beyond the reach of smaller brands.

Many organisations attempt to measure the size of the media audience and then treat this as an indicator of effectiveness. This is misleading, as advertising and sponsorship are considered to work in different ways and cannot be measured in a similar way. Audiences consider events (a sports match, exhibition or TV programme) as their primary focus, not which organisation is sponsoring the activity, unlike advertising, where the message either dominates the screen or a page of a magazine and viewers attend according to their perceptual filters. The focus of attention is different, and so should be the means of evaluation.

Marshall and Cook (1992) found that sports sponsors preferred to use consumer surveys to examine customer (not audience) profiles, brand-related images, attitudes and purchasing activities. This was accomplished through the use of personal interviews and telephone and postal surveys. Because the level of funding in many of the smaller sponsorships is relatively low, few if any resources are allocated to evaluative practices.

The main way in which sponsorship activities should be measured is through the objectives set at the outset. By measuring performance rigorously against clearly defined sales and communications-based measures it is more likely that a reasonable process and outcome to the sponsorship activity will be established.

Summary of key points

1. Public relations, whether oriented primarily to product support or to the development of corporate goodwill, plays an important role within the communications mix. It is now recognised as a communications discipline that can develop and maintain a portfolio of relationships with a range of key stakeholder audiences.

2. Public relations enables organisations to position themselves and provide stakeholders with a means of identifying and understanding an organisation.

3. The main characteristics of public relations are that it represents a very cost-effective means of carrying messages with a high degree of credibility. However, the degree of control that management is able to exert over the transmission of messages can be limited.

4. There are several activities and tools used in the name of public relations. These are media relations (consisting mainly of press releases, interviews, press kits and press conferences), and publicity and events, which can include product-, organisational- and community-related activities.

5. Public relations might be considered an umbrella term that incorporates lobbying, crisis management, corporate advertising and sponsorship.

6. Sponsorship allows access to specific target audiences and can enhance an organisation's image. Through association with events, activities and organisations the introduction of new products and brands can be assisted by the use of appropriate sponsorships and can be used to prepare markets for the arrival and penetration of new brands.

7. The evaluation of sponsorship arrangements poses a problem in that measurement is little better than that used for advertising. However, the impact and approach that sponsorship can have suggest that the two tools should be used together, coordinated, if not integrated, to develop awareness and strong brand associations and triggers.

Review questions

1. Define public relations, set out its principal characteristics and identify the main objectives of using public relations.

2. What is the difference between corporate public relations and marketing public relations? Is this difference of importance?

3. Why do you think an increasing number of organisations are using sponsorship as a part of their communications mix?

4. Discuss the view that public relations can only ever be a support tool in the communications mix.

5. What are the main opportunities that sponsorship opens up for organisations?

6. If the objective of using sponsorship is to build awareness (among other things), then there is little point in using advertising. Discuss this view.

References

Allen, D. (2000), 'TV sponsorship rules are eased', *Media Week*, 14 April, p. 3.

Armstrong, C. (1998), 'Sport sponsorship: a case study approach to measuring its effectiveness', *European Research*, **16**(2), pp. 97–103.

Barrett, P. (1997), 'A marriage of PR and ads', *Marketing*, 30 October, p. 15.

Boyle, E. (2004), 'Press and publicity management: the Dyson case', *Corporate Communications: An International Journal*, **9**(3), pp. 209–22.

Bruning, S.D. and Ledingham, J.A. (2000), 'Perceptions of relationships and evaluations of satisfaction: an exploration of interaction', *Public Relations Review*, **26**(1), pp. 85–95.

Calvert, J. and Walsh, G. (2005), 'How to get ahead in advertising at the BBC', *Sunday Times*, 18 September, pp. 1, 10–11.

Cutlip, S., Center, A.H. and Broom, G.J. (1985), *Effective Public Relations*, Englewood Cliffs, NJ: Prentice-Hall.

Ehling, W.P. (1992), 'Estimating the value of public relations and communication to an organisation', in *Excellence in Public Relations and Communication Management* (eds J.E. Grunig, D.M. Dozier, P. Ehling, L.A. Grunig, F.C. Repper and J. Whits), pp. 617–38, Hillsdale, NJ: Lawrence Erlbaum.

Ehrenberg, A.S.C. (1974), 'Repetitive advertising and the consumer', *Journal of Advertising Research*, **14** (April), pp. 25–34.

Fill, C. (2006), *Marketing Communications: engagement, strategies and practice*, 4th edn, Harlow: FT Prentice Hall.

Fry, A. (1997), 'Keeping the right company', *Marketing*, 22 May, pp. 24–5.

Goften, K. (1999), 'The measure of PR', *Campaign Report*, 2 April, p. 13.

Gray, R. (2005), 'Samsung rides blue wave', *Marketing*, 5 May, p. 17.

Gregory, A. (2004), 'Scope and structure of public relations: a technology driven view', *Public Relations Review*, **30**(3) (September), pp. 245–54.

Grimes, E. and Meenaghan, T. (1998), 'Focusing commercial sponsorship on the internal corporate audience', *International Journal of Advertising*, **17**(1), pp. 51–74.

Grunig, J. (1992), 'Models of public relations and communication', in *Excellence in Public Relations and Communications Management* (eds J.E. Grunig, D.M. Dozier, P. Ehling, L.A. Grunig, F.C. Repper and J. Whits), pp. 285–325, Hillsdale, NJ: Lawrence Erlbaum.

Grunig, J. and Hunt, T. (1984), *Managing Public Relations*, New York: Holt, Rinehart & Winston.

Harverson, P. (1998), 'Why IT companies take the risk', *Financial Times*, 2 June.

Hastings, G. (1984), 'Sponsorship works differently from advertising', *International Journal of Advertising*, **3**, pp. 171–6.

Hauss, D. (1993), 'Measuring the impact of public relations', *Public Relations Journal*, February, pp. 14–21.

Hawtin, L. (2004), 'Imperial Leather: a winning performance', *Admap*, **39** (April), pp. 23–5.

Hedburg, A. (2000), 'Bumper crop', *Marketing Week*, 19 October, pp. 28–32.

Hoek, J., Gendall, P., Jeffcoat, M. and Orsman, D. (1997), 'Sponsorship and advertising: a comparison of the effects', *Journal of Marketing Communications*, **3**, pp. 21–32.

Iacono, E. (2004), 'Making measurement count', *PR Week* (USA), 15 November. Retrieved 4 January 2005 from www.brandrepublic.com/news/newsArticle.

Kent, M.L. and Taylor, M. (2002), 'Toward a dialogic theory of public relations', *Public Relations Review*, **28**(1) (February), pp. 21–37.

Kitchen, P.J. and Proctor, R.A. (1991), 'The increasing importance of public relations in FMCG firms', *Journal of Marketing Management*, **7**(4) (October), pp. 357–70.

Marshall, D.W. and Cook, G. (1992), 'The corporate (sports) sponsor', *International Journal of Advertising*, **11**, pp. 307–24.

Miller, G. (1989), 'Persuasion and public relations: two "Ps" in a pod', in *Public Relations Theory* (eds C. Botan and V. Hazelton), Hillsdale, NJ: Lawrence Erlbaum.

Reed, D. (1994), 'Sponsorship', *Campaign*, 20 May, pp. 37 8.

Summers, D. (1995), 'Sponsors' careful link with TV', *Financial Times*, 2 March, p. 14.

Thorncroft, A. (1996), 'Business arts sponsorship: arts face a harsh set of realities', *Financial Times*, 4 July, p. 1.

Thwaites, D. (1994), 'Corporate sponsorship by the financial services industry', *Journal of Marketing Management*, **10**, pp. 743–63.

Tripodi, J.A. (2001), 'Sponsorship – a confirmed weapon in the professional armoury', *International Journal of Sports Marketing and Sponsorship*, **3**(1) (March/April), paper 5.

Walker, J.-A. (1995), 'Community service', *Marketing Week*, 20 October, pp. 85–90.

Witcher, B., Craigen, G., Culligan, D. and Harvey, A. (1991), 'The links between objectives and functions in organisational sponsorship', *International Journal of Advertising*, **10**, pp. 13–33.

Direct marketing, personal selling and evaluation

11

Aims and objectives

The aims of this chapter are, first, to consider the characteristics of direct marketing, and second, to explore some of the principal issues and concepts associated with personal selling. There are four primary topics in this chapter:

Direct marketing, Personal selling, Multiple sales channels, Evaluation

The learning objectives are to enable readers to:

1. define direct marketing and set out its key characteristics;
2. describe the different methods used to implement direct marketing;
3. explain the significance of the database in direct marketing and consider different direct-response media;
4. consider the different types, roles and tasks of personal selling;
5. consider the strengths and weaknesses of personal selling as a form of communication;
6. introduce the concept of multiple sales channels;
7. consider how direct marketing and personal selling might best be integrated with the other tools of the marketing communications mix;
8. explain the main ways in which both of the tools can be evaluated.

Introduction

This chapter explores both direct marketing and personal selling. These are vast topics so it is only possible to include a certain amount of material here; readers interested in more detailed information are referred to Fill (2006) and to specialised texts such as Tapp (2005).

Direct marketing is a term used to refer to all media activities that generate a series of communications and responses with an existing or potential customer. Primarily, direct marketing is concerned with the management of customer behaviour and is used to complement the strengths and weaknesses of the other communication disciplines. To put this another way, advertising and public relations provide information and develop brand values but sales promotion, direct marketing and personal selling drive response, most notably behaviour. Both direct marketing and personal selling have the potential to engage customers directly and explicitly, and can provide both an intellectual as well as an emotional basis upon which interaction and dialogue can be developed.

The role of direct marketing

For a long time direct mail was the main tool of direct marketing but the development of IST and, in particular, the database have enabled the introduction of a range of other media. These are used to communicate directly with individual customers and often carry a behavioural (call-to-action) message. Typically, direct-marketing agencies work across a variety of media including the telephone, Internet, direct mail, email, press and posters. No single media channel dominates their work. In an era when the talk is about integration and media neutrality, the direct-marketing industry is in a strong position to provide a wide range of client-communication services. All the elements of the mix can be used with direct marketing to support and build meaningful relationships with consumers and members of the various stakeholder networks.

> Typically, direct-marketing agencies work across a variety of media including the telephone, Internet, direct mail, email, press and posters.

ViewPoint 11.1   Sainsbury's says Happy Birthday

One of the advantages of direct marketing is the opportunity to personalise messages and in doing so create a stronger opportunity to engage an audience, and secure loyalty through one-to-one communication. Sainsbury's now sends 400,000 birthday cards, and a gift, each month, to selected customers. Each gift is determined by marrying the age of the recipient with their purchases so that the gift is individually relevant.

The scheme involves suppliers who welcome the opportunity to present brands and not have to devalue them through discounts and price promotions. So, one such involved Heineken when they launched their keg-shaped ID can. Sainsbury's identified males who had purchased premium lagers and sent a card with a voucher for a free six-pack of Heineken. With redemption rates as high as 70 per cent and little chance to annoy customers through overfamiliarity, Sainsbury's is optimistic that this approach cuts through the mass mailings delivered by competitors.

Source: Adapted from McElhatton (2005)

Direct marketing is a tool of marketing communications and is used to create and sustain a personal and intermediary-free communication with customers, potential customers and other significant stakeholders. In most cases this is a media-based activity and offers great scope for the collection and utilisation of pertinent and measurable data. There are a number of important issues associated with this definition. The first is that the activity should be measurable. That is, any response(s) must be associated with a particular individual, a particular media activity and a particular outcome, such as a sale or enquiry for further information. The second issue concerns the rewards that each party perceives through participation in the relationship. The customer receives a variety of tangible and intangible satisfactions. These include shopping convenience, time utility and the satisfaction and trust that can develop between customers and a provider of quality products and services when the customers realise and appreciate the personal attention they appear to be receiving.

Underpinning the direct-marketing approach are the principles of trust and commitment.

Underpinning the direct-marketing approach are the principles of trust and commitment, just as they support the validity of the other communications mix tools. If a meaningful relationship is to be developed over the long term and direct marketing is an instrumental part of the interaction, then the promises that the parties make to develop commitment and stability are of immense importance (Ganesan, 1994).

The direct marketer derives benefits associated with precision target marketing and minimised waste, increased profits and opportunities to provide established customers with other related products, without the huge costs of continually having to find new customers. In addition, direct marketing represents a strategic approach to the market. It actively seeks to remove channel intermediaries (at least from the initial communication), reduce costs, and improve the quality and speed of service for customers, and through this bundle of attributes presents a new offering for the market, which in itself may provide competitive advantage. First Direct, Virgin Direct and the pioneer, Direct Line, all provide these advantages, which have enabled them to secure strong positions in the market.

Types of direct brand

Direct marketing is assumed to refer to direct communication mix activity, but this is only part of the marketing picture. Using direct-response media in this way is an increasingly common activity used to augment the communications activities surrounding a brand and to provide a new dimension to the context in which brands are perceived.

Direct marketing can be used by organisations in a number of different ways.

However, direct marketing can be used by organisations in a number of different ways, very often reflecting the business strategy of the organisation. Four types can be identified and they should not be regarded as hierarchical, in the sense that there has to be progression from one type to another. They are reflections of the ways different organisations use direct marketing and the degree to which the tool is used strategically.

Type 1: complementary tool

At this level, direct-response media are used to complement the other communications mix activities used to support a brand. Their main use is to generate leads and to some extent awareness, information and reinforcement. For example, financial services companies, tour operators and travel agents use DRTV to stimulate enquiries, loans and bookings, respectively.

Type 2: primary differentiator

Rather than be one of a number of communications mix tools, at this level direct-response media are the primary form of communication. They are used to provide a distinct point of differentiation from competitor offerings. They are the principal form of communication. In addition to the Type 1 advantages they are used to cut costs, avoid the use of intermediaries and reach finely targeted audiences (for example, book, music and wine clubs).

Type 3: sales channel

A third use for direct marketing and telemarketing in particular concerns its use as a means of developing greater efficiency and as a means of augmenting current services. By utilising direct marketing as a sales tool, multiple sales channels can be used to meet the needs of different customer segments and so release resources to be deployed elsewhere and more effectively. This idea is developed further later in this chapter.

Type 4: brand vehicle

At this final level, brands are developed to exploit market space opportunities. The strategic element is most clearly evident at this level. Indeed, the entire organisation and its culture are normally oriented to the development of customer relationships through direct-marketing activities: prime examples are lastminute.com and amazon.

The growth of direct marketing

There can be little doubt that, of all the tools in the marketing communications mix, direct marketing has experienced the most growth in the last ten years. The reasons for this growth are many and varied, but two essential drivers behind the surge in direct marketing have been technological advances and changing buyer lifestyles and expectations. These two forces for change demonstrate quite dramatically how a change in the context can impact on marketing communications.

Two essential drivers behind the surge in direct marketing have been technological advances and changing buyer lifestyles and expectations.

Growth driver 1: technology

As discussed previously in Chapter 6, rapid advances in technology have heralded the arrival of new sources and forms of information. Technology has enabled the collection, storage and analysis of customer data to become relatively simple, cost-effective and straightforward. Furthermore, the management of this information is increasingly available to small businesses as well as the major blue chip multinational organisations.

Computing costs have plummeted, while there has been a correspondingly enormous increase in the power that technology can deliver.

The technological surge has in turn stimulated three major developments. The first concerns the ability to capture information, the second to process and analyse it and the third to represent part or all of the information as a form of communication to stimulate interaction and perhaps dialogue to collect further information.

Growth driver 2: changing market context

The lifestyles of people in Western European and North American societies, in particular, have evolved and will continue to do so. Generally, the brash phase of *selfishness* in the 1980s gave way to a more caring, society-oriented *selflessness* in the 1990s. The start of the twenty-first century suggests that a *self-awareness* lifestyle might predominate and be reflected in brand-purchase behaviour and a greater emphasis on long-term value and different brand values. Continued fragmentation of the media and audiences requires finely tuned segmentation and communication devices. Direct marketing offers a solution to this splintering and micro-market scenario and addresses some of the changing needs of management, namely for speed of response and justification for the use and allocation of resources.

The twin impact of these drivers can be seen within the emergence of ideas about integrated marketing communications and an overall emphasis on relationship-marketing principles. The enhanced ability of organisations to collect, store and manage customer lifestyle and transactional data, to generate personalised communications and their general enthusiasm for retention and loyalty schemes have combined to provide a huge movement towards an increased use of direct and interactive marketing initiatives.

The role of the database

At the hub of successful direct-marketing and CRM activities is the database.

At the hub of successful direct-marketing and CRM activities is the database. A database is a collection of files held on a computer that contain data that can be related to one another and which can reproduce information in a variety of formats. Normally the data consist of information collected about prospects and customers that are used to determine appropriate segments and target markets and to record responses to communications conveyed by the organisation. A database therefore plays a role as a storage, sorting and administrative device to assist direct and personalised communications.

Age and lifestyle data are important signals of product usage.

Age and lifestyle data are important signals of product usage. However, there will be attitudinal variances between people in similar groups demanding further analysis. This can, according to Reed (2000), uncover clues concerning what a direct-mail piece should look like. So, older customers do not like soft colours and small type and sentences should not begin with 'and' or 'but'.

Increasingly, the information stored is gathered from transactions undertaken with customers, but on its own this information is not enough and further layering of data is required. The recency/frequency/monetary (RFM) model provides a base upon which lifestyle data, often bought in from a list agency, can be used to further refine the information held. Response analysis requires the identification of an organisation's best customers, and then another layer of data can be introduced that points to those

ViewPoint 11.2   Supermarkets direct

The lead organisations in the UK grocery market use databases to hold detailed information about their customers' purchases. The database holds information about its customers that they can mine and then target sales promotions, advertising and direct-marketing communications. For example, each quarter Tesco sends out a statement to its 10 million regular Clubcard users and includes communication mix vouchers and coupons mirroring each customer's purchases. As a result, there are 100,000 different promotional messages reflecting the preferences and buying habits of customers rather than the supermarket's desire to sell particular products (Marsh, 2001).

that are particularly responsive to direct-response marketing activity (Fletcher, 1997). It is the increasing sophistication of the information held in databases that is enabling more effective targeting and communications.

ViewPoint 11.3   Data-rich BSkyB

It is generally assumed that members of loyalty schemes are less likely to leave, although it is recognised that they will probably be members of several other schemes, some in the same sector. First T, a joint venture of the British Market Research Bureau and Dunnhumby designed to bring together market research with database marketing, represents an attempt at achieving a level of consilience. BSkyB used First T to analyse its subscribers using Target Group Index data to find out about their aspirations, hobbies, pastimes and interests; what inspired them; what drove and what motivated them. From this information BSkyB was better placed not only to adapt the rewards offered within its loyalty scheme but also better placed to communicate with prospects and potential new members.

Source: Adapted from Pearson (2003); used with permission

Databases provide the means by which organisations, large and small, can monitor changes in customer lifestyles and attitudes or, in the business-to-business sector, the changing form of the interorganisational relationships and their impact on other members in the network as well as the market structure and level of competitive activity (Gundach and Murphy, 1993). It is through the use of the database that relationships with participants can be tracked, analysed and developed. Very importantly, database systems can be used not only to identify strategically important customers and segments but also to ascertain opportunities to cross-sell products (Kamakura et al., 2003).

> Database systems can be used not only to identify strategically important customers and segments but also to ascertain opportunities to cross-sell products.

Direct-response media

The choice of media for direct marketing can be very different from those selected for general advertising purposes. The main reason for using direct-response media is that direct contact is made with prospects and customers in order that a direct response is solicited and a dialogue stimulated or maintained. In reality, a wide variety of media can be used, simply by attaching a telephone number, website address or response card. However, if broadcast media such as television and radio are the champions of the general advertiser, their adoption by direct marketers in the UK has been relatively slow. Direct mail, telemarketing and door-to-door activities are the main direct-response media, as they allow more personal, direct and evaluative means of reaching precisely targeted customers.

Direct mail

Direct mail refers to personally addressed advertising that is delivered through the postal system. It can be personalised and targeted with great accuracy, and its results are capable of precise measurement.

The generation of enquiries and leads together with the intention of building a personal relationship with customers are the most important factors contributing to the growth of direct mail. Management should decide whether to target direct mail at current customers with the intention of building loyalty and retention rates, or whether they should chase new customers. The decision, acquisition or retention, should be part of the marketing plan but often this aspect of direct marketing lacks clarity, resulting in wastage and inefficiency. Direct mail can be expensive, at anything between £250 and £500 per 1,000 items dispatched. It should, therefore, be used selectively and for purposes other than creating awareness.

Organisations in the financial services sectors are the main users of this medium and the financial health of the sector is dependent to a large extent on some of the major financial services companies maintaining their spend on direct mail. However, an increasing number of other organisations are experimenting with this approach, as they try to improve the effectiveness of their investment in the communications mix and seek to reduce television advertising costs. The growth in consumer-based direct-mail activities has outstripped that of the business-to-business sector. The number of direct-mail items sent to consumers has increased considerably in comparison with the b2b sector.

Telemarketing

The prime qualities of the telephone are that it provides for interaction, is flexible and permits immediate feedback and the opportunity to overcome objections, all within the same communication event. Other dimensions of telemarketing include the development and maintenance of customer goodwill, allied to which is the increasing need to provide high levels of customer service. Telemarketing also allows organisations to undertake marketing research which is both highly measurable and accountable in that the effectiveness can be verified continuously and call rates, contacts reached and the number and quality of positive and negative responses are easily recorded and monitored.

Telemarketing also allows organisations to undertake marketing research which is both highly measurable and accountable.

Growth in telemarketing activity in the business-to-business sector has been largely at the expense of personal selling. The objectives have been to reduce costs and to utilise the expensive sales force and their skills to build on the openings and leads created by telemarketing and other lead-generation activities.

All the advantages of interaction, immediate feedback, flexibility and opportunity to overcome objections can be executed by personal selling, but the speed, cost, accuracy and consistency of the information solicited through personal visits can often be improved upon by telemarketing. The complexity of the product will influence the degree to which this medium can be used successfully. However, if properly trained professional telemarketers are used, the sales results, if measured on a call basis, can outperform those produced by personal selling.

The costs of telemarketing are high: for example, £15 to reach a decision-maker in an organisation. When this is compared with £5 for a piece of direct mail or £150+ for a personal sales call to the same individual, it is the effectiveness of the call and the return on the investment that determines whether the costs are really high.

Carelines

Another reason to use telemarketing concerns the role that carelines can play within consumer/brand relationships. Manufacturers use contact centres to enable customers to:

- complain about product performance and related experiences;
- seek product-related advice;
- make suggestions regarding product or packaging development;
- comment about an action or development concerning the brand as a whole.

What binds these together is the potential all of these people have for repurchasing the brand, even those who complain bitterly about product performance and experience. If these people have their complaints dealt with properly then there is a reasonable probability that they will repurchase.

The majority of careline calls are not about complaints but seek advice or help about products. Food manufacturers can provide cooking and recipe advice, cosmetic and toiletries companies can provide healthcare advice and application guidelines, and white goods and service-based organisations can provide technical and operational support.

> The majority of careline calls are not about complaints but seek advice or help about products.

Carelines are essentially a post-purchase support mechanism that facilitates market feedback and intelligence gathering. They can warn of imminent problems (product defects), provide ideas for new products or variants and, of course, provide a valuable method to reassure customers and improve customer-retention levels. Call operators, or agents as many of them are now being called, have to handle calls from a variety of

ViewPoint 11.4   Careline approaches

Nestlé Purina, whose petfood brands include Purina ONE, Felix, Go Cat, Bakers and Winalot, refers to its contact centre as a relationship centre. Using a strapline 'Your pet, our passion'™, the careline is used not only to get feedback on campaigns and products – it is also used by a variety of people internally who 'listen in' in an attempt to get close to the consumer.

The extent of the company's involvement with consumers is demonstrated by the fact that contact staff have been trained in bereavement counselling, to help people who have recently lost a pet.

Source: Bashford (2004)

new sources – the Web, email, interactive TV and mobile devices – and it is appreciated that many are more effective if they have direct product experience. Instant messaging channels enable online shoppers to ask questions that are routed to a call centre for response. Sales conversion ratios can be up by 40–50 per cent and costs are about £1 to answer an inbound question, compared with £3.50 by phone (Murphy, 2000). Kellogg's reports that its careline makes a 13:1 return on investment (Bashford, 2004).

Although the Internet has provided further growth opportunities, it will also take on a number of the tasks currently the preserve of telemarketing bureaux. Websites enable product information and certain support advice to be accessed without the call-centre costs and focus attention on other matters that are of concern to the customer. Chat-room discussions, collaborative browsing and real-time text conversations are options to help care for customers in the future. However, it is probably the one-to-one telephone dialogue between customer and agent that will continue to provide satisfaction and benefits for both parties.

Inserts

Inserts are media materials that are placed in magazines or direct-mail letters. These not only provide factual information about the product or service but also enable the recipient to respond to the request of the direct marketer. This request might be to place an order or post back a card for more information, such as a brochure.

Inserts have become more popular, but their cost is substantially higher than a four-colour advertisement in the magazine in which the insert is carried. Their popularity is based on their effectiveness as a lead generator, and new methods of delivering inserts to the home will become important to direct-mailing houses in the future. Other vehicles, such as packages rather than letter mail, will become important.

Print

There are two main forms of direct-response advertising through the printed media: first, catalogues, and second, magazines and newspapers.

Catalogues mailed direct to consumers have been an established method of selling products for a long time. Mail-order organisations such as Freeman's, GUS and Littlewoods have successfully exploited this form of direct marketing. Organisations such as Tchibo and Kaleidoscope have successfully used mini-catalogues, but instead of providing account facilities and the appointment of specific freelance agents, their business transactions are on a cash-with-order basis.

Business-to-business marketers have begun to exploit this medium, and organisations such as Dell and IBM now use online and offline catalogues, partly to save costs and partly to free valuable sales personnel so that they can concentrate their time selling into larger accounts. Direct-response advertising through the press is similar to general press advertising except that the advertiser provides a mechanism for the reader to take further action. The mechanism may be a telephone number (call free) or a coupon or cut-out reply slip requesting further information. Dell has transformed its marketing strategy to one that is based around building customised products for both consumers and business customers. Consumer direct print ads that offer an incentive are designed explicitly to drive customers to the Dell website, where transactions are completed without reference to retailers, dealers or other intermediaries.

> Organisations such as Dell and IBM now use online and offline catalogues.

Dell Home & Home Office   **Offer due to end Wednesday 24th November 2004**

Free Double Memory: Unforgettable Value!

512MB SDRAM

DVD Rewriter Drive

Dell™ recommends Microsoft® Windows® XP Professional

Twice the incentive to buy early for Christmas

You now get double the memory absolutely free with these Dell Home systems. Take this superb Dimension 3000 desktop system with 256MB RAM (was 128MB), flat panel monitor and a great DVD Rewriter Drive – all for just £499. Or enjoy total mobile freedom with this Inspiron 510M for just £829.

What's more, with our Buy Now, Pay Later deal, you won't have to start payments till next November! Call Dell or go online now!

INSPIRON™ 510m

- **Intel® Centrino™ Mobile Technology** with Intel® Pentium® M processor 725 (1.60GHz, 2MB L2 cache, 400MHz FSB) & Intel® Pro/Wireless 2100 (802.11b)
- **Microsoft® Windows® XP Home Edition**
- 512MB 266MHz DDR SDRAM (Was 256MB)
- 40GB Hard Drive
- 15" XGA TFT (1024x768) Screen
- Modular 8xDVD/24x CDRW Combo Drive
- 56k data fax modem with unlimited AOL Broadband from £19.99 p.m. [1]
- 1 Year Euro Collect and Return Service
- Microsoft® Works 7.0

	36 Monthly Payments of
£829	**£38.17***
Incl. Del. & VAT	Incl. Del. & VAT

Typical Example for Inspiron™ 510m*

Deposit required	£82.90
No payments & option to settle loan for up to 12 months	
and then 36 monthly payments of	£38.17
Total amount payable	£1,456.85

RECOMMENDED UPGRADES

• 3 Year Intl. Next Business Day On-Site	£199 Incl. VAT[3]
• Microsoft® Office 2003 Basic	£130 Incl. VAT[2]

E-Value Code: PPUK5 N1121A

DIMENSION™ 3000

- Intel® Celeron® D Processor 330 (2.66GHz, 533fsb, 256k cache)
- Microsoft® Windows® XP Home Edition
- 256MB DDR RAM (Was 128MB)
- 40GB Hard Drive (7200 RPM)
- 15" Flat Panel Monitor
- 16x DVD+RW Drive
- 56k data fax modem with unlimited AOL Broadband from £19.99p m [1]
- Microsoft® Works 7.0

	36 Monthly Payments of
£499	**£22.97***
Incl. Del. & VAT	Incl. Del. & VAT

Typical Example for Dimension™ 3000*

Deposit required	£49.90
No payments & option to settle loan for up to 12 months	
and then 36 monthly payments of	£22.97
Total amount payable	£876.92

RECOMMENDED UPGRADES

• Microsoft® Office 2003 Basic[2]	£130 Incl. VAT
• 80GB Hard Drive (7200 RPM)	£36 Incl. VAT

E-Value Code: PPUK5 D1127D

0870 907 5262
8am – 9pm weekdays, 9am – 6pm Sat, 10am – 5pm Sun.

www.dell.co.uk/special

GO ONLINE Go Online for the Latest Offers

An individual PC. Easy as **D≪LL**™

intel inside
centrino™
MOBILE TECHNOLOGY

APR*
29.5%

EXHIBIT 11.1 Direct-response print ad from Dell. Used with permission

Door to door

This delivery method can be much cheaper than direct mail as there are no postage charges to be accounted for. However, if the costs are much lower, so are the response rates. Responses are lower because door-to-door drops cannot be personally addressed, as can direct mail, even though the content and quality can be controlled in the same way.

Avon (cosmetics) and Betterware are traditionally recognised as professional practitioners of door-to-door direct marketing. Other organisations, such as the utilities companies (gas, electricity and water), are using door to door to create higher levels of market penetration.

Radio and television

Of the two main forms discussed earlier, radio and television, the former is used as a support medium for other advertising, often by providing enquiry numbers. Television has greater potential because it can provide the important visual dimension, but its use in the UK for direct-marketing purposes has been limited. One of the main reasons for this has been the television contractors' attitude to pricing. However, the industry has experienced a period of great change and has introduced greater pricing flexibility, and a small but increasing number of direct marketers have used the small screen successfully, mainly by providing freephone numbers for customers. Direct Line, originally a motor-insurance organisation, has been outstanding in its use of television not only to launch but also to help propel the phenomenal growth of a range of related products.

The Internet and new media

The explosion of activity around new media, the Internet and email communications has been quite astonishing in recent years and now represents a major new form of interactive marketing communications. The establishment of digital television services and the imminent withdrawal of analogue services have driven new forms of interactivity. Initially, home shopping and banking facilities were attractive to those whose lifestyles complemented the benefits offered by the new technology, but fully interactive services now bring increased leisure and entertainment opportunities. For more information on the impact of technology on marketing communications, readers are referred to Chapter 6 and to Fill (2006).

Personal selling

Personal selling characterises the importance of strong relationships between vendor and buyer.

At a time when relationship marketing has become increasingly understood and accepted as the contemporary approach to marketing theory and practice, so personal selling characterises the importance of strong relationships between vendor and buyer.

The traditional image of personal selling is one that embraces the hard sell, with a brash and persistent salesperson delivering a volley of unrelenting, persuasive messages at a confused and reluctant consumer. Fortunately, this image has receded as the professionalism and breadth of personal selling has become more widely recognised and as the role of personal selling becomes even more important in the communications mix.

Personal-selling activities can be observed at various stages in the buying process of both the consumer and business-to-business markets. This is because the potency of personal communications is very high, and messages can be adapted on the spot to meet the requirements of both parties. This flexibility, as we shall see later, enables objections to be overcome, information to be provided in the context of the buyer's environment and the conviction and power of demonstration to be brought to the buyer when the buyer requests it.

Personal-selling messages can be tailored and made much more personal than any of the other methods of communication.

Personal selling is different from other forms of communication in that the transmitted messages represent, mainly, dyadic communications. This means that there are two persons involved in the communication process. Feedback and evaluation of transmitted messages are possible, more or less instantaneously, so that these personal-selling messages can be tailored and made much more personal than any of the other methods of communication.

Using the spectrum of activities identified by the hierarchy of effects, we can see that personal selling is close enough to the prospective buyer to induce a change in behaviour. That is, it is close enough to overcome objections, to provide information quickly and to respond to the prospects' overall needs, all in the context of the transaction, and to encourage them directly to place orders.

The tasks of personal selling

The generic tasks to be undertaken by the sales force have been changing because the environment in which organisations operate is shifting dramatically. These changes, in particular those associated with the development and implementation of new technologies, have had repercussions on the activities of the sales force and are discussed later in this chapter.

The tasks of those who undertake personal selling vary from organisation to organisation and in accord with the type of selling activities on which they focus. It is normally assumed that they collect and bring into the organisation orders from customers wishing to purchase products and services. In this sense the order aspect of the personal-selling tool can be seen as one of four order-related tasks:

1. *Order takers* are salespersons to whom customers are drawn at the place of supply. Reception clerks at hotels and ticket-desk personnel at theatres and cinemas typify this role.

2. *Order getters* are sales personnel who operate away from the organisation and who attempt to gain orders, largely through the provision of information, the use of demonstration techniques and services and the art of persuasion.

3. *Order collectors* are those who attempt to gather orders without physically meeting their customers. This is completed electronically or over the telephone. The growth of telemarketing operations was discussed in the previous chapter, but the time saved by both the buyer and the seller using the telephone to gather repeat and low-value orders frees valuable sales personnel to seek new customers and build relationships with current customers.

TABLE 11.1 Tasks of personal selling

Prospecting	Finding new customers
Communicating	Informing various stakeholders and feeding back information about the market
Selling	The art of leading a prospect to a successful close
Information-gathering	Reporting information about the market and reporting on individual activities
Servicing	Consulting, arranging, counselling, fixing and solving a multitude of customer 'problems'
Allocating	Placing scarce products and resources at times of shortage
Shaping	Building and sustaining relationships with major customers

4. *Order supporters* are all those people who are secondary salespersons in that they are involved with the order once it has been secured, or are involved with the act of ordering, usually by supplying information. Order processing or financial advice services typify this role. In truly customer-oriented organisations, all customer-facing employees will be order supporters.

However, this perspective of personal selling is narrow because it fails to set out the broader range of activities that a sales force can be required to undertake. Salespersons do more than get or take orders. The tasks listed in Table 11.1 provide direction and purpose, and also help to establish the criteria by which the performance of members of the personal selling unit can be evaluated. The organisation should decide which tasks it expects its representatives to undertake.

Personal selling is the most expensive element of the communications mix. The average cost per contact can easily exceed £250 when all markets and types of businesses are considered. It is generally agreed that personal selling is most effective at the later stages of the hierarchy of effects or buying process, rather than at the earlier stage of awareness building. Therefore, each organisation should determine the precise role the sales force is to play within the communications mix.

> Each organisation should determine the precise role the sales force is to play within the communications mix.

The role of personal selling

Personal selling is often referred to as interpersonal communication, and from this perspective Reid et al. (2002) determined three major sales behaviours, namely getting, giving and using information:

● Getting information refers to sales behaviours aimed at information acquisition – for example, gathering information about customers, markets and competitors.

● Giving information refers to the dissemination of information to customers and other stakeholders – for example, sales presentations and seminar meetings designed to provide information about products and an organisation's capabilities and reputation.

● Using information refers to the sales person's use of information to help solve a customer's problem. Associated with this is the process of gaining buyer commitment through the generation of information (Thayer, 1968, cited by Reid et al., 2002).

These last authors suggest that using the information dynamic appears to be constant across all types of purchase situations. However, as the complexity of a purchase situation increases so the amount of giving information behaviours decline and getting information behaviours increase. This finding supports the need for a salesperson to be able to recognise particular situations in the buying process and then to adapt their behaviour to meet the buyer's contextual needs.

Sales people undertake numerous tasks in association with communications activities.

However, sales people undertake numerous tasks in association with communications activities. Guenzi (2002) determined that some sales activities are generic simply because they are performed by most salespeople across a large number of industries. These generic activities are selling, customer-relationship management and communicating to customers. Other activities such as market analysis, pre-sales services and the transfer of information about competitors to the organisation are industry-specific. Interestingly, he found that information-gathering activities are more likely to be undertaken by organisations operating in consumer markets than in b2b, possibly a reflection of the strength of the market orientation in both arenas.

The role of personal selling is largely one of representation. In business-to-business markets, sales personnel operate at the boundary of the organisation. They provide the link between the needs of their own organisation and the needs of their customers. This linkage, or boundary-spanning role, is absolutely vital, for a number of reasons that will be discussed shortly, but without personal selling, communication with other organisations would occur through electronic or print media and would foster discrete closed systems. Representation in this sense therefore refers to face-to-face encounters between people from different organisations.

Many authors consider the development, organisation and completion of a sale in a market-exchange-based transaction to be the key part of the role of personal selling. Sales personnel provide a source of information for buyers so that they can make the right purchase decisions. In that sense they provide a good level of credibility, but they are also perceived, understandably, as biased. The degree of expertise held by the salesperson may be high, but the degree of perceived trustworthiness will vary, especially during the formative period of the relationship, unless other transactions with the selling organisation have been satisfactory. Once a number of transactions have been completed and product quality established, trustworthiness may improve.

As the costs associated with personal selling are high, it is vital that sales personnel are used effectively. To that end, some organisations are employing other methods to decrease the time that the sales force spends on administration, travel and office work and to maximise the time spent in front of customers, where they can use their specific selling skills.

The amount of control that can be exercised over the delivery of the messages through the sales force depends upon a number of factors. Essentially, the level of control must be regarded as low, because each salesperson has the freedom to adapt messages to meet changing circumstances as negotiations proceed. In practice, however, the professionalism and training that many members of the sales force receive and the increasing accent on measuring levels of customer satisfaction mean that the degree of control over the message can be regarded, in most circumstances, as very good, although it can never, for example, be as high as that of advertising.

This flexibility is framed within the context of the product strategy. Decisions that impact upon strategy are not allowed. There is freedom to adapt the manner in which products are presented, but there is no freedom for the sales representatives to decide the priority of the products to be detailed.

Strengths and weaknesses of personal selling

There are a number of strengths and weaknesses associated with personal selling. It is interesting to note that some of the strengths can in turn be seen as weaknesses, particularly when management control over the communication process is not as attentive or as rigorous as it might be.

Strengths

Dyadic communications allow for two-way interaction that, unlike the other communications mix tools, provides for fast, direct feedback. In comparison with the mass media, personal selling allows for the receiver to focus attention on the salesperson, with a reduced likelihood of distraction or noise.

There is a greater level of participation in the decision process by the vendor than in the other tools.

There is a greater level of participation in the decision process by the vendor than in the other tools. When this is combined with the power to tailor messages in response to the feedback provided by the buyer, the sales process has a huge potential to solve customer problems.

Weaknesses

One of the major disadvantages of personal selling is the cost.

One of the major disadvantages of personal selling is the cost. Costs per contact are extremely high, and this means that management must find alternative means of communicating particular messages and improve the amount of time that sales personnel spend with prospects and customers. Reach and frequency through personal selling are always going to be low, regardless of the amount of funds available.

Control over message delivery is very often low and, though flexibility is an advantage, there is also the disadvantage of message inconsistency. This in turn can lead to confusion (a misunderstanding, perhaps with regard to a product specification), the ramifications of which can be enormous in terms of cost and time spent by a variety of individuals from both parties to the contract.

The quality of the relationship can, therefore, be jeopardised through poor and inconsistent communications.

Team selling

Three distinct selling strategies can be identified: transactional, consultative and alliance sales (Rackman and DeVincetis, 1999). See Table 11.2. These strategies represent different eras of thought and approaches to selling and sales management. However, they also represent phases through which individual organisations can develop their selling practices.

In order that partnership and more collaborative selling approaches are implemented it has become increasingly necessary and common for organisations to assign a team of salespeople to meet the needs of key account customers. A variety of different skills

TABLE 11.2 Three selling strategies

Selling strategy	Explanation
Transactional selling	This is the traditional form of selling, and the strategy is characterised by the planned development of a large volume of sales accounts, each of which has individual and unrelated buyers.
Consultative selling	Because of better understanding about relationships and the need to limit the number of buyers, consultative selling evolved in the mid-1980s. Partnerships were formed with customers and a form of preferred-supplier status was established. Sometimes referred to as solution selling.
Alliance sales	An alliance sales strategy was developed when various processes of the selling organisation were integrated with those of the partner. Sales moved from a quantitative perspective (transactional) to a qualitative perspective (both consultative and alliance-based).

Source: *Rethinking the Sales Force; Redefining Selling to Crente and Capture Customer Value*, N. Rackham & J. DeVincentis, © 1999 The McGraw-Hill Companies, Inc.

are thought necessary to meet the diversity of personnel making up the DMUs of the larger organisations. Consequently, a salesperson may gain access to an organisation, after which a stream of engineers, analysts, technicians, programmers, training executives and financial experts follow.

For example, when a car manufacturer plans a new model, a salesperson from a potential (or established) supplier opens the door to provide a communication link between the two organisations. Soon, a project team evolves, consisting of engineering, manufacturing, purchasing, production and quality staff, all working to satisfy the needs of their client. It is common practice for suppliers to use the same project code number as the client to provide for clarity and avoid confusion. It also helps to build the relationship and identification between the partners.

Most leading IT-based organisations used to sell the hardware and then leave the customer to work out how to use it. Team selling is now used by Digital, Hewlett-Packard, IBM and others to provide customised combinations of hardware, software and technical support as solutions to their customers' business problems. This requires teams of salespeople and technical experts working closely with the customer's DMU throughout the sales/purchasing cycle and beyond.

The sales-team approach requires high levels of coordination and internal communication.

The sales-team approach requires high levels of co-ordination and internal communication if it is to be successful and sell across product lines from various locations (Cespedes et al., 1989). In addition, the range of activities associated with team selling requires a culture that is focused on customers' needs and the team must be supported and self-driven to deliver on these internally recognised performance barriers. Indeed, Workman et al. (2003) refer to the need to develop an *esprit de corps* in order that selling teams, primarily used for key accounts, may be successful. Team selling requires a different approach to both the customer and also the associated internal activities from those required for regular field-force selling. Both the levels of commitment and costs associated with cross-functional team selling are large, and these reasons alone restrict the use of this selling approach to those accounts that are strategically important.

When personal selling should be a major part of the communications mix

In view of the role and the advantages and disadvantages of personal selling, when should it be a major part of the communications mix? The following is not an exhaustive list, but is presented as a means of considering some of the important issues: complexity, network factors, buyer significance and communication effectiveness.

Complexity

Personal selling is very important when there is a medium to high level of relationship complexity.

Personal selling is very important when there is a medium to high level of relationship complexity. Such complexity may be associated either with the physical characteristics of the product, such as computer software design, or with the environment in which the negotiations are taking place. For example, decisions related to the installation of products designed to automate an assembly line may well be a sensitive issue. This may be owing to management's attitude towards the operators currently undertaking the work that the automation is expected to replace. Any complexity needs to be understood by buyer and seller in order that the right product is offered in the appropriate context for the buyer. This may mean that the buyer is required to customise the offering or provide assistance in terms of testing, installing or supporting the product.

When the complexity of the offering is high, advertising and public relations cannot always convey benefits in the same way as personal selling. Personal selling allows the product to be demonstrated so that buyers can see and, if necessary, touch and taste it for themselves. Personal selling also allows explanations to be made about particular points that are of concern to the buyer or about the environment in which the buyer wishes to use the product.

Buyer significance

The significance of the product to the buyers in the target market is a very important factor in the decision on whether to use personal selling. Significance can be measured as a form of risk, and risk is associated with benefits and costs.

The absolute cost to the buyer will vary from organisation to organisation and from consumer to consumer. The significance of the purchase of an extra photocopier for a major multinational organisation may be low, but for a new start-up organisation or for an established organisation experiencing a dramatic turnaround, an extra photocopying machine may be highly significant and subject to high levels of resistance by a number of different internal stakeholders.

The timing of a product's introduction may well be crucial to the success of a wider plan or programme of activities. Only through personal selling can delivery be dovetailed into the client's scheme of events.

Communications effectiveness

There may be a number of ways to satisfy the communications objectives of a campaign, other than by using personal selling. Each of the other communications tools has strengths and weaknesses; consequently, differing mixes provide different benefits. Have they all been considered?

One of the main reasons for using personal selling occurs when advertising alone, or any other medium, provides insufficient communications.

One of the main reasons for using personal selling occurs when advertising alone, or any other medium, provides insufficient communications. The main reason for this inadequacy surfaces when advertising media cannot provide buyers with the information they require to make their decision. For example, someone buying a new car may well observe and read various magazine and newspaper advertisements. The decision to buy, however, requires information and data upon which a rational decision can be made. This rationality and experience of the car, through a test drive perhaps, balances the former, more emotional, elements that contributed to the earlier decision.

The decision to buy a car normally evokes high involvement, so car manufacturers try to provide a rich balance of emotional and factual information in their literature. From this prospective buyers seek further information, experience and reassurance from car dealers. Car buyers sign orders with the presence and encouragement of salespersons. Very few cars are bought on a mail-order basis, although some are bought over the Internet.

Personal selling provides a number of characteristics that make it more effective than the other elements of the mix. As discussed, in business-to-business marketing the complexity of many products requires salespeople to be able to discuss with clients their specific needs; in other words, to be able to talk in the customer's own language, to build source credibility through expertise and hopefully trustworthiness, and build a relationship that corresponds with the psychographic profile of each member of the DMU. In this case, mass communications would be inappropriate.

There are two further factors that influence the decision to use personal selling as part of the communications mix. When the customer base is small and dispersed across a wide geographic area it makes economic sense to use salespersons, as advertising in this situation is inadequate and ineffective.

Personal selling is the most expensive element of the communications mix. It may be that other elements of the mix may provide a more cost-effective way of delivering the message.

Channel-network factors

If the communications strategy combines a larger amount of push rather than pull activities, then personal selling is required to provide the necessary communications for the other members of the channel network. Following on from this is the question regarding what information needs to be exchanged between members and what form and timing the information should be in. Handling objections, answering questions and overcoming misconceptions are also necessary information-exchange skills.

When the number of members in a network is limited, the use of a sales force is advisable, as advertising is inefficient. Furthermore, the opportunity to build a close collaborative relationship with members may enable the development of a sustainable competitive advantage. Cravens (1987) suggested that the factors in Table 11.3 are important and determine when the sales force is an important element of the communications mix.

The roles of personal selling and the sales force are changing because the environment in which organisations operate is also shifting dramatically. The repercussions of these changes will become evident following the discussion of the tasks that personal selling is expected to complete.

TABLE 11.3 When personal selling is a major element of the communications mix

	Advertising relatively important	Personal selling relatively important
Number of customers	Large	Small
Buyers' information needs	Low	High
Size and importance of purchase	Small	Large
Post-purchase service required	Little	A lot
Product complexity	Low	High
Distribution strategy	Pull	Push
Pricing policy	Set	Negotiate
Resources available for promotion	Many	Few

Source: *Strategic Marketing*, 5E, D. Cravens, © 1997 The McGraw-Hill Companies, Inc.

Integration and supporting the sales force

In an effort to increase the productivity of the sales force and to use their expensive skills more effectively, direct marketing has provided organisations with an opportunity to improve levels of performance and customer satisfaction. In particular, the use of an inside telemarketing department is seen as a compatible sales channel to the field sales force. The telemarketing team can accomplish the following tasks: they can search for and qualify new customers, so saving the field force from cold calling; they can service existing customer accounts and prepare the field force should they be required to attend to the client personally; they can seek repeat orders from marginal or geographically remote customers, particularly if they are low-unit-value consumable items; finally, they can provide a link between network members that serves to maintain the relationship, especially through periods of difficulty and instability. Many organisations prefer to place orders through telesales teams, as it does not involve the time costs associated with personal sales calls. The routine of such orders gives greater efficiency for all concerned with the relational exchange and reduces costs.

Direct mail activities are also becoming more important in areas where personal contact is seen as unnecessary or where limited field sales resources are deployed to

Direct mail is often used to supplement the activities of the field force.

key accounts. As with telesales, direct mail is often used to supplement the activities of the field force. Catalogue and electronic communications such as fax can be used for accounts that may be regarded as relatively unattractive.

In addition to this, use of the Internet and mobile-based communications have provided new opportunities to reach customers. The website itself symbolises the changing orientation of marketing communications. Whereas once the brochure, mass-media advertising and perhaps a communications mix incentive represented the central channels of communication, now the website and the database serve to integrate directed, sometimes interactive, one-to-one communications. These are supported in many cases by more call-to-action messages channelled through a variety of coordinated offline and digital media.

All of these activities free the field sales force to increase their productivity and to spend more time with established customers or those with high profit potential.

Multichannel selling

A number of different sales channels have been identified so far and many organisations, in their search to reduce costs, have restructured their operations in an attempt to better meet the 'touchpoints' of their different customers.

Restructuring has often taken the form of introducing multiple sales channels with the simple objective of using less expensive channels to complete selling tasks that do not require personal, face-to-face contact.

Restructuring has often taken the form of introducing multiple sales channels with the simple objective of using less expensive channels to complete selling tasks that do not require personal, face-to-face contact. Technology-enhanced channels, mainly in the form of Web-based and email communications, have grown considerably, often at the expense of telephone and mail facilities. Payne and Frow (2004) have developed a categorisation of sales channels, and these are depicted in the vertical column of Table 11.4.

ViewPoint 11.5   Oarsman uses many channels

FiveGold is a company developed by five times Olympic gold medallist Sir Steve Redgrave. The company supplies good-quality clothing to catalogue retailers such as Freeman's and Grattan, independent menswear clothing shops and department stores. In addition the brand uses the Internet, which accounts for 20 per cent of sales. Online catalogues, email and viral marketing campaigns are used online. FiveGold uses advertising in Sunday newspaper supplements and attends particular sporting events to merchandise the brand. Sir Steve was even dressed in FiveGold clothing when commentating for the BBC and being seen greeting the British Olympic rowers after their latest famous victory.

The range of channels used by FiveGold is designed to meet the needs of particular target audiences. The chosen channels do not cannibalise sales from other channels and serve the mass market that the brand was designed to serve.

Source: Adapted from Crush (2004)

TABLE 11.4 Comparison of channel characteristics

Channel	Breadth	Dominant form of communication	Cost/contact
Field sales	Key account, service and personal representation	Dialogue	High
Outlets	Retail branches, stores, depots and kiosks	Interactive	Medium
Telephony	Traditional telephone, facsimile, telex and contact centres	One way and two way	Low to Medium
Direct marketing	Direct mail, radio and traditional television	One way and two way	Low
ecommerce	Email, Internet, interactive television	Interactive	Very low
m-commerce	Mobile telephony, SMS, WAP and 3G	Interactive	Very low

In order to better meet the needs of customers, organisations need to evolve their mix of channels. Customers will then be able to interact with their supplying organisations using the mix of channels that they prefer to use. Therefore, marketing communications needs to be used in order to best complement the different audiences, channel facilities and characteristics. Through mixing channels and communications in a complementary way higher levels of customer service can be achieved. The proliferation of channels may, however, lead organisations to believe that the greater the number of channels the greater the chances of commercial success. In addition to the view that multichannel customers are known to spend up to 30 per cent more than single-channel customers, the Internet and overseas call centres also offer substantial (short-term) cost savings (Myers et al., 2004).

Categorising customers

One simple approach to managing channels is to categorise accounts (customers) according to their potential attractiveness and the current strength of the relationship between supplier and buyer.

One simple approach to managing channels is to categorise accounts (customers) according to their potential attractiveness and the current strength of the relationship between supplier and buyer. See Figure 11.1. A strong relationship, for example, is indicative of two organisations engaged in mutually satisfying relational exchanges. A weak relationship suggests that the two parties have no experience of each other or, if they have, that it is not particularly satisfying. If there have been transactions, it may be that these can be classified as market-exchange experiences. Attractiveness refers to the opportunities a buying organisation represents to the vendor: how large or small the potential business is in an organisation.

For reasons of clarity, these scales are presented as either high or low, strong or weak. However, they should be considered as a continuum, and with the use of some relatively simple evaluative criteria accounts can be positioned on the matrix and strategies formulated to move accounts to different positions, which in turn necessitate the use of different sales-channel mixes.

Based on the original approach developed by Cravens et al. (1991), appropriate sales channels are superimposed on the grid so that optimum efficiency in selling effort and costs can be managed (Figure 11.2). Accounts in Section 1 vary in attractiveness, as some will be assigned key account status. The others will be very important and will require a high level of selling effort (investment), which has to be delivered by the field sales force. Accounts in Section 2 are essentially prospects because of their weak relationship but high attractiveness. Selling effort should be proportional to the value of

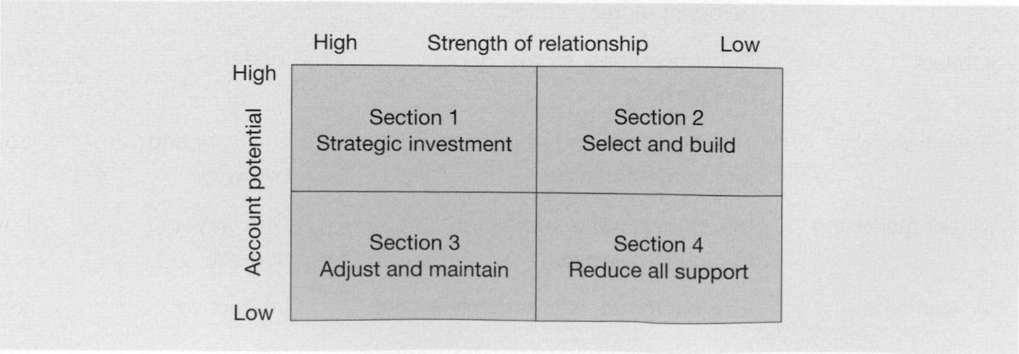

	High Strength of relationship Low	
High	Section 1 Strategic investment	Section 2 Select and build
Low	Section 3 Adjust and maintain	Section 4 Reduce all support

(Account potential — vertical axis, High to Low)

FIGURE 11.1 Account investment matrix

ViewPoint 11.6   Multichannel BUPA Wellness

BUPA Wellness offers an on-site corporate dental service. Rather than use the expensive and time-poor field sales force to generate leads and new business it decided to manage the process of customer acquisition through technology. BUPA outsourced the task to Inbox Media, whose goals were to develop a database as a foundation for the project, create awareness and impact in the market and generate leads for the sales force to convert.

Inbox Media used telemarketing to create a list of HRM managers who agreed to receive emails from it in the future. Their details were used in the database and then each were sent personalised video emails informing them about the services of BUPA Wellness and, more particularly, the number of days that their organisation lost each year through dental visits and associated oral health problems. While the results were entirely satisfactory (52 per cent of emails were opened, 21 per cent clicked through and approximately 50 leads were turned into appointments), one of the interesting elements of the campaign concerned the dynamics associated with the email part of the programme. Inbox Media was able to monitor who opened the emails, how long they spent reading them and who they forwarded them to. It thus built a picture of email opening and behaviour characteristics.

Although the opportunity was declined it was technically possible to use the sales team to call recipients as they opened their video email or even when or just after it had been played. However, this co-ordinated approach was considered inappropriate as it would raise strong concerns about privacy, trust, intrusion, reputation and the ethics associated with over-aggressive selling strategies.

Source: Adapted from Anon. (2003)

the prospects: high effort for good prospects and low for the others. Care should be given to allocating a time by which accounts in this section are moved to other parts of the grid, and in doing so save resources and maximise opportunities for growth. All the main sales channels should be used, commencing with direct and email to identify prospects, telesales for qualification purposes, field-sales-force selling directed at the strong prospects and telesales and website for the others. Website details provide support and information for those accounts that wish to remain distant. As the relationship becomes stronger, so field selling takes over from telemarketing and the coordinating activities of the contact or call centre. If the relationship weakens, then the account may be discontinued and selling redirected to other prospects.

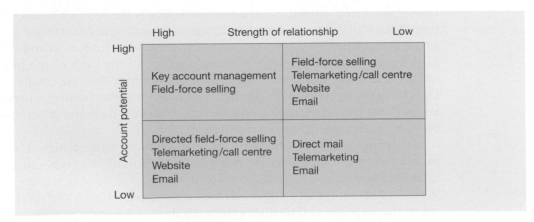

FIGURE 11.2 Multichannel mix allocation

Accounts in Section 3 do not offer strong potential and, although the relationship is strong, there are opportunities to switch the sales-channel mix by reducing, but not eliminating, the level of field-force activity and to give consideration to the introduction of telemarketing for particular accounts. Significant cost reductions can be achieved with these types of accounts by simply reviewing the means and reasoning behind the personal-selling effort. Accounts in Section 4 should receive no field-force calls, the prime sales channels being telesales, email, the website and perhaps catalogue selling, depending upon the nature of the website.

Establishing a multiple-sales-channel strategy based on the grid suggested above may not be appropriate to all organisations. For example, the current level of performance may be considered as exceeding expectations, in which case there is no point in introducing change. It may be that the costs and revenues associated with redeployment are unfavourable and that the implications for the rest of the organisation of implementing the new sales-channel approach are such that the transition should be either postponed or rejected. Payne and Frow (2004) suggest that a range of channel options or strategies can be identified that relate to the channel needs of target segments. These can be a single dominant channel such as those used by Amazon and Egg; a customer-segment approach designed for use with different channel types such as intermediaries, b2b end-user customers and consumers; one based on the different activity channels that customers prefer to use, such as a mix off online and offline resources to identify, see, demonstrate, select and pay for a computer; and a truly integrated multichannel strategy utilising CRM systems to integrate all customer information at whichever contact point the customer chooses to use. These strategies reflect some of the approaches that can be used, and indeed various combinations can be used to meet customers' channel needs. However, experience has shown that costs can be reduced through the introduction of a multiple-sales-channel approach and that levels of customer satisfaction and the strength of the relationship between members of the network can be improved considerably. In addition, it is vital to remember that customers will move into and use new channel mixes over the customer life cycle and that channel decisions should be regarded as fluid and developmental.

> **Costs can be reduced through the introduction of a multiple-sales-channel approach and that levels of customer satisfaction and the strength of the relationship between members of the network can be improved considerably.**

Evaluating performance

One of the many attractions of direct marketing is the ease with which the effectiveness of the tool can be measured. In an age of increasing accountability managers prefer to use performance measures that are easily calculated, understood and communicated. Sales figures have always been a key measure for all the tools of the mix, despite the fact that in many instances (for example, advertising) they are totally inappropriate. Direct marketing seeks to change behaviour, and it should deliver a personalised, customised and precisely targeted call to action. Therefore, measures of performance should be sales or response-behaviour oriented.

Measuring responses, whether they be in terms of forms returned, emails opened, websites visited or calls made for brochures, representatives or other such information, is largely relevant and helpful. However, in an age of increasing reference to integrated (coordinated) campaigns, difficulties arise concerning which tool(s) of the mix actually led to the response and to what extent did direct marketing provide a suitable return on the overall investment.

The measurement of personal selling needs to accommodate two main elements: the performance of individual salespeople and the performance of the sales force. In both cases the unit of measurement concerns the inputs and outcomes of the overall personal-selling process. At a broad level outputs can be regarded as sales and profits resulting from exchanges with customers, and productivity can be deemed to be the ratio of inputs to outputs.

The measurement of personal selling needs to accommodate two main elements.

Evaluating the performance of a salesperson

There are two main types of inputs to the sales process. The first consists of the activities undertaken and the costs incurred as a result. The second concerns the knowledge and skills necessary to achieve the required outputs. Measuring and then evaluating the activities of each salesperson, the inputs, is an important and frequently used measuring stick. The number of planned and unplanned sales calls, the number of presentations, the frequency with which the showroom has been used and the mix of accounts visited, plus the expenses, cost of samples used and time associated with these activities, can be measured and evaluated against organisational standards and expectations. These simple quantitative measures provide for objectivity and measurement; what they do not do is provide an insight into why the input and the ultimate performance rating did or did not achieve the required standard.

Measuring and evaluating the knowledge component of the input dimension requires greater subjectivity and reliance on qualitative measures. How well a salesperson uses their selling skills and presents themselves to customers is vitally important. In addition, the depth of knowledge that the subject has of the products, customers, territory and market will probably have a greater bearing on the performance outcome than the number of visits made. In other words, it is the quality of the sales call that is important, not the number of sales calls made, a process that relies on a personal judgement made by the people charged with evaluation.

Outputs are more easily measured than inputs.

Outputs are more easily measured than inputs. The most common technique used is that of the ratings attached to the volume or value of sales generated in a particular period in a designated area. Using a quota to measure achievement can be important for consistent tracking of performance and for motivational purposes. Volume analysis allows management to measure the effectiveness of the sales process, as comparisons can be drawn with last year's performance, with other salespersons (with similar territory potential) and with the potential in the territory.

Ratios provide a further insight into the overall performance and productivity of a salesperson. Expense ratios are a useful tool for understanding the way in which a salesperson is managing the territory. The cost/call ratio, for example, reveals the extent to which the subject is making calls and the costs of supporting the individual in the territory. Further detailed analyses are possible: for example, servicing ratios reveal the extent to which a territory's business potential has been acquired, such as what percentage of a territory's accounts has been won, how many prospects become customers, how many customers are lost and what level of sales are achieved on average per customer or per call. Activity ratios determine the effort that is put into a territory, and calls/day, calls/account type and orders/call reveal the amount of planning and thought that is being put into an area.

In isolation, these ratios provide some objectivity when attempting to measure the performance of a salesperson. Used in combination they become a more powerful tool, but only to the extent that they are an aid to decision-making. One major advantage of ratio analysis is the benchmarking effect. Comparisons become possible not only across the sales force but also across the industry, as norms become established through time.

Evaluating the performance of a sales force

An overall measure of the effectiveness of the sales force is also necessary. The following constitute the main areas of evaluation: the objectives set in the promotion mix, the level of interaction with the other elements of the promotion mix, activity measures and achievement against quota, the effectiveness of the sales channels used and the quality of the relationships established with customers.

The sales force, as a part of the promotion mix, has a responsibility to achieve the sales objectives set out in the promotion objectives. To do this, the sales force needs the support of the other elements of the mix. Measuring this interdisciplinary factor is extremely difficult, but there is no doubt that each of the elements works more efficiently if they are coordinated with one another and the messages conveyed dovetail with and reinforce each other.

One further area of evaluation that is necessary is that of the sales channels themselves. The increased use of multiple sales channels and the contribution that direct marketing will make to the sales force cannot be ignored. Measures are required of the effectiveness of the field sales force, the key account selling team and the array of direct-marketing techniques. Constant monitoring of the market is required to judge whether the classification of an account should be changed, and whether different combinations of selling approaches should be introduced.

Finally, customers need to be involved in the sales-channel-decision process and in the evaluation of the field sales force. If customers are happy with a sales channel, then they are more likely to continue using it. It is vital that the views of customers are monitored regularly and that they contribute to the evaluation process.

The evaluation of the sales force and its individual members has for a long time been oriented to quantitative measures of input and output productivity. These are useful, as they provide for comparison within the organisation and with the industry norms. However, in future, evaluation is moving from a revenue to a profit perspective and a much greater emphasis will be placed upon the quality of the relationships that the sales force develops with its customers. The current imbalance between the use of quantitative and qualitative measures will shift to a position where qualitative measures become more important in evaluating the performance of the sales force.

Summary of key points

1. The use of direct marketing has grown considerably in recent years mainly because of developments in technology and changing market conditions and customer preferences.

2. Direct marketing uses direct-response media based on database support and permits the generation and feedback of messages with individual customers. The overarching objectives are to build and sustain two-way communication.

3. One of the outcomes from two-way communication is interaction, and then comes dialogue. This can lead to a mutually rewarding relationship with each customer, reduce media costs and improve effectiveness and measurement.

4. There are four different ways in which direct marketing is used by organisations. For some organisations their whole marketing approach has been built around the direct concept (e.g. First Direct in financial services), whereas for others the approach has been used to complement their use of the other tools in the communications mix.

5. Direct marketing will not replace mass-media-based communications but it is likely that an increasing proportion of marketing budgets will continue to move towards direct communication activities.

6. There are a number of different personal-selling tasks, but increasingly telemarketing and direct mail is being used to free the sales force from non-selling activities. This allows management to focus the time of the sales force upon getting in front of valued customers and prospects, with a view to using their particular selling skills.

7. As organisations move to more relational exchanges, so the sales force will need to play a complementary role. This role will necessitate the execution of tasks such as managing customer relationships and integrating with the other tools of the marketing communications mix.

8. The use of the field sales force as the only means of reaching customers is unlikely to remain. Technological advances, tighter cost constraints, and the need for increasing levels of communications mix effectiveness and accountability, have driven many progressive organisations to introduce multiple sales channels.

Review questions

1. Explain the different levels of direct marketing, highlighting the key differences.

2. Discuss the role of the database as the hub of marketing communications.

3. Describe the role of personal selling and highlight its main strengths and weaknesses.

4. What are the different types of personal selling and what are the tasks that salespersons are normally expected to accomplish?

5. Which factors need to be considered when determining the significance of personal selling in the communications mix?

6. Write brief notes outlining the ways in which direct marketing might be used to assist personal-selling activities.

References

Anon. (2003), 'Royal Mail', Data 2003, *Marketing Direct*, sponsored supplement.

Bashford, S. (2004), 'Telemarketing: customers calling', *Marketing*, 8 September; retrieved 16 October from www.brandrepublic.com/news/.

Cespedes, F.V., Doyle, S.X. and Freedman, R.J. (1989), 'Teamwork for today's selling', *Harvard Business Review*, March/April, pp. 44–55.

Cravens, D.W. (1987), *Strategic Marketing*, Homewood, Ill.: Richard D. Irwin.

Cravens, D.W., Ingram, T.N. and LaForge, R.W. (1991), 'Evaluating multiple channel strategies', *Journal of Business and Industrial Marketing*, 6(3/4), pp. 37–48.

Crush, P. (2004), 'FiveGold', *Marketing*, 1 December, p. 21.

Fill, C. (2006), *Marketing Communications: engagement, strategies and practice*, 4th edn, Harlow: FT Prentice Hall.

Fletcher, K. (1997), 'External drive', *Marketing*, 30 October, pp. 39–42.

Ganesan, S. (1994), 'Determinants of long-term orientation in buyer–seller relationships', *Journal of Marketing*, **58** (April), pp. 1–19.

Guenzi, P. (2002), 'Sales force activities and customer trust', *Journal of Marketing Management*, **18**, pp. 749–78.

Gundach, G.T. and Murphy, P.E. (1993), 'Ethical and legal foundations of relational marketing exchanges', *Journal of Marketing*, **57** (October), pp. 93–4.

Kamakura, W.A., Wedel, M., de Rosa, F. and Mazzon, J.A. (2003), 'Cross-selling through database marketing: a mixed factor analyzer for data augmentation and prediction', *International Journal of Research in Marketing*, **20**(1) (March), pp. 45–65.

McElhatton, N. (2005), 'Many happy returns', *Marketing Direct*, June, pp. 29–30.

Marsh, H. (2001), 'Dig deeper into the database goldmine', *Marketing*, 11 January, pp. 29–30.

Murphy, D. (2000), 'Call centres ponder price of technology', *Marketing*, 14 September, pp. 43–4.

Myers, J.B., Pickersgill, A.D. and Metre van, E.S. (2004), 'Steering customers to the right channels', *McKinsey Quarterly*, **4**, 16 November.

Payne, A. and Frow, P. (2004), 'The role of multichannel integration in customer relationship management', *Industrial Marketing Management*, **33**(6) (August), pp. 527–38.

Pearson, S. (2003), 'Data takes centre stage', Data 2003, *Marketing Direct*, sponsored supplement.

Rackman, N. and DeVincetis, J.R. (1999), *Rethinking the Sales Force: Redefining Selling to Create and Capture Customer Value*, New York: McGraw-Hill.

Reed, D. (2000), 'Too much, too often', *Marketing Week*, 12 October, pp. 59–62.

Reid, A., Pullins, E.B. and Plank, R.E. (2002), 'The impact of purchase situation on salesperson communication behaviors in business markets', *Industrial Marketing Management*, **31**(3), pp. 205–13.

Tapp, A. (2005), *Principles of Direct and Database Marketing*, 3rd edn, Harlow: FT Prentice Hall.

Workman Jr, J.P., Homburg, C. and Jensen, O. (2003), 'Interorganisational determinants of key account management effectiveness', *Journal of Academy of Marketing Science*, **31**(1), pp. 3–21.

Part 3 summary

Review

The tools or disciplines of the communications mix are a key aspect of marketing communications activities. This part of the book considered the main marketing communications tools: advertising, sales promotion, direct marketing, public relations and personal selling. Each chapter examined the main characteristics of particular tools, including issues about the ways in which each main communications tool can be measured and evaluated. It should be recognised that there are a host of sub-tools and derivative approaches such as field marketing, packaging, exhibitions and brand-experience activities. Space restrictions preclude their consideration here but readers interested in such topics should read Fill (2006).

The balance of the communications mix used by organisations has, as a generalisation, changed and the process of transition is continuing. Whereas once mass-media-led communications, dominated by advertising, were directed at huge audiences, now direct and personal communications allow for interactivity with small, niche audiences. Direct marketing, and sales promotion in combination with digital technologies, are now the leading disciplines.

Advertising is still a powerful form of communication and has a significant role to play in both offline and online contexts. Earlier models about how advertising works, such as AIDA, Dagmar and other sequential models, have been largely discarded because they are too generalised and only explain how advertising works in a particular context.

More recent ideas are based around the strong and the weak theories, about the underlying informational and emotional needs of the target audience and the motivations that drive attitudes and purchase intentions.

Media selection and planning used to be most associated with advertising activities. In many ways this is still relevant, but now sales promotion and direct marketing make use of paid media in order to reach the target audience.

Each medium has a set of characteristics that enables it to carry messages to target audiences and for it to affect the audience in particular ways. The selection of media, therefore, should be based partly on the ability of each medium to deliver the client's message in an effective and compelling way and in such a manner that it reinforces other media activity. One of the other primary factors in media selection are the costs associated with message delivery. These can vary considerably.

The third chapter in this part considered sales promotion. This tool should be used to offer buyers additional value, an inducement in order to generate an immediate sale. These inducements can be targeted at consumers, distributors, agents and members of the sales force.

Although there may be some doubts about the overall effectiveness of sales promotions they can be used strategically and can complement the other activities in the promotional mix. By attempting to develop a consistent theme to a promotional plan, sales promotions can follow advertising's awareness-building activities with a series of messages that continue the theme already established.

Chapter 10 considered public relations and sponsorship, both of which play an important role within the communications mix. Public relations can be used to support products and services (marketing PR) or the development of corporate goodwill (corporate PR). Although some brands have been launched entirely through the use of public relations, its main role has been to complement other communications activities, as part of coordinated or integrated marketing communications.

One of the earlier ideas concerning public relations was that its key role was to develop interest and goodwill with key stakeholders. The contemporary view is that it should be used to develop and maintain a portfolio of relationships with a range of key stakeholder audiences.

Sponsorship is used to gain access to specific target audiences. Through involvement with events, activities and other organisations it is possible to develop associations that the target audience perceives as positive.

Chapter 11 dealt with two major marketing communications tools, direct marketing and personal selling. These two tools are being used increasingly by some organisations in a complementary way. In order to focus the sales force on its core activities, namely identifying new customers and building relationships, direct marketing is being used to maintain the smaller, less-profitable accounts.

Direct marketing uses direct-response media, to enable the generation and feedback of messages with individual customers. One of the outcomes from such two-way, personal communication is interaction and, in some cases, dialogue. This can lead to a mutually rewarding relationship with each customer, a reduction in media costs and an improvement in effectiveness and measurement.

The costs associated with operating a sales force can be extremely high. As a result many organisations are using personal selling to develop relationships with specific customers, and using the other tools of the communications mix to reach the other customers in their portfolio. Key account management develops these principles and uses high-calibre members of the sales force to manage these strategically important accounts.

The tools of the mix set out in this chapter are the main headline tools. There are many other activities undertaken in the name of marketing communications, too many to explore here. Exhibitions, merchandising, field marketing, crisis communications, lobbying and packaging are some of these other activities.

The tools of the marketing communications mix should be used to complement each other and to reinforce messages. Some argue that this is the foundation of what is regarded as integrated marketing communications. Whether or not this is true, the effectiveness and efficiencies associated with such an approach cannot be doubted or ignored by those responsible for managing an organisation's marketing communications.

Questions and exercises

1. Compare and contrast the characteristics of both advertising and public relations. Explain why some organisations might use public relations rather than advertising, and find appropriate examples.

2. Identify the different types of sales promotion and find contemporary examples of each, from a country or region of your choice.

3. Explore the main characteristics of both art and sports-based sponsorship and offer reasons for its continued popularity in the twenty-first century.

4. Identify an organisation that uses direct marketing, collect information about its communications activities, and evaluate the outcomes. What do they do well, what could be improved?

5. Write notes in response to the following. If personal selling is expensive, what is the justification for its use by organisations?

6. How might the marketing communications mix evolve?

MINI CASE STUDY
On the road to recovery

In the UK car recovery and breakdown market the Royal Automobile Club (RAC) is regarded as the challenger brand with the Automobile Association (AA) as the undisputed market leader. In addition, Direct Line Rescue (DLR) has entered the market and taken a 10 per cent market share.

Customers in this market are no longer simply users of the vehicle breakdown services but also expect a broad range of products and services, which the motoring organisations aim to satisfy in different ways.

Traditionally, marketing communications messages have been based on advertising and the development of brand values. Messages have been very product-focused, typified by ads for speed of recovery, get-you-home services, helpfulness of their staff and a range of ancillary products such as car finance and legal and advisory services.

The perceived benefits of motor organisation membership have changed. Factors concerning reassurance have become more important, whereas economic factors have become less important. Motorists express more concern about the need to get home quickly with or without their car than they do about the economic arguments between motorist organisation membership and ad hoc services.

One of the main reasons for the change in attitude towards motor organisation membership is the change in profile of the UK motorist. The dominance of middle-aged male drivers has diminished as the percentage of young and female drivers has increased. Drivers are less willing to perform roadside repairs while, at the same time, cars are becoming more complex – cars are certainly becoming more reliable but it is also increasingly difficult for drivers to repair them by the roadside, partly as a result of the need for specialised diagnostic equipment and sealed accessories.

During the 1990s, the promotional thrust of the main motoring organisations changed from one that emphasised economic and tangible attributes to one that gave higher prominence to driver safety and reassurance. In addition to changes in the core messages used by the RAC and the AA, greater emphasis has been placed on the other promotional tools, partly in response to the entry and aggression of DLR.

One of the strategies used by both the AA and the RAC has been to change the organisational culture, but some commentators feel this has been at the expense of customer service. A recently published *Which?* magazine survey revealed that the RAC fared badly against the AA. In addition, a BBC consumer affairs programme, *Rogue Traders*, revealed that some RAC patrolmen were selling car batteries to stranded drivers who didn't need them.

In face of competitive pressures, profit margins declining on recovery services and private membership rising only slightly, the RAC has moved into direct-response TV (DRTV) to support their ancillary services. This required a move to a more emotional-based message to convey the idea that the RAC can help people afford their dream car, regardless of what it is, and secure the finance from a trusted brand to help them buy it. The ads encouraged viewers to call an 0800 number to apply for a loan and get an instant decision. Every successful loan applicant received free RAC Breakdown cover. In addition, the RAC has developed a 36-page RAC Magazine as a means of communicating with their different markets. Of the several million copies mailed out three times a year, everyone receives the standard 20 pages of content but, in addition, there is also a 16-page insert that takes account of a person's lifestage and their length of membership.

Direct Line Rescue (DLR) is a very strong brand that lends itself to strong imagery and no-nonsense messaging. DLR want to develop a much closer relationship with their customers and they too have strategies that are designed to offer more than just vehicle breakdown services. A recent campaign was designed to target customers of the RAC and the AA and to reinforce the Rescue brand, which has nearly a million customers. Through their DM agency they developed a series of mail packs, each containing a letter, envelope and insert, targeting different messages to existing AA and RAC members. These messages instructed recipients to 'Stop Paying Too Much' by switching to Direct Line. Direct Line's own car insurance customers received a third pack that said, 'First we save u money, then we save u'. This was intended to highlight the breakdown cover offer from £35 and to reassure people about the high level of service while also prompting them to respond through bold calls to action and guaranteed low prices.

Questions

1. Explain the characteristics of rational and emotional-based messages and provide examples based on the car recovery market.

2. Examine the ways in which marketing communications can be used to change motorists' attitudes towards vehicle recovery services.

3. Evaluate the extent to which customer magazines can help develop relationships with customers.

4. Recommend the key processes and procedures necessary to develop and implement an effective direct-mail campaign.

MINI CASE STUDY
Farmers' Kitchens

The general kitchen furniture market in the UK is worth over £900 million p.a. Farmers' Kitchens (FKs) is a privately owned company located in a small country town. The company makes medium-quality kitchen furniture that is designed around kitchens used by farmers and cottagers. The units are available in both finished and self-assembly format and unit sales currently reflect a 35/65 per cent split. The move into the self-assembly market proved successful as it enabled the company to reach customers in a wider geographic area. An installation facility is available for the finished units but the trend appears to be in favour of self-assembly products.

Farmers' Kitchens sales have grown steadily over the 45 years of trading, and currently stand at £13.7 million p.a. with net profit at 8.2 per cent. Products are sold through both direct and indirect marketing channels. The indirect channels consist of a small number of appointed distributors who sell a range of kitchen and bathroom products from many different manufacturers. They hold limited stock but work from brochures and their own showrooms.

Staff are very supportive of the company and appear to have a strong identification with the country-style positioning. Over 50 per cent have been with the company in excess of 15 years. It should be noted that many of the internal systems and procedures are old, slow and in need of updating, perhaps a reflection of the slower, rural culture that identifies the Farmers' Kitchens company.

In addition to these internal challenges the company has begun to experience increased competition from major national kitchen-furniture manufacturers. These companies either buy in prefabricated panels and apply a (rural) design template or import them direct from overseas manufacturers. In addition, they have sufficient resources to use broadcast media and offer lower prices.

In recognition of some of these problems facing the company, management have developed a marketing plan that seeks growth of 15 per cent p.a. to be achieved by market penetration and, in particular, the attraction of new customers. It now needs a marketing communications programme to deliver the marketing strategy.

The competition, as Farmers' Kitchens see it, have huge resources that can be used to invest in promotional campaigns to drive awareness and action. For example, these companies have authentic websites, unlike Farmers' Kitchens site, which is little more than an online brochure. Many of the large, national, standardised companies can produce promotional literature in large production runs and are happy to ignore wastage. Using expert photography of pretend kitchens, the quality and impact of the literature is high. Farmers' Kitchens' smaller budgets dictate that photographs of real customer's kitchens are required, which seldom look perfect and can appear amateurish. It costs £5 to produce each of the Farmers' Kitchens' brochures, so the vetting of each request for literature is important if it is to avoid those people merely intent on collecting brochures. A high conversion rate is necessary and although 50 per cent of quotations are converted into sales, the company cannot afford this figure to be lowered.

Current promotional activities centre on small space advertising in the supplements of weekend newspapers to generate leads and the use of brochures distributed via direct mail using bought-in lists. In addition to this, a small number of largely commission-based sales consultants work the geographic areas not covered by the distributors. This sales team is supported by a few office staff who advise clients by telephone, should they have any product-assembly-related problems. They also liaise with the distributors. Sales promotions are used seasonally to promote sales and to reduce any excess stock. Word of mouth is important, although little is undertaken to manage or develop it.

Farmers' Kitchens' customers want self-assembly country-style kitchen units but at mid- to low-range prices. Because they are bought direct there is little opportunity to inspect the quality before purchasing, so it is important that all customer contact is reassuring. For many, price is a key issue and a high degree of trust is necessary in order that a sale be completed.

Questions

1. Evaluate the current and future roles of marketing communications at Farmers' Kitchens.

2. Consider the importance of perceived risk to end-user customers of Farmers' Kitchens and, in the light of this knowledge, make recommendations about how marketing communications might best be used.

3. How might the development of Internet and digital-based technologies influence relationships with the distributors?

4. Recommend and justify a suitable coordinated marketing communications mix.

Industry, relationships and operations

Relationships: value, loyalty and trust

12

Aims and objectives

The aims of this chapter are, first, to consider the nature and significance of marketing relationships, and second, to explore the influence marketing communications can have on the relationships between organisations and various stakeholder audiences. There are four primary topics in this chapter:

Relationships, Customer life cycle, Loyalty, Internal communications

The learning objectives are to enable readers to:

1. discuss the concept of value and explain the main characteristics of relationship marketing;

2. explain the importance of customer retention and the use of loyalty programmes to reduce customer defection;

3. discuss issues concerning the development of trust in online environments;

4. examine trust and commitment as important relationship concepts;

5. explain the principles of the customer life cycle;

6. explore ways in which marketing communications can help organisations develop relationships;

7. understand the ideas about internal marketing communications;

8. discuss the concept of organisational identity and the impact that employees can bring to the way that organisations are perceived.

Introduction

Relationship marketing has become a key aspect of both consumer and business marketing. There are a number of dimensions associated with organisational and consumer relationships, many of which encompass established concepts such as trust, commitment and loyalty. The role that marketing communications can play in establishing and nurturing key relationships can be pivotal, yet the ways in which marketing communications might best be deployed depends to a large extent on the context in which both the relationship and the communications are configured.

> The role that marketing communications can play in establishing and nurturing key relationships can be pivotal.

Value has become an increasingly significant concept, to both marketing practitioners and academics. Indeed, many believe that the only viable marketing strategy should be to deliver improved shareholder value (Doyle, 2000). However, the importance of providing value for customers is not a new idea. Concepts of differentiation, unique and emotional selling propositions (USPs and ESPs) and positioning are founded on the idea that superior perceived value is of primary significance to customers. It has long been understood that customers buy benefits not features, that they buy products and services as solutions that enable them to achieve their goals. Most women buy lipstick because of a mixture of both tangible and intangible attributes or even features and benefits. They buy particular brands because they feel different as a result of using them. What they buy will vary from person to person, but in terms of tangible attributes they prefer to buy colour and smudge-free lips (no 'bleed'), that the lipstick stays on the lips, prevents dryness, is long lasting and smooth (Puth et al., 1999). However, among the intangible attributes are self-confidence, a coordinated fashion accessory, trust, perhaps an alter ego or, as Revlon once claimed, hope.

> Concepts of differentiation, unique and emotional selling propositions (USPs and ESPs) and positioning are founded on the idea that superior perceived value is of primary significance to customers.

The same principle applies to organisational marketing. Business customers buy solutions to business problems, not just stand-alone products. These benefits and solutions constitute added value for the customer, and represent the reason why one offering is selected in preference to another. For both consumers and business customers, value is determined by the net satisfaction derived from a transaction, not the costs incurred to obtain it.

Thus, if customers seek to satisfy their needs through their purchase of specific products and services, then it can be said that the satisfaction of needs is a way of delivering value. Kothandaraman and Wilson (2001) argue that the creation of value is dependent upon an organisation's ability to deliver high performance on the benefits that are important to the customer, and this in turn is rooted in their competency in technology and business processes, or core competences. According to Doyle (2000), the creation of customer value is based on three principles:

- Customers will choose between alternative offerings and select the one that (they perceive) will offer them the best value.
- Customers do not want product or service features, they want their needs met.
- It is more profitable to have a long-term relationship between a customer and a company rather than a one-off transaction.

Value is the customer's estimate of the extent to which a product or service can satisfy their needs.

Value is the customer's estimate of the extent to which a product or service can satisfy their needs. However, normally there are costs associated with the derivation of benefits such that a general model of value would identify the worth of the benefits received for the price paid (Anderson and Narus, 1998). Therefore, value is relative to customer expectations and experience of competitive offerings within a category and can be derived from sources other than products, such as the relationships between buyers and sellers (Simpson et al., 2001).

The value concept

The value-chain concept developed by Porter (1985) is based on the premise that organisations compete for business by trying to offer enhanced value, which is developed, internally, through a coordinated chain of activities. The value chain was devised as a tool to appraise an organisation's ability to create what Porter terms 'differential advantage'. It consists of nine activities, five primary and four support, all of which incur costs but together can (and should) lead to the creation of value. The primary activities are those direct actions necessary to bring materials into an organisation, to convert them into final products or services, to ship them out to customers and to provide marketing and servicing facilities. Support activities facilitate the primary activities. Customers perceive they are getting superior value when these activities are linked together, and these linkages can be achieved through systems and processes such as those offered by new technology. Doyle refers to three processes:

- innovation processes to generate a constant stream of new products and hence ability to maintain margins;
- operations processes to deliver first-class performance and costs;
- customer creation and support processes to provide a consistent and positive cash flow.

ViewPoint 12.1   Added value OnAir

As part of its customer development Airbus has developed facilities for airlines to offer a range of consumer communications while in flight. The system will enable passengers to use email and text messages, send and receive voice messages and Web browse, all through the use of their own phones, laptops and PDAs.

Airbus has identified a major opportunity in the market and believes the system, branded as OnAir, represents significant added value for major premium-travel airlines to offer their passengers. It is expected that Boeing will offer a similar system, with both manufacturers recognising the need for their customers to offer passengers additional value in what is a highly competitive market.

The processes used by an organisation become a critical part of the ways in which they can add value. However, it is customers who lie at the heart of the value chain. Only by understanding particular customer needs and by focusing and linking value-chain activities on satisfying them can superior value be generated. Value might be perceived in terms of price, low cost and accessibility. For others, price may be relatively inconsequential and the other benefits associated with a brand or organisation, such as continuity of supply, innovation and prestige, are signals that a longer-term association is of greater value to them. However, according to Ryssel et al. (2004), there is an increasing amount of evidence that the relationships organisations form are themselves generators of value and hence an important aspect of contemporary marketing.

Development of the relationship-marketing concept

Interaction between customers and sellers is based around the provision and consumption of perceived value. However, the quality, duration and level of interdependence between customers and sellers can vary considerably. The reasons for this variance are many and wide-ranging, but at the core are perceptions of shared values and the strength and permanence of any relationship that might exist. Relationship value can be visualised as a continuum (see Figure 12.1).

At one end of the continuum are transactional exchanges, characterised by short-term, product- or price-oriented exchanges, between buyers and sellers coming together for one-off exchanges independent of any other or subsequent exchanges. Both parties are motivated mainly by self-interest. Movement along the continuum represents the acceptance and desire for increasingly valued relationships. Interactions between parties are closer and stronger. The focus moves from initial attraction to retention and mutual understanding of each other's needs.

At the other end of the continuum are relational exchanges or what Day (2000) refers to as 'collaborative exchanges'. These are characterised by a long-term orientation, where there is complete integration of systems and processes and where the relationship is motivated by partnership and mutual support.

Trust and commitment underpin these relationships. Trust and commitment underpin these relationships and these variables become increasingly important as relational exchanges become established.

Perceived value may take many forms and be rooted in a variety of attributes, combined in different ways to meet segment needs. However, the context in which an

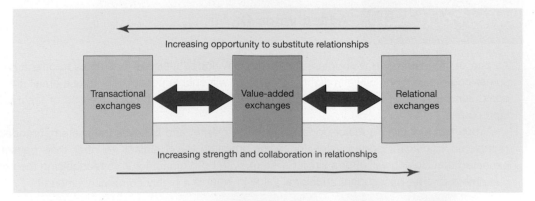

FIGURE 12.1 A continuum of value-oriented exchanges. Adapted from Day (2000)

TABLE 12.1 Key differences between transactional and relationship marketing

Attribute	Discrete exchange	Relational exchange
Chronological aspects of exchange	● Defined beginning ● Short term ● Sudden end	● Beginning can be traced back to earlier agreements ● Long term ● Reflects a continuous process
Expectations of the relationship	● Conflicts of interest/goals are expected ● Immediate settlement ('cash payment') ● No problems expected in future	● Conflicts of interest expected ● Future problems are overcome by trust and joint commitment
Communications	● Minimal personal relations ● Ritual-like communications predominate	● Both formal and informal communications used
Transferability	● Totally transferable ● It makes no difference who performs contractual obligations	● Limited transferability ● Exchanges are highly dependent on the identity of the parties
Cooperation	● No joint efforts	● Joint efforts at both planning and implementation stages ● Modifications endemic over time
Division of burden and benefit	● Sharp distinction between parties ● Each party has its own, strictly defined obligations	● Burdens and benefits likely to be shared ● Division of benefits and burdens likely to vary over time

Source: Wagner and Boutellier (2002). Reprinted with permission from *Business Horizons*, **45**(6) (November–December 2002). Copyright © (2002) by The Trustees at Indiana University, Kelley School of Business

exchange occurs between a buyer and a seller provides a strong reflection of the nature of their relationship. If the exchange is focused on the product (and the price) then the exchange is considered to be essentially transactional. If the exchange is focused around the needs of both the customer and the seller then the exchange is considered to be relational. The differences between transactional and relational exchanges are set out in Table 12.1 and provide an important starting point in understanding the nature of relationship marketing.

The product-marketing approach is rooted in the traditional 4Ps model of marketing and to a large extent reflects the transactional approach. Consumer marketing has long been regarded as something that generally takes place between anonymous individuals. Relationship marketing considers the value inherent in a longer-term series of exchanges that occurs between individuals who are, in general, known to each other. Relationship marketing acknowledges the changing lifetime needs of customers and emphasises the importance of both the product and customer life cycles. This in turn leads to a focus on customer retention.

Relationship marketing is also characterised by the frequency and intensity of the exchanges between customers and sellers.

Relationship marketing is also characterised by the frequency and intensity of the exchanges between customers and sellers. As these exchanges become more frequent and more intense so the strength of the relationships between buyers and sellers improves. It is this that provided the infrastructure for a new perspective of marketing, one based on relationships (Spekman, 1988; Rowe and Barnes, 1998), rather than the objects of a transaction, namely products and services.

Principles of retention

Marketing has been characterised by its potential to influence and attract customers. Indeed, early ideas considered marketing to be a social anathema due to the perception that it persuaded and manipulated people into purchasing goods and services they did not want. Although these fears and misgivings have generally been overcome, a further fallacy concerned the notion that all customers are good customers. As most commercial organisations will now agree, some customers are far more attractive than other customers, on the grounds that some are very profitable, others are marginally profitable but offer great potential and others offer little and/or incur losses.

Through the use of relationship cost theory it was possible to identify the benefits associated with stable and mutually rewarding relationships. Such customers avoid costly switching costs that are associated with finding new suppliers, whereas suppliers experience reduced quality costs incurred when adapting to the needs of new customers. Reichheld and Sasser (1990) identified an important association between a small (e.g. 5 per cent) increase in customer retention and a large (e.g. 60 per cent) improvement in profitability. Therefore, a long-term relationship leads to lower relationship costs and higher profits. Since this early work there has been general acceptance that customers who are loyal not only improve an organisation's profits but also strengthen its competitive position (Day, 2000) because competitors have to work harder to dislodge or destabilise their loyalty. It should be noted that some authors suggest the link between loyalty and profitability is not that simple (Dowling and Uncles, 1997), while others argue that much more information and understanding is required about the association between profitability and loyalty, especially when there may be high costs associated with customer acquisition (Reinartz and Kumar, 2002).

By undertaking a customer-profitability analysis it is possible to identify those segments that are worth developing, and hence build a portfolio of relationships, each of varying dimensions and potential. These relationships provide mutually rewarding benefits and offer a third dimension of the customer dynamic, namely customer development.

Relationships provide mutually rewarding benefits.

The customer life cycle

Customer relationships can be considered in terms of a series of relationship-development phases: customer acquisition, development, retention and decline. Collectively these are referred to as the customer life cycle. The duration and intensity of each relationship phase in the life cycle will inevitably vary, and it should be remembered that this representation is essentially idealistic. A customer-relationship cycle is represented at Figure 12.2.

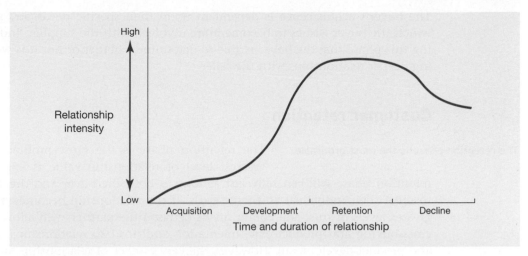

FIGURE 12.2 The customer-relationship cycle

Customer acquisition

The acquisition phase is characterised by three main events: search, initiation and familiarisation. See Table 12.2.

The logical sequence of acquisition activities moves from search and verification through the establishment of credentials. The length of this initiation period will depend partly on the importance of the buying decision and the complexity of the products, and partly upon the nature of the introduction. If the parties are introduced by an established and trusted source then certain initiation rites can be shortened. Once a transaction occurs the buyer–seller start to become more familiar with each other and gradually begin to reveal more information about themselves. The seller receives payment, delivery and handling information about the buyer, and as a result is able to prepare customised outputs. The buyer is able to review the seller's products and experience the service quality of the seller.

Customer development

The development phase is characterised by the seller attempting to reduce buyer risk and enhance credibility. This is achieved by encouraging cross-selling whereby the buyer consumes other products, by improving the volume of purchases, by engaging the buyer with other added-value services and by varying delivery times and quantities.

TABLE 12.2 Customer-acquisition events

Acquisition event	Explanation
Search	Buyers and sellers search for a suitable pairing
Initiation	Both parties seek out information about the other before any transaction occurs
Familiarisation	The successful completion of the first transaction enables both parties to start revealing more information about themselves

The buyer's acquiescence is dependent upon their specific needs and the degree to which the buyer wishes to become more involved with the supplier. Indeed, it is during this phase that the buyer is able to determine whether or not it is worth developing deeper relationships with the seller.

Customer retention

The retention phase is the most profitable.   The retention phase is the most profitable, where the greatest level of relationship value is experienced. The retention phase will generally last as long as both the buyer and the seller are able to meet their individual and joint goals. If the relationship becomes more involved greater levels of trust and commitment between the partners will allow for increased cross-buying and product experimentation and, for b2b relationships, joint projects and product development. However, the very essence of relationship marketing is for organisations to identify a portfolio of customers with whom they wish to develop a range of relationships. This requires the ability to measure levels of retention and also to determine when resources are to be moved from acquisition to retention and back to acquisition.

ViewPoint 12.2   Retaining office accounts

The office products division of the Cantrell Corporation had been an important part of the company's overall performance, with 40 per cent of its revenue derived online. However, office products customers rely on flawless ecommerce performance by their suppliers to help reduce their administrative overhead, and as a result competition within this sector is strong.

One of the challenges facing Cantrell is that its website was not integrated with customer-account information, so customers with questions about order status or account balances flooded the call centres. Costs were rising, customers were leaving and performance targets were increasingly being missed. Cantrell resolved to reassert its prominence in the market by creating a world-class shopping experience, with CRM capabilities, automatic fulfilment and integration with its largest customers.

The company developed a new website and as a result customers are now able to research their questions on the Web, and the company no longer needs to fund an additional call centre.

Customers can now shop online for office supplies, order online training courses and read online newsletters that are customised for them. They can quickly and efficiently find the items they need in the online catalogue, order them and check stock. Cantrell's order-fulfilment system now reads Web orders just as if they had been generated from the call centre, and fulfils them automatically. As a result, instead of customers leaving, new accounts are being registered at record levels, order-fulfilment cycles have been reduced and costs lowered, all by using technology to improve customer management and retention.

Customer decline

Customer decline is concerned with the closure of a relationship. Termination may occur suddenly as a result of a serious problem or episode between the parties. The more likely process is that the buying organisation decides to reduce its reliance on the seller because its needs have changed, or an alternative supplier that offers superior added value has been found. The buyer either formally notifies the established supplier or begins to reduce the frequency and duration of contact and moves business to other, competitive organisations.

This cycle of customer attraction (acquisition), development, retention and decline represents a major difference to the 4Ps approach. It is, above all else, customer-focused and more appropriate to marketing values. However, even this approach is questionable as, although the focus of analysis is no longer the product but the relationship, the focus tends to be oriented towards the 'customer relationship' rather than the relationship per se. In other words, there is a degree of asymmetry inherent in the relationship-marketing concept.

Trust, commitment and loyalty

Among the many concepts associated with the development of relationship marketing, three stand out: trust, commitment and loyalty. These are considered in turn.

Trust

Many writers contend that one of the crucial factors associated with the development and maintenance of both personal and interorganisational relationships is trust (Morgan and Hunt, 1994; Doney and Cannon, 1997). Trust is an element of personal, intraorganisational and interorganisational relationships, and is both necessary for and results from their perpetuation of others. As Gambetta (1988) argues, trust is a means of reducing uncertainty in order that effective relationships can develop.

Cousins and Stanwix (2001) suggest that, although trust is a term used to explain how relationships work, often it actually refers to ideas concerning risk, power and dependency, and that these propositions are used interchangeably. From their research of vehicle manufacturers it emerges that b2b relationships are about the creation of mutual business advantage and the degree of confidence that one organisation has in another.

Interorganisational trust is based on two main dimensions: credibility and benevolence. Interorganisational trust is based on two main dimensions: credibility and benevolence. Credibility concerns the extent to which one organisation believes (is confident) that another organisation will undertake and complete its agreed roles and tasks. Benevolence is concerned with goodwill, that the other organisation will not act opportunistically, even if the conditions for exploitation should arise (Pavlou, 2002). In other words, interorganisational trust involves judgements about another organisation's reliability and integrity.

Institutional trust is clearly vital in b2c markets where online perceived risk is present and known to prevent many people from purchasing online. In the b2b market, institutional trust is also important but more in terms of the overall reputation of the organisation. The development and establishment of trust is valuable because of the outcomes that can be anticipated. Three major outcomes from the development of trust have been identified by Pavlou, namely satisfaction, perceived risk and continuity. Trust can reduce conflict and the threat of opportunism and that in turn enhances the probability of buyer satisfaction, an important positive outcome of institutional trust.

Perceived risk is concerned with the expectation of loss. Perceived risk is concerned with the expectation of loss and is therefore tied closely with organisational or brand performance. Trust that a seller will not take advantage of the imbalance of information between buyer and seller effectively reduces risk. Continuity is related to business volumes, necessary in online b2b marketplaces, and the development of both online and offline enduring relationships. Trust is associated with continuity and when present is therefore indicative of long-term relationships. Ryssel et al. (2004, p. 203) recognise that trust (and commitment) have a 'significant impact on the creation of value and conclude that value creation is a function of the atmosphere of a relationship rather than the technology employed'.

Trust within a consumer context is equally important as a means of reducing uncertainty. Brands are an important means of instilling trust mainly because they are a means of condensing and conveying information so that they provide sufficient information for consumers to make calculated purchase decisions in the absence of full knowledge. In a sense, consumers transfer their responsibility for brand decision-making, and hence brand performance, to the brand itself. Through extended use of a brand, purchasing habits develop or what is termed routinised response behaviour emerges. This is important not just because complex decision-making is simplified but because the amount of communication necessary to assist and provoke purchase is considerably reduced.

The establishment of trust can be based around the existence of various components. Morrison and Firmstone (2000) identify reputation, familiarity/closeness, performance and accountability as four critical elements. According to Young and Wilkinson (1989) the presence of trust within a relationship is influenced by four other factors. These are the duration of the relationship, the relative power of the players, the presence of cooperation and various environmental factors that may be present at any one moment. Extending these ideas into what is now regarded by many as a seminal paper in the relationship-marketing literature, Morgan and Hunt (1994) argued, and supported with empirical evidence, that the presence of both commitment and trust leads to cooperative behaviour and this in turn is conducive to successful relationship marketing.

Online trust and security

These components can be substantiated through experience but in terms of information systems and technology, and the Internet in particular, problems arise when attempting to apply these criteria. There is a total lack of accountability on the Internet that may explain why a substantial proportion of the population are reluctant to engage in ecommerce exchanges. Many consumers do not understand the performance characteristics of the Internet and of various aspects of the modern digital world, which suggests to Morrison and Firmstone that there is too much missing knowledge for a sufficient level of trust to be present. This factor may dissipate as successive generations become more conversant and confident with technology and its performance characteristics. However, at the moment a lack of familiarity might partly explain why sufficient numbers of consumers do not place their trust when there is so much that is unknown. In addition, the cues by which trust is established offline have yet to become established in the online world. Symbols, trademarks and third-party endorsements need to be available so that the trust-inducing cues can be interpreted and relied on. Lastly, brand reputation is a summary statement of performance, and reputation conveys signals that others do and, for long-established brands, have in the past trusted the brand. Morrison and Firmstone (2000, p. 621) argue that 'existence confers an invitation to trust and a long existence gives strength to the presumption that one should trust'. This means that pure play ecommerce operations will have a more challenging task to establish reputation than bricks and clicks operations that are able to transfer part of their offline reputation into their online world.

Technology is available to provide virtually secure online transactions yet, despite the relatively small amount of online crime, there is a strong consumer perception that online transactions are not safe, even though many of these same people willingly give their credit-card details over the telephone to complete strangers. E-retailers should use marketing communications to reduce levels of perceived risk associated with online shopping and to provide a strong level of consumer reassurance. Thomas (2000) suggests that there are a number of things that can be done to provide such reassurance. These are:

1. Strong offline brands immediately provide recognition and an improved level of security, although care needs to be taken to convince audiences that the operator's online work is as effective as that of the offline brand.

2. Ensure that the Web pages where sensitive data are stored are hosted on a secure server. Use the most up-to-date security facilities and then tell consumers the actions you have taken to create a feel-good association and trust with the online brand. It is also worthwhile listing any physical, tangible addresses the company might have in order that consumers feel they are dealing with a modern yet conventional business.

3. Provide full contact details, fax, telephone, postal addresses and the names of people they can refer to. Again, this enables a level of personalisation and may soften the virtual atmosphere for those hesitant to immerse themselves in online transactions.

4. Provide an opportunity for the consumer to lock into the online brand by registering and subscribing to the site. Many organisations offer an incentive such as a free email newsletter or introductory offer.

5. By satisfying criteria associated with transparency, security and customer service it is possible to earn accreditation or cues that signal compatibility and compliance. The Academy of Internet Commerce operates a best practice called the Academy Seal of Approval. The logo appears on the site and when clicked provides a full text of the charter itself, a powerful form of reducing functional and financial risk.

6. Post-purchase communications are just as important in the online as well as the offline environment. Email acknowledgement of an order provides reassurance that the company actually exists and prompt (immediate/next-day) delivery or, if on extended delivery, an interim progress report (email) will provide confidence. Online order tracking is now quite common, so that it is possible to see the exact location of an order.

ViewPoint 12.3   Online trust

A survey of 1,700 online users by Thomson (2004) found that 1 in 20 online consumers have been victims of attempts to defraud or steal financial or personal details while undertaking transactions online. The study also found that 73 per cent of UK consumers were more concerned about security than convenience, price or quality when shopping online. In the UK 20 million consumers shop online, so a security failure should represent a crisis for online retailers. The study revealed that 24 per cent of discontented buyers defect to alternative online brands after security failures and 12 per cent made (word-of-mouth) complaints to friends and family about the companies that had let them down.

The overall finding is that if consumers lose trust when shopping in an online environment they will switch brands readily, so the need for online security systems and processes is absolutely fundamental and cannot be overstressed.

Source: Adapted from Thomson (2004)

Commitment

Morgan and Hunt (1994) regard commitment as the desire that a relationship continue (endure) in order that a valued relationship be maintained or strengthened. They postulated that commitment and trust are key mediating variables between five antecedents and five outcomes. See Figure 12.3.

According to the KMV model the greater the losses anticipated through the termination of a relationship the greater the commitment expressed by the exchange partners. Likewise, when these partners share the same values commitment increases. Trust is

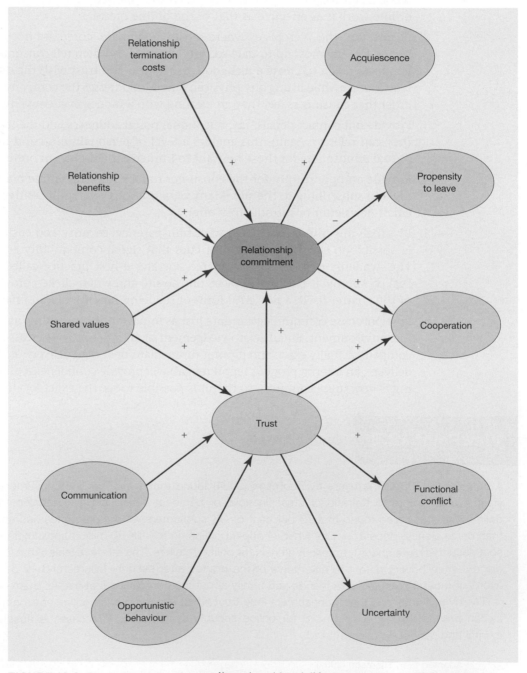

FIGURE 12.3 The KMV model of commitment and trust (Morgan and Hunt, 1994); used with kind permission of the American Marketing Association

enhanced when communication is perceived to be of high quality but decreases when one organisation knowingly takes action to seek to benefit from the relationship that will be to the detriment of the other.

The centrality of the trust and commitment concepts to relationship marketing has thus been established, and they are as central to marketing-channel relationships as to other b2b relationships (Achrol, 1991; Goodman and Dion, 2001).

Customer loyalty and retention

Implicit within this customer-relationship cycle is the notion that retained customers are loyal. However, this may be misleading as 'loyalty' may actually be a term used to convey convenience or extended utility. Loyalty, however presented, takes different forms, just as there are customers who are more valued than others. Christopher et al. (2002) depict the various types of relationships as stages or steps on a ladder, the Relationship Marketing Ladder of Loyalty. See Figure 12.4.

A prospect becomes a purchaser, completed through a market or discrete exchange. Clients emerge from several completed transactions but remain ambivalent towards the seller organisation. Supporters, despite being passive about an organisation, are willing and able to enter into regular transactions. Advocates represent the next and penultimate step. They not only support an organisation and its products but actively recommend it to others by positive, word-of-mouth communications. Partners, who represent the top rung of the ladder, trust and support an organisation just as it trusts and supports them. Partnership status, discussed in greater detail later in this chapter, is the embodiment of relational exchanges and interorganisational collaboration.

The simplicity of the loyalty-ladder concept illustrates the important point that customers represent different values to organisations.

The simplicity of the loyalty-ladder concept illustrates the important point that customers represent different values to organisations. The perceived value (or worth) of a customer may or may not always be fully reciprocated,

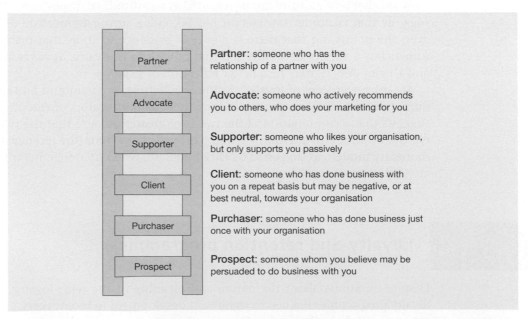

FIGURE 12.4 Relationship Marketing Ladder of Loyalty (Christopher et al., 2002). Reprinted from *Relationship Marketing: Creating Stakeholder Value*, Copyright (2002), with permission from Elsevier

TABLE 12.3 Types of loyalty

Emotional loyalty	This is a true form of loyalty and is driven by personal identification with real or perceived values and benefits.
Price loyalty	This type of loyalty is driven by rational economic behaviour, and the main motivations are cautious management of money or financial necessity.
Incentivised loyalty	This refers to promiscuous buyers: those with no one favourite brand who demonstrate through repeat experience the value of becoming loyal.
Monopoly loyalty	This class of loyalty arises where a consumer has no purchase choice owing to a national monopoly. This, therefore, is not a true form of loyalty.

understood or recognised, so it is not surprising that there is a wide variety and complexity of relationships.

Types and levels of loyalty

In addition to the popularity of the loyalty concept shown by organisations, manifest in the increasing number of loyalty-based schemes, the term loyalty has attracted much research attention. As a result there are a variety of interpretations, definitions and depictions of the concept. Table 12.3 represents some of the more general types of loyalty that can be observed.

These hierarchical schemes suggest that consumers are capable of varying degrees of loyalty. Loyalty at one level can be seen to be about increasing sales volume, that is, fostering loyal purchase behaviour. High levels of repeat purchase, however, are not necessarily an adequate measure of loyalty, as there may be a number of situational factors determining purchase behaviour, such as brand availability (Dick and Basu, 1994).

At another level, loyalty can be regarded as an attitudinal disposition. O'Malley (1998) suggests that customer satisfaction has become a surrogate measure of loyalty. However, she points out that there is plenty of evidence to show that many satisfied customers buy a variety of brands and that polygamous loyalty, as suggested by Dowling and Uncles (1997), may be a better reflection of reality.

At whichever level of loyalty, customer retention is paramount and neither behavioural nor attitudinal measures alone are adequate indicators of true loyalty. O'Malley suggests that a combination of the two is of greater use and that the twin parameters, relative attitudes (to alternatives) and patronage behaviour (the recency, frequency and monetary model), as suggested by Dick and Basu, when used together offer more accurate indicators of loyalty.

Loyalty and retention programmes

Despite questions about the nature and meaning of the term loyalty, the growth of loyalty programmes has been a significant development in recent years. Often developed inappropriately in the name of relationship marketing, loyalty schemes have received a great deal of attention. One of the more visible schemes has been the ClubCard offered by Tesco, which has been partly responsible for Tesco dominating the UK retail market. The response of its nearest rival at the time, Sainsbury's, was to publicly reject loyalty cards, but some 18 months later it launched its Reward Card and then subsequently joined the group scheme, Nectar.

Loyalty schemes have been encouraged through the use of swipe cards. Users are rewarded with points each time a purchase is made. This is referred to as a 'points accrual programme', whereby loyal users are able to build up the necessary points, which are stored (often) on a card, and 'cashed in' at a later date for gifts or merchandise. The benefit for the company supporting the scheme is that the promised rewards motivate customers to accrue more points and in doing so increase their switching costs, effectively locking them into the loyalty programme and preventing them from moving to a competitor brand.

Recent technological developments mean that smart cards (a card that has a small microprocessor attached) can record enormous amounts of information, which is updated each time a purchase is made.

ViewPoint 12.4   Loyalty to Qantas

The reasons behind the development of the Frequent Flyer Programme (FFP), run by the airline Qantas, are very similar to other loyalty programmes. Essentially they are used to nurture brand loyalty and repeat business, to deter smaller airlines from entering the market and to collect information about their customers in order to provide them with more personalised communications and product offers.

Points are awarded according to the distance flown and class of travel or fare paid. There are four different levels of membership: bronze at entry level, silver, gold and platinum, and each level confers different privileges.

To some extent all airlines need such a programme but each incurs heavy administrative and IT costs and a potential liability in terms of the accumulation of unredeemed points. Apart from a small number of very loyal customers, these types of loyalty schemes do not appear to reflect true relationship development. In view of the financial problems facing the airline industry the long-term value of FFPs has to be questioned (although some frequent flyer loyalty schemes have been very successful).

Source: Adapted from Whyte (2004)

Not only have loyalty schemes for frequent flyers (e.g. BA Executive Club and Virgin Freeway) been very successful, but the cards are also used to track individual travellers. Airlines are able to offer cardholders particular services, such as special airport lounges and magazines; the card through its links to a database also enables a traveller's favourite seat and dietary requirements to be offered. In addition, the regular accumulation of air miles fosters continuity and hence loyalty, through which business travellers reward themselves with leisure travel. However, the airlines' desire to develop relationships with their customers might not be fully reciprocated as customers seek only convenience.

The potential number of applications for smart cards is tremendous. However, just like swipe cards the targeting of specific groups of buyers can be expected to become more precise and efficient, and it is also easier to track and target individuals for future communications activities.

Perhaps the attention given to loyalty and retention issues is misplaced because marketing is about the identification, anticipation and satisfaction of customer needs (profitably). If these needs are being met properly it might be reasonable to expect that customers would return anyway, reducing the need for overt 'loyalty' programmes. The absence of any loyalty card at ASDA suggests that they do not see such investment as a suitable (profitable) way of achieving competitive advantage and differentiation. There is an argument that these schemes are important not because of the loyalty aspect but because they allow for the collection of up-to-date customer information that can be used to make savings in the supply chain. It was estimated that Tesco had saved over £500 million through the use of its customer data (Jardine, 2000). That information has not been updated, but what was one of the main logistical problems concerning the management and analysis of the huge volumes of data collected has largely been overcome. Some organisations use less than half the data they collect, and then it was argued that the data actually used can be bought in at a much lower cost than these loyalty schemes cost to run. This may be partly true but vastly improved data-mining and warehousing techniques have led to more effective use of customer data.

> **Improved data-mining and warehousing techniques have led to more effective use of customer data.**

There has been a proliferation of loyalty cards, reflecting the increased emphasis upon keeping customers rather than constantly finding new ones, and there is evidence that sales lift by about 2 or 3 per cent when a loyalty scheme is launched. Such schemes enable organisations to monitor and manage stock, use direct marketing to cross- and up-sell customers, and manage their portfolio in order to consolidate (increase?) customers' spending in a store. Whether loyalty is being developed by encouraging buyers to make repeat purchases or whether the schemes are merely sales-promotion techniques that encourage extended and consistent purchasing patterns is debatable. Customer retention is a major issue and much emphasis has been given to loyalty schemes as a means of achieving retention targets.

Hallberg (2004) reports a major study involving in excess of 600,000 in-depth consumer interviews. The study identifies different levels of loyalty and concludes that significant financial returns are gained only when the highest level of loyalty is achieved. These levels of loyalty are set out in Figure 12.5.

Hallberg refers to the impact of emotional loyalty, a non-purchase measurement of attachment to a brand:

● At the 'No presence' level consumers are unaware of a brand and so there is no emotional loyalty.

● At the 'Presence' level there is awareness but emotional loyalty is minimal.

● At the 'Relevance and performance' level the consumer begins to feel that the brand is acceptable in terms of meeting their needs.

● At the 'Advantage' level consumers should feel that the brand is superior with regard to a particular attribute.

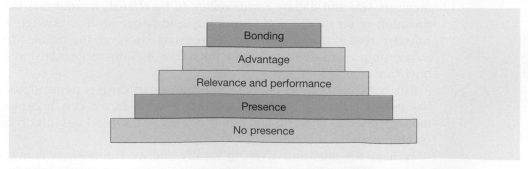

FIGURE 12.5 Levels of loyalty: the brand emotional loyalty pyramid (Hallberg, 2004); used with permission

TABLE 12.4 Five loyalty trends

Trend	Explanation
Ubiquity	Loyalty programmes have proliferated in most mature markets and many members have little interest in them other than the functionality of points collection. Managers are trying to reduce communications costs by moving the scheme online but also need to be innovative.
Coalition	Schemes run by a number of different organisations in order to share costs, information and branding (e.g. Nectar) appear to be the dominant structure industry model.
Imagination	Opportunities to exploit technologies and niche markets will depend on creativity and imagination in order to get customer data to feed into the loyalty system. Employ IST imaginatively.
Wow	To overcome consumer lethargy and boredom with loyalty schemes, many rewards in future will be experiential, emotional, unique, in an attempt to appeal to lifestage and aspirational lifestyle goals – wow them. Differentiate to stand out.
Analysis	To be competitive the use of customer data analytics and business intelligence is becoming critical, if only to feed CRM programmes. Collect and analyse customer information effectively.

Source: Adapted from Capizzi et al. (2004)

● At the 'Bonding' level emotional loyalty is at its highest because consumers feel the brand has several unique properties. They love the brand.

Loyalty schemes are exponentially effective when the consumers reach the bonding stage. Although sales generally increase the further up the pyramid consumers move it is only at the Bonding stage that sales start to reflect the emotional attachment people feel towards the brand. Hallberg refers to the success and market leadership that Tesco has achieved, but the principles established through this study should apply to loyalty programmes regardless of category or sector.

There are a proliferation of loyalty programmes to the extent that Capizzi et al. (2004) suggest that the market is mature. They also argue that five clear trends within the loyalty market can be identified. These are set out in Table 12.4.

These trends suggest that successful schemes will be those that enable members to perceive significant value associated with their continued association with a scheme. That value will be driven by schemes run by groups of complementary brands, which use technology to understand customer dynamics and communications that complement their preferred values. The medium-term goal might be that these schemes should reflect customers' different relationship needs and recognise the different loyalty levels desired by different people.

The role of marketing communications in relationships

Having considered ideas about relationship marketing and established its centrality within contemporary marketing thought, it now remains to explore ways in which marketing communications can contribute to relationship marketing. Transaction

TABLE 12.5 Source of messages about an organisation

Message source	Explanation
Planned marketing communications	Make promises about how solutions to customer problems should occur – for example, mass communications, brochures, sales, direct response, www pages
Product messages	For example, the design, technical features, utility, appearance, production process, durability and distribution
Service messages	Derived from interactions with an organisation's customer service – deliveries, invoicing, claims handling, product documentation
Unplanned messages	News stories, references, gossip, Internet chat groups, word-of-mouth communications
Absence	A lack of communication or silence following service breakdown

Source: Derived from Gronroos (2000) who acknowledges the work of Duncan and Moriarty (1997) and Calonius et al. (1989)

marketing, where the focus is on product and price, uses mass communications with persuasion as a central element. Relationship marketing, with its focus on the relationship between the participants, encourages interaction and dialogue with individual customers. This is compatible with the concepts of integrated marketing communications (IMC). Gronroos (2004) suggests that although IMC cannot be synonymous with relationship marketing, IMC is an important aspect of it. He argues that within an interaction and planned communication context customer messages can be divided into five groups. These are set out in Table 12.5.

> Relationship marketing encourages interaction and dialogue with individual customers.

Gronroos develops the view that there are two main types of message that customers receive, process and use to determine the extent to which a relationship delivers value. The first of these messages are planned marketing communications messages, those that are predetermined and delivered through various media and tools of the communications mix. These planned messages set out an organisation's promises. In addition, there are messages generated through the product and service aspects of the interaction that occurs between organisations and their customers. The degree to which these two streams of messages support or counter each other will influence the type of unplanned communications that ensue. The greater the degree that the two sets of messages support or reinforce one another the more favourable the unplanned communication that should result in positive word-of-mouth communication (Gronroos and Lindberg-Repo, 1998). This can lead to an increasing propensity to share information, the establishment of two-way communication and the development of a shared reasoning approach. Reasoning is important because it enables a sharing of values and a deeper understanding of the other parties' needs and position. From here dialogue emerges out of interaction and through shared meaning trust increases. Gronroos argues that relationship marketing develops, not from planned marketing communications, but through the interaction and personal experience of products and services and the degree to which these two sets of messages and meanings complement the promises and messages transmitted previously. He suggests that when these two processes come together a single, two-way

> Reasoning is important because it enables a sharing of values and a deeper understanding of the other parties' needs and position.

communication process emerges. Put precisely, he says (p. 107), 'the two processes merge into a relationship dialogue'.

Marketing communications and the customer life cycle

Marketing communications can play an important role throughout all relationship phases and at all stages of the customer life cycle. Indeed, marketing communications should be used to engage with audiences according to the audiences' needs, whether transactional and remote or relational and close. According to Ryssel et al. (2004) the use of IST, which enables communication to be timely, accurate and direct, has a positive impact on trust. During the acquisition phase marketing communications needs to be geared towards creating awareness and providing access to the brand. Included within this period will be the need to help potential customers become familiar with the brand and help them increase their understanding of the key attributes, possible benefits from use and know how the brand is different and represents value that is superior to the competition. Indeed, marketing communications has to work during this phase because it needs to fulfil a number of different roles and be targeted at precise audiences. Perhaps the main overriding task is to create a set of brand values that are relevant and that represent significant value for the target audience. In DRIP terms differentiation and information will be important and, in terms of the communications mix, advertising and direct marketing in the b2c market and personal selling and direct marketing in the b2b market.

> Marketing communications should be used to engage with audiences according to the audiences' needs.

The main goals during the development phase are for the selling organisation to reduce buyer-perceived risk and to simultaneously enhance its own credibility. In order to reduce risk a number of messages will need to be presented through marketing communications. The selection of these elements will depend upon the forms of risk that are present either in the market sector or within individual customers. Marketing communications needs to engage by communicating messages concerning warranties and guarantees, finance schemes, third-party endorsements and satisfied customers, independent testing and favourable product-performance reports, awards and the attainment of quality standards, membership of trade associations, delighted customers, growth and market share, new products and alliances and partnerships, all of which seek to reduce risk and improve credibility. In DRIP terms information and persuasion will be important, and in terms of the communications mix public relations, sales promotion and direct marketing in the b2c market and personal selling, public relations and direct marketing in the b2b market.

> The length of the retention phase will reflect the degree to which the marketing communications is truly interactional and based on dialogue.

The length of the retention phase will reflect the degree to which the marketing communications is truly interactional and based on dialogue. Messages need to be relational and reinforcing. Incentive schemes are used extensively in consumer markets as a way of retaining customers and minimising customer loss (or churn, defection or attrition). They are also used to cross-sell products and services and increase a customer's commitment and involvement with the brand. Through the use of an integrated programme of communications, value can be enhanced for both parties and relational exchanges are more likely to be maintained. In business markets personal contact and key account management are crucial to maintaining interaction, understanding and mutual support. Electronic communications have the potential to automate many routine transactions and allow for increased focus on one-to-one communications. In DRIP terms reinforcement and information will be important and, in terms of the communications mix, sales promotion and direct marketing in the b2c market and personal selling (and key accounts), public relations and direct marketing in the b2b market.

The final phase of decline concerns the process by which a relationship is eventually terminated. This process may be sharp and sudden or slow and protracted. Marketing communications plays a minor role in the former but is more significant in the latter. During an extended termination, marketing communications, especially direct marketing in the form of telemarketing and email, can be used to deliver orders and profits. These forms of communication are beneficial because they allow for continued personal messages, but they also incur the heavy costs associated with field selling (b2b) or advertising (b2c). In DRIP terms reinforcement and persuasion will be important, and in terms of the communications mix direct marketing in both markets and sales promotion in the b2c will be significant.

Internal relationships

Traditionally, external stakeholders (customers, intermediaries and financiers) are the prime focus of marketing communications. However, recognition of the importance of internal stakeholders as a group who should receive marketing attention has increased, and the concept of *internal marketing* emerged in the 1980s.

Recognition of the importance of internal stakeholders as a group who should receive marketing attention has increased.

It can be argued that the role of the employee is changing. Once they could be just part of the company but now this role has been extended so that they are now recognised as, and need to adopt the role of, brand ambassadors (Freeman and Liedtka, 1997; Hemsley, 1998). This is particularly important in service environments where employees represent the interface between an organisation's internal and external environments and where their actions can have a powerful effect in creating images among customers (Schneider and Bowen, 1985; Balmer and Wilkinson, 1991). It is evident that many now recognise the increasing importance of internal communications (Storey, 2001).

Employees are important to external stakeholders not only because of the tangible aspects of service and production they provide but also because of the intangible aspects, such as attitude and the way in which the service is provided: 'How much do they really care?' Images are often based more on the intangible than the tangible aspects of employee communications.

Management is responsible for the allocation of resources and the process and procedures used to create added value. Its actions effectively constrain the activities of the organisation and shape the nature and form of the communications the organisation adopts, either consciously or unconsciously. Each organisation is a major influence upon its own marketing communications and can influence the perception others have of the character and personality of the organisation.

The purpose of internal marketing

Research by Foreman and Money (1995) indicates that managers see the main components of internal marketing as falling into three broad areas, namely development, reward and vision for employees. These will inevitably vary in intensity on a situational basis.

TABLE 12.6 The roles of internal marketing communications

DRIP factors	To provide information
	To be persuasive
	To reinforce – reassure/remind
	To differentiate employees/groups
Transactional	To coordinate actions
	To promote the efficient use of resources
	To direct developments
Affiliation	To provide identification
	To motivate personnel
	To promote and coordinate activities with non-members

All of these three components have communication as a common linkage.

All of these three components have communication as a common linkage. Employees and management (members) need to communicate with one another and with a variety of non-members, and do so through an assortment of methods. Communication with members, wherever they are located geographically, needs to be undertaken for a number of reasons. These include the DRIP factors (Chapter 1), but these communications also serve the additional purposes of providing transaction efficiencies and affiliation needs; see Table 12.6.

The values transmitted to customers, suppliers and distributors through external communications need to be reinforced by the values expressed by employees, especially those who interact with these external groups. Internal marketing communications are necessary in order that internal members are motivated and involved with the brand such that they are able to present a consistent and uniform message to various stakeholders. This is an aspect of integrated marketing communications and involves product- and organisation-centred messages. If there is a set of shared values then internal communications are said to blend and balance the external communications. This process whereby employees are encouraged to communicate with customers helps ensure that what is promised by an organisation is realised and delivered, sometimes referred to as 'living the brand'.

ViewPoint 12.5   'Living the brand' – British Airways

Back in the 1980s British Airways introduced a training programme that all staff attended. This was referred to as 'Putting People First', and a part of each weekly session was attended by a senior director, very often the CEO (now Lord Marshall), to reflect the importance and significance of the training and to be customer-oriented. This scheme has been reintroduced as 'Putting People First – Again', partly in an effort to remind staff what the brand represents and to involve them in its development. Goften (2000) reports that the programme is about the past, the present and the future – that is, pride in the past, passion for the present and faith in the future. In doing so staff are developed and encouraged to live the brand and, in a service-based business, the quality of the customer-service encounter can seriously enhance or damage brand reputation. In 2003 BA started to use a similar scheme but this time called 'Passion for Service', which again is concerned about the employee contribution to the BA brand.

Organisational identity

Organisational identity is concerned with what individual employees think and feel about the organisation to which they belong. When their perception of the organisation's characteristics accords with their own self-concept then the strength of organisational identity will be strong (Dutton et al., 1994). Organisational identity also refers to the degree to which feelings and thoughts about the distinctive characteristics are shared among employees (Dutton and Dukerich, 1991). There are therefore both individual and collective aspects to organisational identity.

Organisations must make three main decisions: who they are, what business they are in and what they want to be.

Albert and Whetten (1985) stated that organisations must make three main decisions: who they are, what business they are in and what they want to be. In order that these decisions can be made they claim that consideration must be given to what is central, what is distinctive and what is enduring about the character of the organisation.

Those external to an organisation also develop feelings and thoughts about what are the central, enduring and distinctive characteristics of an organisation. It is highly probable that there will be variances between the perceptions and beliefs of those internal and external to an organisation and this may be a cause of confusion, misunderstanding or even conflict.

For employees, organisational identity may be seen as their perception of their organisation's central and distinctive attributes, including its positional status and relevant compositional group. Consequently, external events that refute or call into question these defining characteristics may threaten the perception that employees have of their organisational identity (Dutton and Dukerich, 1991).

Organisational culture

According to Beyer (1981), organisational identity is a subset of the collective beliefs that constitute an organisation's culture. Indeed, internal marketing is shaped by the prevailing culture, as it is the culture that provides the context within which internal marketing practices are to be accomplished.

Corporate culture is 'the deeper level of basic assumptions and beliefs that are shared by members of an organisation.

Corporate culture, defined by Schein (1985), is 'the deeper level of basic assumptions and beliefs that are shared by members of an organisation, that operate unconsciously and define in a basic taken-for-granted fashion an organisation's view of itself and its environment'. A more common view of organisational culture is 'the way we do things around here'. It is the result of a number of factors, ranging through the type and form of business the organisation is in, its customers and other stakeholders, its geographical position, and its size, age and facilities. These represent the more tangible aspects of corporate culture. There are a host of intangible elements as well. These include the assumptions, values and beliefs that are held and shared by members of the organisation. These factors combine to create a unique environment, one where norms or guides to expected behaviour influence all members, whatever their role or position.

ViewPoint 12.6   Changing values at QinetiQ

The Defence Evaluation and Research Agency (DERA) owned by the Ministry of Defence (MoD) in the United Kingdom has recently moved from public to private ownership. Many of the staff at the organisation are scientists and engineers who under public ownership had no real need to interact with a diverse external audience and indeed knew little of the work in other divisions and parts of DERA. However, the success of the QinetiQ organisation depended on employees adopting a commercially focused value set, one that is very different from that engrained through working in a publicly owned organisation. They also needed to be committed and engaged with the new organisation.

This transformation was achieved partly through the use of CEO-led roadshows plus printed matter, cascade briefings, desk drop packs and online Web chats (with the CEO). Internal direct-looped radio, accessed through telephones and later desktop PCs, is used by the CEO to communicate key developments, to provide divisional results or just to encourage feedback. One broadcast attracted an audience of 2,000 people, of whom 300 provided immediate feedback. In addition, the use of an intranet, a variety of posters and noticeboards plus face-to-face staff meetings all reflect the organisation's drive to reach employees, to actively encourage involvement and, in doing so, engage them within the QinetiQ brand.

Source: Hardaker and Fill (2005)

Internal engagement

Ideas about engagement, explored elsewhere in this book, have their roots in employee-based communications. It is generally accepted that employees need to buy in to their workplace values in order that they be fully motivated and effective (Thomson and Hecker, 2000). This buy-in or process of engagement consists of two main components: an intellectual and an emotional element (Hardaker and Fill, 2005). The intellectual element is concerned with employees buying in and aligning themselves with the organisation's strategy, issues and overall direction. The emotional element is concerned with employees taking ownership of their contribution and becoming committed to the achievement of stated goals. Communication strategies should be based on the information-processing styles of employees and access to preferred media. Ideally these communications should reflect a suitable balance between the need for rational information to meet the intellectual needs and expressive types of communication to meet the emotional needs of the workforce. It follows that the more effective the communication, the higher the level of engagement.

Communication strategies should be based on the information-processing styles of employees and access to preferred media.

The development of internal brands based around employees can be accomplished effectively and quickly by simply considering the preferred information-processing style of an internal audience. By developing messages that reflect the natural processing style and using a diversity of media that best complements the type of message and the needs of each substantial internal target audience, the communication strategy is more likely to be successful.

Client/agency relationships

There are a vast number of relationships that form between various clients and agencies, disciplines, and within individual organisations. The nature of the relationships that exist in the marketing communications industry undoubtedly shapes and influences the strategies and operations of its member organisations.

There are a number of agency/client relationships that have flourished over a very long period of time, and some for several decades. However, these appear to be in the minority, as many relationships appear to founder as clients abandon agencies and search for better, fresher solutions, because a contract expires, the client needs change or because of takeovers and mergers between agencies, which require that they forfeit accounts that cause a conflict of interest.

From a contextual perspective these buyer/seller relationships can be seen to follow a pattern of formation, maintenance and severance, or pre-contract, contracting process and post-contract stages (Davidson and Kapelianis, 1996). Clients and agencies enter into a series of interactions (West and Paliwoda, 1996) or exchanges through which trust and commitment are developed. Hakansson (1982) identified different contexts or atmospheres within which a relationship develops. These contexts had several dimensions: closeness/distance, cooperation/conflict, power/dependence, trustworthiness and expectations. Therefore, the client/agency relationship should be seen in the context of the network of organisations and interactions (or exchanges) that occur in a network. It is through these interactions that the tasks that need to be accomplished are agreed, resources made available, strategies determined and goals achieved. The quality of the agency/client relationship is a function of trust, which is developed through the exchanges and that fosters confidence. As discussed earlier, commitment is derived from a belief that the relationship is worth continuing and that maximum effort is warranted at maintaining the relationship (Morgan and Hunt, 1994). The development of new forms of remuneration, based around payment by results, also signifies a new client focus and a willingness to engage with clients and to be paid according to the success and contribution the agency can provide (Lace and Brocklehurst, 2000).

> Poor relationships between agencies and clients are likely to result from a lack of trust and falling commitment.

Poor relationships between agencies and clients are likely to result from a lack of trust and falling commitment. As it appears that communication is a primary element in the formation and substance of relational exchanges, clients might be advised to consider the agencies in their roster as an extended department of the core organisation and to use internal marketing communications procedures to assist the development of identity and sense of belonging.

ViewPoint 12.7   Agency relationships

Timex is a well-known brand but its overall share in the UK is relatively small compared with the 30 per cent market share it holds in the USA. There it sells more watches than the next 18 best-selling brands combined.

In 2002 Timex USA decided to end its 16-year relationship with its lead agency Fallon Worldwide. According to Timex spokesman Jim Katz, 'After 16 years, we feel we want to see what else is out there.' The account is thought to be worth around £6 million.

Summary of key points

1. Value is a key concept and is relative to customer expectations and experience of competitive offerings. Customers lie at the heart of the value chain, and only by understanding particular customer needs and by focusing and linking value-chain activities on satisfying them can superior value be generated.

2. The development of customer-perceived value is now regarded not only as crucial for commercial success but there is an increasing amount of evidence that indicates that the relationships organisations form, with a range of stakeholders, not just customers, are themselves a generator of value and hence an important aspect of contemporary marketing.

3. There is a range of exchange transactions: at one extreme transactional exchanges are typified by the 4Ps approach, where the focus is on prices and products, and at the other end relational exchanges are characterised by collaboration and focus is on the relationship itself. Trust and commitment underpin these relationships, and these variables become increasingly important as relational exchanges become established.

4. Relationship marketing is based upon various ideas about costs and profitability, but at the heart of the concept is the premise that it is more profitable to have a long-term relationship between a customer and a company rather than a one-off transaction.

5. An organisation's marketing activities should be directed towards servicing those customer groups that offer the highest (potential) lifetime value. Understanding the characteristics of relationship concepts can help organisations manage and direct their resources more profitably.

6. Customer relationships can be considered in terms of a series of relationship-development phases: customer acquisition, development, retention and decline. Collectively these are referred to as the customer life cycle. The duration and intensity of each relationship phase in the life cycle will inevitably vary, and it should be remembered that this representation is essentially idealistic.

7. At the heart of many relationship-marketing strategies are loyalty or customer-retention programmes. Whether these are loyalty or perhaps convenience programmes may be debatable, but organisations in the b2c market should always question whether consumers really desire a relationship with a brand and whether their actions are those bred of loyalty or inertia.

8. The centrality of the trust and commitment concepts to relationship marketing has thus been established, and they are as central to marketing-channel relationships as to other b2b relationships. Interorganisational trust involves judgements about another organisation's reliability and integrity. Questions concerning trust and commitment have far-ranging implications for marketing communications, whether these be delivered offline or in an online context.

9. Increasingly, organisations understand the importance of employees in the customer-experience process. By using marketing communications to engage employees with an organisation's values, strategy and goals it may be possible to close the gulf between how customers perceive a brand and how an organisation presents it.

10. The quality of the agency/client relationship is a function of trust, which is developed through the exchanges and which fosters confidence. As discussed earlier, commitment is derived from a belief that the relationship is worth continuing and that maximum effort is warranted to maintain the relationship.

Review questions

1. Identify the three principles Doyle established for the development of customer value.

2. Make a list of the main differences between transactional and relationship marketing.

3. Explain the concepts of trust and commitment, and outline the linkages between them. What are the implications for client/agency relationships?

4. Evaluate reasons why it has been difficult for organisations to establish online customer trust.

5. Prepare brief notes explaining different types of loyalty. Identify two different commercial loyalty programmes and consider the marketing communications used to support them.

6. Discuss ways in which marketing communications should be used to develop relationships with employees and customers.

References

Achrol, R.S. (1991), 'Evolution of the marketing organisation: new forms for turbulent environments', *Journal of Marketing*, **55**(4), pp. 77–93.

Albert, S. and Whetten, D.A. (1985), 'Organisational identity', in *Research in Organisational Behavior* (eds L.L. Cummings and B.M. Staw), Greenwich, Conn.: Jai Press.

Anderson, J.C. and Narus, J.A. (1998), 'Business marketing: understand what customers value', *Harvard Business Review*, **76** (June), pp. 53–65.

Balmer, J.M.T. and Wilkinson, A. (1991), 'Building societies: change, strategy and corporate identity', *Journal of General Management*, **17**(2), pp. 22–33.

Beyer, J.M. (1981), 'Ideologies, values and decision making in organisations', in *Handbook of Organisational Design* (eds P. Nystrom and W. Swarbruck), London: Oxford University Press.

Calonius, H., Avlontis, G.J., Papavasiliou, N.K. and Kouremeos, A.G. (1989), 'Market communication in service marketing', *Marketing Thought and Practice in the 1990s*, Proceedings from the XVIIIth Annual Conference of the European Marketing Academy, Athens.

Capizzi, M., Ferguson, R. and Cuthbertson, R. (2004), 'Loyalty trends for the 21st century', *Journal of Targeting Measurement and Analysis for Marketing*, **12**(3), pp. 199–212.

Christopher, M., Payne, A. and Ballantyne, D. (2002), *Relationship Marketing: Creating Stakeholder Value*, Oxford: Butterworth Heinemann.

Cousins, P. and Stanwix, E. (2001), 'It's only a matter of confidence! A comparison of relationship management between Japanese and UK non-owned vehicle manufacturers', *International Journal of Operations and Production Management*, **21**(9), October, pp. 1160–80.

Davidson, S. and Kapelianis, D. (1996), 'Towards an organisational theory of advertising: agency–client relationships in South Africa', *International Journal of Advertising*, **15**, pp. 48–60.

Day, G. (2000), 'Managing market relationships', *Journal of the Academy of Marketing Science*, **28**(1), Winter, pp. 24–30.

Dick, A.S. and Basu, K. (1994), 'Customer loyalty: toward an integrated framework', *Journal of the Academy of Marketing Science*, **22**(2), pp. 99–113.

Doney, P.M. and Cannon, J.P. (1997), 'An examination of the nature of trust in buyer–seller relationships', *Journal of Marketing*, **62**(2), pp. 1–13.

Dowling, G.R. and Uncles, M. (1997), 'Do customer loyalty programmes really work?', *Sloan Management Review* (Summer), pp. 71–82.

Doyle, P. (2000), *Value Based Marketing*, Chichester: John Wiley.

Duncan, T. and Moriarty, S. (1997), *Driving Brand Value*, New York: McGraw-Hill.

Dutton, J.E. and Dukerich, J.M. (1991), 'Keeping an eye on the mirror: image and identity in organisational adaptation', *Academy of Management Review*, **34**, pp. 517–54.

Dutton, J.E., Dukerich, J.M. and Harquail, C.V. (1994), 'Organisational images and member identification', *Administrative Science Quarterly*, **39**, pp. 239–63.

Foreman, S.K. and Money, A.H. (1995), 'Internal marketing: concepts, measurements and application', *Journal of Marketing Management*, **11**, pp. 755–68.

Freeman, E. and Liedtka, J. (1997), 'Stakeholder capitalism and the value chain', *European Management Journal*, **15**(3), pp. 286–96.

Gambetta, D. (1988), *Trust: Making and Breaking Co-operative Relations*, New York: Blackwell.

Goften, K. (2000), 'Putting staff first in brand evolution', *Marketing*, 3 February, pp. 29–30.

Goodman, L.E. and Dion, P.A. (2001), 'The determinants of commitment in the distributor–manufacturer relationship', *Industrial Marketing Management*, **30**(3) (April), pp. 287–300.

Gronroos, C. (2004), 'The relationship marketing process: communication, interaction, dialogue, value', *Journal of Business and Industrial Marketing*, **19**(2), pp. 99–113.

Gronroos, C. and Lindberg-Repo, K. (1998), 'Integrated marketing communications: the communications aspect of relationship marketing', *IMC Research Journal*, **4**(1), pp. 3–11.

Hakansson, H. (1982), *International Marketing and Purchasing of Industrial Goods: An Interaction Approach*, Chichester: John Wiley.

Hallberg, G. (2004), 'Is your loyalty programme really building loyalty? Why increasing emotional attachment, not just repeat buying, is key to maximizing programme success', *Journal of Targeting Measurement and Analysis for Marketing*, **12**(3), pp. 231–41.

Hardaker, S. and Fill, C. (2005), 'Corporate service brands: the intellectual and emotional engagement of employees', *Corporate Reputation Review: an International Journal*, **7**(4) (Winter), pp. 365–76.

Hemsley, S. (1998), 'Internal affairs', *Marketing Week*, 2 April, 49–53.

Jardine, A. (2000), 'Why loyalty's not as simple as ABC', *Marketing*, 18 May, p. 19.

Kothandaraman, P. and Wilson, D. (2001), 'The future of competition: value creating networks', *Industrial Marketing Management*, **30**(4) (May), pp. 379–89.

Lace, J.M. and Brocklehurst, D. (2000), 'You both win when you play the same game', *Admap*, October, pp. 40–2.

Morgan, R.M. and Hunt, S.D. (1994), 'The commitment–trust theory of relationship marketing', *Journal of Marketing*, **58** (July), pp. 20–38.

Morrison, D.E. and Firmstone, J. (2000), 'The social function of trust and implications of ecommerce', *International Journal of Advertising*, **19**, pp. 599–623.

O'Malley, L. (1998), 'Can loyalty schemes really build loyalty?', *Marketing Intelligence and Planning*, **16**(1), pp. 47–55.

Pavlou, P.A. (2002), 'Institution-based trust in interorganisational exchange relationships: the role of online b2b marketplaces on trust formation', *The Journal of Strategic Information Systems*, **11**(3–4) (December), pp. 215–43.

Porter, M.E. (1985), *Competitive Advantage: Creating and Sustaining Superior Performance*, New York: Free Press.

Puth, G., Mostert, P. and Ewing, M. (1999), 'Consumer perceptions of mentioned product and brand attributes in magazine advertising', *Journal of Product Brand Management*, **8**(1), pp. 38–50.

Reichheld, F.F. and Sasser, E.W. (1990), 'Zero defections: quality comes to services', *Harvard Business Review*, September, pp. 105–11.

Reinartz, W.J. and Kumar, V. (2002), 'The mismanagement of customer loyalty', *Harvard Business Review*, July, pp. 86–94.

Rowe, W.G. and Barnes, J.G. (1998), 'Relationship marketing and sustained competitive advantage', *Journal of Market-Focused Management*, **2**(3), pp. 281–97.

Ryssel, R., Ritter, T. and Gemunden H.G. (2004), 'The impact of information technology deployment on trust, commitment and value creation in business relationships', *Journal of Business and Industrial Marketing*, **19**(3), pp. 197–207.

Schein, E.H. (1985), *Organisational Culture and Leadership*, San Francisco, Calif.: Jossey-Bass.

Schneider, B. and Bowen, D. (1985), 'Employee and customer perceptions of service in banks: replication and extension', *Journal of Applied Psychology*, **70**, pp. 423–33.

Simpson, P.M., Sigauw, J.A. and Baker, T.L. (2001), 'A model of value creation: supplier behaviors and their impact on reseller-perceived value', *Industrial Marketing Management*, **30**(2) (February), pp. 119–34.

Spekman, R. (1988), 'Perceptions of strategic vulnerability among industrial buyers and its effect on information search and supplier evaluation', *Journal of Business Research*, **17**, pp. 313–26.

Storey, J. (2001), 'Internal marketing comes to the surface', *Marketing Week*, 19 July, p. 22.

Thomas, R. (2000), 'How to create trust in the net', *Marketing*, 2 March, p. 35.

Thomson, J. (2004), 'Businesses need help with e-security'. Retrieved 5 January 2005 from www.nuriskservices.co.uk/news/articles/.

Thomson, K. and Hecker, L.A. (2000), 'The business value of buy-in', in R.J. Varey and B.R. Lewis (eds), *Internal Marketing: Directions for Management*, pp. 160–72, London: Routledge.

Wagner, S. and Boutellier, R. (2002), 'Capabilities for managing a portfolio of supplier relationships', *Business Horizons*, November–December, pp. 79–88.

West, D.C. and Paliwoda, S.J. (1996), 'Advertising client–agency relationships', *European Journal of Marketing*, **30**(8), pp. 22–39.

Whyte, R. (2004), 'Frequent flyer programmes: Is it a relationship, or do the schemes create spurious loyalty?', *Journal of Targeting, Measurement and Analysis for Marketing*, **12**(3), pp. 269–80.

Young, L.C. and Wilkinson, I.F. (1989), 'The role of trust and co-operation in marketing channels: a preliminary study', *European Journal of Marketing*, **23**(2), pp. 109–22.

Stakeholders: channels, business-to-business and international communications

13

Aims and objectives

The aims of this chapter are, first, to consider the nature, role and influence stakeholders can have on an organisation's marketing communications, and then to explore some of the essential aspects of business-to-business and international marketing communications. There are four primary topics in this chapter:

Stakeholders, Marketing channels, Business-to-business MCs, International MCs

The learning objectives are to enable readers to:

1. discuss the nature of stakeholder networks;

2. describe the reasons and ways in which organisations combine to form marketing-channel relationships;

3. explain the structure of conventional marketing channels;

4. examine the role of marketing communications within marketing channels;

5. explore some of the behavioural issues involved with the management of marketing channels, including power, conflict and leadership;

6. discuss some of the key issues associated with international-based marketing communications.

Introduction

The distribution of products and services concerns the management of not only the tangible elements of a product's availability but also the intangible aspects or issues of ownership, control and flows of communication between parties responsible for making the offering accessible to customers. It is generally agreed that the relationship between any two organisations is contingent upon the direct and indirect relationships of many other organisations (Andersson, 1992). Contemporary marketing communications should therefore attempt to incorporate the whole network of relationships that exist between interacting organisations, particularly those in the distribution or marketing channels.

Products flow through a variety of organisations, which coordinate their activities to make the offering readily available to the end-user. Coordination is necessary to convert raw materials into a set of benefits that can be transferred and be of value to the end-user. These benefits are normally bundled together and represented in the form of a product or service. The various organisations that elect to coordinate their activities each perform different roles in a chain of activity. Some perform the role of manufacturer, some act as agents and others may be distributors, dealers, value-added resellers, wholesalers or retailers. Whatever their role, it is normally specific and geared to refining and moving the offering closer to the end user.

Each organisation is a customer of the previous organisation in an industry's value chain. Some organisations work closely together, coordinating and integrating their activities, while others combine on a temporary basis. In both cases, however, these organisations can be observed to be operating as members of a partnership (of differing strength and dimensions) with the express intention of achieving their objectives with their partner's assistance and cooperation. So, in addition to the end-user, a further set of customers (partners) can be determined: all those who make up the distribution channel.

Organisations should identify which other organisations interact with them.

Organisations should identify which other organisations interact with them and determine the nature and the form of the relationships between organisations both inside and outside of the distribution channel. For example, organisations operating within the 'fast-moving consumer goods' or the 'over-the-counter' markets will invariably be able to identify two particular clusters: first, all those that contribute to the value-adding activities and directly affect the performance of the focus organisation, such as dealers, distributors, wholesalers and retailers, and second, all those that affect the performance in an indirect way, such as banks, market research agencies, recruitment organisations and local authorities. All of these make up the various networks in which most organisations operate.

The stakeholder concept

All organisations develop a series of relationships with a wide variety of other organisations, groups and indeed consumers who buy their products. These relationships and individual partnerships vary considerably in their intensity, duration and function. Nevertheless, these partnerships are entered into on the grounds that each organisation anticipates benefit from mutual cooperation.

The concept of different groups influencing an organisation and in turn being influenced is an important element in the development of marketing communications. The concept enables an organisation to identify all those other organisations and individuals who can be or are influenced by the strategies and policies of the focus organisation. Understanding who the stakeholders are also helps to determine where power is held, and this will in turn influence strategy at a number of levels within the focus organisation. According to Freeman (1984), stakeholders are 'any group or individual who can affect or is affected by the achievement of an organisation's purpose'. These stakeholders may be internal to the organisation, such as employees or managerial coalitions, or external to the organisation in the form of suppliers, buyers, local authorities, shareholders, competitors, agencies or the government.

The essential purpose of stakeholder analysis is to determine which organisations influence the focus organisation.

The essential purpose of stakeholder analysis is to determine which organisations influence the focus organisation and what their aims, objectives and motivations are. This enables the development of a more effective strategy, one that considers the power and interests of those who have a stake in the focus organisation. It also influences the nature of the marketing communications used. Freeman suggested that the stake held by any organisation could be based upon one of three forms. The first is a stake based upon the equity held in the organisation, the second is a stake based upon an economic perspective, reflecting a market-exchange-based relationship, and the third is a stake based upon the influence of organisations that affect the focus organisation but 'not in marketplace terms'.

The horizontal dimension reflects the type of power that stakeholders can have over the focus organisation. Again, Freeman highlights three elements. The first is the formal power to control the actions of the organisation. The second is economic power to influence the organisation through the markets in which they operate, and the last element is political power generated by the stakeholders' ability to influence an organisation through legislation and regulation. He constructed a matrix, Figure 13.1, which represents the dominant influence of each stakeholder. This acknowledges that stakeholders could be placed in a number of different cells, but as Stahl and Grigsby (1992) point out, by showing their dominant role the focus organisation is in a better position to gauge the influence of each stakeholder group.

It is therefore logical to expect that organisations develop networks in which they collaborate and work closely together in order to be competitive, add value and provide superior end-user satisfaction.

Stake	Power	Formal or voting	Economic	Political
	Equity	Shareholders Directors Minority interests	Employers/owners	Dissident shareholders
	Economic	Preferred debt holders	Suppliers Debt holders Customers Employees Competitors	European Union Local governments Foreign governments Consumer lobbies Unions
	Influencers	Outside directors Licensing bodies	Regulatory agencies	Trade associations Environmental groups

FIGURE 13.1 Participant stakeholders: the grid location denotes the primary but not necessarily sole orientation of the stakeholder. From Freeman (1984); used with kind permission

ViewPoint 13.1   Networking pallets

Palletways is a growing haulage business that was originally based on the principle of carrying clients' goods on pallets stacked on lorries to destinations all over the country. Of several problems, two were crucial. The first concerned collecting sufficient orders to make the outward journey profitable and hoping that there might even be an order to contribute to the costs of the homeward journey. The second concerned the fragmented nature of the market and the territories that were owned by local 'warlords'.

Palletways introduced a new approach, whereby it coordinated networks of hauliers from across the country. By bringing the different constituents of the industry together, it has reduced conflict and brought some new values to this part of the distribution system. Hauliers now bring their clients' goods to a central depot in the Midlands where they offload and pick up other loads from other members, for distribution in their own geographic areas. This helps ensure economic load factors, reduces costs and environmental damage and improves the service for all clients.

Source: Adapted from Gracie (2001)

Marketing channels

Most organisations have primary or perhaps key networks. These normally consist of those organisations that join together (either formally or informally) to enable the end-user customers access to the products and services. These particular networks are called marketing channels. There are two main types of marketing channel: direct and indirect. By definition the direct channel does not make use of intermediaries, and organisations using this approach prefer to work independently and are relatively confident about the market and associated conditions. Most organisations choose to sacrifice some independence and in return are able to share risks and uncertainties with other intermediaries or channel members. The decision to adopt one or the other is really a function of the uncertainty surrounding the performance of the customers, products and services, intermediaries, competitors and suppliers. See Table 13.1.

> There are two main types of marketing channel: direct and indirect.

TABLE 13.1 Stakeholder uncertainties and channel selection

Stakeholder	Type of uncertainty
Customers	In terms of their location, types and buying characteristics, their perceived value and desirable satisfaction levels.
Products/services	In terms of their attributes, availability, speed of perishability, customisation and support.
Intermediaries	In terms of their capability in terms of selling, distribution and financing, their ability to add real value.
Competitors	In terms of their channel decisions, skills and level of interaction.
Suppliers	In terms of their size, resources, level of openness and reliability.

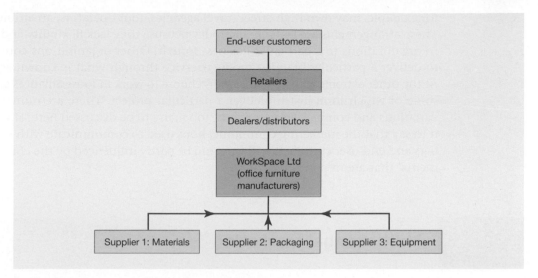

FIGURE 13.2 A conventional marketing channel

All organisations experience uncertainty, and they use a variety of strategies, methods and techniques to contain and reduce specific risks to an acceptable level. Cooperating with organisations that have particular skills and competences is a strategic approach to reducing and sharing such uncertainty. Indirect channels are selected when the degree of uncertainty concerning the delivery of end-user value exceeds acceptable levels.

Marketing channels consist of all those stakeholder organisations who choose to work together in order to make products and services available to end user customers. Each organisation has a specific role to play in this process of distribution, which directly adds value to a product or service as it passes from manufacturer to retailer. Traditionally, marketing channels are made up of manufacturers and producers, distributors, wholesalers and dealers, and retailers and added-value resellers of various descriptions. The exact configuration will vary for a number of reasons that are particular to the nature of the market, the products and the strategy and culture of the participant organisations. Figure 13.2 sets out the structure of a conventional marketing channel.

Organisations group together because independently their objectives cannot be achieved.

Traditionally, organisations group together because independently their objectives cannot be achieved. By working together each member can concentrate upon those activities that it does best. This may be retailing, broking or manufacturing, but, whatever it is, the objectives of each organisation are best served by allowing others to perform alternative, specialist functions for them. Through this approach, organisations form temporary, often loosely aligned, relationships with a range of organisations.

Organisations make decisions about the balance between the level of independence and the level of interdependence that they wish to adopt. A decision to work through intermediaries enables a focus on core skills to be retained but reduces their independence and autonomy. Conversely, a decision to remain relatively independent decreases the level of interdependence and increases an organisation's perceived level of control over its business activities.

Marketing channels have evolved from this simple configuration to reflect issues concerning power, control and market influence. For example, some organisations seek to own all the companies that make up the whole marketing channel, known as a corporate vertical marketing system. They do this in order to maintain service levels and take a margin from each stage of the industry value chain. Travel organisations, for example, may own high-street travel agencies, tour operators, an airline and hotels. These arrangements are less popular today because they lack flexibility and tend to lock in organisations to a particular business format. Other organisations contract retailers to deliver a particular branded product/service through what is known as a franchise. At the other extreme some organisations choose to work in loose alliances and networks, some of which form just to deliver a particular project. There are numerous network variations and complex arrangements, too many to be discussed here. However, suffice it to say that the marketing communications used to communicate with channel members and end-user customers will vary and be partly influenced by the channel 'arrangements' that are in position.

Multichannel marketing

Of course, organisations today operate through a variety of marketing channels, not just one. Multichannel marketing is important because it recognises that different people are able and prefer to access products and services in different ways. Figures 13.3 and 13.4 show some of the main channels used in both the consumer and business markets. For a fuller explanation of these and the roles each member undertakes readers should read Chapter 7 in Fill and Fill (2005).

Many organisations now incorporate a range of direct and indirect channels within their channel strategy.

Thus, many organisations now incorporate a range of direct and indirect channels within their channel strategy. Internet technologies have brought a new dimension to the direct channel. Through the use of ecommerce, organisations that once relied on the distribution of catalogues or the use of a sales force can now reach wider, even global, audiences.

Direct-channel marketing in the business-to-business sector has grown as new technology enables organisations to build relationships directly with each of their customers. Electronic channels represent opportunities for manufacturers to reach end-user customers and to also provide intermediaries with higher levels of service and support.

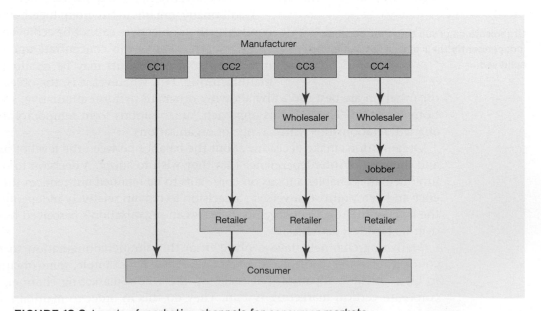

FIGURE 13.3 Levels of marketing channels for consumer markets

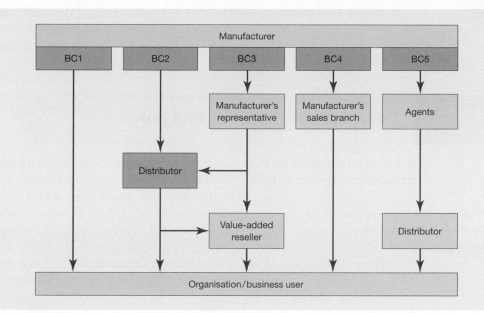

FIGURE 13.4 Levels of marketing channels for business-customer markets

ViewPoint 13.2   Direct-channel marketing at BOC Gases

For more than 10 years, BOC Gases have developed innovative products and processes designed to reduce the total cost of ownership for compressed gas products and services. For example, the recent expansion of BOC Arrowhead's cylinder tracking system, a networked customer application, enables customised cylinder tracking, buy-site access and exchange connectivity, for compressed gases and equipment users. This has now been equipped to provide wireless communications access. BOC customers are equipped with hand-held devices that provide real-time connectivity to the Arrowhead system or other BOC services such as its online catalogue and configurator, which allows customers to customise their gas mixtures.

Customers can now use the hand-held device to place orders or conduct stock transactions while walking around their facilities. In addition, this device can be used to connect to other online services offered by BOC such as online product specifications, certificates of analysis, shelf-life expiration tracking and other technologies.

Companies in industries such as chemicals, petroleum, pulp and paper, pharmaceuticals and power generation use a variety of compressed and special gases to control processes, perform testing and track emissions. For organisations with multiple locations that may have numerous purchasers ordering a wide range of compressed gases and equipment, this technology offers easy access to the most up-to-date data and transactions.

BOC's wide range of service offerings – from vendor-managed inventory (VMI) systems that manage customers' gas and equipment requirements, to BOC's *Sentry* Site Services™ for on-site staffing, to e-business systems that allow customers to track their cylinders and transactions – are tailored to meet each customer's specific needs and to achieve reductions in the total cost of ownership for compressed gases.

Wireless technology represents the next logical step and, by enabling wireless access to BOC's Web-based tools, customers benefit from improved supply-chain management and overall convenience.

Organisations employ multichannel strategies because different segments prefer to use (value) different channels. In addition, a multichannel strategy is necessary in order that production efficiencies can be achieved and resources utilised more effectively.

Coordination, conflict and power

If a marketing channel is to function effectively, cooperation between members is paramount. To work effectively and efficiently the interdependence, specialisation and expertise of individual organisations should be encouraged (Rosenbloom, 1983). However, interdependence is rarely distributed in a uniform and equitable way and this inequality is a major source of power for some channel members. This disproportionate distribution means that relationships between members are a reflection of the balance of power that exists between them.

Interdependence is rarely distributed in a uniform and equitable way.

Sources of power

French and Raven (1959), in a classic study, determined five bases for power: rewards, coercion, expertise, legitimate and reference bases. *Rewards* are one of the more common, where, for example, a manufacturer might grant a wholesaler particular discounts dependent upon the volume of products bought during an agreed period. *Coercion* is the other side of the 'reward-based' coin, where negative measures may be brought in to sanction a channel member. If a wholesaler becomes dissatisfied with the payment cycle adopted by a retailer, deliveries may be slowed down or the discount structure revised. Power based upon *expertise*, perceived by other channel members, makes them dependent upon the flow of information from the source. Interestingly, the expert power exercised by leading pharmaceutical manufacturers is derived from the dependence of the pharmacies and general practitioners (GPs) on them and not so much on the dependence of the wholesalers. *Legitimate* power, whereby the authority to manage the channel is recognised rather like a manager recognises the authority of an executive director, is uncommon in conventional channels. Only in contractual and corporate vertical marketing systems (for example, franchisors) can legitimate power be exercised. Lastly, *reference* power works on the basis of association and identification – 'being in the same boat' as Rosenbloom (1983) refers to it. If members of a network are able to share and empathise with the problems of their 'network partners', then a channel-wide solution to a common problem may well result in increased understanding, collaboration and trust.

By recognising and understanding the bases of power, the levels of cooperation and the form of the relationships between members, the nature of communication, its pattern, its frequency and its style can be adjusted to complement the prevailing conditions. Furthermore, such an understanding can be useful to help shape the power relationships of the future and to enhance the corporate/marketing strategy. Once the current and expected power bases are determined, marketing communications can assist the shaping process. Of the power propositions provided by French and Raven, reward and coercion seem more apt for use within channels, where market-exchange-based transactions predominate. Legitimate and expert power might be better applied in channels with a high level of relational exchanges.

Channel conflict

Conflict within and between all channels is endemic and is widely prevalent in channel relationships.

Conflict within and between all channels is endemic and is widely prevalent in channel relationships (Hunt and Nevin, 1974). Conflict represents a breakdown or deterioration in the levels of cooperation between partners (Shipley and Egan, 1992). The reasons for conflict need to be clearly appreciated, as identification of the appropriate cause can lead to communications strategies that remedy, or at least seek to repair, any damage. Some of the more common reasons for channel conflict, suggested by Stern and Gorman (1969), are failure to enact a given or agreed role, issues arising among the participant organisations, selective perception and inadequate communications. For example, because channel members undertake particular *roles*, any failure to fulfil the expected role may be a cause of conflict. An *issue* may arise within the channel that causes conflict. For example, a wholesaler and a manufacturer may disagree about margins, training, marketing policies or, more commonly, territorial issues. McGrath and Hardy (1986) see conflict emanating from manufacturers' policies, such as sales-order policies. The tighter and more constricting they are, the greater the likelihood that conflict will erupt than if the policies are flexible and can be adjusted to meet the needs of both parties.

All of these reasons can be distilled into three main factors (Stern and Heskett, 1969). These concern differences relating to:

● competing or incompatible goals;
● domains;
● perceptions of reality.

Underpinning all of them is inadequate communication.

Competing goals

This is a common form of conflict and typically occurs when one upstream member changes strategy so that its goals become difficult for downstream members to support. For example, a manufacturer may decide that it wants to reach new market sectors, but current dealers might resist this strategy as it is not in their interest to supply other (new) channels with the same products. Indeed, if actioned it might give rise to increased channel competition and then impact on dealer revenues and profits.

Another example of competing goals can be seen when retailers try to increase performance by lowering their stock levels. Conflict is likely as the manufacturer's goal is to increase the level of stock in the channel, whereas intermediaries prefer to be able to pull down stock on demand and hence avoid working-capital costs.

Alternatively, a department manager in a retail organisation may not be too concerned which of its product offerings in a particular category helps the department achieve its volume and margin contributions. However, the manufacturer of an individual brand will be most concerned if its brand is not included as part of the retailer's portfolio of category brands. Different goals, yet same product focus.

Domain differences

A channel domain refers to an area, field or sphere of operations. According to Stern et al. (1996) it has four main elements: population, territory, member roles and issues concerning technology and marketing. Disputes can thus arise because one channel member perceives another member operating outside the previously designated (agreed) area, perhaps geographically, or in terms of its role. For example, a wholesaler and a manufacturer may disagree about margins, training, marketing policies or, more commonly, territorial issues. McGrath and Hardy (1986) see conflict emanating from manufacturers' policies, such as sales-order policies. The tighter and more constricting they are, the greater the likelihood that conflict will erupt than if the policies are flexible and can be adjusted to meet the needs of both parties.

ViewPoint 13.3   Domain-based conflict at Miller Electric

Miller Electric, a manufacturer of welding equipment, and Linweld, a key distributor of industrial and medical gases and welding supplies, experienced domain-based conflict concerning a change in channel strategy.

Miller Electric's website receives 60,000 visitors every month and over half result in sales. Miller Electric wanted to move to a direct-channel strategy, with distributors responsible for delivering the goods. However, ownership of the sales transaction meant that Miller Electric would be able to set prices and eventually cut the channel out completely. The intermediaries rejected the strategy.

Miller Electric compromised and sales leads generated by Miller Electric's website were given to distributors. Once customers designate items they want to buy on Miller Electric's site, they must choose from a list of nearby distributors. The customers and their shopping lists are then whisked off to the selected distributor's website, where they receive pricing and availability information prior to completing the order.

However, another problem arose concerning which distributor gets the lead. Miller Electric's process for listing distributors works on the basis that when a customer inputs a zip code, the three closest distributors pop up. Moreover, only the distributor's name, address and contact information are provided. Such a simple process does not reflect Linweld's power, importance and size of investment compared with many smaller and more provincial distributors. In reaching a solution, Miller had to recognise Linweld's powerful position based on the volume and value of business placed through Miller Electric.

Source: Adapted from Kaneshige (2001) http://www.line56.com/articles/default.asp?NewsID=2382 (accessed 3 December 2003); used with kind permission

So a wholesaler who starts to sell direct to end-user consumers, or retailers who begin to sell to other retailers, are blatantly adopting a new role and this may infringe upon another member's role and prevent or impede them from achieving their objectives.

A more common example exists when a manufacturer decides to sell through a dealer's competitors, to the extent of even breaking an exclusivity arrangement. The reverse of this intra-channel type of conflict can also cause conflict, when a manufacturer perceives an intermediary selling another (competing) manufacturer's products at the expense of its own range of products.

The reverse of this intra-channel type of conflict can also cause conflict.

Another cause of domain-based conflict concerns the emergence of multiple channels. An intermediary might feel threatened by increased competition and reduced financial performance opportunities.

Disagreements about pricing, sales areas or sales-order processing, for example, are sensitive issues that can also lead to channel conflict. Once agreement has been made about policy terms or operational formats, any changes should be negotiated and managed in a cooperative and considered way. Indeed, some channels often stipulate the way that changes to key domain-based issues should be managed.

Perceptions of reality

Through the process of selective perception any number of members may react to the same stimulus in completely different and conflicting ways. The objectives of each of the channel members are different, however well bonded they are to the objectives of the distribution system. It is also likely that each member perceives different ways of achieving the overall goals, all of which are recipes for conflict. As each member organisation perceives the world differently, their perception of others and their actions may lead to tensions and disagreements. So, an action taken by member X might be perceived differently by member Y from that intended. Any action that Y takes as a result of this perception may result in conflict. Perceptions about a product attribute, its applications and appropriate segments can all give rise to perceptually based conflict.

Apart from poor or incomplete communication, the main reason for this tendency to see different information or actions differently from that intended may arise because, in the absence of a strong cooperative relationship, different channel members are focused on different business elements (Coughlan et al. (2001)). A manufacturer might be focused on products and processes and a dealer may be focused on their customers and the functions and processes necessary to meet their needs. Differences in perception may arise because member focus is culturally driven. What may be an appropriate behaviour in one culture may not be understood by, known to or be just different from that in another. This can obviously be a problem for internationally based organisations.

What may be an appropriate behaviour in one culture may not be understood by, known to or be just different from that in another.

The final reason is perhaps one of the most important, and central to the issue of this particular key factor. *Communication* is a coordinating mechanism for all members of the system. Its absence or failure will inevitably lead to uncoordinated behaviour and actions that are not in the best interests of the channel system. The channel can become destabilised through poor or inadequate communication, as the processes of selective perception can distort encoded messages and lead to conflict and disunity.

Conflict can be beneficial.

Conflict can be beneficial, and can be harnessed to help relationships in many different ways. For example, conflict, once resolved, might just clear the air and enable the parties to resume their focus on core rather than peripheral activities. Early conflict resolution can be used to avoid potential end-user problems and so maintain levels of production, service and support. Conflict can help to recharge relationships, promote problem-solving arrangements for the future, encourage parties to better understand how conditions have changed and what that means for future operations and relationships. Conflict can also be used, once resolved, to reduce complacency, encourage opportunities for market, product and customer development. Conflict can be used to challenge existing beliefs and to show that there are better, more efficient ways of doing things. In much the same way, conflict can assist new product and systems development.

Conflict is generally regarded as having negative consequences but this is not necessarily the case. Channel relationships can be made stronger simply because members learn more about each other having experienced conflict and its resolution by working as part of a team. However, it should be understood that conflict can only help a relationship if managed appropriately. Conflict resolution methods such as arbitration, domination (coercion) and harsh words may accentuate matters and lead to a further deterioration in the health of the relationship, rather than help it flourish.

Channel relationships can be made stronger simply because members learn more about each other.

Management of channel communications

Communications between members of marketing channels are normally the responsibility of a particular member in the channel. This member assumes the dominant role by virtue of the dependence of the other members. The organisations that are perceived to be powerful in the context of the distribution channel are said to be channel leaders or channel captains.

Channel leadership carries a responsibility to coordinate the activities of the other members.

Channel leadership carries a responsibility to coordinate the activities of the other members. Therefore, all communications should be designed to assist the network as a whole and not just those of the leader. As Frazier and Sheth (1985) suggest, the objective of channel leadership is to contribute to the improved performance of the channel network. If the channel performance improves, then the channel leader is likely to benefit and its role as leader will be reaffirmed.

The communications that the channel leader masterminds consist of two main strands. The first is the operational data flow, enhancing the performance of the network at an operational level. The advances in information technology (IT) have been crucial to the distribution of data between organisations. Indeed, IT now provides an opportunity for organisations to develop competitive advantage. For example, the installation of computerised reservation systems in travel agencies by tour operators not only helps to provide for a high level of customer satisfaction through real-time processing but also signals the existence of a considerable mobility barrier. Those travel agents who wish to exit the network and those tour operators wishing to enter a more compelling relationship with certain travel agents must now account for all the costs of changing systems, including the hardware, software, training and support associated with information technology.

The second strand is marketing communications. This concerns the deployment of the range of tools in the promotional mix, established earlier. These flows of largely persuasive information are designed to influence organisations and individuals to take a particular course of action. Information is distributed in order to influence the decisions that members make about the marketing mix they each adopt.

ViewPoint 13.4   Li & Fung: the orchestrators

Li & Fung, a Hong Kong-based trading company, outsources the production of all its goods to others. Li & Fung make no products at all. By orchestrating its global network of highly focused providers it arranges private-label manufacturing, primarily on behalf of US and European clothiers. For a specific product or client, Li & Fung puts together a set of partner organisations to manage product development, the sourcing of raw materials, production planning and management, manufacturing and shipping. Any problems are resolved by shifting activities from one network partner to another.

Brown et al. (2002) argue that this level of flexibility 'promotes high-output performance'. Li & Fung gains efficiencies through the specialisation of suppliers rather than by squeezing supply-chain costs by tightly integrating activities. Loose coupling frees up processes and enables greater levels of specialisation. The results confirm the efficacy of this approach. The return on equity has been over 30 per cent a year for each year since 1996, and in 2001 revenues amounted to just over $1 million per employee.

Source: Adapted from Brown et al. (2002); used with permission

Marketing communications in the channels

The marketing channel represents a part of business-to-business marketing and requires distinct marketing communications strategies and methods. Marketing communications is an audience-centred activity and the characteristics, motivations and nature of organisational buyer behaviour are so dissimilar to the consumer market that different messages, tools and media are required.

It was established earlier that, from a managerial perspective, communication is important because many of the causes of tension and conflict in interorganisational relationships stem from inadequate or poor communication.

The role of communications within marketing channels can be considered through use of the DRIP framework.

The role of communications within marketing channels can be considered through use of the DRIP framework, considered in Chapter 1. Manufacturers and producers need to provide messages that serve to differentiate their offerings from those of competitors, in order that intermediaries see value in continuing the relationship and that end-users will also see value in the differences. Dealers and distributors will need reminding of the value of the products and services provided and in doing so serve to reinforce the existing relationship. One of the most important aspects of marketing communications in the channels is the provision of timely and accurate information. When lacking, this can be the cause of considerable discontent and even conflict. Extranet technologies enable channel members fast access to discreet Web pages that can provide detailed information about products, prices, stock, availability and new developments. This is an important facility that serves to provide intermediaries with not just the information to do better business faster, but which also helps reassure dealers by providing a stable platform on which they can do business. Intermediaries will need to be persuaded to sign up as a distributor in the first place, to take increased stock at particular times in the trading cycle and agree to certain promotional activities or perhaps changes in contract arrangements.

Marketing communications in the marketing channel are necessary to provide information, foster participative decision-making and provide for the coordination and exercise of power and the encouragement of loyalty and commitment, as this can reduce the likelihood of tension and conflict.

ViewPoint 13.5   Novell

Novell, a highly influential and well-regarded network computing company, had strong relationships with IT professionals. However, in order to progress it needed to develop stronger relationships with senior business executives and those involved in strategic IT purchase decisions. Otherwise it faced losing business and clients.

J. Walter Thompson decided to use a three-part strategy to reach the target market. First, rather than talk to these key influential people using technology as the main vocabulary, it was decided to converse on a business basis and to communicate messages based on the business issues and needs faced by clients. Second, the strategy needed to stress Novell's ability to deliver on the promises it made, and third, help clients achieve their profit targets. 'We speak your language' became a meaningful tagline and became Integrated B2B campaign of the year (2003).

Source: www.jwt.com/case studies/; used with permission

The b2b communications mix

As stated earlier, the use of the tools of the communications mix in the marketing channels is very different from that in consumer markets. The prime tool is personal selling supported by both above- and below-the-line activities. The Internet and related digital technologies have had a very significant role in changing the way business is conducted and the speed at which transactions can be undertaken and costs reduced. The Web is, of course, both a new distribution channel and a communication medium. As a form of communication it is impersonal and more disposed to information search and retrieval than to information that is heavily branded and has emotional overtones. The nature of b2b communications is that they are very personal, they often require face-to-face interaction and the interactive nature lends itself to tailored messages and rapid feedback.

> It is impersonal and more disposed to information search and retrieval than to information that is heavily branded and has emotional overtones.

Advertising and b2b

Apart from increasing use of online b2b advertising, the most important form is print advertising in trade journals and newspapers. Perhaps the most important role of advertising in this context is to inform and remind, whereas differentiation and persuasion are delivered through other tools of the communications mix, namely sales promotion and personal selling.

Direct marketing and b2b

Telemarketing has played an important role in recent years as a support mechanism for the sales force. It is used to facilitate customer enquiries, to establish leads, make appointments, and in certain circumstances provide a direct sales channel. One of the more common uses is as a sales-order processing system to collect routine low-value orders. This frees up the sales force to concentrate on other, more profitable, activities.

Direct mail has been an important part of the communications mix in b2b markets for some time. Direct mail can be used to support personal selling by building awareness, enhancing image, establishing credibility and taking orders, and it can provide levels of customer management. The significance of this part of the communications mix is not in doubt, even though some of it is being surpassed by the use of the Internet and ecommerce practices.

It would thus appear sensible to be able to measure direct-mail activities, and in the b2b sector this is usually accomplished through measurement of response rates. However, this has not always been entirely satisfactory because there are a number of stages through which a receiver of direct mail moves. These are the opening, scanning, (re)reading and response behaviours. Vriens et al. (1998) suggest that there are three main parts to the process. The first is the opening behaviour that is influenced by the attractiveness of the envelope and situational factors. Reading behaviour is influenced by the opening behaviour, the reader's situational characteristics and the attractiveness of the mailing and its contents. The final behaviour concerns the response generated, which is affected by the attractiveness of the offer, by the reading behaviour that preceded the response and the characteristics of the individual reader and their situation.

Wulf et al. (2000) used this framework to find ways in which response rates to direct mail could be increased. They found that the attractiveness of the envelope did impact on opening behaviour but so did the envelope size, material, colour and even type of postage. Surprisingly, the volume of direct mail each manager received had no impact on opening behaviour. With regard to reading behaviour, it was the attitudes of the reader that were found to be significant, not the situational factors. Lastly, response behaviour appeared to be determined more by the reading behaviours of the individual rather than any other factor.

Sales promotions and b2b

The use of sales- or rather trade-based promotions is very often unnoticed by consumers. However, trade promotions and interorganisational incentives are common and generally effective. Manufacturers will use competitions and sweepstakes to incentivise the sales forces of its distributors, to motivate technical- and customer-support staff in retail organisations and as an inducement to encourage other businesses to place orders and business with them.

ViewPoint 13.6   Dulux targets decorators

In an effort to consolidate its position as market leader and to increase sales, Dulux used a trade-based promotion in the spring of 2004. Targeting decorators who choose paints on behalf of their largely domestic customers, rather than contractors who work on commercial accounts where the brand choice of paint is decided by the customer, a cash prize fund of £2 million was a significantly attractive promotion. The sales promotion instrument or mechanic was a scratchcard that was distributed through 1,200 trade outlets across the UK. Rather than use premium give-aways or price cuts, the scratchcard was attached to cans of white paint so that the benefit went to the buyer (the decorator) rather than the counter staff who tend to feed their largest, by volume, customers.

Source: Adapted from Mistry (2004) and Dulux-provided materials; used with kind permission

Price-based promotions and delayed discounts are used to encourage organisations to place business.

Price-based promotions and delayed discounts are used to encourage organisations to place business. Another popular approach is to discount technical support and bundle up a range of support facilities. Whatever the package, the purpose remains the same: to add value in order to advance (or gain) a purchase commitment.

Public relations and b2b

The effectiveness of public relations in a b2b context should not be underestimated. The range of public relations tools and techniques enables credibility to be developed in an environment where advertising is relatively ineffective, personal selling critical to the development of relationships and sales promotion limited to short-term sales shifts. Direct marketing and particularly interactively based communications are increasingly important in this sector, but public relations provides credibility and richness to an organisation's communications.

Personal selling and b2b

Personal selling is the most important tool of the b2b marketing communications mix, simply because of the need for interaction, dialogue and relationship development and maintenance. Although exhibitions are also a major part of the communications mix used in b2b markets, the one area that has developed in recent years, owing to the use of direct marketing and interactive technology, is the management of those customers who are of strategic importance to an organisation. This is referred to as key account management and is explored in the next section.

What is important is the use of a coordinated mix within a multichannel strategy in order to deliver messages that seek to develop relationships.

However, b2b marketing communications is not just about the use of particular tools of the communications mix. What is more important is the use of a coordinated mix within a multichannel strategy in order to deliver messages that seek to develop relationships. In this case the goal is to enable channel partners to meet their business-performance goals so that their trust, commitment and satisfaction is maximised.

Key account management

One of the major issues concerning the development and maintenance of interorganisational relationships is the method by which very important and/or valuable customers are managed. Key account management, an extension of personal selling, has emerged as an important way of managing significant business-to-business relationships.

The increasing complexity of both markets and products, combined with the trends towards purchasing centralisation and industrial concentration, mean that a small number of crucial accounts have become essential for the survival of many organisations.

The growth in the significance of key account management (KAM) is expected to continue.

The growth in the significance of key account management (KAM) is expected to continue and one of the results will be the change in expectations of buyers and sellers, in particular the demand for higher levels of expertise, integration and professionalism of sales forces.

It has long been recognised that particular customer accounts represent an important, often large, proportion of turnover. Such accounts have been referred to variously as national accounts, house accounts, major accounts and key accounts. Millman and Wilson (1995) argue that the first three are oriented towards sales, tend to the short term and are often only driven by sales-management needs. However, Ojasalo (2001) sees little difference in the terminology KAM, national account marketing (NAM) and strategic account management (SAM).

Key accounts may be of different sizes compared with the focus organisation, but what delineates them from other types of 'account' is that they are strategically important. Key accounts are customers that, in a business-to-business market, are willing to enter into relational exchanges and that are of strategic importance to the focus organisation.

There are two primary aspects of this definition. The first is that both parties perceive relational exchanges as a necessary component and that the relationship is long term. The second aspect refers to the strategic issue. The key account is strategically important because it might offer opportunities for entry to new markets, represent access to other key organisations or resources, or provide symbolic value in terms of influence, power and stature.

The key account is strategically important because it might offer opportunities for entry to new markets.

The importance of the long-term relationship as a prime element of key account identification raises questions about how they are developed, what resources are required to manage and sustain them, and what long-term success and effectiveness results from identifying them. Essentially this comes down to who in the organisation should be responsible for these key accounts. Generally there are three main responses: to assign sales executives, to create a key account division or to create a key account sales force.

The assignment of sales executives to these important accounts is common in smaller organisations. Those organisations that have the resources are able to incorporate the services of senior executives. They assume this role and with it they bring the flexibility and responsive service that are required as the account grows in stature. They can make decisions about stock, price, distribution and levels of customisation.

These accounts may be major or national accounts, as very often their strategic significance is not recognised. There is a tendency for these accounts to receive a disproportionate level of attention, as the executives responsible for these major customers lose sight of their own organisation's marketing strategy.

A further way of managing these accounts is to create a key account division. The main advantage of this approach is that it offers close integration of production, finance, marketing and sales. The main disadvantage is that resources are duplicated and the organisation can become very inefficient. It is also a high-risk strategy as the entire division is dependent upon a few customers.

Should a key account sales force be preferred then issues concerning the management of this resource arise. Key account managers require particular skills, as indeed do the executives themselves.

Key account managers

Abratt and Kelly (2002) report Napolitano's (1997) work, which found that, to be successful, a KAM programme requires the selection of the right key account manager. This person should possess particularly strong interpersonal and relationship skills and be capable of managing larger, significant and often complex customers. Key account managers act as a conduit between organisations, through which high-value information flows, in both directions.

Key account managers act as a conduit between organisations, through which high-value information flows.

They must be prepared and able to deal with organisations where buying decisions can be protracted and delayed (Sharma, 1997).

Among the key success factors, Abratt and Kelly report that, in addition to selecting the right key account manager, the selection of the right key account customers is also important for establishing KAM programmes. Not all large and high-volume customers are suitable for KAM programmes. Segmentation and customer prioritisation according to needs and an organisation's ability to provide consistent value should be used to highlight those for whom KAM would not be helpful.

In addition, particular sales behaviours are required at this level of operation. As the majority of key account managers are drawn internally from the sales force (Hannah, 1998, cited by Abratt and Kelly, 2002) it is necessary to ensure that they have the correct skills mix. It is also important to take a customer's perspective on what makes a successful KAM programme. Pardo (1997) is cited as claiming that the degree of impact a product has on the customer's business activity will determine the level of attention offered to the supplier's programme. In addition, the level of buying-decision centralisation will impact on the effectiveness of the KAM programme.

Abratt and Kelly found that six factors were of particular importance when establishing a KAM programme. These are the 'suitability of the key account manager, knowledge and understanding of the key account customer's business, commitment to the KAM partnership, delivering value, the importance of trust and the proper implementation and understanding of the KAM concept'.

Key account relationship cycles

A number of researchers have attempted to gain a greater understanding of KAM by considering the development cycles through which relationships move. Millman and Wilson (1995) offer the work of Ford (1980), Dwyer et al. (1987) and Wotruba (1991) as examples of such development cycles. See Table 13.2.

Millman and Wilson have attempted to build upon the work of the others and have formulated a model that incorporates their own research as well as that established in the literature. McDonald (2000) has since elaborated on their framework, providing further insight and explanation.

The cycle develops with the *Exploratory KAM* level, where the main task is to identify those accounts that have key account potential and those that do not, in order that resources can be allocated efficiently. Both organisations are considering each other: the buyer in terms of the supplier's offer as regards its ability to match their own requirements, and the seller in terms of the buyer providing sufficient volumes, value and financial suitability.

The next level is *Basic KAM*, where both organisations enter into a transactional period, essentially testing each other as potential long-term partners. Some relationships may stabilise at this level while others may develop as a result of the seller seeking and gaining tentative agreement with prospective accounts about whether they would become 'preferred accounts'.

At the *Cooperative KAM* level more people from both organisations are involved in communications.

At the *Cooperative KAM* level more people from both organisations are involved in communications. At the Basic KAM level both parties understand each other and the selling company has established its credentials with the buying organisation through experience. At this next level, opportunities to add value to the relationship are considered. This could be encouraged by increasing the range of products and services transacted. As a result, more people are involved in the relationship.

At the *Interdependent KAM* level of a relationship both organisations recognise the importance of the other to their operations, with the supplier either first-choice or only

TABLE 13.2 Comparison of relational models

Ford (1980), Dwyer et al. (1987)	Wotruba (1991)	Millman and Wilson (1995)	McDonald (2000)
Pre-relationship awareness	Provider	Pre-KAM	Exploratory
Early stage exploration	Persuader	Early KAM	Basic
Development stage expansion	Prospector	Mid-KAM	Cooperative
Long-term stage commitment	Problem-solver	Partnership KAM	Interdependent
Final stage institutionalisation	Procreator	Synergistic KAM	Integrated
		Uncoupling KAM	Disintegrated

Source: Updated from Millman and Wilson (1995)

supplier. Retraction from the relationship is now problematic as 'inertia and strategic suitability', as McDonald phrases it, holds the partners together.

Integrated KAM is achieved when the two organisations view the relationship as consisting of one entity where they create synergistic value in the marketplace. Joint problem-solving and the sharing of sensitive information are strong characteristics of the relationship, and withdrawal by either party can be traumatic at a personal level for the participants involved, let alone at the organisational level.

The final level is *Disintegrating KAM*. This can occur at any time and for a variety of reasons, ranging from company takeover to the introduction of new technology. The relationship may return to another, lower level and new terms of business are established. The termination, or readjustment, of the relationship need not be seen as a negative factor as both parties may decide that the relationship holds no further value.

McDonald develops Millman and Wilson's model by moving away from a purely sequential framework. He suggests that organisations may stabilise or enter the model at any level – indeed, he states that organisations might readjust to a lower level. The time between phases will vary according to the nature and circumstances of the parties involved. The labels provided by McDonald reflect the relationship status of both parties rather than of the selling company (e.g. prospective) or buying company (e.g. preferred supplier). Although the Millman and Wilson and the McDonald interpretations of the KAM relationship cycle provide insight they are both primarily dyadic perspectives. They neglect to consider the influence of significant others, in particular those other network member organisations that provide context and interaction in particular networks and that do influence the actions of organisations, and those key individuals who are strategic decision-makers.

Some final aspects of KAM

In mature and competitive markets, where there is little differentiation between the products, service may be the only source of sustainable competitive advantage. Key account management allows senior sales executives to build a strong relationship with each of their customers and so provide a very high level of service and strong point of differentiation. This approach enables an organisation to select its most experienced and able salespersons and, in doing so, provide a career channel for those executives who prefer to stay in sales rather than move into management. Administratively, this structure is inefficient as there is a level of duplication similar to that found in the customer-type structure discussed earlier. Furthermore, commission payable on these accounts is often a source of discontent, both for those within the key account sales force and those aspiring to join the select group.

International marketing communications

For organisations the differences between operating within home or domestic markets as compared with overseas or international markets are many and varied. Most of these differences can be considered within an economic, cultural, legal, technological and competitive framework. If the core characteristics of a home market (such as prices, marketing channels, finance, knowledge about customers, legislation, media and competitors) are compared with each of the same factors in the international markets in which an organisation might be operating, then the degree of complexity and uncertainty can be easily illustrated.

Key variables affecting international marketing communications

There are a large number of variables that can impact upon the effectiveness of marketing communications that cross international borders. Many of these are controllable by either local or central management. However, there are a large number that are uncontrollable, and these variables need to be carefully considered before communications are attempted.

Culture

The values, beliefs, ideas, customs, actions and symbols that are learned by members of particular societies are referred to as culture. The importance of culture is that it provides individuals with identity and the direction of what is deemed to be acceptable behaviour. Culture is acquired through learning. If it were innate or instinctual, then everyone would behave in the same way. Human beings across the world do not behave uniformly or predictably. Different cultures thus exist, and from this it is possible to appreciate that there must be boundaries within which certain cultures, and hence behaviours and lifestyles, are permissible or even expected. These boundaries are not fixed rigidly, as this would suggest that cultures are static. They evolve and change as members of a society adjust to new technologies, government policies, changing values and demographic changes, to mention but a few dynamic variables.

Culture is passed from generation to generation.

Culture is passed from generation to generation. This is achieved through the family, religion, education and the media. These conduits of social behaviour and beliefs serve to provide consistency, stability and direction. The extent to which the media either move society forward or merely reflect its current values is a debate that reaches beyond the scope of this book. However, there can be no doubt as to the impact that the media have on society and the important part that religion plays in different cultures around the world.

Culture has multiple facets, and those that are of direct relevance to marketing communications are the values and beliefs associated with *symbols*, such as language and aesthetics, *institutions* and *groups*, such as those embracing the family, work, education, media and religion, and finally *values*, which according to Hofstede et al. (1990) represent the core of culture.

Media

The rate of technological change has had a huge impact on the forms and types of media that audiences can access. However, media availability is far from uniform, and the range and types of media vary considerably across countries. These media developments have been accompanied by a number of major structural changes to the industry and the ways in which the industry is regulated. Many organisations (client brands, media and agencies) have attempted to grow through diversification and the development of international networks (organic growth and alliances), and there has been an

TABLE 13.3 General trends in worldwide media

Electronic media expenditures have grown at the expense of print.

The worldwide adspend on newspapers has fallen considerably.

The number of general-interest magazines has fallen and the number of specialist-interest magazines has grown.

The growth of satellite facilities has helped generate the development of television and cable networks.

Online adspend is increasing faster than for any other medium.

Television programming and distribution have become more important.

Cinema capacity is beginning to outstrip demand.

Out-of-home media, in particular outdoor and alternative new media (e.g. ambient), have grown significantly.

increase in the level of concentration as a few organisations/individuals have begun to own and hence control larger proportions of the media industry. For example, Goodman and Goodman (2005) listed the following: Rupert Murdoch's News Corporation (Fox, HarperCollins, *New York Post*, *Weekly Standard*, *TV Guide*, DirecTV and 35 TV stations), General Electric (NBC, CNBC, MSNBC, Telemundo, Bravo, Universal Pictures and 28 TV stations), Time Warner (AOL, CNN, Warner Bros., *Time* and its 130-plus magazines), Disney (ABC, Disney Channel, ESPN, 10 TV and 72 radio stations), Viacom (CBS, MTV, Nickelodeon, Paramount Pictures, Simon & Schuster and 183 US radio stations), Bertelsmann (Random House and its more than 120 imprints worldwide, and Gruner + Jahr and its more than 110 magazines in 10 countries). These seven organisations now have substantial cross-ownership holdings of international media. This concentration is partly the result of the decisions of many governments to deregulate their control over the media and to create new trading relationships. As a result, this cross-ownership of the media (television, newspapers, magazines, cable, satellite, film, publishing, advertising, cinema, retailing, recorded music) has created opportunities for client advertisers to have to go to only one media provider, who then provides access to a raft of media across the globe.

> Cross-ownership of the media has created opportunities for client advertisers to have to go to only one media provider, who then provides access to a raft of media across the globe.

In addition to changes in ownership and structure, the global media industry has experienced major deregulation. This has served to enable clients, agencies and media greater flexibility in terms of when and where media can be used, which in turn has had a profound impact on media provision in nearly all parts of the world. Table 13.3 sets out some of the more general worldwide trends in advertising media. The net impact of all these changes has been principally the emergence of satellite television and cable provision and the development of the international consumer press.

Cross-border marketing communications strategy

The degree to which organisations should adapt their external messages to suit local or regional country requirements has been a source of debate since Levitt (1983) published his landmark work on global branding. The standardisation/adaptation issue is unlikely to be resolved, yet is an intuitively interesting and thought-provoking subject. The cost savings associated with standardisation policies are attractive and, when these are combined with the opportunity to improve message consistency, communication effectiveness and other internally related efficiencies such as staff morale, cohesion and organisational identity, the argument in favour of standardisation seems difficult to counter. However, in practice there are very few brands that are truly global. Some, such as McDonald's, Coca-Cola and Levi's are able to capitalise upon the identification and inherent brand value that they have been able to establish across cultures. The majority of brands lack this depth of personality, and because individual needs vary across cultures so enterprises need to retune their messages in order that their reception is as clear and distinct as possible.

Adaptation

The arguments in favour of adapting messages to meet the needs of particular local and/or regional needs are as follows:

1. Consumer needs are different and vary in intensity. Assuming there are particular advertising stimuli that can be identified as having universal appeal, it is unlikely that buyers across international borders share similar experiences, abilities and potential either to process information in a standardised way or to ascribe similar sets of meanings to the stimuli they perceive. Ideas and message concepts generated centrally may be inappropriate for local markets.

2. The infrastructure necessary to support the conveyance of standardised messages varies considerably, not only across but often within broad country areas.

3. Educational levels are far from consistent. This means that buyers' ability to give meaning to messages will vary. Similarly, there will be differing capacities to process information, so that the complexity of message content has to be kept low if universal dissemination is to be successful.

4. The means by which marketing communications are controlled in different countries is a reflection of the prevailing local economic, cultural and political conditions. The balance between voluntary controls through self-regulation and state control through legislation is partly a testimony to the degree of economic and political maturity that exists. This means that what might be regarded as acceptable marketing communications activities in one country may be unacceptable in another. For example, cold calling is not permissible in Germany and, although not popular with either sales personnel or buyers, is allowed in the Netherlands and France.

5. Local management of the implementation of standardised, centrally determined messages may be jeopardised because of a lack of ownership. Messages crafted by local 'craftsmen' to suit the needs of local markets may receive increased levels of support and motivation.

Standardisation

Just as the arguments for adaptation appear convincing at first glance, then so do those in favour of standardisation:

1. Despite geographical dispersion, buyers in many product categories have a number of similar characteristics. This can be supported by the various psychographic typologies that have been developed by advertising agencies for their clients. As

ViewPoint 13.7   Adaptive Guinness

When Guinness appointed AMV and Saatchi & Saatchi as its two creative agencies (reducing the number of roster agencies substantially) the decision was made in recognition that the brand's heritage and promotional requirements were essentially twofold.

Tylee (2001) explains that in the relative sophistication of Europe and the USA the brand is perceived as a premium product supported by very emotionally led advertising reflecting years of development. In Africa and other parts of the world, the brand established itself originally because it was able to be shipped long distances and still be drinkable. Now, Guinness is a mass-market brand and is supported in Africa by a James Bond character, Michael Power, a black all-action hero.

Guinness recognises the need to utilise different creative approaches in respect of market perceptions.

brand images and propositions are capable of universal meaning, there is little reason to develop a myriad of brand messages.

2. Many locally driven campaigns are regarded as being of poor quality, if only because of the lack of local resources, experiences and expertise (Harris, 1996). It is better to control the total process and at the same time help exploit the opportunities for competitive advantage through shared competences.

3. As media, technology and international travel opportunities impact upon increasing numbers of people, so a standardised message for certain offerings allows for a strong brand image to be developed.

> A standardised message for certain offerings allows for a strong brand image to be developed.

4. Just as local management might favour local campaigns, so central management might prefer the ease with which they can implement and control a standardised campaign. This frees local managers to concentrate on managing the campaign and removes from them the responsibility of generating creative ideas and associated issues with local advertising agencies.

5. Following on from this point is one of the more enduring and managerially appealing ideas. The economies of scale that can be gained across packaging, media buying and advertising message creation and production can be enormous. In addition, the prospect of message consistency and horizontally integrated campaigns across borders is quite compelling. Buzzell (1968) argued that these economies of scale would also improve levels of profitability.

However, although a few organisations do operate at either end of the spectrum, the majority prefer a contingency approach. This means that there is a degree of standardisation, where for example creative themes, ideas and campaign planning are driven centrally and other campaign elements such as language, scenes and models are adapted to the needs of the local environment. Bold (2000) refers to pharmaceutical companies that have generally made the product the centre of their communications strategy, not brands. Drugs are launched in different countries using different names and different strategies targeted at the medical professionals. He comments that while this approach was prevalent the structure of pharmaceutical companies tended to be nation-focused even to the extent that there would be separate regionalised budgets. Merger and consolidation activity together with the rapid rise in patient involvement in healthcare (e.g. AIDS) has resulted in the formation of centralised marketing departments and the development of multinational brands.

Organisations rarely decide on a polarised strategy of total adaptation or complete standardisation. In practice, a policy of 'glocalisation' seems to be preferred. Under this

In practice, a policy of 'glocalisation' seems to be preferred.

approach, organisations develop standard messages centrally but expect the local country areas to adapt them to meet local cultural needs by adjusting for language and media components. There are, of course, variations on this theme. For example, head office might decide on the strategic direction and thrust of the campaign and leave the local country management to produce its own creatives.

Summary of key points

1. All organisations develop a series of relationships with a wide variety of other organisations, groups and, indeed, consumers who buy their products. These organisations are referred to as stakeholders and the relationships and individual partnerships vary considerably in their intensity, duration and function.

2. Organisations need to work together with particular stakeholders in order that products and services can be made available at times and places that are of convenience to end-user customers. These chains of stakeholder organisations are referred to as marketing channels. Each organisation seeks to add value to the product/service as the product is passed towards the end user.

3. In marketing channels each organisation is a customer of the previous organisation. Some organisations work closely together, coordinating and integrating their activities, while others combine on a temporary basis. In both cases, however, these organisations can be observed to be operating as members of a partnership (of differing strength and dimensions) with the express intention of achieving their objectives with their partner's assistance and cooperation.

4. Increasingly, organisations are providing multichannel facilities in order to reach a variety of audiences. Many organisations now incorporate a range of direct and indirect channels within their channel strategy as Internet technologies have brought a new dimension to the direct channel.

5. There are five types of power bases: reward, coercion, reference, expertise and legitimate. Through recognising and understanding the bases of power, the levels of cooperation and the form of the relationships between members, the nature of communications, its pattern, its frequency and its style can be adjusted to complement the prevailing conditions.

6. Conflict is endemic in marketing channels and three main types of conflict have been observed. These are: competing or incompatible goals, domains and perceptions of reality.

7. The marketing channel represents a part of business-to-business marketing and requires distinct marketing communications strategies and methods. Key account management, an extension of personal selling, has emerged as an important way of managing significant business-to-business relationships.

8. There are a large number of variables that need to be carefully considered before communications are attempted in an international or global arena. Two of the more important ones are culture, and media availability.

9. Organisations that operate in an international environment need to consider whether their messages should be adapted to meet the needs of country or regional audiences or whether they should use a single message that is delivered to all audiences.

Review questions

1. Determine the main stakeholders for an organisation with which you are familiar and rank them in order of importance.

2. Select those stakeholders that directly influence the value-adding processes performed by the organisation.

3. What are the differences between conventional channel networks and vertical marketing systems?

4. French and Raven identified several bases for power. What are they?

5. Identify the different types of conflict that are considered to prevail in marketing channels. Using newspapers, magazines and online resources, find examples of each type of conflict.

6. Write brief notes explaining the advantages of both an adapted and standardisation approach to international marketing communications.

References

Abratt, R. and Kelly, P.M. (2002), 'Perceptions of a successful key account management program', *Industrial Marketing Management*, **31**(5) (August), pp. 467–76.

Andersson, P. (1992), 'Analysing distribution channel dynamics: loose and tight coupling in distribution networks', *European Journal of Marketing*, **26**(2), pp. 47–68.

Bold, B. (2000), 'Unlocking the global market', *PR Week*, 11 August, pp. 13–14.

Brown, J.S., Durchslag, S. and Hagel III, J. (2002), 'Loosening up: how process networks unlock the power of specialization', *McKinsey Quarterly*, No. 2, retrieved from www.mckinseyquarterly.com/article/page.aspx?ar=1202&L2=1&L3=24.

Buzzell, R. (1968), 'Can you standardise multinational marketing?', *Harvard Business Review*, **46** (November/December), pp. 102–13.

Coughlan, A.T., Anderson, E., Stern, L. and El-Ansary, A. (2001), *Marketing Channels*, 6th edn, Englewood Cliffs, NJ: Prentice-Hall.

Dwyer, F.R., Shurr, P.H. and Oh, S. (1987), 'Developing buyer–seller relationships', *Journal of Marketing*, **51**(2), pp. 11–28.

Fill, C. and Fill, K.E. (2005), *Business to Business Marketing*, Harlow: FT Prentice Hall.

Ford, I.D. (1980), 'The development of buyer–seller relationships in industrial markets', *European Journal of Marketing*, **14**(5/6), pp. 339–53.

Frazier, G.L. and Sheth, J. (1985), 'An attitude–behavior framework for distribution channel management', *Journal of Marketing*, **43**(3), pp. 38–48.

Freeman, R.E. (1984), *Strategic Management*, Boston, Mass.: Pitman.

French, J.R. and Raven, B. (1959), 'The bases of social power', in D. Cartwright (ed.), *Studies in Social Power*, Ann Arbor, Mich.: University of Michigan Press.

Goodman, A. and Goodman, D. (2005), 'Why media ownership matters', *Seattle Times*, 3 April. Retrieved 7 November, from www.commondreams.org/views05/0403-25.htm.

Hannah, G. (1998), 'From transactions to relationships: challenges for the national account manager', *Journal of Marketing and Sales* (SA), **4**(1), pp. 30–3.

Harris, G. (1996), 'International advertising: developmental and implementational issues', *Journal of Marketing Management*, **12**, pp. 551–60.

Hofstede, G., Neuijen, B., Ohayv, D.D. and Sanders, G. (1990), 'Measuring organisational cultures: a qualitative and quantitative study across twenty cases', *Administrative Science Quarterly*, **35**(2), pp. 286–316.

Hunt, S.B. and Nevin, J.R. (1974), 'Power in channels of distribution: sources and consequences', *Journal of Marketing Research*, **11**, pp. 186–93.

Kaneshige, T. (2001), 'Avoiding channel conflict', *Line56 Magazine*, March.

Levitt, T. (1983), 'The globalization of markets', *Harvard Business Review*, May/June, pp. 92–102.

McDonald, M. (2000), 'Key account management: a domain review', *Marketing Review*, **1**, pp. 15–34.

McGrath, A. and Hardy, K. (1986), 'A strategic paradigm for predicting manufacturer–reseller conflict', *European Journal of Marketing*, **23**(2), pp. 94–108.

Millman, T. and Wilson, K. (1995), 'From key account selling to key account management', *Journal of Marketing Practice: Applied Marketing Science*, **1**(1), pp. 9–21.

Mistry, B. (2004), 'Dulux sets out to steal share', *Promotions and Incentives*, March, pp. 32–3.

Napolitano, L. (1997), 'Customer–supplier partnering: a strategy whose time has come', *Journal of Selling and Sales Management*, **17**(4), pp. 1–8.

Ojasalo, J. (2001), 'Key account management at company and individual levels in business-to-business relationships', *Journal of Business and Industrial Marketing*, **16**(3), pp. 199–220.

Pardo, C. (1997), 'Key account management in the business-to-business field: the key accounts point of view', *Journal of Selling and Sales Management*, **17**(4), pp. 17–26.

Rosenbloom, B. (1983), *Marketing Channels: A Management View*, Hinsdale, Ill.: Dryden Press.

Sharma, A. (1997), 'Who prefers key account management programs? An investigation of business buying behaviour and buying firm characteristics', *Journal of Personal Selling and Sales Management*, **17**(4), pp. 27–39.

Shipley, D. and Egan, C. (1992), 'Power, conflict and co-operation in brewer–tenant distribution channels', *International Journal of Service Industry Management*, **3**(4), pp. 44–62.

Stahl, M. and Grigsby, D. (1992), *Strategic Management for Decision Making*, Boston, Mass.: P.W.S. Kent.

Stern, L.W. and Gorman, R.H. (1969), 'Conflict in distribution channels: an exploration', in L.W. Stern (ed.), *Distribution Channels: Behavioural Dimensions*, Boston, Mass.: Houghton Mifflin.

Stern, L.W. and Heskett, J.L. (1969), ' Conflict management in interorganisational relations: a conceptual framework', in L.W. Stern (ed.), *Distribution Channels: Behavioural Dimensions*, Boston, Mass.: Houghton Mifflin.

Stern, L.W., El-Ansary, A. and Coughlan, A.T. (1996), *Marketing Channels*, 5th edn, Englewood Cliffs, NJ: Prentice-Hall.

Tylee, J. (2001), 'AMV and Saatchis prepare to meet over Guinness', *Campaign*, 12 January, p. 23.

Vriens, M., van der Scheer, H.R., Hoekstra, J.C. and Bult, J. (1998), 'Conjoint experiments for direct mail response optimisations', *European Journal of Marketing*, **32**(3/4), pp. 323–40.

Wotruba, T.R. (1991), 'The evolution of personal selling', *Journal of Personal Selling and Sales Management*, **11**(3), pp. 1–12.

Wulf, K.D., Hoekstra, J.C and Commandeur, H.R. (2000), 'The opening and reading behaviour of business-to-business direct mail', *Industrial Marketing Management*, **29**(2), pp. 133–45.

The industry: structure, budgets and control

14

Aims and objectives

The aims of this chapter are to introduce the various organisations involved in the marketing communications industry, to explore the methods used to determine marketing communications budgets and to examine some of the methods by which the industry is controlled. This last section also includes ideas about how business ethics are relevant to marketing communications. There are four primary topics in this chapter:

Industry structure, Budgets, Ethics, Regulation

The learning objectives are to enable readers to:

1. appreciate the size and characteristics of the UK marketing communications industry;
2. describe the value and usage trends of the individual tools that make up the marketing communications mix;
3. explain the various methods organisations can use to determine the size of their marketing communications budgets;
4. outline some of the statutory and voluntary controls used to regulate the industry;
5. understand how ethical considerations affect specific issues in marketing communications.

Introduction

The marketing communications industry consists of four principal sectors.

The marketing communications industry consists of four principal sectors. These are the media, the clients, the various communications agencies and finally the thousands of support organisations, such as production companies and fulfilment houses, that enable the whole process to function. It is the operations and relationships between these organisations that not only drive the industry but also form an important context within which marketing communications needs to be understood.

The number of relationships that can be developed in this industry, as with others, is enormous. To further complicate matters, the slow yet enduring move towards integrated marketing communications (Chapter 4) requires participants to form new relationships and acquire new skills. The argument that marketing communications activities should be kept in-house is now weak, as manufacturing and service-industry providers continue to increase their level of outsourcing activities and de-layer and hollow out their organisations. There is little or no room to maintain people with skills and expertise who are only drawn upon infrequently and where the notion of critical mass is important for media buying. Most observers would hold that it could only be accomplished by agencies and others that are dealing with a large number of clients and that are, by definition, in constant touch with developments in the industry. In the field of media buying, for example, many would argue that it is unlikely that the necessary expertise could be developed in-house. The increased emphasis on accountability and efficiency means that it is necessary to outsource such activities in order to use expertise and specialised resources, and to take advantage of collective discounts from media houses. Marketing practitioners therefore need to use some of the other organisations in the communications industry. A level of interdependence exists that requires cooperative and collaborative behaviour if the system is to function efficiently.

Dimensions of the UK marketing communications industry

It is useful to consider the size and value of the industry by taking into account the sums of money invested by clients in marketing communications. Some of these figures are acknowledged to be estimates, and there is some evidence of 'double counting' (one or more sectors claiming part of the overall spend for itself), so any figures produced cannot be seen as being totally accurate. That said, however, the total spend for advertising, as can be seen from Table 14.1, was £18.4 billion in 2004 (Advertising Association, 2005).

The total spend for advertising was £18.4 billion in 2004.

The Institute of Sales Promotion claims that the growth of sales promotion has been 'explosive', but measuring growth is difficult because there are no rate cards (price lists) and the breadth of activities that are attributable to sales promotion are many and varied. However, the Institute estimates that expenditure on sales promotion has grown from £9 billion in 1996 to perhaps £15.4 billion in 2004. Although not yet formally exceeding the spend on advertising, this area of activity has been catching up the advertising spend and, despite published figures, it is widely believed inside the industry that sales promotion has already overtaken advertising in terms of the proportion of client spend.

TABLE 14.1 Total UK advertising expenditure (including direct mail) in £m

	2004	2000	1996
Press	8,741	8,604	6,413
Television	4,740	4,646	3,379
Direct mail	2,470	2,049	1,405
Outdoor and transit	986	810	466
Radio	604	595	344
Cinema	192	128	73
Internet	653	153	NA
Total	**18,386**	**16,985**	**12,080**

Source: Advertising Association's *Advertising Statistics Yearbook* published by the World Advertising Research Center

ViewPoint 14.1   Industry issues

In a recent (2005) article the Director-General of the Incorporated Society of British Advertisers, Malcolm Earnshaw, referred to three main issues facing the marketing industry.

The first of these was the need for advertisers to defend their rights to advertise responsibly and not to be constrained by increasing legislation and government regulations. In particular, he referred to a recent government White Paper regarding food advertising and public health (obesity).

The second issue concerned the continuing consolidation in the media and the possible negative impact on clients in the advertising market.

The third issue referred to clients using the services of procurement specialists in order to drive down advertising costs with a consequent impact on agency margins and overall profitability. His argument is based on the need for agencies to offer better value to clients rather than to win pitches based on price alone.

Source: Earnshaw (2005)

Estimates vary, mainly because of problems of definition, but of the other areas in the industry sponsorship has grown significantly to £793 million in 2003. Direct-marketing spend has increased steadily as industry confidence has grown. However, a downturn in the economy brought this increase to an abrupt halt, with two years of little or no growth. Goften (2004) reports that there are some tentative signs of recovery with expenditure on direct mail, the dominant aspect of the industry, rising 2.2 per cent in 2003 to £2.43 billion (Direct Mail Information Service (DMIS)) but the figures remained flat throughout 2003 and 2004.

Other areas of the industry include public relations, which has experienced steady development and was worth approximately £2 billion in 2004, and exhibitions, of which there were 858 in 2003, each over 2,000 sq. ft. and in total worth approximately £1,800 million. Expenditure patterns do change, however, albeit at different rates, and, given the domination of advertising and sales promotion, the overall balance is unlikely to change dramatically in the short term. Nevertheless, it is clearly important for those responsible for the future and current planning of marketing communications activities to monitor trends, particularly those in the fastest-growing sectors of the industry, in order to identify and target creative opportunities.

Structure and development of the UK marketing communications industry

As with any industry, growth and development spawn new organisational types and structures. Adaptation to the environment is crucial for survival. The same applies to the marketing communications industry, where many different organisational configurations have evolved. Before considering some of the structural issues it is useful to establish the main types of organisations that populate the industry. These are set out in Table 14.2.

Clients can decide to manage the entire range of communications activities themselves, and this is referred to as the in-house approach. However, this is both costly and inefficient, and most organisations decide to outsource their requirements. Of the four main groups the production and media houses require that the clients and agencies agree and specify campaigns in order that they are able to contribute. So, to some extent, agencies and clients are the lead players in this industry.

Agency types and structures

The marketing communications industry consists of a number of different types of organisations whose purpose is to enable clients to communicate effectively and efficiently with their target audiences. Originally, these organisations acted as agents on behalf of media owners who wanted to sell media time and space; this was basically a production and selling role but one that has changed drastically. These agents learned to work more closely with their clients and in doing so became more customer-oriented. As will be seen later, agents undertook two main roles: creative message design and media planning and buying. The media component

Agents undertook two main roles: creative message design and media planning and buying.

TABLE 14.2 The main organisations in the communications industry

Type of organisation	Key role in the industry
Clients	Clients underpin the communications process by providing activities to be undertaken and the funding to support it.
Agencies	Agencies act on behalf of clients to develop, implement and evaluate either part or all of a marketing communications campaign.
Media owners	Media owners sell space and time in their media vehicles so that a message can be seen and/or heard by the client's target audience.
Production houses	Production houses produce the communications piece (e.g. film, video, soundtrack, mailer) that constitutes part or all of a campaign.

has subsequently been spun off to specialist agencies and might be regarded as a direct function of the media owners yet again. However, the interest and drive towards integrated communications, including media neutrality, means that agents will probably assume new, more independent roles in the future. The result of this development is that a number of different types of agency have emerged.

Full-service agencies

The first and most common type of agency (advertising) is the full-service agency. This type of organisation offers the full range of services that a client requires in order to advertise its products and services. Agencies such as J. Walter Thompson and Leo Burnett offer a full service consisting of strategic planning, research, creative development, production and media planning. Some of these activities may be subcontracted, but overall responsibility rests with the full-service agency. Further discussion of some of the issues concerning full-service agencies follows later.

Creative shops

A derivative of this type of agency is the creative shop, which often forms when creative personnel (teams) leave full-service agencies to set up their own business. These 'HotShops' provide specialist services for clients who wish to use particular styles and approaches for their creative work.

ViewPoint 14.2   It's not advertising, it's communication

Many aspects of the marketing communications industry have changed and are continuing to change. Some of these changes concern the nature and size of agencies. Many large, dominant groups are emerging, such as the four major organisations that pitched for Samsung's worldwide branding account: Interpublic (using its FCB operation), Omnicom (using BBDD agency), WPP (using J. Walter Thompson and Red Cell) and Publicis Groupe (using Leo Burnett and Saatchi & Saatchi). The fact that WPP won the account is not the point.

These organisations evolved as advertising agencies but have now transformed themselves into 'communications partners'. This reflects the increasing attention given to relationship marketing, the development of integrated marketing communications and the relative decline in the dominance of advertising within the communications mix. Organisations now seek to communicate different messages and this involves using a variety of (neutral) media. The term 'communications agencies', or partners, suggests variety and flexibility and reflects a change in core business.

Media independents

Similarly, media independents provide specialist media services for planning, buying and monitoring the purchase of a client's media schedule. There are two main forms: media independents, where the organisation is owned and run free of the direction and policy requirements of a full-service agency, and media dependents, where the organisation is a subsidiary of a creative or full-service organisation. The largest dependent in the UK is Mediacom, and the largest independent is Carat.

À la carte

Partly in response to the changing needs of clients and consumers, many organisations require greater flexibility in the way their advertising is managed, and consequently these clients prefer to use the services of a range of organisations. In this way, the planning skills of a full-service agency, the creative talent of a particular HotShop and the critical mass of a media-buying independent provide an à la carte approach. This process needs to be managed by the client, because when the services of other marketing communications providers are included flexibility is increased but coordination and control become more complex and problematic.

New media

New media agencies have developed as a result of the growth of the new media industry, which has seen huge growth in recent years. The growth has come from two main areas. The first concerns the surge of online brands that hit the market full of expectation of transforming the way business is conducted, and the second concerns established offline brands seeking to reach customers by adding to their marketing channels.

The provision of Internet facilities has been the main area of work, mainly communications and business-operations activities. This has been followed by WAP technology activity and interactive television (see Chapter 6). The market appears to have formed into three main parts of a spectrum of activities. At one end are those agencies that are marketing-oriented and at the other are technology-based organisations. Murphy (2000) feels that the real growth is likely to develop in the middle, with organisations referred to as 'interactive architects' that can offer a blend of skills and consultancy services. Merger and acquisition activity has been intense, mainly a reaction to rapid industry growth that was not capable of being sustained. The move towards what is referred to as 'integrated marketing communications' (see Chapter 4) has been accelerated by the greater efficiency and harmonisation that digital technology brings.

> The move towards 'integrated marketing communications' has been accelerated by the greater efficiency and harmonisation that digital technology brings.

Industry structure

The structure of the industry has changed through time. Some may argue that it has not changed enough, but the shape and size of the industry has developed. Over the last 20 years the size of the industry has increased in response to the growth in the number of marketing communications activities and with it the real value of advertising, sales promotion, public relations and direct marketing. The growth distribution among these tools has been variable, with only direct marketing showing consistent levels of real growth.

> The configuration of the agency-services industry partly reflects the moves made by the larger agencies to consolidate their positions.

The configuration of the agency-services industry partly reflects the moves made by the larger agencies to consolidate their positions. They have attempted to buy either smaller, often medium-sized competitors, in an attempt to protect their market share, or provide an improved range of services for their clients (see the next section on one-stop shopping). This has led to an industry characterised by a large number of very big agencies and an even larger number of very small agencies. These smaller agencies have formed as the result of people formerly employed in large agencies becoming frustrated with having to work within tight margins and increased administration, and leaving and setting up their own fledgling businesses. This is currently evident in the direct-marketing part of the industry, according to Billings (2004). She argues that there are now two distinct structural models emerging: those direct-marketing agencies that are attached to advertising agencies (for example: Elvis; Hall Moore CHI) and those that are entirely independent (for example: Barraclough Edwards Chamberlain; Keevill Lee Kershaw). This pattern was also observed in the 1990s when media-planning houses developed. Some were entirely independent and others, such as Zenith, were dependent upon a parent organisation.

The current preference for loose, independent networks has given some large organisations the ability to offer clients an improved range of services.

Although ownership has been an important factor driving industry development the current preference for loose, independent networks has given some large organisations the ability to offer clients an improved range of services (integrated marketing communications – IMC) and the small agencies a chance to work with some of the bigger accounts. Miln (2004) speculates that structural changes to the way in which clients and agencies work together may give rise to what he refers to as 'new agencies' that will provide a limited range of specific communications services, most commonly involved with the thinking around the creative or media elements, but will outsource or delegate the implementation to a third-party organisation. These organisations possess the core skills associated with project management and are better placed to fulfil this specialist role. The agency will remain responsible to the client for the implementation but is in a better position to continue advising about the overall communications strategy and media imperatives.

One-stop shopping

As with most industries, the structure of the communications industry has evolved in response to changes in the environment. However, if there is a 'holy grail' of communications it is an organisation's ability to offer clients a single point from which all of their integrated communications needs can be met. In search of this goal, WPP and Saatchi & Saatchi set about building the largest marketing communications empires in the world. According to Green (1991), Saatchi & Saatchi attempted to become the largest marketing services company in the world. The strategy adopted in the early 1980s was to acquire companies outside its current area of core competence, media advertising. Organisations in direct marketing, market research, sales promotion and public relations were brought under the Saatchi banner. By offering a range of services under a single roof, rather like a supermarket, the one-stop-shopping approach made intrinsic sense. Clients could put a package together, rather like eating from a buffet table, and solve a number of their marketing requirements – without the expense and effort of searching through each sector to find a company with which to work.

Green also refers to the WPP experience in the late 1980s. J. Walter Thompson and Ogilvy & Mather were grouped together under the umbrella of WPP, and it was felt that synergies were to be achieved by bringing together their various services. Six areas were identified: strategic marketing services, media advertising, public relations, market research, non-media advertising and specialist communications. A one-stop-shopping approach was advocated once again.

The recession of the early 1990s brought problems to both these organisations, as well as others. The growth had been built on acquisition, which was partly funded from debt. This required considerable interest payments, but the recession brought a sharp decline in the revenues of the operating companies, and cash-flow problems forced WPP and Saatchi & Saatchi to restructure their debt and their respective organisations. As Phillips (1991) points out, the financial strain and the complex task of managing operations on such a scale began to tell.

However, underpinning the strategy was the mistaken idea that clients actually wanted a one-stop-shopping facility. It was unlikely that the best value for money was going to be achieved through this, so it came as no surprise when clients began to question the quality of the services for which they were paying. There was no guarantee that they could obtain from one large organisation the best creative, production, media and marketing solutions to their problems. Many began to shop around and engage specialists in different organisations (à la carte) in an attempt to receive not only the best quality of service but also the best value for money. Evidence for this might be seen in the resurgence of the media specialists whose very existence depends on their success in media planning and buying.

> Underpinning the strategy was the mistaken idea that clients actually wanted a one-stop-shopping facility.

It is no wonder, then, that clients (and indeed many media people working in agencies who felt constrained decided to leave and set up on their own account) felt that full-service agencies were asking too much of their staff, not only in terms of providing a wide range of integrated-marketing services generally, but also in giving full attention and bringing sufficient expertise to bear in each of the specific services it has to offer (account management, creative, production, media research, etc.).

The debate about whether or not to use a full-service agency becomes even more crucial, perhaps, for those in specialist areas. For example, a large number of business-to-business communications agencies have been set up by people leaving full-service agencies. They spotted opportunities to provide specialist services in a market area that at the time was under-resourced, often marginalised or even ignored. In many ways it comes back to the quality of relationships. Arguments for the specialist agency are based upon the point that, while there may be some convergence of approaches between consumer-goods marketing and business-to-business advertising, it can be easier for a business-to-business advertising agency to do consumer advertising than it is to do the reverse.

As a general view, business-to-business shops survive on their ability to execute some very fundamental techniques for clients, such as direct mail or sales promotion. In contrast, the large, consumer-goods-oriented shops, whose traditional skills are market research, planning and media advertising, often lack the core skills, initiative or expertise to deliver business-to-business marketing services.

The same has been said of direct marketing, where there appears to be the same sort of disenchantment with the full-service agency. Criticisms include the exclusion of direct-marketing experts from presentations to clients, a lack of education among mainstream agency types as to what direct marketing actually does, or the complaint that clients don't want to be force-fed a direct-marketing subsidiary that may be incompetent or inappropriate. The experience of those involved in direct marketing has been further destabilised by the growth in the Internet. Direct mail has gained rather than lost because many online brands have used direct mail as offline promotion to drive website traffic. Telemarketing has flourished because call centres have repositioned themselves as multimedia contact centres and have extended their range of services.

> Clients can find an agency that can provide all of the required marketing communications services under one roof, or find a different agency for each of the services, or mix and match.

There is a spectrum of approaches for clients. They can find an agency that can provide all of the required marketing communications services under one roof, or find a different agency for each of the services, or mix and match. Clearly the first solution can be used only if the budget holder is convinced that the best level of service is being provided in *all* areas, and the second only if there are sufficient gains in efficiency (and savings in expenditure) to warrant the amount of additional time he or she would need to devote to the task of managing marketing communications.

One area that has experienced significant change has been media. Industry concentration and the development of global networks have shifted the structure and composition of the industry. Clients have responded by centralising their business into a single media-network agency in search of higher discounts and improved efficiency. As a general rule, the stronger the competitive forces, the lower the profitability in the market. An organisation needs to determine a competitive approach that will allow it to influence the industry's competitive rules, protect it from competitive forces as much as possible and give it a strong position from which to compete. The media networks have yet to find a competitive form of differentiation, although some are offering additional services as a way of trying to enhance brand identities (Griffiths, 2000).

It appears that the power of the media agencies, the low switching costs of buyers and the large threat of substitute products make this a relatively unattractive industry in its current form. Finer segmentation to determine markets that permit higher margins and a move to provide greater differentiation among agencies, together with a policy to reduce the threats from substitute products, perhaps through more visible alliances and partnerships, would enable the industry to recover its position and provide greater stability. It is interesting to note that many leading agencies have moved into strategic consultancy, away from the reliance on mass media, where a substantially higher margin can be generated. Many direct-marketing companies have evolved out of sales-promotion agencies. According to Goften (2000) both have tried to reposition themselves, with the sales-promotion houses adopting a wide variety of promotional activities and direct-marketing agencies moving their focus of business activity to one that is either oriented towards ecommerce or customer-relationship management.

Agency structures and IMC

The development of integrated marketing communications has been mentioned earlier in Chapter 4, and although the concept is subject to considerable debate and uncertainty the underlying good sense inherent in the concept has started to resonate with clients and agencies. As a result, the influence of IMC on agencies and clients should not be underestimated.

In order for messages to be developed and conveyed through an integrated approach, the underlying structure supporting this strategy needs to be reconsidered. Just as the structure of the industry had a major impact on the way in which messages were developed and communicated as the industry developed, so the structural underpinning needs to adapt to the new and preferred approaches of clients.

The structural underpinning needs to adapt to the new and preferred approaches of clients.

The use of outside agencies that possess the skills, expertise and purchasing advantages that are of value to clients is unlikely to change. However, the ways in which these outsourced skills are used and how they are structured has been changing. Aspects of client–agency relationships are important and are considered in the next chapter. What is important for this part of the text is a consideration of the way in which those organisations that provide outsourcing facilities and contribute to a client's IMC can be configured to provide optimal servicing and support. Gronstedt and Thorsen (1996) suggest several ways in which agencies could be configured to provide integrated marketing communications. They determined that there was a continuum of services. At one end there are highly centralised agencies that can provide a high level of integration, for a variety of communications disciplines, from within the agency itself. Staffed by generalists with no particular media bias, these organisations are structured according to client needs, not functional specialisms. High levels of integration are offered at the expense of in-depth and leading-edge knowledge in new and developing areas.

At the other end of the continuum are those providers that group themselves in the form of a network. Often led by a main advertising agency that has divested itself of expensive overheads, the independent yet interdependent network players each provide specialist skills under the leadership of the main contractor agency. One of the two main weaknesses associated with this model concerns the deficiency associated with communications across the players in the network. This horizontal aspect means that individual members of the network tend to identify with their own area of expertise and advance their specialism, possibly at the expense of the client's overriding requirements. The other main weakness concerns the transitory or temporary nature of a member organisation's involvement within such networks. Therefore, the level of potential integration is possibly weakest in this model, although the level of expertise available to clients is highest at this end of the continuum.

> The level of potential integration is possibly weakest in this model, although the level of expertise available to clients is highest at this end of the continuum.

One of the essential points emerging from this research is that there seems to be a trade-off between levels of integration and the expertise provided by different agencies. Clients who want to retain control over their brands and to find an integrated agency where all the required services are of the exact level and quality demanded may be expecting too much. The inevitability of this position is that clients may choose to select marketing communications expertise from a variety of sources, and the integrated agency may well lose out.

It is suggested therefore that clients who seek a campaign that draws on more than one marketing communications discipline have a basic choice of four main options. These are set out in Table 14.3.

Neither of these four approaches can provide a perfect solution, and the variety of integrated possibilities reflects different client structures and cultures and hence different needs and relationships that need to be satisfied (Murphy, 2004). The mini-group option is a relatively recent development and can include the use of product development, research, design and interactive services. This means that this approach serves a broad range of needs, typical of smaller client organisations whose budgets do not match those of mainstream firms. Furthermore, environmental factors should not be ignored,

TABLE 14.3 Integrated agency options

Type of agency	Explanation
Integrated agency	A single agency that provides the full range of communications disciplines from within.
Complementary agencies	The client selects a range of different agencies, each from a different discipline, and self-manages or appoints a lead agency.
Networked agencies	A single group agency is appointed (e.g. WPP or Interpublic), which then appoints agencies within its own profit-oriented network.
Mini-group agencies	Clusters of small, independent, specialist agencies that work on a non-competitive basis for a client.

and it may be that clients in the future will state their preferred structural requirements at the pitching or client-briefing stage of the agency–client relationship. Increasingly, agencies may well be required to mix and match their structures and provide structural flexibility to meet the varying needs of their clients.

A further point concerns global branding and the standardisation/adaptation debate when considered in the light of IMC. One argument is that standardisation is the only

> **One argument is that standardisation is the only way in which IMC can be achieved.**

way in which IMC can be achieved. However, as it is generally accepted that there are few examples of truly standardised global brands, does that suggest that IMC is not possible for global brands? A strong counter-view is that globalisation encourages integration where it matters, at the point of implementation. Furthermore, to have adaptation, there must be strong internal integration between head office (and business/marketing strategies) and those responsible for local adaptation and implementation. For example, Fielding (2000) shows that many Japanese and Korean advertising messages emphasise product-related information, whereas many Western brands require an emphasis on the development of brand personality and character. For IMC to succeed, a consistent core message and local or regional flavour need to be delivered if such a difference is to be overcome.

Client, agency and industry issues

New technology has led to changes in the balance of the tools used by many organisations. Most notably, those operating in the FMCG sector that spend vast sums on above-the-line media in order to develop brand values have begun to spend more below the line in an effort to impact on behaviour rather than just brand development. Direct marketing has also impacted on the advertising spend, and with the development of IMC and related concepts such as media-neutral planning the balance of the communications spend has moved towards either sales promotions and/or direct marketing.

The content of many marketing communications messages has therefore swung, and with it the work of advertising agencies. Agencies have had to adapt to a new environment, one in which clients expect their agencies to present strategies that involve a much broader range of tools and media and to offer new skills and resources. This has been achieved mainly through acquisition and the development of international networks of agencies, from all disciplines, pooling their talents in order to secure domestic and international business.

Tapp and Hughes (2004) refer to the impact of information systems and technology (IST) on the company–customer interface and on the internal processes and marketing resources within client companies. They report on the major impact IST has had internally and the struggle organisations have experienced coping with the disruption new technology has stimulated. In terms of marketing communications this disruption is potentially enormous. With websites becoming the focus of much internal communications activity, forces propelling ideas concerning the desire to integrate marketing communications, and planning and strategy processes having to accommodate uncertain industry, media and audience expectations, marketing communications has been severely buffeted by IST.

> **These changes should be seen positively, as a primary means of moving organisations forward.**

However, although the changes driven by new technology might bring about an unwelcome internal production focus, these changes should be seen positively, as a primary means of moving organisations forward. New technology can help organisations communicate more effectively and more efficiently, both internally and externally. By adopting a stronger customer focus, organisations can deliver improved levels of customer value and be better placed to meet their marketing goals and improve shareholder value.

Marketing communications budgets

Investment in advertising in 2004 grew 4.5 per cent on the previous year, and early in 2005 there were signs that investment in advertising was growing again after several years of relative stagnation. Within the sector online advertising has grown substantially in percentage terms, and is currently the fastest-growing medium.

This noticeable cutback in offline advertising expenditure when trading conditions tighten reflects the short-term orientation that some organisations have towards brand development or advertising. What is also of interest is the way in which the communications mix has been changing over the past 10–15 years. For many years the spend on media advertising dominated the promotional budget of consumer products and services. Then sales promotion became a strong influence, but spend on this tool has stagnated over the past few years. Now sponsorship, direct marketing and online activities show the greatest investment. The reasons for this shift are indicative of the increasing attention and accountability that management is attaching to the communications spend. Increasingly, marketing managers are being asked to justify the amounts they spend on their entire budgets, including advertising and sales promotion. Senior managers want to know the return they are getting for their promotional investments, in order that they meet their objectives and that scarce resources may be used more effectively in the future.

Some organisations have deliberately reallocated their budgets in order to make more funds available for price cutting and discounting.

In recent years some organisations have deliberately reallocated their budgets in order to make more funds available for price cutting and discounting. Procter and Gamble, Citröen, and Heinz are just some of the organisations that have made these decisions. The Royal Mail slashed its advertising budget in May 2004 (see ViewPoint 14.3).

ViewPoint 14.3   Slashed Mail

The Royal Mail announced in May 2004 that it was cutting back on its advertising by at least 40 per cent, approximately £8m. It also announced that it was postponing further marketing activities, including £5m assigned to promoting its Parcelforce brand. These cuts were made in the light of strikes the previous autumn, a series of reported financial losses and the reduction in headcount of about 350 staff.

The news of the reduction in communications spend coincided with a report from the industry watchdog Postwatch that over 14m items of post are lost each year.

Although the cuts affect a number of roster agencies and the brand was receiving poor publicity, the Royal Mail was under huge pressure to turn the operation around. Interestingly, in November 2004 the Royal Mail reported that its six-monthly results had shown a turnaround from a previous loss to a profit of £217m. So were the £8m cuts in advertising really necessary? Was it perhaps the need to avoid publicity when so many items were not being delivered?

It is not uncommon to find companies who are experiencing trading difficulties deciding to slash their adspend, if only on a temporary basis. Marks & Spencer and Sainsbury's have experienced difficulties but have either increased or maintained their above-the-line spend. According to Hall (1999), Procter and Gamble set 'strict guidelines about how much can be spent below the line if a brand's equity is to be maintained'. Research by Profit Impact on Market Strategy (PIMS) (Tylee, 1999; Tomkins, 1999) found that companies that maintain or even increase their adspend during a recession are likely to grow three times faster than those companies that cut the adspend when the economy turns round. The Renault Clio and the Nescafé Gold Blend brands were cited as examples of advertisers that had increased their investment during the last downturn and succeeded in increasing their profitability and market performance.

The role of the promotional budget

The role of the promotional budget is the same whether the organisation is a multi-national trading from numerous international locations, or a small manufacturing unit on an industrial estate outside a semi-rural community. Both organisations want to ensure that they achieve the greatest efficiency with each pound they allocate to promotional activities. Neither can afford to be profligate with scarce resources, and each is accountable to the owners of the organisation for the decisions it makes.

There are two broad decisions that need to be addressed. The first concerns how much of the organisation's available financial resources (or relevant part) should be allocated to promotion over the next period. The second concerns how much of the total amount should be allocated to each of the individual tools of the promotional mix.

> The second concerns how much of the total amount should be allocated to each of the individual tools of the promotional mix.

ViewPoint 14.4   What is the right level of spend?

Back in 1987 Nike's marketing president was pitching to the board for a revised advertising budget. The previous year Nike spent $8m and the marketing chief wanted to raise this to $34m, an astronomical increase, particularly for a company that was just getting going. The CEO, Philip Knight, turned to the marketing man and asked the question, 'How do I know if you are asking for enough?'

Source: Holmes (2004)

There are four main stakeholder groups that contribute to the budget decision. These are the focus organisation, any communication agencies, the media whose resources will be used to carry the designated messages and the target audience. It is the ability of these four main stakeholders to collaborate effectively that will impact most upon the communications budget. However, determining the 'appropriate appropriation' is a frustrating exercise for the marketing communications manager. The allocation of scarce resources across a promotional budget presents financial and political difficulties, especially where the returns are difficult to identify. The development and significance of technology within marketing can lead to disputes concerning ownership and the control of resources. For example, in many companies management of and responsibility for the website rests with the IT department, which understandably takes a technological view of issues. Those in marketing, however, see the use of the website from a marketing perspective and need a budget to manage it. Tension between the two can result in different types of website design and effectiveness, and this leads to different levels of customer perception and support.

Readers may have noticed that the terms 'spend' and 'investment' have been used alternatively in this chapter. Conventional terminology refers to adspend, but the word *spend* suggests that communications represents a cost and as such is reflected in the profit and loss account. Increasingly, communication is understood to represent an investment and as such should be capable of measurement in terms of the return that the investment generates on the balance sheet. Although there is certain disagreement about how and what represents a suitable return, the idea that marketing communications is an investment is one that should be encouraged.

> Increasingly, communication is understood to represent an investment.

Techniques and approaches

Marginal analysis is the main theoretical approach to setting optimal budgets. This determines the point at which maximum returns are achieved based on an extra unit of investment in promotional activities. The main problem with this approach is that it has little practical application because the data to run the analysis is either non-existent in many organisations or insufficient to withstand the analysis. It is not surprising, therefore, that other, more practical approaches have been developed. These are set out in Table 14.4.

Competitive parity

In certain markets, such as the relatively stable fast-moving consumer goods (FMCG) market, many organisations use promotional appropriation as a competitive tool. The underlying assumption is that advertising is the only direct variable that influences sales. The argument is based on the point that while there are many factors that impact on sales, these factors are all self-cancelling. Each factor impacts upon all the players in the market. The only effective factor is the amount that is spent on planned communications. As a result, some organisations deliberately spend the same amount on advertising as their competitors spend: competitive parity.

Competitive parity has a major benefit for the participants. As each organisation knows what the others are spending and while there is no attempt to destabilise the market through excessive or minimal promotional spend, the market avoids self-generated turbulence and hostile competitive activity.

There are, however, a number of disadvantages with this simple technique. The first is that, although information is available, there is a problem of comparing like with like. For example, a carpet manufacturer selling a greater proportion of output into the trade will require different levels and styles of advertising and promotion from another manufacturer selling predominantly to the retail market. Furthermore, the first organisation may be diversified, perhaps importing floor tiles. The second may be operating in a totally unrelated market. Such activities make comparisons difficult to establish, and financial decisions based on such analyses are highly dubious.

TABLE 14.4 Practical approaches to setting promotional budgets

Budget-setting methods	Explanation
Arbitrary	This approach is based on a guess made by the chairman or CEO. Very often the budget is decided on the hoof, and as each demand for communications resources arrives so decisions are made in isolation from any overall strategy. Not recommended.
Inertia	This approach directs that the same amount as last time is spent. Here, all elements of the environment and the costs associated with the tasks facing the organisation are ignored. Not recommended.
Media multiplier	Here, last year's spend is increased by the rate at which media costs have increased. Not recommended.
Percentage of sales	This requires a budget to be set at a level equal to a predetermined percentage of past or expected sales. More market-oriented organisations invariably select a percentage that is traditional to the organisation, such as 'we always aim to spend 5 per cent of our sales on advertising'. Not recommended.
Affordable	This requires that each unit of output is allocated a proportion of all the input costs and all the costs associated with the value-adding activities in production and manufacturing, together with all the other costs in distributing the output. After making an allowance for profit, what is left is to be spent on advertising and communication. In other words, what is left is what we can afford to spend. Not recommended.
Objective and task	This approach attempts to determine the resources required to achieve each marketing communications objective. For example, the costs associated with buying a DM list, for the creative, envelope and mailing, for the telemarketing follow-up, plus costs for sales promotion and public relations and campaign analysis, are aggregated into an overall budget. Recommended.

The competitive-parity approach fails to consider the qualitative aspects of the advertising undertaken by the different players. Each attempts to differentiate itself, and very often the promotional messages are one of the more important means of successfully positioning an organisation. It would not be surprising, therefore, to note that there is probably a great range in the quality of the planned communications. Associated with this is the notion that, when attempting to adopt different positions, the tasks and costs will be different, so seeking relative competitive parity may be an inefficient use of resources. The final point concerns the data used in such a strategy. The data are historical and based on strategies relevant at the time. Competitors may well have embarked upon a new strategy since the data were released. This means that parity would not only be inappropriate for all the reasons previously listed, but also because the strategies are incompatible.

Advertising-to-sales ratio

An interesting extension of the competitive-parity principle is the notion of advertising-to-sales (A/S) ratios. Instead of simply seeking to spend a relatively similar amount

This approach attempts to account for the market shares held by the different players and to adjust promotional investment accordingly.

on promotion as one's main competitors, this approach attempts to account for the market shares held by the different players and to adjust promotional investment accordingly.

If it is accepted that there is a direct relationship between the volume of advertising (referred to as weight) and sales, then it is not unreasonable to conclude that if an organisation invests more on advertising then it will see a proportionate improvement in sales. The underlying principle of the A/S ratio is that, in each industry, it is possible to determine the average advertising spend of all the players and compare it with the value of the market. Therefore, it is possible for each organisation to determine its own A/S ratio and compare it with the industry average. Those organisations with an A/S ratio below the average may conclude either that they have advertising economies of scale working in their favour or that their advertising is working much harder, pound for pound, than some of their competitors. Organisations can also use A/S ratios as a means of controlling expenditure across multiple product areas. Budgets can be set based upon the industry benchmark, and variances quickly spotted and further information requested to determine shifts in competitor spend levels or reasons leading to any atypical performance.

Each business sector has its own characteristics, which in turn influence the size of the advertising expenditure. In 2003 the A/S ratio for soaps and shower gels was 12.07 per cent, baby foods 0.53 per cent, butter 2.06 per cent, facial skincare 17.94 per cent, hair colourants 18.58 per cent and washing up/dishwasher products 9.95 per cent (Advertising Association, 2005). It can be seen that the size of the A/S ratio can vary widely. It appears to be higher (that is, a greater proportion of revenue is used to invest in advertising) when the following are present:

1. The offering is standardised, not customised.
2. There are many end-users.
3. The financial risk for the end-user customer is small.
4. The marketing channels are short.
5. A premium price is charged.
6. There is a high gross margin.
7. The industry is characterised by surplus capacity.
8. Competition is characterised by a high number of new-product launches.

A/S ratios provide a useful benchmark for organisations when they are trying to determine the adspend level.

A/S ratios provide a useful benchmark for organisations when they are trying to determine the adspend level. These ratios do not set out what the promotional budget should be, but they do provide a valuable indicator around which broad commercial decisions can be developed.

Share of voice

Brand strategy in the FMCG market has traditionally been based upon an approach that uses mass-media advertising to drive brand awareness, which in turn allows premium pricing to fund the advertising investment (cost). The alternative approach has been to use price-based promotions to drive market share, though this latter approach has often been regarded as a short-term approach that is incapable of sustaining a brand over the longer term.

The concept underlying the A/S ratio can be seen in the context of rival supporters chanting at a football match. If they chant at the same time, at the same decibel rating, then it is difficult to distinguish the two sets of supporters, particularly if they are chanting the same song. Should one set of supporters shout at a lower decibel rating, then the collective voice of the other supporters would be the one that the rest of the crowd, and perhaps any television audience, actually hears and distinguishes.

This principle applies to the concept of share of voice (SOV). Within any market the total of all advertising investments, that is, all the advertising by all the players, can be analysed in the context of the proportions each player has made to the total. Should one advertiser invest more than any other then it will be its messages that are received and stand a better chance of being heard and acted upon. In other words, its SOV is the greater. This implies, of course, that the quality of the message transmitted is not important and that it is the sheer relative weight of adinvestment that is the critical factor.

This concept can be taken further and combined with another, share of market (SOM). When a brand's market share is equal to its share of advertising spend, equilibrium is said to have been reached (SOV = SOM).

Ethical issues in marketing communications[1]

Just as organisations send messages about their identity through both formal and informal ways, so organisations send messages, partially through marketing communications, about their attitude and stance on ethical issues. As ethical issues are becoming increasingly prominent so organisations are attempting to become more actively involved in addressing the ethical consequences of their marketing communications (Christy, 2005, p. 88).

Issues about matters that may be right or wrong are manifest in a wide range of marketing communications activities. The way an organisation attends to its duties and responsibilities, the extent to which it plans and considers the consequences of its actions before acting provides a broad measure of its overall attitude towards all of its stakeholders and associated environments. This is referred to as corporate and social responsibility (CSR) and is fast becoming a key agenda item for many organisations.

> There are three main theoretical approaches to CSR, each of which reflects an organisation's perspective of to whom it is primarily responsible.

There are three main theoretical approaches to CSR, each of which reflects an organisation's perspective of to whom it is primarily responsible. The *shareholder* approach suggests that an organisation's actions should be considered in terms of its ability to satisfy shareholders. The *stakeholder* approach recognises the influence of a wider array of stakeholders or constituencies, and the *societal* approach accepts the role organisations play in the fabric and expectations of society. Whichever of these approaches are adopted, the role of marketing communications within CSR is still wide and its use, therefore, should be carefully considered (managed), especially in an era of integrated marketing communications. Some of the different ways in which ethical issues can be considered in this context are listed in Table 14.5.

[1] The author wishes to acknowledge the work of Richard Christy from whose chapter in Fill (2006) much of this material on ethics has been adapted.

TABLE 14.5 Some of the ethical issues in marketing communications

Issue	Explanation
Truth-telling	The use of advertising and public relations to mislead or misrepresent a product, person, object or organisation.
Taste and decency	The use of marketing communications to deliberately shock audiences. Often achieved through the use of tasteless, vulgar or indecent material in unusual or unexpected contexts.
Vulnerability	The use of marketing communications to influence particular audiences who are unable to protect themselves or understand the issues at hand.
Pressure	The use of unorthodox and unacceptable sales techniques designed to overwhelm and manipulate audiences (often vulnerable groups).
Privacy	The disregard for an individual's privacy typified through unsolicited telesales calls, unwelcome direct mail and spam.
Confusion	The use of marketing communications designed to confuse audiences rather than inform and support them. Sometimes referred to as confusion marketing, this approach has been claimed to work in the financial services industry, where many of the products are complex and require considerable thought.
Bribery and inducements	This covers a wide area, including the payment of bribes to win business, decision-making by individual sales managers that may not be in the longer-term interests of the organisation and the use of hospitality.

The importance of context

The importance of context in judging ethical behaviour can be seen in the debate in the UK over the problems arising from the selling of private pensions during the 1980s. In many cases customers were persuaded by salespeople to switch out of existing pension schemes into new schemes whose subsequent performance left them worse off. In these cases the complex nature of the services, together with the unfamiliarity of many of the customers with the various types of product and how to choose between them, led them to place an unusually great reliance on the advice provided by the salesperson. Put another way, the extent to which the buyer was foreseeably *able* to 'beware' in these cases was very limited, which in turn should have placed a greater than normal ethical duty on the salesperson to ensure that customers were properly informed of the consequences and implications of the switch. The fact that these ethical standards were clearly not met in a large number of cases has caused a great deal of loss, anxiety and inconvenience for the customers who lost out, but also a great deal of difficulty, expense and embarrassment for the pensions industry as a whole.

A further critical contextual element concerns the relationship between buyer and seller. In relational exchanges, value for all parties is rooted in the maintenance of trust and commitment, so the communications and associated expectations used in relational exchanges will be different from those used in transactional exchanges. A customer might, for example, feel upset if a car salesperson with whom he had dealt for many years failed to tell him that the model he was buying was about to be superseded, because that would seem to be inconsistent with the trust built up over the years. The

ViewPoint 14.5   Pension confusion

Diacon and Ennew (1996) point out that marketing transactions in financial services have greater than normal potential for ethical complications. The unavoidable complexity of many financial services products is heightened by the fact that the evaluation may depend upon individual calculations carried out for the customer by the salesperson; furthermore, risk for the customer may be significant, in that the actual benefits received will often depend upon the performance of the economy over a long period. The authors highlight a number of other ethical issues relevant to insurance selling, including:

● the issue of 'fitness for purpose' in both the design of the products and the way in which they are matched to customer needs;

● the transparency of the price for these products, such that any commissions payable to the intermediary organisation or individual salesperson are clearly visible;

● the need for truth in promotion, not only in terms of strict factual correctness, but also in terms of what the consumer might be expected to understand from a phrase;

● the effect of the sales targeting and reward systems of the selling organisation on the behaviour of salespeople, particularly in view of the important advisory component of this type of selling.

The serious problems arising from the selling of personal pensions during the 1980s provide an example of how important it is for businesses to maintain an active awareness of the likely effects of their actions. It is difficult to escape the conclusion that a more enlightened assessment of the long-term interests of the business on the part of financial service providers would have helped to avert many of the problems, to the great benefit of all involved. This is easy to conclude with hindsight: the effective ethical businesses are those that manage to cultivate this type of *foresight*.

same customer might not be at all upset to find the same thing happen with a personal computer bought from a discount store in London, not only because computers are known to date more quickly than models of cars, but also because there was no long-term relationship to be brought into question.

ViewPoint 14.6   Types of public complaint

The annual report of the Advertising Standards Authority (ASA) provides a crude barometer of public attitudes towards advertising images.

For example, in its commentary on complaints received in 2003, the ASA pointed out that the number of complaints received had increased to a record level of 14,277, 2.3 per cent higher than for 2002. The ten most complained-about campaigns were responsible for about 11 per cent of these complaints. Complaints about misleading claims in adverts were the most frequent type of complaint, though complaints about matters of taste and decency rose by 18 per cent over 2002 to become the second largest category of complaint. Reflecting developments in communications technology, a fast-growing category of complaint concerned advertising sent by email or SMS: the Internet is now the fifth most-complained-about medium, ahead of regional press. On the other hand, the report gives details of a number of cases in which the ASA had decided that the complaint was 'not justified' – six of the ten most-complained-about campaigns had received this verdict.

Source: ASA website (http://www.asa.org.uk/); accessed 5 January 2005

Regulating marketing communications

It should be clear that a range of marketing communications activities have ample opportunity to mislead or offend, or, at another level, individuals might be subject to more severe distress such as physical injury, psychological suffering or perhaps financial loss. It is important, therefore, to have in place a system that provides a measure of control over the industry, one that regulates marketing communications activities in order to protect and serve society in ways that are regarded as appropriate.

> It is important, therefore, to have in place a system that provides a measure of control over the industry, one that regulates marketing communications activities.

Regulation is managed through a blend of two main approaches. One is based on legislation, that is, the use of law to provide a legal boundary for what is and what is not permitted. The second approach is based on a set of voluntary codes and processes, run by members of the marketing industry. Although the voluntary codes are used to manage day-to-day questions, Harker's (1998) review of approaches to regulation in five countries suggests that a combination of both legal and voluntary approaches can work effectively to regulate the marketing communications industry.

In the United Kingdom, a major change to the regulation of marketing communications was introduced from November 2004. The main thrust of the reform was to introduce a 'one-stop shop' for consumer complaints, with the Advertising Standards Authority taking responsibility for advertising content regulation in both broadcast and non-broadcast advertising (the former by delegation from Ofcom, the general regulator for the communications industry, and the latter by continuance of the ASA's former role). For this purpose the ASA, which will continue to be funded by levies from advertising, will administer a set of codes of advertising practice for the various types of advertising (see www.asa.org.uk for further details). The new system is aimed at providing clearer arrangements for consumers, as well as a better and more consistent structure for dealing with the much more diverse range of communications media that has developed in recent years.

> The new system is aimed at providing clearer arrangements for consumers, as well as a better and more consistent structure for dealing with the much more diverse range of communications media.

Although Ofcom retains backstop powers over the new arrangements for broadcast advertising, the system remains effectively self-regulatory in approach, building on the ASA's four decades of experience as the regulator of non-broadcast advertising content. Strictly speaking, the new system is co-regulatory rather than self-regulatory, in that Ofcom, with its statutory powers, has delegated the responsibility for maintaining and applying codes of practice approved by the regulator (see www.ofcom.org.uk).

Self-regulation

In the UK, a range of specialised codes have been developed to provide guidance on the production of acceptable marketing communications in particular circumstances. The website of the Advertising Standards Authority (http://www.asa.org.uk) provides access to full-text versions of these codes. The ASA's main code for non-broadcast advertising (the Code of Advertising, Sales Promotion and Direct Marketing, published by the Committee of Advertising Practice) begins with a set of general principles. The first two in particular set the tone for the whole code:

- *All marketing communications should be legal, decent, honest and truthful.*

- *All marketing communications should be prepared with a sense of responsibility to con-sumers and to society.*

(ASA Code of Advertising, Sales Promotion and Direct Marketing (2003, p. 6).)

The general rules of the Code discuss the requirements of legality, decency, honesty and truthfulness in more detail and also provide guidance on, for example, the protection of privacy, the use of testimonials and endorsements, on competitor comparisons and product availability.

Later sections of the main Code focus on sales promotion (sections 27–40) and direct marketing (sections 41–45), with guidance on specific issues such as free offers and free trials (section 32) and the increasingly important area of database practice (section 43). The Code also offers detailed guidance on specific marketing communications contexts, such as alcoholic drinks, children, motoring, health and beauty products and therapies, weight control, financial products and tobacco.

Besides the advice and guidance, it defines the processes through which advertisers should comply with the Code and the sanctions that can be applied. A key aim of the Code is to help those in the industry to produce 'marketing communications that are welcomed and trusted' (p. 3).

Since the broadening of its responsibilities in 2004, the ASA also now maintains a range of codes on broadcast advertising:

- The Radio Advertising Standards Code

- The TV Advertising Standards Code

- The Alcohol Advertising Rules

- Advertising Guidance Notes (concerning, for example, the identification of programmes likely to appeal to children and young people)

- Rules on the Scheduling of Advertising

- Code for Text Services

- Guidance on Interactive TV.

As can be seen from this list, the self-regulatory regime is having to encompass the technology-fuelled proliferation of broadcast entertainment and information services. Keeping up to date with this rapid development, as well as remaining sensitive to changes in public sensitivity or taste, is a major challenge for any organisation, and the ASA's library of advertising codes can be expected to continue to evolve in the future.

Summary of key points

1. This chapter has attempted to examine the complex world of the marketing communications industry. Its huge size, diversity, and independent and specialist structure contribute to issues concerning its regulation, development and dynamics.

2. There are four main sectors that make up the core of the marketing communications industry: clients, agencies, production houses and the media. Between them, and supported in various ways by other stakeholders such as the public, the government and shareholders, they interact to generate streams of different messages designed to influence a variety of customer and other stakeholder groups.

3. Communications agencies have evolved in various ways, all designed to meet their clients' needs. They are characterised by their inherent focus on a single marketing

communications discipline. Currently, ideas concerning the provision of the full range of marketing communications services, informally referred to as one-stop shopping, continues to attract interest.

4. Clients use a variety of methods in order to budget for the use of marketing communications. No one single approach can be said to be totally correct and practice suggests that a number of methods should be used, including objective and task approaches.

5. Ethical issues are becoming increasingly prominent, and many organisations are attempting to become more actively involved in addressing the ethical consequences of their marketing communications activities. Concern about telling the truth, their attitude towards vulnerable groups, respect and concern for individual privacy, ensuring all communications are tasteful and decent and that the use of inducements to clients, sales personnel and others are transparent and appropriate, are some of the more obvious areas towards which organisations should direct their attention.

6. The regulation of marketing communications is generally undertaken through a blend of statutory measures, imposed by the government, or voluntary codes, coordinated and implemented by the industry itself, otherwise referred to as self-regulation.

Review questions

1. You have been asked to prepare brief notes for a presentation to be given during an interview for a job with a blue-chip company of your choice. You have to explain the constitution of the marketing communications industry in your country and to select and explore three issues that are of significant concern to the industry.

2. To what extent has new technology impacted on the marketing communications industry?

3. How might an organisation determine the sum to be spent on marketing communications, and how might that sum be apportioned between the various activities available?

4. Choose four product categories and find out their A/S ratios. How have these changed over the past 10 years?

5. How can an organisation best acquaint itself with the relevant controls in a chosen area of marketing communications?

6. Explain how the introduction of Ofcom has changed the way in which the UK industry is regulated.

References

Advertising Association (2005), *Advertising Statistics Year Book*, Henley-on-Thames: NTC.

Billings, C. (2004), 'DM's new wave', *Campaign*, 7 September. Retrieved from http://www.brandrepublic.com/news/newsArticle.cfm.

Christy, R. (2006), 'Ethics in Marketing Communications', in C. Fill, *Marketing Communications: engagement, strategies and practice*, 4th edn, Harlow: FT Prentice Hall.

Diacon, S.R. and Ennew, C.T. (1996), 'Ethical issues in insurance marketing in the UK', *European Journal of Marketing*, **30**(5), pp. 67–80.

Earnshaw, M. (2005), 'New year, new challenges', *Marketing*, 5 January, p. 10.

Fielding, S. (2000), 'Developing global brands in Asia', *Admap*, June, pp. 26–9.

Fill, C. (2006), *Marketing Communications: engagement, strategies and practice*, 4th edn, Harlow: FT Prentice Hall.

Finch, M. (2000), 'How to choose the right marketing agency', *Admap*, October, pp. 46–7.

Goften, K. (2000), 'Mergers shake up DM and SP groups', *Agency 2001 Marketing Report 13*, 30 November, pp. 15–16.

Goften, K. (2004), 'Top 85 direct marketing agencies', *Marketing*, 25 March, pp. 25–31.

Green, A. (1991), 'Death of the full-service ad agency?', *Admap*, January, pp. 21–4.

Griffiths, A. (2000), 'More than a media network', *Campaign Report*, 20 October, pp. 3–4.

Gronstedt, A. and Thorsen, E. (1996), 'Five approaches to organise an integrated marketing communications agency', *Journal of Advertising Research*, March/April, pp. 48–58.

Hall, E. (1999), 'When advertising becomes an expensive luxury', *Campaign*, 10 December, p. 18.

Harker, D. (1998), 'Achieving acceptable advertising: an analysis of advertising regulation in five countries', *International Marketing Review*, **15**(2), pp. 101–18.

Holmes, S. (2004), 'What happened to "just do it"?', *Independent on Sunday*, 12 September, pp. 8–9.

Miln, D. (2004), 'New marketing, new agency?', *Admap*, **39**(7) (July/August), pp. 47–8.

Murphy, C. (2004), 'Small but perfectly formed?', *Marketing*, 15 December, p. 12.

Murphy, D. (2000), 'New media's year of good fortunes', *Agency 2001 Marketing Report 13*, 30 November, p. 33.

Phillips, W. (1991), 'From bubble to rubble', *Admap*, April, pp. 14–19.

Tapp, A. and Hughes, T. (2004), 'New technology and the changing role of marketing', *Marketing Intelligence and Planning*, **22**(3), pp. 284–96.

Tomkins, R. (1999), 'If the return is right, keep spending', *Financial Times*, 19 March, p. 8.

Tylee, J. (1999), 'Survey warns against adspend cuts', *Campaign*, 12 March, p. 10.

Agency operations: selection, personnel and practice

15

Aims and objectives

The aims of this chapter are to explore the operations and processes associated with and used by communications agencies. In addition, consideration is given to the key roles and procedures relating to these operations and the ways in which agencies interact with clients. There are four primary topics in this chapter:

Agency selection, Operations, Briefing, Remuneration

The learning objectives are to enable readers to:

1. explain the role of communications agencies within the marketing communications industry;

2. consider the processes and criteria clients should use when selecting an agency;

3. describe the key agency personnel and their associated roles;

4. explain how the briefing processes work during the development of campaigns;

5. examine ways in which new technology can be used by agencies to improve performance;

6. describe ways in which agencies are remunerated by their clients.

Introduction

One of the many decisions an organisation has to make is whether to employ people on a permanent basis, recruit temporary workers as demand requires or use specialists on a continuous or ad hoc basis. Most organisations use a mixture of these different types and adjust the balance between them according to trading and other environmental factors. With regard to marketing communications, organisations can do it themselves and develop what is called an in-house facility. This provides a good level of control over the tools, messages and media used, and can improve on the speed of decision-making compared with using an outside agency. On the other hand it increases fixed costs, reduces flexibility and introduces political dimensions, often around budgets, which tend to deflect from objectivity and creativity. Perhaps the most critical dimension concerns the lack of access to expertise.

Perhaps the most critical dimension concerns the lack of access to expertise.

In an age where integration is a popular concept, it is important to have access to experts in the various communications disciplines. It is extremely unlikely that such experts can be readily found in-house. Having said this, many retail and business-to-business organisations choose to use in-house facilities.

An alternative route is to use freelancers or self-employed consultants. Although each individual's skills may have been developed within a particular discipline, such as public relations or advertising, freelancers can provide flexibility and access to some experts through their network of personal contacts. However, it should be remembered that the use of freelancers and in-house facilities requires use of the client organisation's resources, if only to manage the freelancers.

The use of agencies is popular because they can provide objectivity and access to expertise and specialist technologies, and at the same time allow the client to concentrate on its core business activities.

The use of agencies is popular because they can provide objectivity and access to expertise and specialist technologies, and at the same time allow the client to concentrate on its core business activities. Indeed, this is the route taken by the vast majority of organisations, which regard the use of communications agencies in the same way as they do accountants, consultants, lawyers and other professionals. By outsourcing these activities, organisations buy experts whose specialist services can be used as and when required. This flexibility has proved to be both efficient and effective for both client and agency. However, the decision to use an agency leads to further decisions concerning which type of agency and what it is required to do, how many agencies should be used and what role the client should play in the relationship with the agency.

These may sound strange questions but consider the question of strategy. Should the client decide on the marketing communications, branding and positioning strategies or is this a part of the agency's tasks? Different client organisations will adopt different positions depending upon their experience, size and the nature of the task that needs to be undertaken. Another question concerns whether a single agency is required to deliver integrated marketing communications activities, whether a single agency should manage the integration process and subcontract tasks to other specialist or group-based agencies (and in doing so act as lead agency) or whether a series of specialist agencies should be appointed, each reporting directly to the client who then needs to marshal the effort and act as ringleader.

Agency selection

In the areas that have traditionally dominated marketing communications, advertising and sales promotion, there has never been a shortage of advice on how to select an agency. Articles informing readers how to select an agency (Young and Steilen, 1996; Woolgar, 1998; Finch, 2000; McKee, 2004) appear regularly, and there are a large number of publications and organisations to assist in the process. However, agency selection is normally part of a review process, one in which the client wants to consider new creative and media ideas. Agency reviews are very often triggered by the appointment of a new marketing manager/director who wants to change strategy and establish their approach as soon as possible. Other reasons include concerns about brand positioning or the quality or appropriateness of the creative work, or there may have been a general deterioration in the relationship between key client and agency personnel. This decline is often caused by disagreements about budgets or remuneration. Anyway, the difference between review and selection is that in a review the current agency may be invited to pitch for the account, whereas a client going into the agency-selection process normally suggests that the incumbent agency has lost the account.

> Agency selection is normally part of a review process, one in which the client wants to consider new creative and media ideas.

ViewPoint 15.1   Direct Line agency selection

In August 2004 Direct Line, a major insurance company, was thought to have called for a review of its £40 million advertising account. It shortlisted four agencies for the pitch and did not invite its current agency to bid for the work, with whom it had worked for eight years.

Recent work by the incumbent agency had not been received well by everyone and was thought to have contributed to the decision to change agency. Direct Line was seeking to launch a major brand campaign, increasing its adspend by 15 per cent.

Source: Adapted from Whitehead (2004)

The process of selecting an agency that is set out below appears to be rational and relatively straightforward. Readers should be aware that the reality is that the process is infused with political and personal issues, some of which can be contradictory. Logically the process commences with a *search*, undertaken to develop a list of potential candidates. This is accomplished by referring to publications such as *Campaign Portfolio* and the *Advertising Agency Roster*, viewing samples of agency work available such as *DigiReels*, together with personal recommendations. The latter is perhaps the most potent and influential of these sources. As many as ten agencies can be included at this stage, although six or seven are to be expected.

Next, the client will visit each of the short-listed candidates in what is referred to as a *credentials presentation*. This is a crucial stage in the process, as it is now that the agency is evaluated for its degree of fit with the client's expectations and requirements. Agencies could develop their websites to fulfil this role, which would save time and costs. The agency's track record, resources, areas of expertise and experience can all be

ViewPoint 15.2   Making agency selection easier

In 2003 discussion began among advertising industry groups (1,500 agencies and 500 clients in the UK) to develop a single database to provide a central online source of information designed to improve the process of finding an ad agency.

Some of the industry's leading websites, including AdForum, ISBA, the Marketing Society, IPA, Media Guardian and Brand Republic, would provide access to the database. Users will be able to view a range of agency credentials and information, plus creative work including TV commercials, print ads, radio, mail packs, discipline-specialist campaigns and interactive work. Creative showreels are also planned with sites carrying text, video and still images, with some ads played live.

Agency profiles can be uploaded and managed online by clicking a button on any of the participating sites to access a data input tool. Agencies need only update their details once to ensure that they reach all UK clients.

This facility should allow client organisations to benchmark their own work on a regular basis, and agency credentials can be considered online as part of the selection process.

made available on the Internet, from which it should be possible to short-list three or possibly four agencies for the next stage in the process: the pitch.

In the PR industry agencies are selected to pitch on the basis of the quality and experience of the agency people, its image and reputation and relationships with existing clients. In addition, Pawinska (2000) reports that the track record of the agency and the extent of its geographical coverage are also regarded as important.

To be able to make a suitable bid the agencies are given a brief that documents information about the client, its markets and the communication task. These agencies are then required to make a formal presentation (the *pitch*) to the client some 6–8 weeks later. This presentation is about how the agency would approach the strategic and creative issues and the account is awarded to whichever agency produces the most suitable proposal. Suitability is a relative term, and a range of factors needs to be considered when selecting an organisation to be responsible for a large part of a brand's visibility. See Table 15.1.

> These agencies are then required to make a formal presentation (the *pitch*) to the client.

The appointment of a communications agency represents the formation of a new strategic alliance, so a strong understanding of the strategic objectives of both parties is necessary, as is an appreciation of the structure and culture of the two organisations. The selection process is a bringing together of two organisations whose expectations may be different but whose cooperative behaviour is essential for these expectations to have any chance of materialising. For example, agencies must have access to comprehensive and often commercially confidential data about products and markets if they are to operate efficiently. Otherwise, they cannot provide the service that is expected. However, it should be noted that pitches are not mandatory and, as Jones (2004) reports, nearly a third of clients move their accounts without involving pitches. One of the reasons for this is the increasing cost involved in running the whole process, as much as £50,000 according to Jones.

> The immediate selection process is finalised when terms and conditions are agreed.

The immediate selection process is finalised when terms and conditions are agreed and the winner is announced to the contestants and made public, often through trade journals such as *Campaign*, *Marketing* and *Marketing Week*.

TABLE 15.1 Key criteria for agency selection

Criteria	Explanation
Industry knowledge and experience	Has the agency significant knowledge and expertise in the client's market? Does it understand the environment in which the client operates?
Conflict of interest	Has the agency another client who is a competitor and that may give rise to a conflict of interest?
International experience and skills	Has the agency sufficient experience or contacts in order to operate successfully in international markets?
Chemistry	Is there a feel-good factor between the agency team and the client? Are the interpersonal relationships likely to be positive?
Costs and contractual terms	Is the agency likely to work within the budget constraints? Does it have a history of overspending? Are the contract terms workable?
Staff credentials	Are the agency staff sufficiently trained and are they experienced enough to manage the account? Do they possess any outstanding features or specialisations that might be of benefit to the client: for example, new media knowledge?
Networking	Is the agency an independent or part of a wider group? Is there access to specialist communications skills, and how will integration be managed?
Size of agency	Is the agency so large that it treats the client as just one of the many or is it of sufficient size to regard the client as a prestige account?
Prestige	Has the agency a track record of success, has it won any awards and how is it regarded by its peers?

This formalised process is now being questioned as to its suitability. The arrival of new media companies and their need to find communications solutions in one rather than eight weeks has meant that new methods have had to be found. In addition, agencies felt that they were having to invest a great deal in a pitch with little or no reward if the pitch failed. Their response has been to ask for payment to pitch, which has not been received well by many clients. Tension arises in that each agency is required to generate creative ideas over which they have little control once a pitch has been lost. The pitching process also gives little insight into the probable working relationships, as it is very often led by senior managers who will not be involved in the day-to-day operations. One solution adopted by Iceland and Dyson (Jardine, 2000) has been to invite agencies to discuss mini-briefs. These are essentially discussion topics about related issues rather than the traditional challenge about how to improve a brand's performance. By issuing the mini-brief on the day it eliminates weeks of preparation and associated staff costs, and enables the client to see agency teams working together.

ViewPoint 15.3   Bring in the consultants

Rather than undertake the agency selection process alone and independently an alternative approach is to appoint a consulting firm. Having taken a detailed brief the agency-selection consultants will then search, filter, negotiate and partially contract with appropriate agencies before shortlisting and recommending an agency to their client. It was reported in September 2005 that one such specialist organisation, the Haystack Group, had helped create a small network of similar agencies in Europe, with the intention of offering a global service. Called SCAN International, the network organisation offers consultancy services to international advertisers who wish to appoint a single agency to handle their pan-European or global advertising work. These types of organisations offer clients the opportunity to outsource agency selection, remuneration, management and evaluation services, all of which are non-core activities.

Source: Adapted from Barrett (2005)

Agency personnel

There are many roles within communications agencies and although the titles may vary according to type of agency, the principal tasks are essentially the same. The key roles are account executive (or manager), account planner, the creative team, media planners and media buyers.

Most communications agencies are generally organised on a functional basis. That is, they are organised according to the job function and its hierarchical position relative to campaign development and customer satisfaction. There have been moves to develop matrix structures where there are two lines of reporting. This has proved to be quite inefficient, however, and the low margins that agencies work on (contrary to popular belief) prohibit the luxury of matrix structures.

A full-service agency consists of several departments, all of which contribute to the development of a client's campaign.

A full-service agency consists of several departments, all of which contribute to the development of a client's campaign. Apart from the obvious need for human resources and finance departments, the main departments are designated for planning campaigns, creating messages and planning and buying media, plus departments that manage the production of communication pieces such as artwork, videos, roughs or mailers. This is sometimes referred to as traffic management.

The account executive (or manager)

The account executive, often referred to as account handler or manager, has a key representational role in the client/agency relationship. The account executive is responsible for representing the interests of the client within the agency and for ensuring that all those working on the client's account are fully informed and working to deadline and budget. They act as gatekeeper and control the flow of communications between the client and the agency so that it is both timely and accurate. The quality of the communications between the two main parties is critical to the success of the overall campaign and to the length of the relationship between the two organisations. Acting at the boundary of the agency's operations, the account executive needs to perform several roles, from internal coordinator and negotiator to presenter (of the agency's work), conflict manager and information gatherer. Very often account executives will experience tension as they seek to achieve their clients' needs while trying to balance the needs of their employer and colleagues. These tensions are similar to those experienced by salespersons and need to be managed in a sensitive manner by management.

The account planner

In addition to the account executive is the role undertaken by account planners (or creative planners). The role of the account planner has been the subject of a flurry of debate (Grant et al., 2003; Hackley, 2003; Collin, 2003; Zambarino and Goodfellow, 2003). The general conclusion of these papers is that the role of the account planner, which has evolved since the beginning of the 1960s, has changed as the communications industry has fragmented and that a new role is emerging in response to integrated marketing communications and media-neutral planning initiatives (see Chapter 4 for details about these concepts).

> The role of the account planner has been the subject of a flurry of debate.

The traditional role of the account planner, which began in full-service agencies, was to understand the client's target consumers, referred to as consumer insight, and to develop strategies for the creative and media departments. Here the role was one largely based on research. As media broke away from full-service agencies so the role of the account planner shifted to the creative aspect of agency work. Media planners assumed the same type of work in media companies, although their work focused on planning the right media mix to reach the target audience. With the development of integrated perspectives and the move towards a broader view of a client's communications needs there is an expectation that the planning role will evolve into a strategic role. The role will be to work with a broad range of marketing disciplines (tools) and media but not to brief the creative team or the media planners directly (Collin, 2003).

The planning role is particularly interesting because it appears to be interpreted in different ways in different agencies or agency networks. In some situations planners support the account executive but in others planners have a more senior role and not only have a strong strategic input but also interact directly with the client (Hackley, 2003). Planners have an important role because their work grounds a campaign and should impact directly on the creative strategy. As Hackley puts it, one of their tasks is to provide the consumer insight and to then ensure that the creative execution reflects the client's marketing goals. This, of course, can be the cause of conflict not only internally but also with the client.

Creative teams

> Creative teams consist of two people, a copywriter and an art director.

Creative teams consist of two people, a copywriter and an art director, supported by a service team. This team is responsible for translating the proposal into an advertisement or communication piece. These two, the art director and copywriter, work together to develop ideas for ads. They work mainly from the creative brief, although there is a balance between the formality of a written document and the inspiration and imagination necessary to communicate ideas about products and services in ways that are memorable and that have meaning for the target audience. The majority of ideas the creatives generate are rejected, but eventually an idea emerges that can be shaped into an ad that can be communicated through particular media (for example, TV, press, magazines, radio, Web or outdoor).

In recent years, partly as a response to the growth of new media, a raft of small entrepreneurial agencies have emerged to exploit the new opportunities arising from the digital revolution. Although these agencies are often founded by people who have started their careers in larger and highly structured agencies, many of them run their own organisations in a more organic manner. Whereas dedicated creative teams might theoretically be the best way to manage a client's project, the reality in many cases is the use of project teams comprising expert individuals working on a number of projects simultaneously. This is not, of course, a new phenomenon, but as a result many people are multitasking and assume many roles with new titles. For example, the title 'head of content' has arisen to reflect the significance of content issues in the new media market. Project managers assume responsibility for the implementation phase and the coordination of all aspects of a client's technological facilities. In addition, there are positions such as head of marketing, mobile (increasing focus on WAP technology), production and technology. The result is no hierarchies, but flat structures and flexible working practices and similar expectations.

Media teams

Media teams perform two main functions, media buying and media planning. The former is concerned with buying the media schedule that has been determined by the latter, the media planners, as the best fit with the target audience.

> Planners undertake a strategic analysis of the target audience and research into their media usage.

Planners undertake a strategic analysis of the target audience and research into their media usage. With such a huge array of media available to buyers and with audiences having access to a variety of media consumption that can change by age, education, geographic location, gender, religion, income and social situation to name just a few, it is critical that the planner pinpoints the best media mix to reach particular targets. From there they build a mix of media that will deliver the message to the target audience the required number of times, within the client's budget and timescale. In other words, the goal is to maximise effectiveness and efficiency by achieving a tight media/audience fit and minimising waste.

The task of media buyers is to purchase the media that the planner has set out in the plan (or schedule) and that best reflects the client's strategy. Buyers negotiate with the sales houses of the media owners to purchase the time and space at the best price, so that their client's messages reach their target audience.

Agency operations

The way an organisation develops its working practices and operations is usually a reflection of the tasks to be undertaken and the environment and context in which it works. The communications industry is no different and has developed processes and operations that reflect a particular approach to the issues and problems they face. One of these is the briefing process.

Briefing

The communications industry has long used briefing as the principal approach to exchanging information within campaign development. Briefing, a process of informing through written documentation, is used because it forces individuals and teams to consider the issues at hand and in such a way that is helpful to others. Client briefs are used to inform the agency of the client's organisation, work and operations and give an insight to the perceived task or communications problem. Creative briefs are used to help agency personnel develop ads and media briefs help those who buy media on the client's behalf. These are all examined in greater detail later in this chapter.

Client briefs should be a snapshot of the strategic thinking and goals.

Briefs are just that, brief. Client briefs should be a snapshot of the strategic thinking and goals associated with the organisation's achievement of key organisational objectives. They should provide clarity and focus and should not contain any detailed embellishment of the issues.

The briefing process has a number of advantages, one of which is that it leads to better use of resources and that it is capable of measurement. A clearly written brief increases the chances of developing a campaign that works at the first attempt. This is far more preferable than having to rework creative ideas, strategy or positioning statements further down the line. Briefing promotes efficiency that in turn leads to improved effectiveness, client satisfaction and ultimately stronger relationships.

A well-written brief contains agreed performance objectives that are absolutely necessary if payment by results (PBR) are to be part of the agency's remuneration package. In an age where accountability is becoming increasingly important, the presence of 'objectives' in the brief enables the return on a client's investment in marketing communications to be better understood, realised and, from the agency's point of view, rewarded.

Briefing is not just about preparing a written document. Briefing is concerned with the development process associated with campaign planning and implementation activities. Through discussion of the various issues that are involved with developing a brief, not only does the client have the opportunity to involve a wider group of people internally, the subsequent discussions involved with the agency also enable clarification of the issues and the various roles other stakeholders are required to play. For example, if there are multiple agencies involved in developing the campaign – for example, direct marketing, sales promotion and advertising (both creative and media) – it can be helpful to brief all parties simultaneously, using a single written brief. At a single subsequent briefing meeting between all the parties, it is more likely that wide agreement can be achieved. This suggests that integrated marketing communications starts with the development of the brief, which of course it does.

Briefing is concerned with the development process associated with campaign planning and implementation activities.

Briefing serves to link together different people, activities and functions.

So, briefing serves to link together different people, activities and functions, both internally and externally. Briefing acts as a conduit through which rich information is communicated to the various agency departments charged with the development and implementation of campaigns.

Briefing is a process that is common across all client/agency relationships in the communications industry. Regardless of whether working in direct marketing, sales promotion, advertising, public relations, media planning and buying or other specialist areas, the brief has a special importance in making the process work and the outcomes significant.

The client brief

Briefs prompt action and provide the information necessary for the designated people to do their jobs. There are several types of brief, but the client brief, the creative brief and the media brief represent the main ones. The client brief is perhaps the key document, as it provides the main platform upon which a campaign is developed. Without it, both the creative and media teams have little idea upon which to build a campaign. The client brief is developed by the client to provide their appointed agencies with key information about their markets, goals, strategies, resources and contacts.

Once an account has been signed a client brief is prepared that provides information about the client organisation (Figure 15.1). It sets out the nature of the industry in which it operates, together with data about trends, market share, customers, competitors and the problem that the agency is required to address. This is used to inform agency personnel. In particular, the account planner will undertake research to determine market, media and audience characteristics and make proposals to the rest of the account team as to how the client problem is to be resolved.

ViewPoint 15.4   Agency operations

New technology has been used to assist different aspects of campaign management. A large majority have been supplier driven but more recent contributions have attempted to enable both clients and agencies to participate more equally in the campaign-development process. For example, Kickfire have developed Marketing Resource Management (MRM), a software system designed specifically to enable organisations to manage the development processes associated with campaigns.

The software application provides for a large degree of ubiquity and freedom as suppliers and clients can work on marketing projects regardless of location. Using a specific password-protected website, parties can share data and documents, develop schedules, allocate individuals to particular tasks, check project progress and produce relevant and timely reports.

The system uses digital asset management functionality to store logos, images and copy that can be utilised by all participants. Public relations activities are also assisted as there are templates for writing press releases. This helps develop coordinated marketing communications through the promotion of image consistency and usage.

Source: Adapted from Murphy (2002)

However, the importance of preparing a brief of suitable quality has for some time been underestimated. With agencies having to brief themselves and some briefs insufficiently detailed, a recent joint industry initiative sought to establish common working practices. The outcome of the process was a briefing template intended to be used by all across the communications agencies in the industry. Seven key headings emerged from the report, and these can be seen at Figure 15.1.

The creative brief

The creative brief is derived partly from the client brief, which illuminates the problem, and the work of the account planner, who has undertaken research to better understand the nature of the problem and who provides direction concerning the solution to the problem.

PROJECT MANAGEMENT
Project Title:
Project Type:
Job/Purchase No.:
Brand:
Company:
Agency(s):
Briefing Date:
Client Team
Agency Team

WHERE ARE WE NOW? What is the current situation?

WHERE DO WE WANT TO BE? What are the goals?

HOW WILL WE KNOW WE'VE ARRIVED? What are the measurement metrics?

WHAT ARE WE DOING TO GET THERE? What is our current thinking?
Marketing Strategy
We plan to achieve our objective(s) by:
Campaign Strategy
Key Messages:
Key Media:
Tonal/Brand Values:

WHO DO WE NEED TO TALK TO? Who are our key audiences?
Definition of target group:
Insights into this target group:

PRACTICALITIES AND APPROVALS
Budgets:
Timings:
Other Considerations:
Approvals:
Appendices (to be attached to brief):

FIGURE 15.1 The client brief – key content (Working Learning Ltd)
This template was developed and endorsed by the main UK trade bodies for the communications industry: CAF, IPA, ISBA, PRCA and MCCA. The project was led by Working Learning with support from the DTI. See www.sslrelay.com/secure.clientbrief.info/site/Brief.aspx for more details

However, the creative brief should be developed by a number of people so that there is agreement on the strategy to be followed and that the communications materials created reflect the research and analysis undertaken. The creative brief is used to inform the creative team about the development of the messages and materials and provide a clear idea of what the communication is meant to accomplish. The creative brief is important because it serves to link not only people but the key processes involved in the development of communications materials. For example, it links research and communications strategy, it translates all background information into actual materials, and helps ensure that the outcomes will address the needs of the client and the needs of their target audiences. See Table 15.2 for a list of key elements that need to be included within a creative brief.

The creative brief, therefore, fulfils the important process role of providing information for those responsible for the creation of the actual message that is communicated. It may be that the creative team responsible for the client's work are external to the lead agency but this should not obscure the vital point that these documents must state quite clearly the campaign objectives and the characteristics of the target audience,

TABLE 15.2 Key elements within a creative brief

Element	Explanation
Target audience	Who should receive (and respond to) the communication?
Communications objective(s)	What is it that the audience should feel, think, believe or do as a result of receiving the communication?
Obstacles	From an audience perspective, what might prevent the communications objectives from being achieved? Are there particular beliefs, social and cultural practices, economic or religious pressures or misinformation present in the audience or market?
Key promise/benefit	What will be the key benefit for the audience as a result of doing, thinking, or feeling what you want them to do?
Support statement/reasons	Why does the key promise outweigh the obstacles?
Tone	What should be the key feeling of this communication?
Media	Which mix of media will be used to reach the target audience?
Creative considerations	Are there any other points/issues that need to be considered?
Budget	What are the financial constraints within which the campaign is to be delivered?

and conveys vital information about the research that has been undertaken, especially the consumer insight material.

The media brief

In a full-service agency, a media brief will also be generated, informing the media planning and buying department of the media required and the type of media vehicles required. However, the vast majority of media-planning work is now undertaken by specialist media agencies and media independents, and these will be briefed by the client, with some support from those responsible for the creative. The media brief, therefore, can be generated by the client or the lead agency, depending upon the circumstances. However, what is common is that the media brief serves to guide the media team with regard to the objectives of the campaign and especially the communications goals, the target audience and their media preferences, the available budget, timescales and the history of previous campaigns, plus the scope of the other tools being used in the campaign.

The vast majority of media-planning work is now undertaken by specialist media agencies and media independents.

Centralised media buying

One of the most important changes in the media-buying landscape happened in the 1990s when media agencies centralised their services into a few buying points. Before this change, the commission system encouraged agencies to offer a full service to their clients. Consequently, clients that had a portfolio of brands used to place their communications business with a range (a roster) of agencies. Each would look after the creative and media requirements and be reimbursed through the commission system, based on the value of the media the client agreed to buy. In a sense there was little incentive for agencies to change this arrangement, and media owners were happy because client organisations were unable to enter into volume purchases and in doing so drive hard discounts.

This began to change with the development of a wider range of available media and the development of creative houses that did not have responsibility for or involvement in media decisions. Client organisations would use a range of creative houses but direct all or most of the media requirements through a single agency. Media houses soon realised that there was an imbalance between the number of media houses or buying points and the number of clients. The result was that through merger and acquisition the number of media houses shrank to just a few core businesses, sufficient to meet the needs of the market. What had happened, of course, was that the market dynamics had changed. Media houses could now bring the needs of various large clients and drive volume discounts from media owners. This benefited clients, whose media investment, in effect, grew smaller through centralised media buying. However, although media owners had to remain price-competitive in order to stay in business, they have added a range of other services and in some media categories have responded by gradually increasing prices.

The centralisation-concentration era has helped transform the way in which agencies, clients and media owners do business. The centralisation–concentration era has helped transform the way in which agencies, clients and media owners do business. Centralisation, the placement of a client's entire media business with a single media house, and concentration, the restructuring of the media-buying market such that there are now just a few, very large media houses through which media is bought and sold, has placed power on the client side and pushed media owners to offer more competitive media packages. This in turn impacts on the relationships between clients and agencies and brings increased pressure for media neutrality and a move away from an over-reliance on above-the-line communications.

The role of technology within agency operations

By and large, the use of technology in agency operations is similar to the ways in which most other organisations use technology. However, it is worth considering some instances where technology not only provides for improved efficiency within client/agency operations but where it can also influence the relationship between the two parties.

Agencies set up extranets and intranets, they provide for online billing and develop databases that process huge amounts of data on clients, campaigns, markets and audiences. Many agencies develop global office facilities or become part of international networks as a way of continuing to support key clients, especially those who operate on a global scale. For these, Internet and digital technologies provide important opportunities to provide added-value services for their clients. For example, through the use of portals, networked agencies can share a range of documents, facilities and information and in doing so save time and costs, all of which can be passed on to the client. In addition, portals enable clients to interact with their agencies much more easily and in doing so improve collaboration and linkages, which are regarded as an important factor when attempting to improve agency performance and reduce client turnover. As

TABLE 15.3 Features and benefits of using a portal within an advertising agency

Feature	Benefit
Content organisation	Workspace views, links to other Web pages and news updates.
Productivity tools	Secure, threaded discussions to foster and enhance collaboration; directories with phone listings; calendar functions; and templates for campaign tracking.
Document routing and management	Expedites the review and approval process and improves workflow. This includes document version controls, distribution list maintenance and automated notification agents to alert clients and account teams when new content is added or modifications are made to existing content.
Server architecture	A distributed architecture that allows several GEM servers to function as a single server. This brings increased scalability, improved load balancing and distribution, and a higher degree of reliability to the agency's portal environment.
Administrative functions	Activity audit trail reports, user-profile maintenance, user definitions and access privileges and default-view definitions.

Source: Kanda Software; used with kind permission

part of the process of enhancing client interaction, a number of features and benefits accrue to the user and their networks. These can be seen at Table 15.3.

Havas, an international agency, claims that its portal has increased efficiency and saved time and money. Turnaround times for client approval of creative work have been reduced by as much as 50 per cent. The ability to manage global research and creative materials within the agency's network has improved dramatically, as has the staff's willingness to share knowledge among account teams. As a result, account teams now have more time to focus on strategic planning and delivering greater value to their clients. The agency can now communicate rapidly and more efficiently with clients, giving both the agency and their clients an improved quality of interaction and a positive working relationship. Through the use of IST this case demonstrates the opportunities to improve agency/client relationships and reduce client turnover.

ViewPoint 15.5   A b2b portal for Havas

Havas, a large advertising agency operating across 131 countries, developed a Web-based system to improve internal and external interaction and collaboration, and to manage the huge and increasing volumes of data and information. However, it found that they did not have the most effective tools to structure and manage the increasing levels of information, and navigation became problematic.

The organisation developed a b2b portal to enable them to manage their diverse and globally distributed agencies. The goal was to enable the agencies and their clients to work more closely together with improved rapport. The portal's features include content authoring and categorisation, threaded discussions, personnel directories, calendars, templates for campaign tracking, as well as document routeing and management.

Source: Adapted from http://www.kandasoft.com/success_GEM2.html (accessed 29 October 2003); used with kind permission

Agency remuneration

One factor that has a significant impact on the quality of the relationship between the parties is the remuneration or reward for the effort.

One factor that has a significant impact on the quality of the relationship between the parties is the remuneration or reward for the effort (added value) the agency makes in attempting to meet and satisfy the needs of its client. One major cause for concern and complaint among marketing managers is the uncertainty over how much their marketing communications programmes will finally cost and the complexity surrounding the remuneration system itself.

There are three main ways in which agencies are paid. These are *commission, fees* and *payment by results*. A fourth is a mixture or combination of these approaches. Traditionally, advertising agencies were paid a commission by media owners for selling space in their publications. A figure of 15 per cent emerged as the norm and seemed a fair reward for the efforts of the agency. However, as relationships between agencies and clients strengthened, it seemed only reasonable that the clients should feel that agencies should act for them (and in their best interests), and not for the media owners. A number of questions were raised about whether the agency was actually being rewarded for the work it did and whether it was being objective when recommending media expenditure. As media independents emerged, questions started to be asked about why media agencies received 3 per cent and the creative agency received 12 per cent.

Client discontent is not the only reason why agency remuneration by commission has been called into question, and alternatives are being considered. In times of recession marketing budgets are inevitably cut, which means less revenue for agencies. Increasing competition means lower profit margins if an agency is to retain the business, and if costs are increasing at the same time the very survival of the agency is in question. As Snowden stated as long ago as 1993, 'Clients are demanding more for less.' She went on to say, 'It is clear to me that the agency business needs to address a number of issues; most important amongst them, how agencies get paid. It is the key to the industry's survival.'

During the early 1990s there was a great deal of discussion and energy directed towards non-commission payment systems. This was a direct result of the recession, in which clients cut budgets and there was a consequent reduction in the quantity of media purchased and hence less revenue for the agencies. Fees became more popular, and some experimented with payment by results. Interestingly, as the recession died and the economy lifted, more revenue resulted in larger commission possibilities, and the death throes of the commission system were quickly replaced by its resuscitation and revival.

It is likely that there will continue to be a move away from a reliance on the payment of commission as the only form of remuneration to the agency. Fees have been around for a long time, either in the form of retainers or on a project-by-project basis. Indeed, many agencies charge a fee for services over and above any commission earned from media owners. The big question is about the basis for calculation of fees (and this extends to all areas of marketing communications, not just advertising), and protracted, complicated negotiations can damage client/agency relationships.

For many, payment by results (PBR) seems a good solution. There are some problems, however, in that the agency does not have total control over its performance, and the final decisions about how much is spent and which creative ideas should be used are the client's. The agency has no control over the other marketing activities of the client, which might determine the degree of success of the campaign. Indeed, this raises the very thorny question of what 'success' is and how it might be measured.

It appears that PBR is starting to become an established form of remuneration.

Despite these considerations, it appears that PBR is starting to become an established form of remuneration, with over 30 per cent of agency–client contracts containing an element of PBR. Lace (2000) explains that this is owing to the inadequacies of both commission- and fee-based systems in the 'new age of cost cutting and accountability'.

A different way of looking at this is to consider what the client thinks the agency does and from this evaluate the outcomes from the relationship. Jensen (1995) proposes that advertising agencies can be seen as *ideas businesses* that seek to build brands for clients. An alternative view is that agencies are *advertising factories*, where the majority of the work is associated with administration, communication, coordination and general running around to ensure that the advertisement appears on the page or screen as desired.

If the 'ideas business' view is accepted then the ideas generated add value for the client, so the use the client makes of the idea should be rewarded by way of a royalty-type payment. If the 'factory concept' is adopted, then it is the resources involved in the process that need to be considered and a fee-based system is more appropriate. Both parties will actively seek to reduce costs that do not contribute to the desired outcomes. These are different approaches to remuneration and avoid the volume of media purchased as a critical and controversial area.

Summary of key points

1. The selection of a communications agency is crucially important if an organisation's marketing communications are to be successful. The agency-selection process should be made against not only an understanding of the market but also of the precise tasks that the appointed agency is required to undertake.

2. The process used to select an agency should be rigorous, systematic and objective. Suggestions that there is no need to do credentials visits, invite and undertake pitches or conduct critical evaluation is invariably misguided and a route to dissatisfaction, frustration and underperformance, without mentioning a waste of time and money.

3. There are a number of roles undertaken by agency people, but essentially the account executive is key because they link the agency with the client to ensure that the client's goals are achieved. Other central personnel are the account planner, the creative team and, if present, the media team.

4. In order that agencies operate effectively the briefing process has become a central process. The client brief details the client's background and communications needs, the creative brief provides specific information about the campaign needs and the media brief informs the media planner of the media requirements necessary to reach the target audience.

5. New technology can enable agencies to collaborate more effectively with both clients and fellow agencies. In addition to the normal benefits arising from digital facilities, portals enable agencies to share information with clients and colleague agencies and in doing so save time, reduce costs and improve opportunities to develop longer-lasting relationships.

6. The traditional way of remunerating agencies was based on a commission system that was related to media spend. This benefited agencies when the economy was buoyant but tended to penalise them when media spend decreased. Today, contracts between client and agency are founded upon a number of criteria, central to which is the notion that agencies should be rewarded according to their performance and the value their services add to a client's business.

Review questions

1. Briefly explain the role agencies fulfil within the marketing communications industry. How might their role be changed?

2. What factors should be taken into consideration and what procedure might be followed when selecting an agency?

3. Examine the key roles in a communications agency.

4. Write short notes evaluating the briefing system.

5. Explain the commission payment system, and outline alternative approaches.

6. Read the trade press such as *Campaign*, *Marketing* or *Marketing Week* (in the UK) to identify three different pitches, and comment on the participants and their relative success.

References

Barrett, L. (2005), 'Haystack joins global agency-selection network', *Marketing*, 14 September, p. 6.

Collin, W. (2003), 'The interface between account planning and media planning – a practitioner perspective', *Marketing Intelligence and Planning*, **21**(7), pp. 440–5.

Finch, M. (2000), 'How to choose the right marketing agency', *Admap*, **35** (October), pp. 46–7.

Grant, I., Gilmore, C. and Crosier, K. (2003), 'Account planning: whose role is it anyway?', *Marketing Intelligence and Planning*, **21**(7), pp. 462–72.

Hackley, C.E. (2003), 'Account planning: current agency perspectives on an advertising enigma', *Journal of Advertising Research*, 43, pp. 235–45.

Jardine, A. (2000), 'Will workshops replace the pitch?', *Marketing*, 13 April, p. 16.

Jensen, B. (1995), 'Using agency remuneration as a strategic tool', *Admap*, **30** (January), pp. 20–2.

Jones, M. (2004), '10 things agencies need to know about clients', *Admap*, **39**(5) (May), pp. 21–3.

Lace, J.M. (2000), 'Payment by results. Is there a pot of gold at the end of the rainbow?', *International Journal of Advertising*, **19**, pp. 167–83.

McKee, S. (2004), 'Pick an agency . . . any agency', *Admap*, **39**(5) (May), pp. 24–5.

Murphy, D. (2002), 'Automation assists business efficiency', *Marketing*, 30 May, p. 23.

Pawinska, M. (2000), 'The passive pitch', *PR Week*, 12 May, pp. 14–15.

Snowden, S. (1993), 'The remuneration squeeze', *Admap*, **28** (January), pp. 26–8.

Whitehead, J. (2004), 'MWO out of running for £40m Direct Line ad account', *Brand Republic*, 17 August. Retrieved from http://www.brandrepublic.com/news/newsArticle.

Woolgar, T. (1998), 'Choosing an agency', *Campaign Report*, 9 October, pp. 6–7.

Young, M. and Steilen, C. (1996), 'Strategy-based advertising agency selection: an alternative to "spec" presentation', *Business Horizons*, **39** (November/December), pp. 77–80.

Zambarino, A. and Goodfellow, J. (2003), 'Account planning in the new marketing and communications environment (has the Stephen King challenge been met?)', *Marketing Intelligence and Planning*, **21**(7), pp. 424–34.

Part 4 Summary

Review

The main theme running through this final part of the book concerns the relationships organisations form with a whole range of stakeholders. Attention is given to the relationships client organisations form with customers, employees and agencies. From an understanding of the nature and development of these relationships, consideration is given to some of the issues that can arise and the ways in which marketing communications can contribute to the development and maintenance of these important relationships.

The first chapter in this part considers relationship-marketing issues, beginning with a consideration of the types of exchanges people and organisations enter into. A range of exchange transactions have been identified and at one extreme transactional exchanges are typified by the 4Ps approach to marketing, where the focus is on prices and products. At the other end relational exchanges are characterised by collaboration, and focus is on the relationship itself. Trust and commitment underpin these relationships and these variables become increasingly important as relational exchanges become established.

Customer relationships can be considered in terms of a series of relationship-development phases: customer acquisition, development, retention and decline. Collectively, these are referred to as the customer life cycle. The duration and intensity of each relationship phase in the life cycle will inevitably vary, and it should be remembered that this representation is essentially idealistic.

At the heart of many relationship-marketing strategies are loyalty or customer-retention programmes. Whether these are loyalty or perhaps convenience programmes may be debatable, but organisations in the b2c market should always question whether consumers really desire a relationship with a brand and whether their actions are those bred of loyalty or inertia.

The centrality of the trust and commitment concepts to relationship marketing has been established, and they are as central to marketing-channel relationships as to other b2b relationships. Interorganisational trust involves judgements about another organisation's reliability and integrity. Questions concerning trust and commitment have far-ranging implications for marketing communications, whether these be delivered offline or in an online context.

In marketing channels each organisation is a customer of the previous organisation. Some organisations work closely together, coordinating and integrating their activities, whereas others combine on a temporary basis. Increasingly, organisations are providing multichannel facilities in order to reach a variety of audiences. Many organisations now incorporate a range of direct and indirect channels within their channel strategy as Internet technologies have brought a new dimension to the direct channel.

The relationship theme continues into the international arena. Not only are customers key audiences but so are agencies and regulators in countries where marketing communications need to operate. However, associated with this dimension is the need to ensure that marketing communications messages can be understood correctly, which may mean adapting messages to meet local needs.

Chapter 14 examined the complex world of the marketing communications industry. Four main sectors were identified: clients, agencies, production houses and the media. Communications agencies are characterised by their inherent focus on a single marketing communications discipline. Currently, ideas concerning the provision of integrated marketing communications services continues to attract interest.

Clients use a variety of methods in order to budget for the use of marketing communications. No one single approach can be said to be totally correct, and practice suggests that a number of methods should be used, including an objective and task approach.

Ethical issues are becoming increasingly prominent, and many organisations are attempting to become more actively involved in addressing the ethical consequences of their marketing communications activities. Concern about telling the truth, their attitude towards vulnerable groups, respect and concern for individual privacy, ensuring all communications are tasteful and decent, and that the use of inducements to clients, sales personnel and others are transparent and appropriate, are some of the more obvious areas towards which organisations should direct their attention.

The final chapter examines agency operations and processes. Although the relationship theme emerges once again it is the rigorous, systematic and objective selection process of the agency in the first place that determines whether the client/agency relationship has a chance to succeed.

The briefing process is used to enable agencies to function and deliver their client's goals. The client brief details the client's background and communications needs, the creative brief provides specific information about the campaign needs and the media brief informs the media planner of the media requirements necessary to reach the target audience.

Today, contracts between client and agency are founded upon a number of criteria, central to which is the notion that agencies should be rewarded according to their performance and the value their services add to a client's business. The traditional way of remunerating agencies, based on a commission system, still operates but its prevalence and significance is much reduced.

The quality of the agency/client relationship is a function of trust, which is developed through the exchanges and which fosters confidence. As discussed earlier, commitment is derived from a belief that the relationship is worth continuing and that maximum effort is warranted to maintain the relationship.

Questions and exercises

1. Identify the principles of relationship marketing and suggest ways in which marketing communications can be used to support these principles.

2. Explain how direct marketing can both assist and hinder the development of effective relationship marketing.

3. Discuss the different types of marketing channels and explain how marketing communications can be used to help ensure that these channels work effectively. How can multichannel marketing improve relationships with intermediaries and end-user customers?

4. Write notes explaining how a move towards international marketing can impact on the marketing communications and relationships of the client organisations.

5. Evaluate the influence of three issues that are currently affecting the marketing communications in a country of your choice. How might these issues evolve or be resolved?

6. Discuss the notion that the key task of communications agencies is to develop sustainable (and in some cases profitable) relationships with various stakeholders, rather than just deliver excellent campaigns.

MINI CASE STUDY
GardenPowerMachines

GardenPowerMachines (GPM) are a long-established medium-sized engineering company, which distributes its range of electrically powered garden equipment products through a variety of retail outlets. One of their leading product ranges is lawnmowers, which traditionally have been distributed through ironmongers and garden centres and more recently through discount stores, hypermarkets and DIY superstores. For a long time GPM's marketing channels and management of its distribution was particularly successful and was regarded as a major competitive strength. This success was attributed to the high reputation that had been established in the trade; the product, service, ordering, delivery, and above all the company, were all perceived to be trustworthy and very reliable. The mainstay of its communications with these outlets was the sales force.

The established market segment that GPM reached through garden centres consisted of men over 45 years old who agreed that they 'took gardening seriously' and 'gardening is my main hobby'. This segment valued solid designs and reliability, and preferred to buy from garden centres where there was experience, advice and support. Information compiled from guarantee-registration cards indicated that customers had much larger gardens than average and that two-thirds were in the south and west of England.

Growth of sales volume was aided by the introduction of new models, often prompted by sales-force suggestions, customers and growing competition.

One of these new products (Whirlybird) had been developed following the recognition of a new customer segment, the convenience gardener. This group wanted a lawnmower that would be simple to use, sufficiently lightweight so that men and women could use it, and be easy to store. The rotary hover mower with grass-collection facilities appeared to satisfy the needs of the convenience gardener. In contrast to traditional buyers, this segment preferred to use DIY superstores to obtain their lawnmowers and related garden equipment. Whirlybird sales soon took off and now contributed 65 per cent of turnover.

Originally, marketing communications had been geared to servicing the garden centres and ironmongers with sales literature, leads and joint promotions with key accounts. Salesmen provided a point of personal contact, they were trained engineers and could provide technical support that was valued by their retail customers. The operation was very successful, profitable and the envy of many of its traditional competitors. However, as the emphasis switched to DIY superstores so the support shifted as well. Now the emphasis was on EDI and stock control with marketing communications oriented to the provision of leaflets and in-store merchandising. Gone was the need for personal support and advice; a salesman's job was now oriented to maintaining relationships with the major buyers of each of the major groups that owned the DIY superstores.

Although sales of Whirlybird-related products were strong, GPM realised that it was losing market share in the traditional market sector. The garden-centre business was no longer central to GPM, and many of the personal friendships and relationships with the garden centres had withered as a result. Sales had slowed partly because GPM could not support each garden centre in the way it used to. Sales-force costs were very high and the reduced size of the sales force meant that they had to be concentrated on the most profitable parts of GPM business, the DIY superstores. Gone, then, was the technical support, the advice for garden-centre sales staff and customers from the traditional gardeners segment.

It was not surprising that garden-centre owners perceived GPM as distant and uncaring about their type of business. GPM had tried to use advertising and direct mail to reach traditional gardeners and build the brand. However, when these potential customers arrived at garden centres to see the products and test them, they were faced with little GPM stock, sales staff with little up-to-date knowledge and large ranges of competitor machines.

GPM began to feel that it would be unable to retrieve its market position. It perceived garden centres as geographically isolated units, too costly to support but potentially profitable if only they could find the right marketing mix. GPM was increasingly concerned about the high levels of dealer dissatisfaction, many of whom had switched their business to GPM's major competitor and other niche manu-facturers. GPM wanted to re-establish its market leadership but knew that to do this it had to re-establish relationships with each garden centre and associated networks. To be competitive it was necessary to provide high levels of support and advice, process sales orders quickly, provide fast customer service and attend to gardeners' needs for advice, not only on machinery but other aspects of lawn and garden care. Support through the sales force was not an option.

Questions

1. Write brief notes about the types of marketing channels you believe exist at GPM. What are their characteristics and how should these change?

2. What value do the intermediaries offer GPM? How is this reflected in their relationships?

3. What technological solution would you propose to GPM in order that it develops its relationships with its intermediaries, and how would you justify it?

4. What might be the benefits for the traditional gardeners and garden centres from this new approach?

5. Using conceptual materials, discuss the ways in which GPM's relationships with its retailers has evolved.

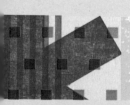

MINI CASE STUDY
EasyHome

EasyHome was one the first furniture retailers in the UK to open large stores at out-of-town locations. Its initial success was founded on sales of flat-pack kitchen and bedroom furniture, which it sold cheaply and discounted regularly. At the time, it was a new retail concept whereby customers took home packs of furniture that they then assembled themselves. Trident, the name of the EasyHome kitchen brand, is still a strong brand name, although many people do not associate the name as part of EasyHome. However, despite the company's success there were quality-related problems typified by broken or missing parts. This association with poor quality has continued to tarnish the brand.

Recently, EasyHome's sales performance has declined and last year turnover fell by approximately 10 per cent. It is still the market leader, but the fall in market share from 11.6 per cent to 8.4 per cent in a market that is actually showing signs of some growth is of concern. More recent entrants to the market, Regents and ASF, are beginning to take market share from both ends of the market. Regents have strong design and quality attributes that are targeted at a niche market (of upwardly mobile professional people). Part of the strength of the ASF chain is its strong distribution and limited (flat-pack) product range. Tougher competition combined with economic pressures and a series of strategy changes have served to confuse consumers' perception of EasyHome so that it is uncertain what the brand now offers customers.

Homeowners are taking an increased interest in their homes as inflation remains low and the housing market booms. New television programmes aimed at people interested in home decoration and design for all types of houses are attracting large audiences. As part of the boom a wave of new magazines has been launched to feed this market.

The style of communications used by EasyHome is largely fast-paced, price-oriented and features happy family couples with their new furniture. Television is the main medium used to promote its sales-promotions activities. These are focused around the price-led sales at different times of the year (e.g. winter sales) and various discount initiatives used to boost store traffic. It has been said that too much reliance was placed on the company's market-leadership position and little was done to communicate the EasyHome offer. Indeed, much has been done to the product to correct the quality and missing-parts problems, but it is clear that these changes have not been communicated.

Although the EasyHome approach to marketing communications has been reasonably innovative, it has been designed to maintain the company's downmarket positioning. Some competitors, however, have been quite radical, both in terms of the message and the variety of media used. Some have featured celebrities to bring personality into their brand-based advertising.

A new marketing team has been introduced, and the company plans to reverse the declining fortunes with a series of measures designed to change customer attitudes towards the EasyHome brand. The company will continue its focus on bedroom and kitchen furniture but, instead of regular discounting, will move towards a value-for-money proposition. To accomplish this a range of other communications tools and media were considered. Rather than just change brand attitudes, some members of the team believe that EasyHome should increase its below-the-line spend as this will help improve sales immediately and complement the value-for-money orientation.

Some of this material has been amended and/or disguised to provide a suitable context for the mini case study and is not intended to imply good or bad management or current timescales.

Questions

1. Explain the sequence of events associated with the appointment of a new marketing communications agency and suggest the key criteria EasyHome should use when deciding which agency to appoint.

2. Briefly describe the role and content of a client brief and explain in note form the key tasks undertaken by account managers, creative teams and media planners.

3. Prepare some brief notes explaining how relationship marketing might be of use to EasyHome.

4. How might EasyHome use marketing communications to develop their key relationships?

5. Discuss ways in which client/agency relationships might be developed.

Author index

Subject index